THE OTHER SIDE
OF THE HILL

One of the world's outstanding teacher-historians, Sir Basil
Liddell Hart was born in Paris in 1895 and educated at St Paul's
and Corpus Christi College, Cambridge. He joined the army
(King's Own Yorkshire Light Infantry) and served in the First
World War; in 1924 he was invalided and three years later retired
with the rank of Captain. He evolved several military tactical
developments including the Battle Drill system and was an early
advocate of airpower and armoured forces. In 1937 he became
personal adviser to the War Minister, but reorganization of the
army was so slow that he resigned a year later to press the need
publicly.

Liddell Hart was military correspondent to the *Daily Telegraph*
from 1925 to 1935 and to *The Times* until the outbreak of the
Second World War. He lectured on strategy and tactics at staff col-
leges in numerous countries and wrote more than thirty books.
He died in 1970.

LIDDELL HART

THE OTHER SIDE OF THE HILL

PAN GRAND STRATEGY SERIES

Germany's Generals
their rise and fall,
with their own account of
military events, 1939–1945

PAN BOOKS

First published 1948 by Cassell and Company Ltd
Revised and enlarged edition 1951

First published by Macmillan General Books in Papermac 1978

This edition published 1999 by Pan Books
an imprint of Macmillan Publishers Limited
25 Eccleston Place London SW1W 9NF
and Basingstoke

Associated companies throughout the world

ISBN 0 330 37324 2

1 3 5 7 9 8 6 4 2

A CIP catalogue record for this book is available
from the British Library

Printed and bound in Great Britain

CONTENTS

MAPS

PREFACE TO THE FIRST EDITION

THE story is told in Croker's *Correspondence and Diaries* how, on a journey with Wellington, he and the Duke passed the time by guessing what kind of country they would find on the other side of each hill on the way. When Croker expressed surprise at Wellington's successes in forecasting it, the latter replied: "Why, I have spent all my life in trying to guess what was at the other side of the hill."

Wellington's remark was subsequently extended into a definition of the imaginative requirement in generalship, in the wider sense of guessing what was happening "at the other side of the hill"—behind the opposing front and in the opponent's mind. It has also served to epitomize the functions of Intelligence.

When the late war ended, I was fortunate in having an early opportunity of exploring the "other side of the hill". Some work I was doing for P.I.D. brought me in contact with the German generals and admirals over a lengthy period. In the course of many discussions with them I was able to gather their evidence on the events of the war before memories had begun to fade or become increasingly coloured by after-thoughts.

Understanding of what happened was helped by studying the German generals, as well as hearing their accounts. Few of them resembled the typical picture of an iron Prussian soldier. Rundstedt came nearest it, but in his case the impression was offset by his natural courtesy and light touch of humour. His quiet dignity in adversity, and uncomplaining acceptance of hard conditions—that were no credit to his captors—won the respect of most British officers who encountered him. In contrast to him were a number of aggressive young generals, blustering and boorish, who owed their rise to Nazi favour. But the majority were of a different type to both, and by no means a dominating one. Many would have looked in their natural place at any conference of bank managers or civil engineers.

They were essentially technicians, intent on their

professional job, and with little idea of things outside it. It is easy to see how Hitler hoodwinked and handled them, and found them good instruments up to a point.

In sifting and piecing together their evidence it was useful to have a background knowledge of the military situation in the pre-war period. It was a guide, not only in saving time, but in avoiding misconceptions that were still widely prevalent at the end of the war. The idea that the General Staff had played a dominant part in Germany's aggressive course, as it did before 1918, still coloured the prosecution proceedings at the Nuremberg Trial. Earlier, that fixed idea had hindered the British and American Governments from giving timely and effective encouragement to the underground movement in Germany which, with military backing, had long been planning Hitler's overthrow. That the prevailing conception of the General Staff's influence was an out-of-date notion had become clear to anyone who dispassionately followed the trend of the Germany Army between the wars. But legends are persistent, and delusions tenacious. They had the unfortunate effect of postponing Hitler's downfall and prolonging the war months, and probably years, after it would otherwise have ended. The ill-consequences for Europe are now beginning to be realized.

I would like to acknowledge my indebtedness to the help and historical sense of those who facilitated the early exploration of events. Also, to Captain F. S. Kingston, whose mastery of the German language and intuitive teamwork were of great assistance in the discussions. At the same time I would express my appreciation of the ready help given by so many of those "on the other side of the hill", in contributing to this piece of historical research, and of the objective attitude most of them showed in discussing events. Finally, I wish to thank Major-General Sir Percy Hobart, Chester Wilmot, G. R. Atkinson and Desmond Flower for valuable comments and suggestions while the book was in preparation.

TILFORD HOUSE, TILFORD
January, 1948

PREFACE TO THE 1951 EDITION

THE original edition of this book was composed from evidence I gathered in discussions with the German generals five years ago, soon after their capture. Since then I have collected a large amount of fresh material, much of it from generals whom I did not have an opportunity of seeing in 1945, while I have also been able to check such evidence by reference to documentary records. The present book is the revised and enlarged product.

In Parts II and III, where the generals' evidence is set forth in their own words, most of the chapters have been enlarged as well as revised, while three new chapters have been added. In Part I, which is my own summary of events and personalities, the revision has been much less, but one fresh chapter has been added—on Guderian, the subordinate commander who was insubordinately responsible for producing the staggering German victory in 1940.

Even in its more fully developed form, however, this book is not an effort to "write history". It is still too early to compile a history of the Second World War—one should wait until the evidence is more complete. In the present book my concern is to assemble, and present in an intelligible form for the public, an important section of the necessary material for history. Nothing is more important as a preparation for writing the history of a great war than to collect the evidence from the opposite side, for to watch a struggle only from one's "side of the hill" is bound to produce a view that is not merely incomplete but distorted.

This lesson had been deeply impressed on me in the course of my earlier researches into the history of the First World War. To speak only of the military field, I found that none of the accounts of any campaign or battle came near the truth unless they were written with awareness of the enemy's intentions, decisions, resources, and moves. Hence as soon as the Second World War ended I

hastened to take an opportunity of exploring the "other
side of the hill" by personal interrogation of the German
military leaders—while their memory of events was still
fresh and before their impressions were affected by post-
war knowledge or trends.

The German leaders will doubtless publish their own
memoirs and narratives eventually, as many of the Allied
leaders have already done. In the case of the former this
memoir-writing was delayed, and with some of them is
still delayed, by prolonged post-war imprisonment and
other restrictions on their freedom. From the historian's
point of view such a delay—or, indeed, any delay—in the
publication of historical material is regrettable. On the
other hand, it must be recognized that the writers of
autobiographies are usually more concerned with their
own interests and the service of their own reputations
than with the service of history. Nothing can be more
misleading than the carefully-framed account of their own
actions that statesmen and generals, of any country,
provide when they compile their accounts in their own
time and way. There is a better chance of reaching the
truth by a searching process of questioning them, combined
with progressive exploration of other sources to provide
cross-checks.

This book of mine presents the digested essence of the
product, as objectively as I can, by assembling a fair
sample of their replies—on many different issues. To have
presented the material "in the raw", through an inter-
minable series of questions and answers, would not only
fill several volumes but confuse the reader—all the more
so because, in probing for the truth, the best way to
penetrate a "defence" is to vary the method of approach.
As any experienced investigator knows, when questioning
is frequently inconsecutive and indirect it is more likely
to elicit facts that might otherwise be concealed. And
here in fairness, I am bound to say that the witnesses came
well enough out of this test, in meeting awkward questions,
as to cause me to modify to a large extent the views with
which I started—especially as their evidence was often
borne out by captured documents.

The accuracy and honesty of their evidence varied individually, as it does with individuals everywhere. But in my experience of investigating events I have found that Germans tend to be rather more objective than most people when discussing professional matters, such as the course of military operations—which was the main subject of my investigations here. Moreover, many of them have a passion for preciseness about the facts, although their conclusions may be like froth on beer. That passion for factual preciseness, and for recording things in detail, led to the discovery and hanging of many of those who were connected with the 1944 plot against Hitler! But it is a definite asset from the historical point of view.

At the same time I took care, wherever possible, to check from other sources the account and answers given by any particular general I was questioning. Most of the statements used in this book were submitted to such cross-checks—and the exceptions are indicated in the text, particularly where there was a divergence in the evidence.

Naturally, the generals tended to excuse themselves for their part in Hitler's aggressions—but not without reason. On this score I had a pre-war background knowledge wider than that of the prosecutors at Nuremberg, and was thus aware of the fallacy of some of their assumptions before I began my post-war investigations.

Between the wars, my work as a military correspondent required me to keep a watchful eye on developments in Europe, and I always sought to keep touch with the trends in Germany. This task was eased, directly and indirectly, by the extent to which my own military books were read in Germany, some of the leading soldiers themselves undertaking the translation.

The warnings I gave about the Nazi menace, and the emphatic line I took in opposing the policy of "appeasement" will be known to most people who followed my pre-war writings. I pointed out the ominous signs even before Hitler came into power. At the same time it was evident to me that the German General Staff had little influence with Hitler compared with what it had exercised in the Kaiser's time, and that it tended to be more of a brake upon his aggressive plans than an impetus to them.

That fact has been amply confirmed by the documents in the captured archives. It is made even clearer by the diaries of Goebbels, which are full of bitter denunciation of the generals for their persistent opposition to Hitler and to the Nazi creed.

It is time for a deeper understanding of the paralysing dilemma in which they were placed, as patriots anxious to preserve their country, between the Allies' demand for unconditional surrender and Hitler's mesmerizing power over their troops—reinforced by the tyrant's police and spy system. I have criticized their "blind eye" in my book, but I doubt whether generals of other countries, in similar circumstances, would have done more to overthrow such a régime.

What is really more remarkable than the German generals' submission to Hitler is the extent to which they managed to maintain in the Army a code of decency that was in constant conflict with Nazi ideas. Many of our own soldiers who have been prisoners of war have borne testimony to this. Moreover, in visiting France, Belgium, and Holland since the war I have often been candidly told, by staunch anti-Nazis, that the general behaviour of the occupying German *Army*—as distinct from the S.S.—was better than that of the Allied Armies which came to liberate them. For that due credit has to be given to the generals, and to Rundstedt in particular.

Where the German generals can be justly criticized is for the way they tended to close their minds to the excesses of the Nazis, and for their lack of moral courage, with some exceptions, in protesting against things they would not have done themselves. Nevertheless, it is obvious from any study of Hitler's brutal orders that the scale of atrocities, and the sufferings of the occupied countries, would have been much worse still if his sweeping intentions had not been tacitly disregarded or at least modified by the military commanders.

Moral courage in protest is not a common characteristic in any army. I met numerous generals on the Allied side who privately deplored the inhumanity of the Allied bombing policy—where it was aimed primarily at terrorizing the civil population—yet I do not know of any who ventured to make a public or official protest on that score. Likewise, they tended to turn a blind eye to other examples of "barbarism" on the part of the Allied forces. Yet they ran no such personal risk in making a protest as the German generals did—merely the risk of damaging their career prospects.

WOLVERTON PARK,
  BUCKINGHAMSHIRE.

June, 1950.

To
MY SON, ADRIAN
and
to all who helped
in this effort to be of service to history

PART I

HITLER'S GENERALS

CHAPTER I

THE SUICIDAL SCHISM

EVERYTHING in war looks different at the time from what it looks in the clearer light that comes after the war. Nothing looks so different as the form of the leaders. The public picture of them at the time is not only an unreal one, but changes with the tide of success.

Before the war, and still more during the conquest of the West, Hitler came to appear a gigantic figure, combining the strategy of a Napoleon with the cunning of a Machiavelli and the fanatical fervour of a Mahomet. After his first check in Russia, his figure began to shrink, and towards the end he was regarded as a blundering amateur in the military field, whose crazy orders and crass ignorance had been the Allies' greatest asset. All the disasters of the German Army were attributed to Hitler; all its successes were credited to the German General Staff.

That picture is not true, though there is some truth in it. Hitler was far from being a stupid strategist. Rather, he was too brilliant—and suffered from the natural faults that tend to accompany such brilliance.

He had a deeply subtle sense of surprise, and was a master of the psychological side of strategy, which he raised to a new pitch. Long before the war he had described to his associates how the daring coup that

captured Norway might be carried out, and how the
French could be manœuvred out of the Maginot Line.
He had also seen, better than any general, how the bloodless conquests that preceded the war might be achieved
by undermining resistance beforehand. No strategist
in history has been more clever in playing on the
minds of his opponents—which is the supreme art of
strategy.

It was the very fact that he had so often proved right,
contrary to the opinion of his professional advisers, which
helped him to gain influence at their expense. Those
results weakened their arguments in later situations which
they gauged more correctly. For in the Russian campaign
his defects became more potent than his gifts, and the
debit balance accumulated to the point of bankruptcy.
Even so, it has to be remembered that Napoleon, who
was a professional strategist, had been just as badly dazzled
by his own success, and made the same fatal mistakes in
the same place.

Hitler's worst fault here was the way he refused to
"cut his loss" and insisted on pressing the attack when
the chances of success were fading. But that was the
very fault which had been most conspicuous in Foch and
Haig, the Allied commanders of the last war, as well as
in Hindenburg and Ludendorff, who then held the German
Supreme Command. All these had been professional
soldiers. Hitler also did much to produce the German
armies' collapse in France by his reluctance to sanction
any timely withdrawal. But, here again, his attitude was
exactly the same as that of Foch. The vital difference
was that in 1918 the commanders on the spot did not
obey Foch more than they deemed wise, whereas in
1944–45 the German generals were afraid to disobey
Hitler's orders.

It is the cause of that fear, and the internal conflict
in the High Command, that we have to probe in order
to find the real explanation why the German plans mis-

carried. Hitler's strategic intuition and the General Staff's strategic calculation might have been an all-conquering combination. Instead, they produced a suicidal schism that became the salvation of their opponents.

The older school of generals, products of the General Staff system, had been the chief executants of German strategy throughout the war, but in the days of success their part had not received full recognition. After the tide turned, they filled an increasing part in the public picture, and came to be regarded by the Allied peoples as the really formidable element on the opposing side. During the last year the spotlight was largely focused on Rundstedt, their leading representative. The constant question became, not what Hitler would do, but what Rundstedt would do—both in the military field and in a political coup to wrest power from the Nazis.

The German generals have been regarded as such a closely-knit body, and so much of one mind, as to be capable of wielding tremendous political power. That impression accounts for the persistent expectation, on the Allies' side, that the generals would overthrow Hitler—an expectation that was never fulfilled. It also accounts for the popular conviction that they were as great a menace as he was, and shared the responsibility for Germany's aggressions. That picture was true of the First World War, but was now out of date. The German generals had little effect on the start of the Second World War—except as an ineffectual brake.

Once the war had started, their executive efficiency contributed a lot to Hitler's success, but their achievement was overshadowed by his triumph. When they came into more prominence in the eyes of the outside world, as Hitler's star waned, they had become more impotent inside their own country.

That was due to a combination of factors. They stood for a conservative order and tradition which had little

appeal to a generation brought up in the revolutionary
spirit and fanatical faith of National Socialism. They
could not count on the loyalty of their own troops in any
move against the régime—and especially its faith-inspiring
Führer. They were handicapped by the way they had
isolated themselves from public affairs, and by the way
Hitler cunningly isolated them from sources of knowledge.
Another factor was their ingrained discipline and profound
sense of the importance of the oath of loyalty which they
had sworn to the Head of the State. Ludicrous as this may
seem in regard to one who was himself so outstanding as
a promise-breaker, it was a genuine feeling on their part,
and the most honourable of the factors which hampered
them. But along with it often ran a sense of personal
interest which undercut their loyalty to their fellows, and
their country's best interests, in face of a common threat.
The play of individual ambitions and the cleavage of
personal interests constituted a fatal weakness in their
prolonged struggle to maintain their professional claim in
the military field, and to preserve it from outside interference. This struggle went on throughout the twelve
years from Hitler's rise to Germany's fall.

The first phase ended in a definite advantage to the
professionals that was indirectly gained when Himmler
played on Hitler's fears so effectively as to prompt him to
carry out a murderous purge of Captain Roehm and
other Brownshirt leaders. It is by no means clear whether
the latter designed to overthrow Hitler, but there is no
doubt that they were aspiring to fill a big place in the
military system. Once they were killed off, Hitler became
more dependent on the generals' support, and the latter
were able to re-establish their own supremacy in the
Army.

The second phase reached a climax in January,
1938, when the professionals themselves were caught in
another of Himmler's traps. In 1933 Hitler had chosen
General von Blomberg as War Minister. His fellow-generals

became increasingly disturbed at his susceptibility to Hitler's influence, and were then shocked to hear that he was marrying a typist in his office. That alienated their sympathies still further. But Hitler gave this "democratic" marriage his blessing and graced the wedding. Soon after it, Himmler produced a police dossier purporting to show that the bride had been a prostitute. Thereupon Hitler, in real or simulated fury, dismissed Blomberg from office. Himmler followed this up by producing another dossier in which homosexual charges had been fabricated against General von Fritsch, the Commander-in-Chief of the Army, whereupon he in turn was removed from his post by Hitler—and never reinstated, though subsequently vindicated after a court of inquiry. (A fuller account of this crisis is given in Chapter III.)

Hitler exploited the moral shock that the officers' corps had suffered by seizing the opportunity to assume supreme command of the German armed forces. This paved the way for his ultimate control of strategy, while enabling Himmler to strengthen his own influence. General Keitel, whose wire-pulling had weakened the united front of the generals in their protest against Fritsch's treatment, was appointed to succeed Blomberg, but with a lower status, and henceforth only kept that place by subservience to Hitler. A more reputable soldier, General von Brauchitsch, who belonged neither to the reactionary nor the Nazi school, was made head of the Army. By this shrewd step, Hitler sought to placate the Army, while assuring himself of an executive commander who would be easier to handle than Fritsch.

Brauchitsch, however, made a stronger rally in defence of the professional class than had been expected. He also sought to slow down the pace of Nazi foreign policy by a warning that the Germany Army was not ready for war and that Hitler must not push his aggressive moves so far as to produce a fight. He was stiffened in his protests by the Chief of the General Staff, General Beck, who

came out with such open condemnation of Hitler's war-
like policy as to spur Hitler to dismiss him. Even then,
Brauchitsch and Halder, Beck's successor, made a stand
when Hitler looked like proceeding to extremes against
Czecho-Slovakia, but the ground was cut away beneath
their feet when the French and British Governments bowed
to Hitler's threat of war.

With the added prestige of his bloodless conquest of
Czecho-Slovakia Hitler was able to force the pace over
Poland. The generals were little check on him here
beyond helping to convince him that no risk of war on
that issue must be taken unless he first secured Russia's
neutrality. On the other hand, once he had done that,
he was able to persuade most of them that Britain and
France would stand aside, and that a stroke against Poland
would carry no serious risk of involving Germany in a
major war.

A fresh strain developed between Hitler and his
generals when, after the conquest of Poland, they found
that he was intent on precipitating the wider conflict they
feared by taking the offensive in the West. Apart from
the long-term risks, they did not believe that it was even
possible to overcome France. But once again their protests were overruled, and their subsequent talk of a concerted move to overturn Hitler came to nothing. It
would be unjust to blame them for their ineffectiveness
at this stage, for it is clear that they had good reason to
doubt whether their troops would have followed them in
turning against Hitler, and they had a natural repugnance to appearing as traitors to their country when at
war.

The invasion of France was ordered by Hitler in
face of their doubts. Its success was due partly to new
tactics and weapons which he had fostered when the older
generals were still conservatively sceptical; partly to an
audacious new plan, suggested by a junior, which he had
pushed them into adopting; partly to blunders by their

fellow-professionals in France on which they had not reckoned.

Nevertheless their executive skill was an indispensable factor in Hitler's conquest of France—while it was through his sudden and strange hesitation that the full fruits of the swift cut through to the Channel were not reaped. But their great contribution to victory resulted, ironically, in a further weakening of their own position. It was Hitler who filled the world's eye after that triumph, and the laurels crowned his brow, not theirs. He took care to crown himself. In his mind, too, he now became convinced that he was the greatest of all strategists, and henceforth interfered increasingly in the generals' sphere of activity, while becoming even less willing to listen to any arguments from them that ran counter to his desires.

Most of them were fearful when they found that he was intending to plunge into Russia. But, like so many specialists, they were rather naïve outside their own sphere, and Hitler was able to overcome their doubts about his Russian adventure with the aid of political "information" designed to convince them of its necessity, and that Russia's internal weakness would affect her military strength. While the opening stages brought great victories, these fell short of being completely decisive—partly because Russian resistance had been miscalculated, and partly because of a divergence of views in the German Command about the objective. When winter approached, wisdom would have counselled a halt, but Moscow looked so close that neither Hitler nor his generals could resist the temptation to push on. The attack was pressed at all costs, though the chances were fading. It ended in a reverse that nearly proved fatal.

Hitler, however, managed to turn the failure to his own advantage. For when Brauchitsch, who was a sick man, asked to be relieved, Hitler himself took over Brauchitsch's post as Commander-in-Chief of the Army. That step not only increased his own power but cleverly shifted the public blame for the failure on to the generals, since Brauchitsch's departure was so announced as to make it look like the customary polite way of removing a commander who has bungled a campaign. Thus Hitler scored doubly.

For the rest of the war, he was able to brush aside the generals' views on policy, and even to override their judgment in their own field. If one of them made a protest, he could always find another one ambitious to fill the vacancy, and ready to express faith in continued attack—as most soldiers are, by instinct, always inclined to do. At the same time the *Waffen* S.S. was increasingly strengthened at the expense of the Army, while Nazi spies were placed in all headquarters to keep watch on the commanders. The possibility of a successful revolt of the generals progressively diminished. All they could do was to make the best of their orders—or to make the worst of them. For there is reason to suspect that some of the generals became ready to carry out orders that they considered hopelessly rash, simply as a way of sabotaging Hitler's designs and hastening the end of the war.

CHAPTER II

THE MOULD OF SEECKT

The German general who had the primary influence on the First World War died the year before it began—and had retired seven years before it. This was Alfred von Schlieffen, who came from Mecklenburg on the Baltic coast. It was he who designed the master-plan for the invasion of France, prepared the "tin-openers" to pierce the fortress barrier, and trained the staff to handle them. That plan embraced the violation of Belgium's neutrality —for the sake of outflanking France—and thus brought Britain into the war. Although its execution was bungled by Schlieffen's successor, it came dangerously close to winning the war within a month.

The German general who had the primary influence on the Second World War died three years before the war— and retired ten years earlier still. This was Hans von Seeckt, who came from Schleswig-Holstein, the land between Mecklenburg and Denmark. He was the man who contrived to rebuild an effective German Army after the last war, and laid the foundations on which a much greater structure could arise. His plans had to be designed and carried out under the extremely hampering conditions of the victors' peace settlement—itself designed to frustrate any serious rebuilding of the German Army. Those restrictions make his performance the more significant. The achievements of the Wehrmacht, especially in the victorious early phase of the war, owed much to the way that Seeckt had moulded the Reichswehr.

No attempt to assess Hitler's generals in the Second World War can be of adequate value unless it first assesses the influence of Seeckt—so important for the future was the reconstruction period of the German Army. Having treated it at length, the individual treatment of the military leaders who rose to fame in 1939–45 can be correspondingly condensed. For here we have a background common to all, and can see the mould in which their doctrine was cast. Naturally there were differences of interpretation, but these were less important than the broad foundation that had been built up afresh in the days when the General Staff, banned by the Versailles Treaty, was working underground.

In the 1914–18 war Seeckt, then a lieutenant-colonel, had begun as chief of staff of a corps in Kluck's First Army, and thus had a close view of the steps by which a masterly design went wrong in the execution, and decisive victory was forfeited just as it appeared within reach. Seeckt made his own mark a year later, in 1915, as the cool brain that guided a dashing Hussar general, the *beau sabreur* Field-Marshal von Mackensen, in the deadly break-through at Gorlice in Galicia, which split the Russian armies—a stroke from which they never fully recovered. It was here that Seeckt introduced a method of attack that contained the germ of modern infiltration tactics— pushing in reserves at the soft spots, and thrusting on as deep as possible, instead of the former method of trying to advance uniformly and using the reserves to break down the tough spots.

Seeckt not only made his mark but also his name. For the concealed brain behind Mackensen became known more and more widely, so that the saying spread through the German Army—"Where Mackensen is, Seeckt is; where Seeckt is, victory is." He continued to play an important part in the Eastern campaign, but it was his misfortune to be outside of, and unpopular with, the Hindenburg–Ludendorff ring which acquired supreme control of the German Army from 1916 to the end of the war. That, however, saved his reputation from being involved in the final collapse in the West, and he became adviser to the German delegation at the Peace Conference. From this it was a natural step for him to become Commander-in-Chief of the Reichswehr, the small army of 100,000 officers and men to which Germany was restricted under the terms of peace.

It was even more natural that he should have dedicated himself to the task of stretching these bonds and preparing the way for Germany to regain her military strength—as any soldier of any country would have done in similar circumstances. As a guide, he had the example of how Scharnhorst had managed to evade the disarmament of the Prussian Army that France had imposed after 1806, and had built up a camouflaged army that turned the tables on Napoleon seven years later. But Seeckt and his pupils in some ways improved on Scharnhorst's process, under more difficult conditions.

The first obstacle that Seeckt had to overcome was the natural mistrust of the leaders of the new Republic for the military caste that had treated civilians with disdain, and then led the nation to a crushing defeat. Here Seeckt was helped by the impression that his polished manner, diplomatic tact, and apparent understanding of civil problems made upon men who had been accustomed to the domineering brusqueness of Hindenburg and Ludendorff. Seeckt was a pleasing contrast to the browbeating Prussian general of whom they had bitter experience. His elegance, artistic interests, and knowledge of the world added a subtle flavour to the self-contained personality that had gained him the nickname of the "Sphinx". While his somewhat cynical attitude and ironical comments had been distasteful in higher military circles, they appealed to the politicians as evidence of a lack of fanaticism, and an assurance that he blended military efficiency with moderation in militarism.

Seeckt kept the army as a whole out of politics, and by his apparent loyalty to the new republican régime at an awkward time, he was the better able to cloak his military

development schemes, as well as the half-veiled political
activities in which numerous officers of the older school
indulged. So far as vested interests allowed, he ensured
that the cadres of the new Reichswehr should represent
the pick of the officers and N.C.O.s who had undergone
the test of war. He aimed to make this small force of
4,000 officers and 96,000 men a corps of qualified instructors
and leaders, capable of serving as the framework for
rapid expansion—when this might become possible. Their
training was developed to a high pitch and on new lines,
so that they should become more intensely professional in
spirit and skill than the unlimited army of the past had
been.

He supplemented this framework with a variety of
underground schemes by which officers could gain wider
experience than was practicable in an army compulsorily
deprived of the major modern weapons, and by which
ex-officers could be kept from getting rusty. Many staff
officers and technicians found temporary employment in
Japan, China, the South American countries, the Baltic
States and Soviet Russia—where they could have some
practical experience with tanks. Other officers gained
flying experience with civil airways. A considerable proportion of the demobilized army was able to get some
continued military practice in unofficial organizations that
were running inside Germany, and many subterfuges were
used to preserve extra weapons for their training.

These devices were testimony to the ingenuity of a
keen soldier and his assistants in evading a network of
restrictions. They were also a constant worry to the
Allied officers responsible for seeing that the peace terms
were fulfilled. But it is an historical mistake to overrate
their importance in making possible Germany's renewed
burst of aggression. The total effect was very slight,
compared with the weight that Germany had to regain
before she could again become a serious danger. The
bulk of the material developments that really mattered

was only achieved after Hitler had come into power, in
1933, and launched the large-scale re-armament with
which the former Allies did not attempt to interfere.

Seeckt's more real achievement was in starting a train
of ideas which revitalized the German Army, turned it
into a new line of progress, and enabled it to add a quali-
tative superiority to the quantitative recovery that the
victors' inertia permitted it to carry out. He gave the
Reichswehr a gospel of mobility, based on the view that a
quick-moving, quick-hitting army of picked troops could,
under modern conditions, make rings round an old-
fashioned mass army. That view was in no small measure
due to his experience on the Eastern Front, where the
wide spaces had allowed far more room for manœuvre
than had been possible on the Western Front. The first
post-war manuals of the Reichswehr laid down that
"every action ought to be based on surprise. Without
surprise it would be difficult to obtain great results".
Flexibility was another keynote—"reserves should, above
all, be pushed in to exploit where a success is gained, even
though it becomes necessary, by so doing, to shift the
original centre of gravity". To promote such flexibility
the Reichswehr was quick to develop new means of inter-
communication, and devoted a larger proportion of its
limited strength to this service than any other post-war
army. It also insisted on commanders of all grades being
further forward than was then the custom, so that they
could keep their fingers on the pulse of battle and exert a
quicker influence.

In the exaltation of manœuvre, these post-war German
manuals offered a striking contrast with those of the French
Army, which drew the conclusion that "of the two elements,
fire and movement, fire is preponderant". The French
doctrine obviously visualized the repetition in any future
war of the slow-motion tactics of 1918. That difference
was ominous. But the German view was not merely
governed by the necessity of making the most of their

handicaps under the peace treaty. For Seeckt, in his preface to the new manual, wrote with remarkable frankness—"These regulations are based on the strength, armament, and equipment of the army of a modern great military power, and not only on the German Army of 100,000 men formed in accordance with the Peace Treaty."

Seeckt's active work came to an end in 1926, when he made a slip and was forced to resign following the political storm that arose through his action in permitting the eldest son of the German Crown Prince to take part in the Army manœuvres. The limitations of his outlook—which had appeared broad by comparison with other generals—were still more clearly brought out by his subsequent venture into politics, as a spokesman of the half-baked ideas of the German People's Party. But the influence of his own military ideas continued to grow.

His vision of the future emerged clearly from the book he wrote soon after he left office—*Thoughts of a Soldier* (1928). He there questioned the value of the huge conscript armies of the past, suggesting that the effort and sacrifice was disproportionate to their effect, and merely led to a slow-grinding war of exhaustion. "Mass becomes immobile; it cannot manœuvre and therefore cannot win victories, it can only crush by sheer weight." Moreover, in peace-time, it was important "to limit as far as possible the unproductive retention of male labour in military service". Technical science and tactical skill were the keys to the future. "A conscript mass, whose training has been brief and superficial, is 'cannon fodder' in the worst sense of the word, if pitted against a small number of practised technicians on the other side." That prediction was fulfilled in 1940, when a handful of *panzer* divisions, striking in combination with dive-bombers, paralysed and pulverized the ill-equipped conscript mass of the French Army.

In Seeckt's view "the operating army" should consist of "professional, long-term soldiers, volunteers as far as

possible". The bulk of the nation's manpower would be
better employed during peace-time in helping to expand
the industry required to provide the professional army
with an ample equipment of up-to-date weapons. The
type of weapons must be settled well in advance, and
arrangements for rapid mass production developed.

At the same time a brief period of compulsory military
training should be given to all fit young men in the country,
"preceded by a training of the young, which would lay less
emphasis on the military side than on a general physical
and mental discipline". Such a system would help to
link the army with the people, and ensure national unity.
"In this way a military mass is constituted which, though
unsuited to take part in a war of movement and seek a
decision in formal battle, is well able to fulfil the duty
of home defence, and at the same time to provide from
its best elements a continuous reinforcement of the regular,
combatant army in the field." It was a conscript levy of
this kind which filled the bulk of the German infantry
divisions in 1940. They merely followed up the decisive
armoured spearheads, and occupied the conquered regions.
Later, as their own training improved, they were available
to expand and replenish the striking forces in the way that
Seeckt had foreseen.

"In brief, the whole future of warfare appears to me to
lie in the employment of mobile armies, relatively small
but of high quality, and rendered distinctly more effective
by the addition of aircraft, and in the simultaneous
mobilization of the whole forces, either to feed the attack
or for home defence."

Curiously, Seeckt's book scarcely touched on the subject
of tanks, but dwelt at length on the value of cavalry, as
well as of motor transport, in the mobile operations he
pictured. He even wrote lyrically that "the days of
cavalry, if trained, equipped and led on modern lines, are
not numbered", and that "its lances may still flaunt their
pennants with confidence in the wind of the future".

It has been suggested in later years that Seeckt's neglect of armoured warfare was prompted purely by political discretion, and that the word "tank" should be read into his sentences wherever he used the word "cavalry". Such a view is contradicted by the undisguised way in which he advocated conscription and aircraft both of which were forbidden to Germany by the peace terms.

For all his dynamism, Seeckt was a man of his generation, rather than a forerunner of the next. His military vision was clear enough to see the necessity of mobile warfare for any offensive purpose, but did not reach far enough to see that *armoured* mobility was the only way to make it possible. It was left for others, particularly Guderian, to develop that possibility—and aggressive necessity.

The old military battle-picture also coloured Seeckt's vision when he argued that the immediate object of the air force's attack should be to destroy the opposing air force. The Luftwaffe did that in Poland, and to a lesser extent in France. But when it tried that way of preparing the invasion of Britain, it suffered crippling losses on meeting, for the first time, a strong defending air force.

On the wider issues of war and life his outlook was patchy. With some truth he contended that direct experience of the horrors of war made soldiers more chary than political leaders of becoming involved in a war, but he went too far in trying to show they were really "pacifists" in the best sense of the word. That characteristic professional apologia, familiar in every country, does not find much support in cases where the archives of a warmaking country have been opened to examination. High soldiers have too often failed to show that "pacifism established on knowledge and born of a sense of responsibility" which Seeckt claimed for them.

He was rather weak in his argument that "militarism" and "aggression" were merely catchwords. At the same time he was shrewdly prophetic in his remarks that when-

ever policy aimed at the acquisition of power, "the statesman will soon find himself thwarted in some way or other,
will deduce from this opposition a menace first to his
plans, then to national prestige, and finally to the existence
of the state itself—and so, regarding his country as the
party attacked, will engage in a war of defence".

A sense of humanity, as well as of prophecy, gleamed
through his ironical comment on the modern psychological
tendency to reverse the moral judgments of the past—"I
find it very inconvenient that I may no longer regard
Nero simply as the imperial monster who used to go to
bed by the light of a burning Christian, but rather as a
wise if somewhat peculiar modern dictator." Was he
hinting a doubt of the new morality that men like the
Nazis were starting to proclaim? Again, in emphasizing
the value of "action", there is a significant qualification
conveyed in his epigrammatic judgment—"Intellect without will is worthless, will without intellect is dangerous."
There was a wise warning, too, in another of his wider
reflections—"The statement that war is a continuation of
policy by other means has become a catch-phrase, and is
therefore dangerous. We can say with equal truth—war is
the bankruptcy of policy."

At the same time Seeckt's care to keep his army out
of politics carried a danger of its own. His attitude of
professional detachment, and the sharp dividing line he
drew between the military and political spheres, tended
towards a renunciation of the soldier's potential restraining
influence on adventurous statesmen.

The Seeckt-pattern professional became a modern
Pontius Pilate, washing his hands of all responsiblity for
the orders he executed. Pure military theory deals in
extremes that are hard to combine with wise policy.
When soldiers concentrate on the absolute military aim,
and do not learn to think of grand strategy, they are more
apt to accept political arguments that, while seeming
right in pure strategy, commit policy beyond the point

where it can halt. Extreme military ends are difficult to reconcile with moderation of policy.

That danger would grow because professional opinion, as embodied in a General Staff, is never so united in practice as it should be in principle. It is split by its own "politics" and personal ambitions. Seeckt himself not only recalled the past but foreshadowed the future when he wrote—"A history of the General Staff . . . would be a history of quiet positive work; it would tell of arrogance and haughty acquiescence, of vanity and envy, of all human weaknesses, of the fight between genius and bureaucracy, and of the hidden causes of victory and defeat. It would take the radiance from many a halo, and it would not be lacking in tragedy."

The General Staff was essentially intended to form a collective substitute for genius, which no army can count on producing at need. Of its very nature it tended to cramp the growth of genius, being a bureaucracy as well as a hierarchy, but in compensation it sought to raise the general standard of competence to a high level. The unevenness of its performance was due less to differences of individual talent than to the underlying differences of personal interest, as well as to conflicting personal views. The chance of promotion tended to make any general swallow his doubts for the moment, long enough to enable Hitler to split the solidity of professional opinion. That applies to all armies, but is particularly marked under a dictatorship. A newly-promoted general is always confident that the situation is better than it appeared to his predecessor, and that he can succeed where the latter failed. Such a disposition is a powerful lever in the hands of any ruler.

CHAPTER III

THE BLOMBERG-FRITSCH ERA

SEECKT was succeeded by Heye, and Heye, four years later, by Hammerstein. Neither was quite of Seeckt's calibre, but both on the whole continued to develop his policy. Hammerstein was deeply perturbed by the growing strength of the Nazi movement, finding both its creed and its methods repugnant, and he was led to depart from Seeckt's principle of political detachment to the extent of considering the possibilities of taking forcible measures to check Hitler's accession to power. The ground was cut away beneath his feet, however, by the decision of the senile President of the Republic, Field-Marshal von Hindenburg, to appoint Hitler to be Chancellor—thus making his position constitutionally valid. Moreover, Hammerstein's apprehensions were not shared by other leading generals who were soldiers "pure and simple". He felt, bitterly, that they were dazzled and led astray "by the favourable outlook for army expansion and greater opportunities of promotion".

The next important step came when Hitler, almost immediately after entering office, appointed General von Blomberg as War Minister. That choice was inspired by the ambitious Colonel von Reichenau, who had been Blomberg's Chief of Staff in East Prussia, and was in close contact with Hitler. Blomberg himself did not know Hitler, and his character was in many ways the antithesis of Hitler's. His acceptance of the appointment, as well as his performance in it, was an illustration of how simple the pure soldier can be.

BLOMBERG

During the previous year Blomberg had been chief military adviser to the German delegation at the Disarmament Conference. He was only just over fifty—young by comparison with the average age of the High Command in the German and other armies. This fact in itself naturally excited envy of his sudden elevation. That hostile feeling was increased by the German generals' attitude of disdain for the "Bohemian Corporal". Many of them had been ready to welcome Hitler's rise to power in so far as it seemed likely to favour their own schemes of military expansion, but they scoffed at the idea that an ex-corporal could be credited with any military judgment, and were thus the more quick to question any preference he showed in making military appointments.

This attitude among the senior officers of the Reichswehr prejudiced Blomberg's position from the outset. By becoming suspect in the eyes of his fellows he was thrown back on Hitler's support, and so was forced to follow Hitler's line further than his own judgment would have led him. Ironically, the natural pleasantness of his personality, refreshingly different from the "Prussian" type, became a handicap in such circumstances of dependence. This combination went far to account for the nickname of the "Rubber Lion" that was bestowed on him by other soldiers.

For Werner von Blomberg was of a different type from the violent and unscrupulous leaders of the new régime. If he was more in sympathy with the Nazis than other generals, it was partly because he was more idealistic—while his romantic enthusiasm easily blinded him to aspects he did not care to see. The Nazi movement for a time attracted quite a number of such idealists, though most of them were much younger than Blomberg. Soldiers, however, are slow to grow up. Blomberg was a natural enthusiast, and looked on the profession of arms in the spirit of a knight-errant. This was evident to me when I met him at Geneva in 1932. He showed an eager interest in new military ideas, especially those that promised a new artistry in tactics as a game of skill, but was still more enthusiastic about the possibilities of resuscitating

the code of chivalry. He became almost lyrical in discoursing upon the appeal of "gentlemanliness" in war.
Close observation of the higher military levels over a
long period makes for scepticism, but Blomberg impressed
me as exceptionally genuine, if boyish, in his profession of
faith. Tall and broad physically, he was neither over-
bearing nor grim in his manner, but showed a natural
courtesy combined with a refreshingly frank way of
talking. It was his hard fate to be called on to deal with
two rival groups, and to become a buffer between them.
In a better environment he might have proved a greater
figure.

Yet in one important respect his influence may have
been more effective than it seemed. One of the surprising
features of the Second World War was that the German
Army in the field on the whole observed the rules of war
better than it did in 1914–18—at any rate in fighting its
western opponents—whereas it was reasonable to expect
that the addition of "Nazism" to "Prussianism" would
make its behaviour worse than before. The relative
improvement in behaviour, and the greater care shown
to avoid stains on its record, may be traced to the more
refined conception of soldierly conduct which Blomberg
and a number of others who shared his views had striven
to instil in the Reichswehr. The restraint shown in 1940
by the troops that invaded Belgium and France, compared
with their predecessors of 1914, was also a wise policy.
It went quite a long way to soften the sting of defeat and
conciliate the people of the conquered countries, and
might have had a more lasting effect but for the contrasting
behaviour of the Gestapo and the S.S. forces.

In the tactical sphere Blomberg helped to give an
important turn to the trend of development. Hammerstein
had perpetuated the German Army's old doctrine of the
offensive, without the material means to practise it or a
new technique to sharpen its edge. But, in East Prussia,
Blomberg had experimented with new forms of tactics

which more realistically recognized the existing superiority of modern defence, and sought to turn this to advantage the other way, as an offensive aid. Instead of attacking a strongly defended position, one might lure the enemy out of position, draw him into making a rash advance or hurried assault, catch him in a trap, and then exploit his disorder by delivering one's own real stroke—in the more deadly form of a riposte. The bait might be created by luring withdrawal or by a sudden swoop that threatened the enemy's communications. The potentialities of this "baited move" combining offensive strategy with defensive tactics—like sword and shield—had struck me in the course of my study of Sherman's campaign in Georgia, and in subsequent books I had elaborated its application to modern warfare. It was Blomberg's particular interest in this idea which first brought us into contact.[1]

Blomberg also showed more appreciation than most generals at that date of the new conception of mobile warfare, with tanks fulfilling the historic role of cavalry—a conception which had met with a half-hearted response in the British Army, except in the circle of the Royal Tank Corps. Reichenau was still keener, and had himself translated some of my books, though even he did not embrace the concept of armoured warfare so fully as men like Guderian and Thoma who took a more direct hand in creating German's armoured forces from 1934 onwards.

The triumphs of German tactics and of the German armoured forces in the first two years of the war cast an

[1] Sherman's methods also fired General Patton's imagination—particularly with regard to the way that they exploited the indirect approach and the value of cutting down impedimenta in order to gain mobility. When I met Patton in 1944, shortly before he took his army across to Normandy, he told me how he had earlier spent a long leave studying Sherman's campaigns on the ground with my book in hand, and we discussed the possibilities of applying such methods in modern warfare. They were demonstrated in his subsequent sweep from Normandy to the Moselle. General Wood, who commanded his spearhead, the 4th Armoured Division, was another enthusiast for these ideas, and on reaching the Seine wrote to tell me how successful their application had proved.

ironical reflection on the measures taken to disarm the
defeated country after the previous war. Materially, they
proved effective. For the numerous evasions that German
military chiefs practised were on a petty scale, and in
themselves amounted to no considerable recovery of
strength. Germany's actual progress in material re-
armament constituted no serious danger up to the time
when the Nazi Government openly threw off the restrictions of the peace treaty. It was the hesitancy of the
victors after that time which allowed Germany again to
become formidable. Moreover, an important result of
her enforced disarmament was to give her a clear start,
by freeing her army from such an accumulation of 1914–
1918 weapons as the victorious nations had preserved—a
load of obsolescence that tended to bind them to old
methods, and led them to overrate their own strength.
When the German Army began large-scale re-armament,
it benefited by having more room for the development of
the newer weapons suggested by a fresher current of ideas.

The development of such fresh ideas was, in turn,
helped by another of the measures imposed by the victors
—the suppression of the General Staff. If it had been
left to carry on in its old form, and its old cumbersome
shell, it might have remained as routinely inert and over-
whelmed by its offices as other General Staffs. Driven
underground, its members were largely exempted from
administrative routine, and impelled to concentrate on
constructive thinking about the future—thus becoming
more efficient for war. Any such military organization
can be destroyed in so far as it is a physical substance, but
not in respect of its activities as a thinking organ—thought
cannot be suppressed.

Thus the net effect of the sweeping disarmament of
Germany after the First World War was to clear the path
for the more efficient modernization of her forces when a
political opportunity for re-armament developed. Limitations in the degree of modernization were due more to

internal conservatism and conflicting interests than to the external restrictions that had been placed upon her.

FRITSCH

Blomberg's position as War Minister enabled him to foster the growth of the new tactics he favoured, and to overcome the resistance which the more orthodox generals had shown—as in other countries, especially France. But the weakness of his own position, as a "buffer-state", handicapped him in hastening their spread and development at the pace that might otherwise have been possible. When he tried, at the end of 1933, to secure the appointment of Reichenau as Chief of the Army Command in place of Hammerstein, he was foiled by the concerted opposition of the senior generals. Acting on their advice Hindenburg chose General von Fritsch, a soldier of great all-round ability, who represented the more conservative school, both politically and militarily. He had grasped the value of tanks and aircraft up to a point, but regarded the new arms as "upstarts", and was intent to keep them in their place—a subordinate place, in his view. Moreover, General Beck, who subsequently became Chief of the General Staff, was almost as critical of the tank "revolutionaries" as he was of the Nazi revolution. Thus German military organization, though it forged ahead of other countries in developing mechanized forces, remained a compromise between the old and new patterns.

Werner von Fritsch, as a comparatively young staff officer, had worked under General von Seeckt at the Reichswehr Ministry from 1920 to 1922, in preparing the new organization. Then he went to regimental duty in command of a battery, and subsequently became chief of staff in East Prussia. In 1927, he returned to the Reichswehr Ministry as assistant to Blomberg, who was head of the operations branch. Here he was largely responsible for devising the plan, in case of war, for a swift offensive against Poland combined with a defensive in the West to

hold France in check. It was the embryo of the plan
that was actually executed in 1939, although then amplified
in scale and multiplied in speed—by mechanized forces.

During the pre-Nazi period Fritsch showed a diplomatic talent, unusual among German officers of the old
school, in dealing with democratic deputies who were
inclined to ask awkward questions regarding increases in
the military budget, and the reasons why an army limited
in size required such a disproportionately large framework
of staff and instructional cadres. Fritsch was adept in
explaining away such curious points, and in persuading
critics not to press their inquiries. He knew how to gag them
in subtle ways—by appealing to their patriotism, playing on
their weaknesses, or cultivating their friendship. Normally
he had an ice-cold manner, and nature, but he could turn
on a warm tap of charm, when it served a purpose.

When the Nazis arrived in power the generals realized
that they would need a chief who combined determination
with diplomacy in order to hold their own. It was Fritsch's
possession of these qualities, in addition to his reputation as
a strategist, that led to his appointment early in 1934.
His first moves were directed to curb the ambition of the
amateur soldiers of the Nazi party, headed by Captain
Roehm, and to counter the threat that their advancement
might carry to the authority and interests of the professional
army. He provided Hitler with evidence that their plans for
arming the storm troopers as a supplement to the army were
designed to pave the way for a *coup d' état,* aimed at Hitler
himself. Himmler was working on the same line—from a
different motive. They succeeded in convincing Hitler so
well as to produce the bloody purge of June 30th, 1934.

This had the double effect of strengthening Fritsch's
position with Hitler and with all the elements in Germany
that, for diverse reasons, feared the growth of the Nazi
influence. For a time he established the supremacy of
the Army Command upon the internal balance of power,
and was able to outmanœuvre Himmler.

A strain began to develop, however, over the conduct of external affairs—about the pace more than about the policy. Fritsch and his fellows liked Hitler's vigorous assertion of Germany's right to equality and the way he spoke of freeing her from the restrictions imposed by the Versailles Treaty. (Preparatory measures were taken in 1933, with his backing, for expanding the Army from the existing 8 divisions to a strength of 24, and the manufacture of the necessary equipment.) But they were dubious about Hitler's sudden decision, in October, 1933, to leave the League of Nations—a step that was taken without consulting the heads of the Army—as they felt that it placed Germany in a position of precarious isolation. They were also worried about the violent attacks on Russia which Hitler made in his speeches; and the more so because they had established friendly relations with the leaders of the Red Army, who had given them facilities to carry out practice with new equipment that was debarred to them in Germany.

Then in March, 1935, came Hitler's defiant announcement to the world that he had thrown off the armament fetters of Versailles, constituted an army of 36 divisions, and was reintroducing conscription. The announcement was made without previous discussion with the heads of the Army, who were the more startled because they knew that his claim was hollow and that no arrangements had yet been made for creating 36 divisions. Much as they liked the idea of a larger army, they had regarded a trebling of the Reichswehr strength as the practicable limit of what could be achieved without dangerously diminishing efficiency. Their tendency to question the decision, and the boast, irritated Hitler all the more because of the way that his announcement was swallowed in other countries without serious protest or doubt of its substance. He felt that his generals were lukewarm when they should have been ardent and enthusiastic.

A year later Hitler gave the world a fresh shock by

moving German troops back into the demilitarized zone
of the Rhineland. This time the military chiefs were consulted—but only on the eve of the step. They had less than
twenty-four hours to draft and issue the orders to the
troops. Blomberg expressed grave doubt about the step,
and its risks, especially that of sending troops west of the
Rhine; Hitler yielded to his arguments so far as to agree
that only three battalions should march over the river—
so that it would be easy to withdraw if the French made a
serious threat of counter-action. But no such threat
materialized, and Hitler's exhilaration at the success of his
manœuvre was accompanied by fresh irritation at the way
his generals, while appearing to keep in step with him,
were trying to slow down the pace.

Hitler was much encouraged by the submissive way in
which those defiant steps were accepted by the French and
British Governments. Then, flouting their desire that all
outside powers should abstain from intervention in the
Spanish Civil War, he sent military aid to General Franco.
His primary object, as he explained to his entourage, was
"to distract the attention of the world powers to the
Pyrenean Peninsula in order to complete the German
re-armament without them intervening in Germany". The
success of Franco's revolt would also establish a Fascist power
athwart the sea-communications of France and Britain.

Fritsch, however, was opposed to such a step. He
shrewdly saw that Spain was an awkward place strategically
at which to risk an open challenge to the Western powers.
As a result of his objections the proposed force of three
divisions was reduced to a training contingent merely, with
a tank battalion. His caution was resented by the Nazi
leaders, flushed with their recent successes in defiance. At
the same time his diplomatic efforts to foster better relations
with the Red Army excited violent complaint on their part.
Hitler's anti-Bolshevik obsession provided Fritsch's enemies
with fruitful soil in which to sow suspicion. Friction was
increased by Fritsch's efforts to maintain the old spirit in

the new officer corps, and keep it free from permeation by Nazi ideology.

Meanwhile the rift between Fritsch and Blomberg was growing. Fritsch and his fellows felt that Blomberg was hypnotized by Hitler, and was not standing up for the Army's interests as he should have done. It seemed to them that Blomberg's spirit of subservience was symbolized in the way he wore Nazi emblems on his uniform, and they nicknamed him Hitler-Youth-Quex, after an idealistic boy portrayed in a Nazi film.

THE DOUBLE DISMISSAL

A crisis came in January, 1938, arising out of an affair that was very remote in appearance from its real causes. Blomberg had fallen in love with a typist in his office, and married her. Hitler expressed approval of Blomberg's intention, as a public proof that the military leaders of National-Socialist Germany were broadening their social outlook and identifying themselves with the people, instead of marrying only into their own caste. He graced the wedding, as a witness. Blomberg's fellow-generals regarded the marriage as unseemly, but—contrary to what was widely reported at the time—it is not true that they made a concerted protest and caused Blomberg's removal from office. For any protest they might have made was forestalled—by Himmler.

After Blomberg's marriage had taken place Himmler presented to Hitler a police dossier purporting to show that the bride had been a prostitute. It has been suggested by American investigators since the war, that Himmler had planted her in Blomberg's office as part of a trap. Hitler's reaction to the revelation was violent, for by his own presence at this wedding of "a woman of the streets" he had been made to look ridiculous. He dismissed Blomberg from his post, and even crossed his name off the list of the officers' corps.

That news did not disturb the other generals. But

they were shaken to their roots by a second stroke that immediately followed. For now that the question of appointing a new War Minister had to be considered Himmler brought out a further dossier to show that Fritsch was under police watch for homosexual offences. It was, actually, a dossier about another man of almost the same name. But when Hitler sent for the Commander-in-Chief, Himmler produced a witness who formally identified him as the man in the case. Hitler thereupon removed him from his post.

According to General Röhricht, the reason for this move of Himmler's was to prevent Fritsch succeeding to Blomberg's position and power, which carried with it supreme command of the Wehrmacht—the armed forces as a whole. "Anyone succeeding to that post would become the superior of Goering who was now Commander-in-Chief of the Luftwaffe. It would have been very difficult to appoint any fresh soldier over his head. Fritsch was the only possible one, because of his existing seniority to Goering as a Commander-in-Chief. Himmler's intervention was not for Goering's sake, but for his own ends. All his moves had the aim of paving the way for his ambition of replacing the army by the S.S., step by step."

Fritsch demanded a Court of Inquiry, but it was only with much difficulty that he was granted one—after energetic representations by Rundstedt, as representative of the senior generals. When it was conceded, Himmler wanted to preside over it himself, but the Minister of Justice then came to Fritsch's help by declaring that a military court was necessary. Himmler next tried to get at the witnesses for the defence. To ensure their attendance, and their safety, the generals arranged for them to be guarded by soldiers. At the inquiry Himmler's chief witness recanted his evidence—and paid for this with his life. But Fritsch was completely acquitted.

Meanwhile, Hitler had taken the opportunity to assume supreme command of the Wehrmacht himself, declaring that he had lost confidence in the generals. Blomberg's former post was reduced to a lower status, and filled by General Keitel, who appeared to Hitler to have the qualities of a good lackey. At the same time General von Brauchitsch was appointed to command the Army in place of Fritsch, so no room was left for the latter by the time he was cleared of the charges that had been framed against him. Thus the outcome of the crisis that had been so deliberately engineered was to pave the way for Hitler's ultimate control of strategy, while strengthening Himmler's influence.

Sectional jealousies and conservative instincts played into Hitler's hands at each stage of his progress to personal control of strategy. He was skilful in exploiting them, while careful to limit the development of any directing organ that might provide a check on his aims. Although a General Staff was reconstituted in 1935, it was not given the powers of the old Great General Staff. Its chief was kept subordinate to the Commander-in-Chief of the Army in military matters, while political matters were reserved for the Minister of War. Moreover, Blomberg was made Commander-in-Chief of the Wehrmacht (the armed forces as a whole) in addition to his duties as War Minister.

In the Oberkommando der Wehrmacht (a title commonly shortened to O.K.W.) were centralized the political and administrative matters common to all three services. A small "national defence" section (Landesverteidigung) was now added, to deal with matters on the borderline between policy and strategy, and with the co-ordination of the three services. This appeared to be a step to the creation of a Wehrmacht General Staff—but the theoretical arguments for this further step were outweighed by other considerations, on all sides.

Such a development was repugnant to the Army High Command (Oberkommando das Heeres—O.K.H. for short), since it would tend to diminish their position and displace them as the heir of the old Great General Staff.

They argued that it was unsound to subordinate a long-established organization such as theirs to a newly formed body of an amateur nature, and that as Germany's military problems were predominantly continental the Army High Command ought to have the decisive influence. Their opposition was helped by the Naval High Command's inherent dislike of being directed by landlubbers, and the more personal objections that arose from Goering's position as Commander-in-Chief of the Air Force. Blomberg, anxious not to arouse resistance, constantly emphasized that the new co-ordinating organ was only a small one, and that he did not wish it to become "top-heavy". As for Hitler, although he wanted to diminish the power of the Army General Staff, he had no desire to replace it by a superior General Staff that would become a fresh hindrance to his personal control. So he abstained from backing any move to develop a Wehrmacht General Staff, and when he cut off the head of O.K.W. by dismissing Blomberg he took care to keep the O.K.W. staff down to the position of a mere "bureau" for himself.

For the time being the General Staff of the Army remained in control of strategy, subject to Hitler's broad direction. But he was looking for opportunities of diminishing its influence so that he could fulfil his ambition to play the part of executive strategist—and actually handle the pieces on the board.

A further step was taken the following winter when Hitler revoked the rule—which had persisted since 1813—that in taking military decisions all Chiefs of Staff had co-responsibility with the Commanders they served, and could record a differing opinion. This practice had enabled them to appeal to higher quarters over the head of their Commander. But under the new rule the Chief of the General Staff himself could no longer voice an independent opinion, and became strictly subordinate to whoever was Commander-in-Chief of the Army. The change diminished his influence and that of all other general staff officers.

CHAPTER IV

THE BRAUCHITSCH–HALDER ERA

At first sight it may seem curious that such a man as
Walther von Brauchitsch was appointed to replace Fritsch,
and that he accepted the appointment. For he had
shown himself conspicuously loyal to the former republican régime, and inclined to take a liberal view of political
and economic issues, while outspokenly critical of Nazi
policies. Neither Junker narrowness nor Nazi fanaticism
appealed to him. At the same time he was generally
regarded as a man who had a keen sense of honour and
was by no means self-seeking. For these reasons, coupled
with his strong sense of justice and consideration for others,
he was trusted both by his fellows and his juniors to an
exceptional degree. Was his acceptance of Hitler's offer
in February, 1938, due to a sudden yielding to personal
ambition—when the prize was so big—or to a feeling that
he might be able to help the Service by stepping into the
breach? The second, and better, explanation tends to be
supported by the fact that Brauchitsch continued on good
terms with Fritsch after the latter had been shelved, and
took more than one opportunity of paying tribute to him,
in a way distasteful to the Nazi leaders. Events soon
showed, however, that Brauchitsch had stepped on to a
slippery slope where he would find it hard to keep upright.

The choice of Brauchitsch was a compromise. Hitler
had thought of appointing Reichenau, but was told by
Rundstedt and others that this would arouse strong opposition from the Army. Brauchitsch was generally regarded
as a sound yet progressive soldier—although primarily an
"artillerist" he had a better appreciation of tank potentialities than most of the senior generals. In other respects,

too, he was less conservative than the school that Fritsch had represented. His popularity with all sections was an obvious asset, which would help to offset suspicion of the political motives behind the changes and of the internal struggle that had preceded them. His unassuming manner fostered the hope that he would prove easier to handle than Fritsch.

Hitler soon found, however, that Brauchitsch—though more polite in his manner—was no more disposed than Fritsch had been to allow a political infiltration in the army. His first steps were to introduce a number of welfare measures for improving the condition and post-service prospects of the ordinary soldier, but he insisted on keeping these clear of Nazi organization. At the same time he tightened discipline. He sought to quicken up the process of equipping the forces, but also to put a brake on the tendency of Nazi foreign policy to precipitate an early conflict. His stand was reinforced by General Beck, then Chief of the General Staff. Beck, though a soldier of great ability and strong character, tended towards the "anti-tank" school, so that in his opposition to Hitler's aggressive policy he was inclined to underrate what Hitler might achieve by the use of new instruments.

After Hitler had made his designs clear, Brauchitsch summoned all the senior generals to a conference early in August, and told them that Beck had drafted a memorandum, which, if they approved, he proposed sending to Hitler. Beck then read the memorandum. It argued that German policy ought to avoid the risk of war, especially over such "a small issue as the Sudetenland". It pointed out the weakness of the German forces, and their inferiority to the combination that might be arrayed against them. It emphasized that, even if the United States did not take a direct part, she was likely to use her resources to supply Germany's opponents with arms and equipment.

Rundstedt, giving me his account of the conference, said—"When Beck had finished reading the memorandum,

Brauchitsch got up and asked whether any of those present
had objections to raise before it was sent to Hitler. No one
objected, so the document was delivered. It provoked Hitler
to great wrath". The clash was followed by the departure
of Beck—who was succeeded by Halder.

This momentarily damped opposition, but when the
Czecho-Slovakian crisis came to a head, in September,
Brauchitsch told Hitler that the German Army was not
prepared for war, and warned him against pressing his
demands so hard as to produce a fight. Brauchitsch was
supported by Halder, who followed his predecessor's line
rather than Hitler's—thus showing him that it was still
difficult to drive a wedge into the close-knit German
military corporation. Halder belonged to the more conservative school in military views, but, like Beck, he looked
well ahead in the political field, and was averse to gambling
with Germany's future. He was anxious, too, that the new
Army should avoid a trial of strength while still immature.
When it became clear that Hitler was not to be checked
by counsels of caution, Halder became busy with plans
for a military revolt against Hitler's policy and régime.

The French and British Governments, however, were
even less prepared for war or willing to risk a fight on
behalf of Czecho-Slovakia, so Hitler gained his claims for
the Sudetenland with little difficulty, at Munich.

In the flush of that triumph Hitler became harder to
curb. Next spring he occupied the whole of the Czechs'
territory by a sudden coup, breaking the Munich agreement. He then proceeded, without pause, to put pressure
on Poland for the return of Danzig to Germany and the
right to build an extra-territorial railway and road across
the Polish Corridor into East Prussia. Unable to see
anybody else's point of view, he could not understand
that these limited demands lost their appearance of
moderation in the circumstances of their proposal. When
the Poles refused to consider such readjustments, and were
stiffened by the British Government's offer of support,

Hitler became so angry under his sense of injury as to press matters further and quicker than he had intended. While still hoping that the Poles would climb down, and save his face, he became more inclined to risk war—provided that the risk in a war would not be too big.

When he consulted the military chiefs on this question, Brauchitsch gave a more qualified reply than Keitel. Brauchitsch considered that Germany could "probably" reckon on a favourable result if the opposition were confined to Poland, France and Britain. But he emphatically declared that Germany would not have much chance of winning if she had also to fight Russia. The French Ambassador in Berlin, M. Coulondre, heard of the arguments and reported them to his government early in June.

Brauchitsch's doubts, coupled with his disparaging comments on the value of Italy as an ally, annoyed the more violent Nazis, who had already been complaining of the way he had checked the Nazification of the Army. They developed a campaign against him. This may explain why he was led at this time to make a public declaration of confidence in the Führer, and also to express sentiments in a speech at Tannenberg which sounded threateningly towards Poland—though they could be construed in a strictly defensive sense. But it is understandable that he should feel that there was little danger in such language, since no one who weighed the situation in military scales was likely to imagine that Britain and France would actually carry their support of Poland to the point of war in such a hopeless strategical position as would result if Russia was induced to stand aside. For Hitler was driven to meet Brauchitsch's stipulations so far as Russia was concerned and to recast his whole policy of the past in an effort to secure her neutrality. Once he accepted the necessity of a political turn-about, Hitler moved quickly to arrange a pact with Russia—in striking contrast to the hesitation and delay of the British

Government in their negotiations with Russia at the same
time.

Despite the announcement of the Russo-German pact
the British Government defied logical military calculation
by deciding to fight, and pushed the French into the same
course. But the invasion of Poland had already been
launched, on Hitler's order, before the fallacy of that
calculation was apparent. For the moment Brauchitsch
and Halder were fully occupied in conducting the campaign—and could drown their anxieties by immersing
themselves in their professional task.

The plan was of their design, and the campaign was
swiftly successful. The executive commanders were
allowed a free hand, and demonstrated the value of it by
showing an initiative and flexibility that were in the best
vein of the old tradition. The main rôle was played by
Rundstedt's Army Group in the South which, after breaking
through the Polish front, sent Reichenau's mobile 10th
Army—this had the bulk of the mechanized divisions—on
a northward swerve to Warsaw, to cut astride the rear of
the main Polish armies in the centre. That stroke which
decided the issue, was the more notable because O.K.H.
had ordered that the 10th Army should be sent straight
ahead over the Vistula, as the Poles were thought to be
already retreating to the south-east. But Rundstedt and
his Chief of Staff, Manstein, had gauged that the main
Polish armies were still west of Warsaw, and could thus
be trapped on the near side of the Vistula. On this occasion the commander on the spot was allowed to act on
his own judgment, which the result vindicated—but when
a similar crucial turn came in the next campaign Hitler
imposed his own decision and thereby paid a heavy
forfeit.

The effect of victory in Poland had an intoxicating
effect on Hitler. But with it was mingled a fear of what
might happen to him in the East if he did not soon secure
peace in the West. The intoxication and the fear, working

on one another, impelled him to fresh action while making
him more reckless.

To Brauchitsch and Halder the victory in Poland had
brought no such intoxication. Once the dust of battle had
settled they perceived more clearly the awkward consequences of that victory, and the dangers of becoming
embroiled more deeply. After the campaign was over
they recovered the long view so far as to oppose—even to
the point of contemplating a revolt—Hitler's idea that an
offensive in the West would make the Allies more inclined
towards peace. But something more than a few months'
inactivity would have been required to restore favourable
conditions for peace, and during the winter the Allies'
threats of "opening up the war", publicly voiced by
Winston Churchill in broadcasts, had a natural tendency
to spur Hitler into forestalling them. The dynamism of
war increasingly took charge of the train of events.

The invasion of Norway in April, 1940, was the first
of Hitler's aggressive moves that was not premeditated.
As the evidence brought out at Nuremberg made clear,
he was led into it unwillingly, more by fear than by desire,
under the combined influence of persuasion and provo-
cation. Although he achieved this conquest with ease he
was no longer in control of his own course. The persuasion
started from the arguments of Vidkun Quisling, the Norwegian pro-Nazi, about the likelihood of the British
occupying the coast of Norway, with or without the con-
nivance of the Norwegian Government. It was reinforced
by the anxiety of the Naval High Command about the
danger of such a development, both in tightening the grip of
the British blockade and hampering their own submarine
operations. These fears were increased, after the outbreak
of the Russo-Finnish war at the end of November, by
Franco-British offers of aid to Finland—which, as the Germans shrewdly suspected, concealed an aim of gaining
strategic control of the Scandinavian peninsula. Hitler,
however, still felt that Germany had more to gain by Nor-

way's continued neutrality, and wanted to avoid an enlargement of the war. After he had met Quisling in mid-December, he decided to wait and see whether Quisling could fulfil his hope of achieving a political coup in Norway.

In January, however, nervousness was accentuated when Churchill made an emphatic broadcast appeal to the neutrals to join in the fight against Hitler, while other signs of an Allied move multiplied. On February 18th the British destroyer *Cossack* pushed into Norwegian waters and boarded the German supply ship *Altmark* to rescue captured British seamen it was carrying. This step was taken on orders from the Admiralty, of which Churchill was then head. It not only infuriated Hitler, but made him think that if Churchill was ready to violate Norwegian neutrality for the rescue of a handful of prisoners, he was still more likely to do so in order to cut off the iron-ore supplies from Narvik that were vital to Germany.

In this connection Rundstedt remarked to me in one of our talks: "Churchill's broadcasts used to make Hitler angry. They got under his skin—as did Roosevelt's later. Hitler repeatedly argued to the Army High Command, especially over Norway, that if he did not move first, the British would—and establish themselves in such neutral points." Admiral Voss, who was present, confirmed this account from his experience in the Naval High Command, and also said: "The British attack on the *Altmark* proved decisive, in its effect on Hitler—it was the 'fuse' that touched off the Norwegian offensive."

Immediately after this, Hitler appointed General von Falkenhorst to prepare the forces for a coup to seize the Norwegian ports. At a conference on February 23rd, Admiral Raeder, the Naval Commander-in-Chief, emphasized that: "The best thing for maintaining this (ore) traffic as well as for the situation in general is the maintenance of Norwegian neutrality." But he went on to say: "What must not be permitted, as stated earlier, is the occupation of Norway by Britain. That could not be undone."

By this time reports from Norway showed that Quisling's party was losing ground, while reports from England indicated that some action in the Norwegian area was being planned, together with the assembly of troops and transports. On March 1st Hitler issued his directive for the expedition to Norway. On the 9th the Naval High Command presented their plan, and dwelt on the urgency of the operation in view of the reports that a British landing was imminent. They were very worried, but their own preparations would take some time to complete, and all they could do was to send submarines to lie off the ports in case the British transports appeared.

But the Allies' plans were upset for the moment by Finland's capitulation on the 13th, which deprived them of the pretext on which they were intending to land at Narvik. When Admiral Raeder saw Hitler on the 26th, he expressed the view that the danger of a British landing in Norway was no longer acute for the moment, but considered it certain that a fresh pretext would soon be found and fresh attempts made to interrupt the iron-ore traffic. "Sooner or later Germany will be faced with the necessity of carrying out operation 'Weseruebung' "—the code name for the expedition to occupy Norway. Thus it was advisable to do this soon, rather than be too late. Hitler agreed, and fixed the date. Now that preparations had gone so far, there was an irresistible urge to put them into operation. At almost the same time the Allies decided to put fresh pressure on the governments of Norway and Sweden. A mine-belt was to be laid in Norwegian waters, on April 5th, and the first convoy of troops was to sail for Narvik on the 8th. But the mine-laying operation was delayed until the night of the 7th, and next afternoon the German invading force sailed.

Early on April 9th small detachments of German troops, carried mostly in warships, landed at the chief ports of Norway, from Oslo to Narvik, and captured them with little difficulty. The sequel showed that the Allies' designs had outrun the efficiency of their preparations, and the collapse of their counter-moves left Germany in possession of the whole of Norway, together with Denmark. This conquest was achieved without any material subtraction from the forces on the Western front, or interference with the preparations there. Moreover, the operation was carried out under the direction of O.K.W. and not of O.K.H.

The story of how the plan for the invasion of the West took form is related in later chapters, and is too complex for brief summary here. For the moment it is more useful to trace the outline of the plan, and point out the basic factors that governed its issue—as a background to the more detailed record of personal influences and internal controversies.

While it appeared to the world as a supreme example of the shock-offensive, it was really more remarkable for its subtlety. The essential condition of its success was the way that the Allied armies of the left wing, comprising the pick of their mobile forces, were lured deep into Belgium, and even into Holland. It was only through the left wing being caught in this trap, and wrenched from its socket, that the *panzer* stroke cut through the Allied left centre deeply and quickly enough to have decisive effects. Moreover, as fast as the German armoured divisions drove towards the Channel coast, cutting a pocket in the Allied front, the motorized divisions followed them up to form a defensive lining along the whole length of the pocket. These tactics extracted a maximum advantage from a minimum use of shock, and exploited the power of tactical defence as an aid to the offensive. For the burden of attacking, at a disadvantage, was thereby thrown on the Allied armies in any attempt to force open the trap and reunite their severed parts. Such subtlety is the essence of strategy.

With the failure of the Allied left wing to break out, its fate was sealed, save for the portion that managed to escape by sea from Dunkirk, leaving all its equipment behind. None at all might have escaped but for the fact that Hitler stopped the sweeping advance of the *panzer* forces on the outskirts of Dunkirk—for reasons that are discussed farther on. But this forfeit did not affect the immediate future. After the elimination of the left-wing armies the remainder were left too weak to hold the far-stretching front in France against a powerful offensive, so that their collapse in turn was mathematically probable even before the next German stroke was delivered. In 1914 the aim had been to wheel inwards and round up the opposing armies in one vast encirclement, an effort that proved too great for the Germans' capacity. In 1940 the German Command concentrated on cutting off a portion of the opposing armies by an outward sweep, with the result that in this piecemeal process it eventually succeeded in swallowing them completely.

But it was baffled, as Napoleon had been, when it came to dealing with the problem that remained—the continued resistance of island Britain, and the prospect of her continuous "thorn-in-the-flesh" effects unless and until she was conquered. The Wehrmacht had been prepared for continental warfare, and for a more gradual development of events than had taken place. Having been led on to attempt, and attain, much more than had been foreseen, it was caught unprepared in shipping and equipment for carrying out any such new technique as was involved in a large-scale oversea invasion.

The combined effect of that dilemma and the sweeping success of the continental campaign encouraged the tendency, inherent in the Nazi gospel, to follow in the footsteps of Napoleon and repeat his invasion of Russia. Brauchitsch and Halder tried to curb Hitler's ambition to succeed where Napoleon had failed, but the immensity of the German successes hitherto made it more difficult for them to impose a policy of moderation. Moreover, while they were far from agreeing with the Nazi view that the conquest of Russia would be easy, the relatively high estimate that they had formed of Russia's strength made them more inclined to accept the necessity of tackling Russia before that strength had still further increased.

The plan they framed was designed on the same principle as 1940—that of piercing weak spots in the Red Army's front, isolating large fractions of it, and forcing these to attack in reverse in the endeavour to get out of the net woven round them. They aimed to destroy Russia's armed strength in battles near to their own frontier, and wanted to avoid, above all, being drawn deep into Russia in pursuit of a still unbroken army that retreated before their advance. Conditions in Russia favoured this design in so far as the vast width of the front offered more room to manœuvre for piercing thrusts than there had been in the West, but were unfavourable in the lack of natural back-stops, comparable to the Channel, against which they could hope to pin the enemy after breaking through.

The German plan achieved a series of great piecemeal victories which brought it ominously close to complete success—helped by the initial over-confidence of the Russian leaders. The armoured thrusts cut deep, and successively cut off large portions of the Russian armies, including a dangerously high proportion of their best-trained and best-equipped troops. But, on balance, the advantage which the German offensive derived from the *breadth of space* in Russia was outweighed by the disadvantage of the *depth of space* through which the Russians could withdraw in evading annihilation. That balance of disadvantage tended to increase as the campaign continued.

Another handicap which emerged was the limited scale of the armoured forces on which the success of the German strokes mainly depended. In 1940 the victory in the West had been virtually decided by the thrusts of the 10 panzer divisions used to open the way for the mass of 150 ordinary divisions which the Germans deployed there. For the invasion of Russia in 1941 the number of panzer divisions was raised to 21—but only by halving the number of

tanks in each. The greater power of manœuvre provided
by this increased scale of mobile divisions was valuable on
such a broad front, while the decreased punching power
did not matter much in the earlier phases of the invasion.
Indeed, the consequent rise in the proportion of infantry
in these divisions was welcomed by the orthodox, since it
provided a higher ratio of troops to hold the ground gained.
But the limited punching power became a serious factor
as the campaign continued, especially when the Germans
met a more concentrated defence on approaching the great
cities.

It was on those "rocks" that the German prospect of
victory foundered. The nearer they came to such objectives, the more obvious became the direction of their
attacks and the less room they had for deceptive manœuvre.
Hitler's long-profitable instinct for the strategy of indirect
approach deserted him when such great prizes loomed
before his eyes. In the end Moscow became as fatal a
magnet for him as it had been for Napoleon.

When the German armies failed to fulfil their aim of a
decisive victory west of the Dnieper—to destroy the
Russian armies before they could retreat beyond it—
the German leaders were divided in opinion as to what to
do next, and a prolonged argument ensued. Brauchitsch
and Halder wished to drive on to Moscow, whereas Hitler
wanted to turn south and mop up the Ukraine. As other
generals favoured that course he was strengthened in his
decision to take it. But after a spectacular encirclement of
the opposing forces around Kiev, he reverted to the original
axis. Although the winter was now close, he decided to
continue the advance on Moscow—as well as the southern
advance through the Ukraine towards the Caucasus.
Early in October he staked his prestige on the gamble by
the announcement that the final stage of the offensive to
capture Moscow had begun.

The opening phase was brilliantly successful, and
600,000 Russians were caught by a great encircling move-

ment around Vyasma, carried out by the armies under Bock's command. But it was the end of October before they were rounded up, and by that time winter had set in, with the result that the exploitation of victory was bogged in the mud on the way to Moscow.

When Hitler called for fresh efforts, some of the higher commanders advised that the armies should draw in their horns and consolidate a safe defensive line for the winter, where the troops could gain shelter from the weather as well as from the enemy. But Hitler would not listen to such cautious arguments. Moreover, Brauchitsch and Halder, as well as Bock, were inclined to persevere with the push to Moscow—after all the difficulty and delay in getting Hitler to pursue that line it was natural that they were reluctant to put on the brake. So another great effort was mounted in November. But the obviousness of its aim and the convergence of its thrusts simplified the Russians' problem in concentrating reserves to check each dangerous development. Brauchitsch ceased to be responsible except in a nominal sense for this later stage of the offensive, carried out under Hitler's orders. After its final failure early in December, coupled with the German retreat from Rostov in the south, it was officially announced that Brauchitsch had been relieved of his post, and that Hitler had decided to "follow his intuitions" and take over supreme command of the German Army, in addition to the supreme command of the forces as a whole, which he had assumed when he had parted with Blomberg in February, 1938.

Brauchitsch's replacement by Hitler registered the final defeat of the soldiers' claim to decide questions of strategy and military policy. Henceforth the "Bohemian Corporal" would dictate to the generals in their own sphere, and their power would be limited to advice or protest. Unwilling executants do not make for good execution.

The transition was traced by Dittmar in one of our talks. "The Polish, Western and Balkan campaigns, and

the first stage of the Russian campaign, were conducted
by O.K.H.—with comparatively little interference from
O.K.W. The battle of Kiev was the first occasion when
Hitler attempted to take direct charge of operations. He
justified this on the ground that it was essential to finish
the Russian campaign before the winter. From then on,
O.K.H. was increasingly dominated by O.K.W.—which
really spelt Hitler."

Dittmar went on to emphasize the effect of another
important development: "Hitler decided that O.K.H.'s
sphere of responsibility should be confined to the Russian
front, and that O.K.W. should assume the exclusive
direction of all other theatres of war. As a result, O.K.H.
could not keep a view of the war as a whole, and this
restriction of outlook progressively weakened its ability to
argue the case against errors of strategy. The division
of spheres, and interests, between O.K.W. and O.K.H.
was a grave weakness in the German planning.

"I heard much about the effects from Halder. He said
that Hitler was a mystic, who tended to discount, even
where he did not disregard, all the rules of strategy.

"Hitler taught and believed that reason and knowledge
are nothing, and that the unbending will to victory and
the relentless pursuit of the goal are everything. Mystical
speculation replaced considerations of time and space, and
the careful calculation of the strength of one's own forces
in relation to the enemy's. All freedom of action was
eliminated. Even the highest commanders were subjected
to an unbearable tutelage."

On the other hand, some of the outstanding younger
generals considered that their seniors were at fault,
especially during the period immediately before the war,
and were particularly critical of Halder. They felt that
he, as well as Brauchitsch, had not been tough enough in
standing up to Hitler, nor fulfilled his proper function.
As one of them put it: "It is true that the overwhelming
majority of German officers were merely technical crafts-

men. This applies also to the officers of the General Staff who, owing to the too hurried building up of the Wehrmacht, lacked a thorough education. An operative 'bureaucracy' was created, headed by Halder as the first operative bureaucrat. This system produced but few great soldiers or outstanding personalities."

The old General Staff system had been better designed to encourage initiative within a corporation, and also to give its members a wider outlook. It is ironical that the Western Powers, when they enforced the abolition of the Great General Staff in 1919, as an insurance against the recurrence of war, should have abolished a system which could have been a more effective curb on a man like Hitler than the more technical and unpolitically-minded organ that replaced it.

CHAPTER V

THE CREATOR OF EARLY VICTORY—
GUDERIAN

HITLER's conquests in the first year of the war wrought a
tremendous but temporary change in the map of Europe.
Their consequences have permanently changed the course
of world history. These epoch-making changes were due
less to Hitler than to Guderian—for he was the man of
vision who created the German armoured forces, grasped
the potentialities of deep strategic penetration by fast-
moving forces of this kind, and trained them to carry it
out. Furthermore, as rarely happens in history, the creator
was also the decisive executant. For Guderian made the
break-through at Sedan and led the subsequent tank
drives, to the Channel coast and the Swiss frontier, which
produced the collapse of France.

It is unlikely that these world-changing strokes would
have been delivered but for Guderian. Although Hitler
had the vision to recognize the value of the new military
technique, he had a less sure grasp of it than Guderian.
Moreover, neither the German General Staff as a body
nor any of the topmost generals visualized its revolutionary
possibilities.

In the years before the war the General Staff showed
more concern with the improvement of the Army on familiar
lines than with the potentialities of the armoured forces
and their mode of employment. Guderian had an uphill
struggle to develop this "new model", and met with almost
as much resistance, though not so prolonged, as its original
advocates had suffered in Britain. And when he also
adopted the idea that such fast-moving forces should be
used for long-range strategic thrusts—which meant racing

on ahead of the main mass of the armies—the senior
generals expressed grave doubts. Like their ellows in
Britain, and France, their minds dwelt on the dangers
instead of seeing the decisive potentialities of such strokes.

Even after the swift overrunning of Poland this negative
view continued to predominate in the General Staff and
among the senior generals. It was manifest in their opposition to embarking upon an offensive in the West. Counting
numbers in the customary way, none of them believed
that the German Army was capable of achieving any
decisive result. Their view would certainly have proved
correct *if* the orthodox methods which had been favoured
had been followed. In conference on the plan of the
offensive they insisted that Guderian's spearhead of
armoured divisions, after driving through the Ardennes,
must wait on the Meuse for the arrival of the infantry
mass. They held that a crossing of the river would not be
possible until the ninth or tenth day from the start. In
that case the French High Command would have had time,
ample time, to reshuffle their dispositions, and bring their
reserves to the spot to block the passage.

But Guderian forced a crossing on the day of his arrival
on the Meuse—the fourth day from the start of the offensive.
Then, despite the continued trepidation of the Higher
Command, he drove on 160 miles through the back areas
of the Allied armies, to cut their lines of supply. On the
eleventh day of the offensive he reached the Channel
coast, cutting off the left wing of the Allied armies. That
lightning stroke virtually decided the issue of the campaign.

Even Hitler, though he had backed Guderian's bold
move in face of the doubts of his chief military advisers,
fell short of Guderian's inspired audacity. If Hitler had
not ordered a halt, Guderian would have cut off the
escape of the British Army from Dunkirk. That intervention had fateful consequences for the ultimate prospect
of the war, though it did not affect the immediate issue.
For the French armies never recovered from the first

stroke, and the loss of their whole left wing. Moreover,
it was Guderian's swift thrust from the Aisne to the Swiss
frontier which proved the decisive stroke in producing
the collapse of the remaining armies, and the fall of
France itself.

Heinz Guderian was born at Kulm on June 17th, 1888.
He was the elder of the two sons of Friedrich and Clara
Guderian—the name, un-Germanic in form, is supposed to
have been derived from the Netherlands village of Gouder-
jan, on an island near the mouth of the Rhine. His father
was then an officer in a Pomeranian Jäger battalion, and he
himself on entering the Army was commissioned into a
Hanoverian battalion of this type—corresponding to what
are called "Light Infantry" or "Rifle" regiments in the
British Army. They march at a faster pace and drill at a
quicker tempo than other infantry, as a constant and visible
reminder of their special tradition of mobility. It is a significant coincidence that the three earliest prophets of fast-
moving armoured warfare, in Britain, came from Light
Infantry or Rifle regiments—evidence of a subconscious
stimulus in the tradition of training. Experience of the trench
deadlock during World War I impressed on Guderian's
mind, as on theirs, the need for reviving mobility by new
tactics and new instruments.

Tanks were forbidden to Germany by the Peace Treaty,
so that a long time passed before Guderian could obtain
any direct experience of them or their employment. But
he gathered knowledge from keen study of what was being
written on the subject. Telling me of his progress, he said:
"I first became interested in tanks in 1922, when I held an
appointment in the *Inspektion der Kraftfahrtruppen* (Inspectorate of Motorized Troops) in the old Reichswehr Ministry.
From that date I began to study the experience with tanks
during World War I and the progress made after that
war in foreign armies, with the result that I became
employed as a teacher of tank tactics in 1928. My audience
was composed of officers of all arms assembled at the

Kraftfahr-Lehrstab (Motor Transport Instruction Staff) in Berlin, "germ-cell" of the *Panzer-schule*. During the following years I developed in theory the organization and tactics of tank troops, and, in consequence of this theoretical occupation with tank organization, resolved to establish Panzer divisions if ever Germany should become free". After lengthy study of post-war French and English writings on tank warfare, past and future, he came to reject the prevailing French doctrine that tanks should be regarded as assistants of the infantry attack, and was led to accept the new gospel then being preached in England— that tanks should be employed as a separate arm, operating independently and reviving the decisive rôle that the cavalry arm had played in earlier centuries. This more revolutionary conception of the rôle of tanks appealed to Guderian's progressive mind and dynamic spirit.

In 1930, Guderian became commander of the 3rd *Kraftfahr-Abteilung* near Berlin, a motorized battalion. During the two years he held this command, he developed one of his companies as a tank scout company, one as a tank company and one as an anti-tank defence company— with dummy tanks and dummy guns. "I developed radio-communication from tank to tank with good results." While the scale of these trials was smaller than those of the "Experimental Armoured Force" constituted three years earlier in the British Army, it was a practical start on the same lines. In October 1931, Guderian was appointed Chief of Staff of the Inspectorate of Motorized Troops, under General Lutz. "My general agreed entirely with my ideas and pushed them forward vigorously."

A stronger impetus came after Hitler's advent to power, in January 1933. "In June, 1934, a Command of '*Kraft-fahr-Kampftruppen*' (Motorized Fighting Troops) was estab-lished, which later was given the title of '*Kommando der Panzertruppen*'. I became Chief of Staff of this Command. Under the direction of General Lutz, we carried out the first manœuvres of a panzer division at Munsterlager in

July, 1935—with complete success. Consequently, on
October 1, 1935, three panzer divisions were established,
the 1st at Weimar, the 2nd at Wurzburg, and the 3rd at
Berlin." The command of the 1st was given to Lieut.-
General Baron von Weichs, and of the 3rd to Lieut.-General
Fessmann, but Guderian was made commander of the 2nd,
though he was still only a Colonel.

Two years earlier the British War Office had at last
been led to form a tank brigade on a permanent basis—
the first of its kind in the world. In contrast to what had
been done in the case of the Experimental Armoured
Force of 1927–28, the command of this tank brigade was
given to an expert in handling tanks, Brigadier P. C. S.
Hobart, who had both vision and a dynamic sense of
mobility. He did much to develop the tactical methods
and wireless control required for fast-moving operations.
He also seized the opportunity to try out in practice the
theory of deep strategic penetration—by an armoured
force operating independently—which I had been advo-
cating and expounding for some ten years past. But most
senior soldiers viewed the method with doubt and disapproval, and the Chief of the Imperial General Staff,
Sir Archibald Montgomery-Massingberd, put a curb on
the continuation of such practice in subsequent years.
Moreover, the enlargement of this first tank brigade into an
armoured division was deferred for a further three years.

The demonstration made a greater impression abroad,
particularly on Guderian's highly receptive mind. Shortly
before the war a Bulgarian officer, Colonel Khandyeff,
gave an account of his period of attachment to the German
Army, and dwelt on the training of the *panzer* troops
under Guderian, saying: "His faith in armoured forces
was such that he took tremendous pains in planting the
same enthusiasm in the people under him. He spent his
own money on providing copies of foreign books and
periodicals, as well as on the services of a local tutor for
the rough translations." Khandyeff went on to relate how

"every move" which I had described and Hobart had executed "was copied and put into practical demonstration —it was like the rehearsal of a play". He also related how when "a visiting anti-tank expert spoke of tank limitations", and quoted the opinion of British generals who had criticized the practice of these new methods, Guderian "impatiently dismissed him by saying: 'It is the old school, and already old history. I put my faith in Hobart, the new man'." Guderian himself has since said that: "Colonel Khandyeff's account was correct. It referred to 1935–36, when I was in command of the 2nd Panzer Division at Wurzburg."

It proved difficult, however, to convert the German Higher Command to the new conception of the independent strategic use of armoured forces, executing long-range strokes of their own. For all his strong convictions Guderian had to be careful in proclaiming his full adoption of it. That led some of his fellow generals to believe that he did not definitely embrace it until 1939. But Manteuffel, who was in very close touch with him from 1936 on, and working under him, says: "Guderian favoured from the beginning the strategic use of panzer forces—a deep thrust into the enemy, without worrying about a possible threat to his own unprotected and far-extended flanks. That was why he planned to transport all supporting elements of the panzer forces (infantry, artillery and engineers) in a similar way—that is, on tracks—and why the supply services (petrol, ammunition, food) were organically incorporated with the fighting troops. This enabled them to accompany, and keep up with, the tank core until fused with it—at the same time assuring Guderian's own supplies for three to five days.

"He may not, on some occasions, have stressed this point very emphatically—simply because many of the older officers could not get used to these new methods, and he may have tried to present them in a more acceptable form."

That shows how stiff was the resistance even in the
German Army to the new theory which brought it victory.
For Guderian was by nature frank in expressing his views,
and found it hard to conceal or curb them in deference to
superior authority. He instinctively put truth before tact.
Mr. Nordhoff, a director of the great Opel motor works,
related to a Danish friend of mine what happened when
he and other representatives of motor manufacturers
were invited to see a presentation of army vehicles a few
years before the war, at the time General von Fritsch was
Commander-in-Chief. "After the demonstration, Guderian
shocked both the officers and the civilian guests by going
up to Fritsch and telling him that he considered the demonstration a failure and the vehicles unsuited for their
purpose. He ended by saying: 'Had my advice been
followed, we would by now have had a real armoured
force'."

Some of those who were present regarded Guderian's
remarks as amazingly insubordinate, especially as so many
of his superior officers were standing round. But Guderian
himself was surprised to hear of this view of his remarks,
and felt that he was merely maintaining the old Prussian
tradition of "absolute frankness, even towards the King"
—which had continued from the eighteenth century down
to the twentieth.

His reliance on that tradition and on his military
superiors' respect for it was justified for the time being.
They also gave preference to expert knowledge when it
came to choosing leaders for the new arm—and in that
way he was more fortunate than his fellow tank experts
in Britain. For early in 1938 Guderian was appointed,
over the heads of many seniors, to command the XVI
Army Corps, Germany's first armoured corps. The date
of his appointment, February 4th, 1938, coincided with
that of a much bigger and more suddenly decided change
in the German Higher Command—the simultaneous
removal from office of Generals von Blomberg and von

Fritsch. In retrospect he himself spoke of it as "the black day of the Army", but from an historical point of view it is clear that the prospects of early victory in another war gained far more from Guderian's advancement to command a corps than they lost from the removal of the two highest soldiers.

That summer Guderian was even considered for appointment as Chief of the General Staff in succession to General Beck. This, however, raised trouble that handicapped him later. For the way that his candidature was pressed by those who preferred him to the conservative Halder, and the heated arguments that developed, left considerable animosity on both sides. It increased the tendency on the opposing side to describe him as a "technician", and thus to suggest that he was disqualified for the higher operational posts. His opponents spoke of him disparagingly as "not a War-Academy soldier"—and said it so often that it came to be generally accepted, as I found myself in talking with many of the German generals. In reality, Guderian passed into the War Academy in 1913. Although the outbreak of World War I interrupted that course, he filled various staff posts in the war, and in 1918 definitely became a member of the General Staff. After the war he was for three years an instructor at the small substitute war-academy, or staff college, surreptitiously established at Stettin. "I was therefore familiar with the technique of the General Staff—and also with its limitations." If Guderian was unsuited for Chief of the General Staff it was on the score of temperament rather than of knowledge. Even so, it seems likely that he would have been more effective in that post in 1938 than when he was actually raised to it six years later.

In November, 1938, he was instead made Chief of the Mobile Forces—embracing both the armoured and motorized troops—a post which enabled him to direct policy in this field while acting as Inspector-General of such forces. In the nine months that remained before war came he pressed on with their development, but was not able to exercise much influence on the modernization of the Army in general. Even in his own line he found the General Staff more inclined to put the brake on his efforts than to back them up. Speaking of this period, Guderian remarked: "In regard to armoured forces Field-Marshal von Brauchitsch already showed understanding before the war—from the time when he became commander of Army Group 4, in Leipzig, which embraced the motorized and mechanized forces of the army. He had his own ideas on mechanized operations and tactics—without, however, making full use of these. He liked to drive his car himself, and thus did not reject motorization as a whole. On the contrary, Halder was an officer of routine, of the old school. He did the inevitable, but nothing more. He did not like panzer divisions at all. In his mind the infantry played the leading rôle now and for ever."[1]

When war came, Guderian welcomed the chance of going back to a fighting job, and for the invasion of Poland was given command of an armoured corps, in Bock's "Army Group North". But the bulk of the tanks were allotted to Rundstedt's "Army Group South", and Guderian found himself at first with only one armoured division in his corps. That division (the 3rd) was commanded by Geyr von Schweppenburg, formerly the German Military Attaché in England from 1933 to 1937, who had been senior to Guderian until the latter was put over his head as commander of Germany's first armoured corps in 1938. Both being men of strong wills and strong views they were soon at loggerheads, and friction was naturally increased when, at the start of the Polish campaign, Guderian had only one armoured division on which to exert all his directing thought and driving

[1] It is only just to note that, in the crucial Dunkirk phase of the 1940 campaign, Halder showed more sense of the importance of exploiting the panzer drive to the full than did anyone else on the higher levels of the German Command.

energy. Under such circumstances, it was hard for him to refrain from interference in the divisional commander's sphere—and Geyr bluntly told him to mind his own business and keep to the functions of corps commander. After cutting through the Polish Corridor, however, Guderian was reinforced by another armoured division, and with the two he carried out a deep drive from East Prussia down to Brest Litovsk, southward across the rear of the Polish armies—a deadly stroke, brilliantly executed.

After that, most tankmen hoped that he would be placed in supreme charge of the armoured forces employed in the offensive against France. When the command of the "panzer group" for the main thrust through the Ardennes was given to General von Kleist, they felt that the prejudice of the old school had prevailed. Guderian, however, was placed in charge of the spearhead—a strong corps of three armoured divisions. With that, he succeeded in achieving a clean break-through—and then fulfilled his dream of exploiting it by a deep strategic thrust which cut the communications of the opposing armies and produced a decisive victory.

The story of that dramatic campaign is related in the opening chapters of Part II. But it is worth while here to give his own view of his two immediate superior officers—besides providing a valuable sidelight on Rundstedt and Kleist, it shows indirectly that when Guderian had sympathetic superiors he was not such a "difficult" subordinate as he is often depicted. "Field-Marshal von Rundstedt was a very fine strategic brain, perhaps one of our best. He preferred horse-cavalry to armoured forces, but he did not handicap them as others did. The chivalry of his character made serving under his command very agreeable. Even if he did not share the opinion of his subordinate, he took notice of it and was disposed to discuss it. He expressed his views frankly even to Hitler, who esteemed his uprightness. Field-Marshal von Kleist was a noble character too. At the beginning of the war he did not like panzers at all, but in the course of the campaign he altered his views and learned to employ them in the right manner."

It would seem that Rundstedt, and Kleist too, were better than Guderian in handling men, as well as in weighing different views—and in that sense more fitted for high command. Several of Guderian's pre-war subordinates have expressed such an opinion to me, though they ardently admired him in other ways. One, who had been on his staff, put it thus: "He lacked the psychological faculty of feeling and sensing his way which a 'leading personality', such as a commander-in-chief, should possess." "He had not the gift of listening calmly to his subordinates or men of his own rank, and allowing them to finish what they were about to say, before issuing his orders or decisions—if their opinions differed from his own. He was a 'strong' rider, and successful as such, but he lacked the mind and psychological insight into the spirit of the 'horse' which are essential in a good rider—of 'horses' in classic races. As an organizer and expert leader of the armoured arm, however, he was indispensable."

While these were fair-minded men, it should also be mentioned that they were former cavalrymen, and that I did not hear similar criticism of his ways from those who had been tank-minded from early days. Guderian had suffered so much obstruction from the supporters of the horse that he may have been inclined to be particularly impatient in dealing with former cavalrymen—as Hobart was in the British Army.

Moreover, it becomes very clear in sifting the evidence about the French campaign that the all-out exploitation of the break-through at Sedan—which turned it into a decisive stroke—was mainly due to him, and would not have been maintained to the point of a strategic decision but for him. His superiors, even Hitler himself, followed his course apprehensively and were wondering whether they ought to put a check on it—but Guderian "had the

bit in his teeth". He was checked by them on the last lap,
to Dunkirk, with the result that the British Army managed
to escape by sea, though this "halt order" did not affect
the immediate issue of the French campaign.

The highly appreciative way he speaks of Rundstedt
shows that, for all his instinctive impatience, he had understanding of the problems of the higher command, and
also generosity of spirit. This quality is equally apparent
in many of his comments on the men who worked with
him in developing the new arm and the new idea. (It is
evident, too, in the way he wrote of how much he had
learned from British military thought, and described
himself as one's "disciple". Few men who have won such
brilliant victories by applying a new idea would be "big
enough men" to make such an acknowledgment of the
source of it—especially a foreign source, in a country
opposed to their own.)

Guderian, too, shows little bitterness in his comments
on the Russian campaign. That is the more remarkable
because many of his fellow-soldiers, even outside the new
arm, feel that the most fatal mistake of 1941 was that the
Higher Command would not let him pursue his drive
for Moscow, in the same way as his decisive drives
in the West a year before. That story is related in
Chapter XVI.

Despite his natural sense of frustration, he had become
more equable—not least in dealing with his subordinates.
On this score, the evidence of Geyr von Schweppenburg
is significant, and the more so because of the earlier
discord. Speaking of the Russian campaign, Geyr said:
"My armoured corps formed part of his armoured group
and I became his spearhead throughout, to Moscow. We
worked in a model way together, owing to the tact and
skill of his chief of staff and to Guderian's own discretion
and good will. During six months of daily hard fighting
there was not a single row." Geyr dwelt on the way that
Guderian had "grown up in leadership". The same opinion

came from others who served under him in the 1941 campaign.

But just when he had proved himself increasingly fitted for higher command, his opportunity was snatched away—by coming into conflict with Hitler. Ironically, the clash occurred in a situation where Guderian, so often criticized as too audacious, was firmly insistent on caution —while Hitler, who had forfeited his best chance of defeating Russia by checking Guderian's earlier drive, was demanding a reckless advance on to the rear of Moscow, in mid-winter.

I had accounts of this "row" from other generals before I heard Guderian's own, which is crisper. "On December 20th, 1941, I had a five hours' discussion with Hitler at his headquarters in East Prussia, in order to inform him of the situation of the 2nd Panzer Army under my command. The mission given to this army was to encircle Moscow from the south and south-west, and then to push forward to Gorki (300 miles beyond Moscow). In view of the condition of the troops and the supply possibilities this task could not be fulfilled.

"I tried to convince Hitler of the correctness of my report, but without success. I got the impression that the reports from the front did not reach him unaltered, and suggested to him that he should relieve the officers of his operational staff and appoint officers with fresh experience from the front line. After the audience, Hitler told Keitel: 'This man, I have not convinced.' A few days later, Field-Marshal von Kluge, who succeeded Field-Marshal von Bock as Commander-in-Chief of the Central Army Group, reproached me that I had disobeyed Hitler's orders not to continue the retreat from Tula to the Susha-Oka position —a semi-fortified position which could have been held in spite of the extreme cold of that winter. Von Kluge was wrong—but his report to Hitler was sufficient to induce the latter to send me home. I was removed from command on December 25, 1941." It was a callous "Christmas card" to the man to whom Hitler owed most for his victories. And Hitler paid the heavier cost.

Guderian was left on the shelf until February, 1943, when Hitler called him back to service, as Inspector-General of Panzer Forces, to reorganize and virtually recreate these after the shattering German defeat at Stalingrad. By June 1943, the panzer divisions had been rebuilt and re-equipped to a level not far below their original strength—and then in the abortive Kursk offensive, his final fling, Hitler squandered them: with fatal effects on his chances of continued resistance to the Russian tide of advance. "My influence on operations was restricted to occasional reports to Hitler, when measures of the General Staff did not accord with the possibilities of armoured warfare—as was repeatedly the case."

A year later, in July, 1944, when the German armies were being driven out of Russia and their front was in a state of collapse, Hitler called Guderian to become Chief of the General Staff. The story of that final phase of Guderian's career, and Germany's fight for survival, is related in Chapter VII, where it best fits into the narrative of events.

It is appropriate, however, to end this chapter by recording the verdicts on Guderian's qualities and influence that were given me by two leading soldiers who served with him for a long time and were particularly well qualified to judge his work. I met a number who admired him so much that they praised him unreservedly, but I have chosen to cite these two verdicts because they came from men who had critical minds.

One was Geyr, who spoke frankly about his clashes with Guderian. Geyr's summing-up, however, was as pertinent as it was pithy. "Sixty per cent of what the German Panzer Forces became was due to him. Ambitious, brave, a heart for his soldiers, who liked and trusted him; rash as a man, quick in decisions, strict with officers, real personality, therefore many enemies. Blunt, even to Hitler.

As a trainer—good; thorough; progressive. If you suggest revolutionary ideas, he will say in 95 per cent of cases: 'Yes': at once."

The other was Manteuffel, the most brilliant of the younger and later Panzer army commanders. His verdict was: "*It was Guderian*—and at first he alone—who introduced the tank to the Army and its use as an operative weapon. It was certainly not the General Staff. During my term in the War Ministry (in the Inspectorate of Panzer Forces) I was well acquainted with Guderian's struggle on behalf of the use of this weapon. *In the best sense of the word, this new weapon bears the stamp of his personality.* Its successes during the war are due to him.

"In peacetime he at first stood alone when he insisted that the 'break-through' of tanks should be pressed long and deep, and at first without regard to exposed flanks. On countless journeys and in countless conferences he injected this idea—even into the actual tank commanders.

"If Guderian was not always successful in carrying out his theories everywhere during the war, it was due to the struggle against the mistrust of so many elderly officers who knew nothing, or little, about tanks.

"He was the creator and master-teacher of our Armoured Forces—and I lay particular stress on the word '*master*'."

CHAPTER VI

"SOLDIER IN THE SUN"—ROMMEL

FROM 1941 onwards the names of all other German generals came to be overshadowed by that of Erwin Rommel. He had the most startling rise of any—from colonel to field-marshal. He was an outsider, in a double sense—as he had not qualified for high position in the hierarchy of the General Staff, while he long performed in a theatre outside Europe.

His fame was deliberately fostered—not only by his own efforts but by Hitler's calculated choice. For Hitler, recognizing the public craving in wartime for glamorous military figures, decided to pick two soldiers (and two only) whom he could safely turn into popular heroes—"one in the sun and one in the snow". Rommel in Africa was to be the sun-hero and Dietl in Finland was to be the snow-hero.

Both performed in the wings of the main stage, where Hitler intended to keep the limelight for himself. Both were vigorous fighting soldiers whose qualities promised well for local success, without being of the intellectual calibre that might make them competitors for the higher strategic direction. Both seemed certain to be loyal instruments of Hitler. In the outcome, Rommel did more of the two in performance to justify his selection, but Hitler's confidence in his sustained loyalty was not so well justified. When Rommel came to see that Hitler's survival and Germany's survival were incompatible he put his country first and turned against his patron.

While Rommel owed much to Hitler's favour, it was testimony to his own dynamic personality that he first impressed himself on Hitler's mind, and then impressed his British opponents so deeply as to magnify his fame beyond Hitler's calculation.

As a junior officer in the previous war Rommel gained exceptional distinction, receiving the highest German decoration, *Pour le Mérite*, after the Caporetto offensive of 1917 against the Italians. But his professional knowledge was not regarded as equal to his fighting record, and he was given only minor employment in the post-war army. He was not considered suitable for the select circle of the future General Staff. The story that in the post-war years he was a Nazi storm-troop leader is, however, a legend invented by propagandists in the days when he became famous, in order to associate his reputation with that of the party.

His opportunity arose through his gifts as a military teacher and writer. From 1929 on he was for four years an instructor at the Infantry School at Dresden. He had a remarkable power of exposition and illustrated his lectures with examples, based on his personal experiences in the war, that vividly conveyed the atmosphere of battle and the influence of personal initiative. He also had a talent for drawing diagrammatic maps which brought out the essential points. He developed his lectures into a book on infantry tactics, published in 1937, which had a wide sale in Germany and other countries. It attracted Hitler, a keen reader of military literature, with the result that in 1938 Rommel was chosen to command the battalion that provided Hitler's escort for the march into the Sudetenland. Hitler found Rommel a refreshingly unorthodox soldier with whom to discuss new military ideas. On the outbreak of war he was appointed commander of Hitler's personal headquarters, which naturally increased both the contact and the opportunity. After the Polish campaign he asked Hitler for command of a panzer division, and got it. This was characteristic of Rommel's keen sense of the right opening and his opportunism in grasping it. For, prior to the war, he had been such a keen infantryman that he had opposed the ideas of those who preached the gospel of tank warfare.

He saw the light on the road to Warsaw, and lost no time in "following the gleam".

He was appointed to command the 7th Panzer Division, and led it in the Western offensive. To prepare himself for the task he studied books on tank warfare—in his African notes he speaks of "the outstanding way" in which the theory had been expounded by English writers, and ascribes the British Army's defeats to the fact that its chiefs had not followed their teachings. His division played a leading part in the break-through over the Meuse and on to the Channel coast. In the next stage it broke through the French front on the Somme between Abbeville and Amiens, and led the drive to the Seine near Rouen. Its brilliant performance was still further enhanced by subsequent publicity, and it was retrospectively christened "The Phantom Division".

Then, early in 1941, when Hitler decided to send an armoured and motorized expeditionary force to help his Italian allies in the invasion of Egypt, he appointed Rommel to command this "Africa Corps". By the time it arrived in Tripoli the Italians had not only been thrown back over the frontier, but their army had been destroyed in the pursuit. Rommel was not daunted by the disastrous situation which greeted him. Knowing that the victorious British army was small, and guessing that it was probably at the end of its tether, he promptly launched an offensive with the first instalment of his corps. He still had little experience in tank technique, but he had a tremendous sense of mobility and a flair for surprise. He caught the British distributed piecemeal, and with most of their tanks in need of repair. The speed of his onset and enveloping dust-clouds magnified his strength. The British were swept head-long out of Cyrenaica and back over the Egyptian frontier.

In the next eighteen months Rommel's fame continually grew, owing to the way he baffled successive British offensives, and, above all, through his startling ripostes whenever his annihilation was prematurely announced.

In the process the troops of the British Eighth Army came
to think much more highly of him than they did of their
own commanders, and his Jack-in-the box performance so
tickled their sense of humour that their admiration became
almost affectionate. He reached the peak of his career
in the summer of 1942 when he defeated the Eighth Army
piecemeal between Gazala and Tobruk, and then chased
the remainder of it back through the Western Desert to
the verges of the Nile Delta.

General Auchinleck, the British Commander-in-Chief
in the Middle East, intervened at this crisis by taking over
personal charge of the battered Eighth Army and rallying
the disheartened troops for a definite stand on the El
Alamein position. Rommel's troops were tired and short
of supplies after their long pursuit. In two successive
efforts they were foiled and thrown back. That check
proved fatal to the invader's prospects.

Rommel still appeared confident that he would succeed
at a third attempt, but his inward hopes were fading, while
time was slipping away in the process of accumulating
supplies. During the interval the British were reinforced
by fresh divisions from home. There was also a change of
commanders. Mr. Churchill wanted the British to take
the offensive as soon as the reinforcements arrived. Auchinleck, more wisely, insisted on waiting until they were
accustomed to desert conditions. In the sequel Auchinleck
was replaced by Alexander as Commander-in-Chief, while
Montgomery took over the Eighth Army. But Rommel
struck first, at the end of August, and was again baffled
by the new defence plan. Then the initiative changed
sides. After a long pause for thorough preparation—
longer than Auchinleck had contemplated—Montgomery
launched an offensive in the last week of October that was
now backed by a tremendous superiority in air-power,
gun-power, and tank-power. Even then it was a tough
struggle for a whole week, as there was no wide outflanking
manœuvre. But the enemy, besides being overstretched,

were vitally crippled by the submarine sinkings of their
petrol tankers crossing the Mediterranean. That decided
the issue, and once the enemy began to collapse at their
extreme forward point they were not capable of any
serious stand until they had reached the western end of
Libya, more than a thousand miles back.

For Rommel himself the decisive blow had been the
frustration of his August attack. Following that disappointment, he was so badly shaken that his moral depression
lowered his physical state, and he had to go sick, with
desert sores, for treatment in Vienna. On hearing of
Montgomery's offensive, be insisted on flying back to
Africa at once, regardless of the doctors' protests, but was
not fit enough to do himself justice in the months that
followed. Although he conducted the long retreat skilfully
enough to evade each of Montgomery's attempts to encircle
his forces, he missed some chances to produce a check,
while his sickness may have accounted for his bad slip
in the Battle of Mareth that opened Montgomery's path
into Tunisia, and thus paved the way for the enemy's
final collapse in Africa. He himself left Africa, for further
treatment, in March—over a month before that occurred.
For Hitler it was as important to preserve Rommel's
prestige as to preserve his services for the future.

Since Alamein there has been a tendency to talk of the
"Rommel legend", and to suggest that his reputation was
unduly inflated. Such disparagement is a common accom-
paniment of a change of fortune. But there was a deeper
reason for it in the first place. He had become the hero
of the Eighth Army troops before Montgomery arrived
on the scene—the scale of their respect for him was shown
by the way they coined the term "a Rommel" as a synonym
for a good performance of any kind. This attitude of
admiration carried a subtle danger to morale, and when
Montgomery took over command special efforts were
made to damp the "Rommel legend" as well as to create
a counter-legend around "Monty".

This propaganda gradually spread the view that Rommel was an overrated general. Montgomery's private feelings, however, were shown in the way he collected photographs of Rommel and pinned them up beside his desk. In other ways, too, he showed ample respect for his opponent. Moreover, any comparative estimate should take account of the fact that when they met in battle Rommel was not only weakened by sickness but tactically crippled by a heavy inferiority of force and shortage of petrol supplies.

The outstanding feature of Rommel's successes is that they were achieved with an inferiority of force, and without any command of the air. No other generals on either side gained the victory under such conditions, except for the early British leaders under Wavell, and their successes were won against Italians. That Rommel made mistakes is clear, but when fighting superior forces any slip may result in defeat, whereas numerous mistakes can be effectively covered up by the general who enjoys a big advantage of strength.

A clearer fault was his tendency to disregard the administrative side of strategy—but his staff say that he grew wiser with experience. More persistent was his reluctance to delegate authority, a defect that was very irritating to his chief subordinates. He not only tried to do everything himself but to be everywhere—so that he was often out of touch with his headquarters, and apt to be riding round the battlefield when he was wanted by his staff for some important decision. On the other hand he had a wonderful knack of appearing at some vital spot and giving a decisive impetus to the action at a crucial moment. He also gave dynamic junior officers such opportunities to prove their value as seniority-bound generals would never have dreamt of allowing them. As a result he was worshipped by the younger men. That feeling was shared by many of the Italian soldiers who saw in him such a vital contrast to their own senile and safety-first higher commanders.

In the field of tactics Rommel was often brilliant in

ruse and bluff. In his first attack in Africa he pushed his tanks so hard that many went astray in the desert, but when he reached the main British position he cleverly concealed the scanty number that were present by utilizing trucks to raise a great cloud of dust, and create the impression that tanks were converging from all sides. This produced a collapse.

While extremely daring he was also subtle. A repeated feature of his battles was the way he used his tanks as a bait, to lure the British tanks into traps that were lined with anti-tank guns—thus skilfully blending the defensive with the offensive. These "Rommel tactics" became increasingly adopted by all armies as the war advanced.

When he left Africa his departure was almost regretted by his opponents, so big was the place he had come to fill in their lives, and in their imagination. That was partly due to his remarkably good treatment of British prisoners; indeed, the number who managed to escape and return to their own lines after a personal contact with him suggests that his chivalry was blended with strategy. Much wider still was the impression made by his swiftness of manœuvre and his startling come-backs after being apparently defeated.

As a strategist, his vision, subtlety, and audacity were sometimes offset by defective calculation. As a tactician, his qualities far outweighed any defects. As a commander, his exceptional combination of leading power and driving power was accompanied by a mercurial temperament, so that he was apt to swing from exaltation to depression.

In 1944 Rommel reappeared as army group commander on the Channel coast, to meet the Anglo-American invasion. Here he was under Field-Marshal von Rundstedt, the Commander-in-Chief in the West. Their views differed as to the best way to meet the invasion and also as to the place where it was to be expected. Rundstedt favoured defence in depth, trusting to the effect of a powerful counter-offensive when the invaders had fully committed themselves. Rommel had a natural disposition to favour such a form of strategy, which he had followed so often in Africa, but experience there had modified his view of its practicability against an invader superior in air-power. He was now anxious to concentrate right forward with the aim of checking the invasion before it became established ashore. Rundstedt also held the view that the Allied offensive would come direct across the Channel at its narrower part, between the Somme and Calais, whereas Rommel became more concerned with the possibilities of an invasion of Western Normandy, between Caen and Cherbourg. Here he took the same view as Hitler.

On the latter issue Rommel's anticipation (and Hitler's) was right. Moreover, there is ample evidence that he had striven hard in the last four months to improve the coast defences in Normandy, which had been neglected by comparision with those in the Pas de Calais. His efforts, fortunately for the Allies, were hampered by the shortage of resources—so that both the under-water obstructions and the coast fortifications were far from complete.

On the other issue, the general opinion on the Allied side, especially among the Generals, has been that Rundstedt's plan—of holding the reserves back and then launching a massive stroke at a chosen moment—was a good one, and that Rommel spoilt it by using up strength in the effort to pen the Allied armies within their Normandy bridgehead. That was even more strongly the opinion of most of the German generals—those who belonged to the General Staff "caste" regarded Rommel as only less of an amateur than Hitler. They argued, also, that Rommel had had no war experience comparable to that provided by the Russian campaign, which had taught the importance of disposing forces in great depth.

Rundstedt's plan was certainly more in accord with the basic theory of strategy. But when one takes account of the size of the Allied forces, coupled with their domination of the air, and set against the wide space open for manœuvre, it looks very doubtful whether any deliberate

counter-offensive by the Germans could have stopped the
invading armies once they penetrated deep into France.
In such circumstances the only real hope may have lain
in preventing them from securing a bridgehead big enough
for building up their strength on that side of the Channel.
Rommel went close to depriving them of this opportunity
in the first few days, and his eventual failure to hold them
in check may be traced back, not to his mistakes, but to
the dilution of his plan and to the delay in switching forces
from the Pas de Calais. That was due to the Higher
Command's continued belief that the Normandy landings
were only a prelude to larger landings between Le Havre
and Calais. Beyond that there was the lack of any adequate
general reserve in the West. Rundstedt and Rommel had
wished to create one by evacuating the southern half of
France, but Hitler would not sanction such a step.

The effects were made fatal by Hitler's refusal to allow
a withdrawal in Normandy when it became clear to both
Rundstedt and Rommel that it was no longer possible to
hold the invading forces in check. A timely withdrawal
might have enabled the German forces to make a stand
on the Seine, and a much longer stand subsequently on
the German frontier. But Hitler insisted that there must
be no general withdrawal, and would not allow the
commanders in the West the freedom to carry out a local
withdrawal, even of a few miles, without his approval.
As a result divisions had to cling on until they were hammered to bits—a rigidity which in the end resulted in much
longer retreats than Rundstedt and Rommel had proposed.

A common sense of the hopelessness of Hitler's policy
had brought these two into closer accord than ever before.
At the end of June Hitler came to France at their urgent
request—it was the only visit he paid to the West in 1944
—and they met him at Soissons. But he would not agree
to their very modest proposal to withdraw behind the
Orne, preparatory to an armoured counter-stroke. In
the following week the strain on the front grew worse.

Rundstedt now bluntly said that it was vain to continue the struggle, and that the war ought to be ended. As that solution did not appeal to Hitler, he decided to try a change of commanders, and despatched his leading general in the East, Field-Marshal von Kluge, to replace Rundstedt.

It was significant that Hitler passed over Rommel, though he did not remove him. Rommel's attitude at Soissons had not found favour with Hitler. But Rommel's view of Hitler had changed even more. He had remarked to a number of his own subordinate commanders that Germany's only hope now lay in doing away with Hitler as quickly as possible, and then trying to negotiate peace. It is certain that he was acquainted—at the least—with the plot that culminated in the attempted assassination of Hitler on July 20th.

Three days before that, Rommel was driving along a road near the front when low-flying 'planes attacked it. His car capsized and he was thrown out, fracturing his skull. The scene of this crash was the aptly-named village of Sainte Foy de Montgommery. He was taken to hospital in Paris and when convalescent went to his home at Ulm. By this time the Gestapo had investigated the plot against Hitler. Two generals came to see Rommel at his home and took him out for a drive. Beforehand they gave him a message from Hitler that he could choose between taking poison and coming to Berlin for trial. He was brought back dead to a hospital in Ulm. It was then announced that he had died from a sudden brain-hæmorrhage, the result of his earlier accident, and he was given a state funeral.

Thus ended the career of a soldier who had a real, and rare spark of genius combined with dynamic executive power in applying the new technique of mechanized mobility. He had a flair for the vital spot and the critical moment. Exasperating to his staff officers, he was worshipped by his fighting troops.

The more deeply his record is examined the clearer it becomes that both his gifts and his performance, in a theatre of independent command, qualified him for a place in the rôle of the "Great Captains" of history.

CHAPTER VII

SOLDIERS IN THE SHADOW

IN Chapter IV the pattern of the war on Germany's side was traced as far as the end of 1941. The last chapter, after following the divergent thread of Rommel's career in the African field, came back along with him to the decisive reopening of the Western field in the summer of 1944. But that has left a gap in the pattern; before passing to the final stage it is desirable to pick up the thread of events in Europe from the end of 1941, and carry it through the interval. To avoid anticipating the fuller picture that emerges from the accounts of the generals, in Part III, this interim chapter will be confined to a brief indication of the course of events, still in terms of the chief military personalities concerned. They were "soldiers in the shadow", in a double sense—for the cloud of Hitler's disapproval as well as the cloud of defeat over-hung their course.

HALDER'S LAST LAP

In 1942 the operations in Russia were conducted by General Franz Halder, Chief of the General Staff, but subject to overriding *directives* from Hitler. Halder had a fine strategical brain, and the actual design of the plans which had proved so successful earlier had been mainly his own work, rather than the inspiration of brilliant assistants in the background. But O.K.H., over which he presided after Brauchitsch's removal, was henceforth more definitely under the control of O.K.W., which was scoffingly called "the military bureau of Corporal Hitler".

In this difficult situation Halder missed the support that Brauchitsch, by virtue of his authority, had formerly provided. It had been more possible to argue with the Commander-in-Chief of the Wehrmacht when backed by the Commander-in-Chief of the Army than it now became when the two were one—and when that one was a man of Hitler's temperament. Between Brauchitsch and Halder there was a harmony rare in high quarters, and differences of view hardly ever arose. According to other generals who knew them, the two had worked so closely together that their respective functions and influence could hardly be distinguished, though Halder tended to be the dominating mind. "What Halder thought out, Brauchitsch presented to Hitler. Halder never saw Hitler without Brauchitsch being present to support him." But henceforth Halder had to fight his battles alone.

The summer campaign of 1942 had brilliant initial success and bore evidence of masterly planning by Halder. An artful delay in opening the campaign on the main front, coupled with a startling coup against the Crimean peninsula, incited the Russians to take the initiative with an offensive towards Kharkov. Having got the southern Russian armies deeply embedded here, the main German offensive was launched past their flank, and gained a clear run down the corridor between the Don and the Donetz rivers. But after crossing the Lower Don the German drive split in divergent directions under Hitler's interference. The prospects of the main advance into the Caucasus, and of securing the oilfields there, were sacrificed to his desire to retrieve the check suffered by the subsidiary advance on Stalingrad, the original object of which had merely been to secure flank cover for the avenue of advance into the Caucasus. Worse still, Hitler's eyes became as narrowly focused on Stalingrad as they had been on Moscow the previous year. The very name of the city was a challenge to him. Once again, by the eventual directness of his aim he helped the Russians to concentrate their reserves to frustrate him.

As soon as it became clear that the effort was losing

momentum, Halder argued that it should be broken off. Hitler had grown increasingly impatient of his objections, and this time his unwelcome advice led to his dismissal, at the end of September.

ZEITZLER

Halder was replaced by Kurt Zeitzler, who had recently been Chief of Staff in the West. The fact that he had thus been out of touch with the situation in the East added to his handicap in taking over at such a critical moment—and lessened his chance of disputing Hitler's view of it.

Zeitzler, a much younger man, had been only a colonel commanding an infantry regiment before the war, but subsequently became chief of staff to Kleist's panzer army. It was he who found a way to solve the problem of supplying armoured forces during long-range advances and rapid switches. Able and energetic, he was predominantly the "man of action" type that appealed to the Nazi leaders, in contrast to the "man of reflection" represented in Halder, who was a mathematician and botanist as well as a military writer of distinction.

Less of a strategist than his predecessor, Zeitzler was an outstandingly resourceful organizer of strategic moves, with an exceptional grasp of what could be done with mechanized forces. His brilliant staffwork in organizing and maintaining the panzer drive through the Ardennes and on through France, in 1940, had been excelled in the complex series of manœuvres called for in 1941—when Kleist's panzer forces had first swerved down through the Ukraine towards the Black Sea, to block Budenny's retreat across the Bug and the Dnieper; then turned about and dashed north to meet Guderian and complete the vast encirclement round Kiev; then been switched south again, on to the rear of the fresh Russian forces that were attacking the German bridgehead over the Dnieper at Dnepropetrovsk; and, after producing a Russian collapse here, had

driven down through the Donetz Basin to cut off the
Russian forces near the Sea of Azov. As Kleist emphasized
to me, in paying unstinted tribute to his chief of staff, the
biggest problem in "throwing armies about in this way"
was that of maintaining supplies.

Zeitzler's performance attracted Hitler's attention, and
early in 1942 Hitler summoned him for interview. Hitler's
impression was deepened by what Zeitzler told him of the
emergency measures that had been improvised, in the
1st Panzer Army, to help the troops through the rigours
of the winter. It impressed Hitler all the more because
he had a deep conviction that German professional soldiers
were too imbued with sealed-pattern methods, and could
not improvise. Soon afterwards, Zeitzler was sent to be
Chief of Staff in the West, and reorganize the defences
there. In September, after the repulse of the Dieppe
landing, he was called back to the East, and told by
Hitler that he was to become Chief of the General Staff.
It was a dazzling jump for a young major-general.

Hitler's preference for younger men who understood
mechanized warfare, coupled with Zeitzler's practical
record in that field, might suffice to explain his selection—
but it was not the complete explanation. In placing such
a junior general at the head of O.K.H., Hitler hoped he
would be so grateful to his patron as to sink his professional
loyalty and become Hitler's henchman as Keitel and Jodl
had done. In ridding himself of Halder, Hitler counted
on relief from the constant objections he had endured
from that "turbulent priest" of the established military
order.

Momentarily, Zeitzler was dazzled. Thus he acquiesced
in the continuance of the assault on Stalingrad, as well as
the advance in the Caucasus, until the bulk of the German
reserves had been committed too far to be extricated—in
so far as they had not already been consumed in vain
efforts.

But his doubts soon began to grow, and he questioned

the wisdom of Hitler's intention to hold on to an advanced position at Stalingrad during the winter. When the Russian counter-offensive began, he wanted to withdraw Paulus's army immediately, but Hitler angrily refused. After that, friction was frequent, for even when Paulus's army was encircled Hitler would not agree that it should be ordered to abandon its position and fight its way out to the west. Zeitzler was driven to tender his resignation, but Hitler brushed that aside.

After the army at Stalingrad had been forced to surrender, Zeitzler managed to induce Hitler to sanction withdrawals from two dangerous salients in the north, facing Moscow and Leningrad respectively. This eased the strain and helped to maintain that front intact in face of subsequent assaults, besides releasing reserves for elsewhere. But Hitler was galled by having to make such an unconcealable step-back from Russia's two greatest cities, and he would not consider any general strategic withdrawal. Zeitzler did not lack courage in standing up to Hitler, but he had to fight his battles alone, for Keitel and Jodl always backed Hitler. He was the more handicapped in combating their influence because their offices were at Hitler's headquarters, while his was some distance away. But the separation was more than a matter of mileage, for as time went on and his protests multiplied, Hitler's manner became distant when they met at the daily conferences.

All this tended to augment the influence of General Jodl, the chief of Hitler's personal staff, and thus of Hitler's own control over operations. For Jodl, who kept his place throughout the war, would never have lasted so long if he had not been adept in "keeping his place" within the limits assigned to him. He was a first-rate clerk. Zeitzler, by contrast, was impulsive and far from subservient—he frequently lost his temper in arguing with Hitler. But the latter seems to have been reluctant to part with a man who was such a master of mechanized logistics, with a

practical capacity to solve movement problems that neither
Keitel nor Jodl possessed.

The end came early in July, 1944, soon after the
collapse of the armies on the Upper Dnieper. Zeitzler
went to see Hitler privately and urged him to sanction
the withdrawal of the Northern Army Group, in the Baltic
States, before it was encircled. Hitler refused, and then
both men flared up. Having had his resignation rejected
several times, Zeitzler went sick as the only way out of a
responsibility he was unwilling to share any longer. Hitler
took his revenge by depriving Zeitzler of various privileges
of his rank, and then by giving the humiliating order that
he was to be discharged from the Army without the normal
right to wear uniform.

GUDERIAN'S LAST LAP

To fill Zeitzler's place Hitler called on an earlier and
older tank expert—Guderian. That appointment shocked
many of the members of the General Staff, who regarded
Guderian as a one-sided enthusiast for his speciality and
a "bull" on the battlefield, lacking the strategical sense
and balanced view required in a Chief of the General
Staff. The choice demonstrated Hitler's instinctive preference for revolutionary ideas, and his appreciation of what
he had owed to Guderian's past activities.[1] It appeared to
set the crown on the career of the man who had been the
pioneer in creating Germany's panzer forces, and then
the spearman of Germany's run of victories. But, in reality,
it proved more in the nature of window-dressing.

For Hitler had long since taken the direction of the
war completely into his own hands, and regarded O.K.H.
as little more than a means of transmitting his orders to,
and handling the executive details of, the Eastern Front.
Even if Guderian had been fitted by temperament and
experience to be Chief of the General Staff he would not

[1] See Chapter V and also Chapter X, "The Rise of Armour."

have been allowed to play the part. As things were, he was doubly checked—by an atmosphere of professional mistrust around him, and by Hitler on top of him.

His subordinates on the General Staff patronizingly, and rather resentfully, spoke of him as "a fighting soldier, not a War-Academy soldier." While the remark was not strictly accurate, it expressed the contrast between his outlook and theirs. With Hitler's backing he might have overcome such resistance, but he soon found himself clashing with Hitler as well. It was difficult enough that his entry into office came when Germany's strength was ebbing, but more difficult still that it came just after the plot of July 20th. Hitler was now in such a mood of distrust that he was apt to take any contrary opinion as a symptom of treason. Some of the younger soldiers knew how to disarm his suspicions, and could argue with him up to a point, but Guderian lacked the knack.

Moreover he had burned up his energy not only in blitzkrieg drives but in prolonged battle for new ideas against doubters and disbelievers. The year he had spent on the shelf had been no rest but, rather, a long spell of fretting over the irreparable mistakes he saw being committed. At the end of 1943 he had nearly died from a heart attack. Although his recall acted as a stimulant, the cramping conditions of his second opportunity aggravated the strain, while repeated frustration sharpened his impatience—as so often happens with men of his kind. He was handicapped in other ways too. One of the younger generals who saw much of him, and admired him intensely as a panzer leader, said: "A soldier in a *key* position must also be able to think and act in a political sense. I don't think that Guderian had either the eye or a broad enough outlook, while he was not sensitive enough when faced with political conditions and opportunities."

Nevertheless, this apostle of the new offensive gospel showed that he had more insight than his master into the defensive requirements of the situation. Early in 1944, when he was still Inspector-General of the Panzer Forces, he had urged Hitler to carry out a strategic withdrawal in the East, and for that purpose prepare a strong rearward defensive line along the 1940 frontier. When he became Chief of the General Staff, the front north of the Pripet Marshes had just previously collapsed, but the Russian flood was eventually checked on a line not far behind what he had proposed. Some twenty divisions, however, had been lost or had sacrificed their equipment in the hasty retreat that followed the collapse, and the breach was only filled by rushing back panzer divisions from Rumania. The weakened front in that quarter soon collapsed, and the collapse was deepened by Rumania's quick change of side. This opened the way for the Russians to push up through the Carpathians into Central Europe in a wide flank march.

Guderian's autumn efforts to consolidate the new line covering East Prussia and Central Poland were hampered, not only by the drain of reserves to bolster up the Hungarian forces, but by Hitler's desire to attempt another offensive in the West. All possible reserves were collected for this dream-plan of "dunkirking" the British again by another flank thrust through the Ardennes. Yet even at this late stage, Hitler would not listen to arguments for withdrawing from the Baltic States, the Balkans and Italy in order to provide reserves for the main front in the East.

When the Ardennes stroke had ended in failure, Hitler still resisted Guderian's arguments. He allowed only a paltry reinforcement to be sent eastward, although Guderian warned him that a fresh Russian offensive was imminent there, and that the German front was not strong enough to hold out. Worse still, that small addition was more than cancelled out by Hitler's order that three of the best armoured divisions in Poland were to be sent southward in a vain offensive attempt to break the Russians' encircling grip on Budapest.

When the Russian offensive was launched on January 12th, Guderian had a mobile reserve of only twelve divisions for a front of nearly 800 miles. Moreover, three days earlier, Hitler had refused his appeal for permission to forestall the Russians by withdrawing from the threatened salients. As a result the front in Poland collapsed quickly, and the Russians' onrush could not be stemmed until they had penetrated deep into Germany and reached the Oder. Here there was a momentary chance for a riposte, as they had outrun their supplies and their flanks were exposed. Hitler had now agreed to release the 6th Panzer Army from the West, but instead of allowing it to be used for this counterstroke he sent it to Hungary for another vain bid to relieve Budapest. He was living in a world of dreams, remote from reality.

Reduced to desperation, Guderian now tackled some of the other leading Nazis about the urgency of seeking peace. His activities soon came to Hitler's ears, and he was dismissed from his post, in March, barely a month before the final collapse.

MANSTEIN

The ablest of all the German generals was probably Field-Marshal Erich von Manstein. That was the verdict of most of those with whom I discussed the war, from Rundstedt downwards. He had a superb strategic sense, combined with a greater understanding of mechanized weapons than any of the generals who did not belong to the tank school itself. Yet in contrast to some of the single-track enthusiasts he did not lose sight of the importance of improving alternative weapons, and defence. He was responsible, shortly before the war, for developing the armoured assault-gun, which proved invaluable later.

A Lewinski by birth, he had been adopted by the Manstein family as a boy. He got an infantry commission shortly before the 1914 war, and, although too young to qualify for the Staff College, he made his mark on the staff of General von Lossberg, who in 1917 produced the new system of defence in depth. By 1935 Manstein had become head of the operations section of the General Staff, and next year was made Deputy Chief under Beck. But in February, 1938, when Fritsch was ousted, Manstein was also removed from O.K.H.—as another move in eliminating opposition to O.K.W. and Nazi designs. He was sent to command a division in Silesia. However, on the eve of war in 1939 he was appointed Chief of Staff to Rundstedt's Army Group, which played the decisive rôle in the Polish campaign. After that he accompanied Rundstedt to the West.

Here he was the source of the brain-wave that produced the defeat of France—the idea of the tank-thrust through the Ardennes. But his arguments only prevailed after he had paid personal forfeit. For the top military circles felt that he was too pushing, and at the end of January, 1940, he was pushed out of the way by sending him to command an infantry corps, the 38th—his request for a panzer corps being rejected on the ground that he lacked experience. After his removal he was summoned to see Hitler and seized the chance to explain his idea. Hitler agreed with it; a week later O.K.H. issued the revised plan.

In the first stage of the campaign, Manstein had no chance to show what he could do as a commander of troops, for his corps was merely among the backers-up of the panzer drive. But in the second stage, the attack on the new French defence line along the Somme, his corps was instrumental in achieving the first break-through, west of Amiens. Rommel's tanks exploited the opening, but Manstein raced them in the pursuit, handling his infantry like mobile troops. His corps was the first to reach and cross the Seine, on June 10th—marching over forty miles that day. Then, by rapid strides, he pushed on to the Loire. After that, when it came to a question of

invading England, he was allotted the formidable task of
making the initial landing.

Before the invasion of Russia he was given command
of a new panzer corps—the 56th, in East Prussia. He
broke through the Russian front here, and raced on so
fast that he reached the Dvina (nearly 200 miles distant)
within four days—capturing the main bridges across it.
But he was not allowed to pursue his drive towards
Leningrad or Moscow as he wished, and had to wait on
the Dvina for a week while the other panzer corps and
the 16th Army came up. He then drove as far again
to reach Lake Ilmen, south of Leningrad, by July 15th,
but was there checked by Russian reserves that had now
had time to gather. In September he was promoted to
command the 11th Army, in the far south, and there
opened the gateway to the Crimea, by breaking through
the narrow and fortified Perekop Isthmus—a feat which
proved his mastery of the technique of siege warfare.

When the invasion of Russia became stuck in the mud
and snow before Moscow that winter, and Hitler sought a
scapegoat in sacking Brauchitsch, many of the younger
generals in the German Army hoped that Manstein would
be chosen to succeed him as Commander-in-Chief. But
Hitler wanted to assume the post himself. He thought of
appointing Manstein Chief of the General Staff, but felt
he might prove even more difficult than Halder.

In the summer of 1942, Manstein was responsible for the
attack on the famous fortress of Sevastopol, which preceded
the main offensive. His success in that task deprived the
Russians of their chief naval base in the Black Sea. After
that, he was chosen to command the attack on Leningrad,
with forces transferred for the purpose from one extreme
flank to the other. It looked as though his scope was to
be continually limited by the skill he had shown in this
specialized rôle of siege tactics.

Manstein's mission went unfulfilled, however, for by
the time the forces were being moved to Leningrad, a

call came for them to go to Stalingrad, where Hitler's
advance had become stuck. Soon that impasse developed
into a crisis, and the army there was surrounded. In the
emergency Manstein was given an improvised force, called
Army Group "Don", and sent to the rescue.

It was too late and the effort failed—after some of the
most breathless cut-and-thrust in the war. In the subsequent retreat he rallied the cracking line and prevented
the Russians crossing the Dnieper. A dazzling counter-
stroke threw them back a long way and recaptured
Kharkov, in March, 1943. Manstein now commanded
Army Group "South". That summer, in combination
with Kluge (Army Group "Centre"), he delivered
Germany's last offensive in the East.

He had proposed alternative courses. One was to
strike early in May before the Russians were ready, and
dislocate their preparations by a pincer-stroke against the
Kursk salient. The other—which he thought better—
was to wait for the Russians' offensive, recoil before it,
and then launch a flank stroke from the Kiev area to roll
up their line. Hitler rejected the latter, fearing to run
the risks involved in such a daring strategic gambit. But
after chosing the former he postponed the attack—just
as it was about to be launched—with the idea that by
waiting until his own strength had increased he would
re-insure his chances. In the end he waited until July
before striking—and the Russians profited more by the
delay. Although the southern pincer (Manstein's) penetrated fairly deep, the northern one was blunted by the
combined tenacity and elasticity of the Russian defence,
and then broken by a flank counter-stroke on the part of
the Russians. This developed into a general counter-offensive, which the Germans no longer had strength to resist.

Manstein showed great skill, against heavy odds, in
conducting the step-by-step retreat to the Polish frontier.
But Hitler would not listen to his arguments for shaking
off the Russian pressure by a long step-back. The vigour

with which he argued became an increasing annoyance to
Hitler, who shelved him in March, 1944, in favour of Model
—saying that resistance yard by yard was more needed
than skill in manœuvre. An underlying factor in the change
was Hitler's and Himmler's political distrust of Manstein.
That ended the military career of the Allies' most formidable military opponent—a man who combined modern
ideas of mobility with a classical sense of manœuvre, a
mastery of technical detail and great driving power.

Dwelling regretfully on Manstein's disappearance from
the field, Blumentritt said to me: "He was not only the
most brilliant strategist of all our generals, but he had a
good political sense. A man of that quality was too difficult
for Hitler to swallow for long. At conferences Manstein
often differed from Hitler, in front of others, and would
go so far as to declare that some of the ideas which Hitler
put forward were nonsense."

KLUGE

Hitler had lost his other best-known commander in the
East a few months earlier, when Kluge was injured in an
air crash. But in the summer of 1944, when he was fit again,
Hitler found fresh room for him—in the West. He was
sent · to supersede Rundstedt as Commander-in-Chief
there.

Field-Marshal Guenther von Kluge was the only sur-
vivor of the original army commanders with whom Hitler
embarked on war in 1939. In the Polish campaign, the
French campaign, and the 1941 campaign in Russia he
commanded the Fourth Army. In the first and the third
he had been in Bock's Army Group, and had been entrusted
with the offensive against Moscow, even though he did not
share the optimism of Hitler and Bock. While he was a
strong personality, it was testimony to his forbearing temperament that he endured Bock so long—for Bock was a very
difficult man to serve. In the same way Kluge had sufficient

moral courage to express his views frankly to Hitler, yet
he also refrained from pressing his views to the point of
being troublesome. After Bock was put on the shelf
early in 1942, Kluge succeeded him in command of the
Central Army Group. There he created a well-woven
defence that withstood successive Russian assaults during
the next two years.

His defensive successes, together with his temperament
and loyalty, naturally recommended him to Hitler when
Rundstedt and Rommel failed to give satisfaction by
achieving the impossible—and caused Hitler further
annoyance by pointing out the inevitable. By the time
Kluge took over, the Allies had poured such a volume of
force into their enlarged Normandy bridgehead that the
sheer weight of it was soon bound to burst the too extensive
dam with which the Germans were trying to contain it.
Three weeks later it collapsed at the western end under
the fresh impact of Patton's American Third Army. But
Hitler still forbade any withdrawal.

Kluge was too obedient to disregard such definite
instructions. One effect was seen in the attempted counter-
stroke on August 6th against the bottleneck at Avranches
through which Patton's forces had poured out. Shrewdly
aimed, this stroke could have been deadly if the panzer
divisions there employed had been strong in tanks; but
in their diminished state its chances were desperately
small, even before it was broken up by concentrated air
attack. Worse still, the German forces were not permitted
to break away from the clinch when this forlorn hope
miscarried. Although retreat was now inevitable, every
withdrawal was fatally late and short. In consequence,
the battle ended in a general collapse of the Germans
armies in France. When this developed, Hitler sacked
Kluge and appointed Field-Marshal Model to replace
him.

Kluge took his dismissal with apparent calm, spent a
day and a half explaining the situation to his successor,

then quietly set off for home and swallowed a capsule of poison on the way. That action was due, not to his chagrin at the ending of his career, but to his anticipation that he would be arrested on arriving home. For he had been in close contact, and sympathy, as early as 1942 with the conspiracy that culminated on July 20th, 1944, in the attempt to overthrow Hitler. Characteristically, he had refrained from committing himself, but he knew that his name had been found in the documents when the plot was investigated after the attempt had failed.

MODÈL

Walter Model was fifty-four, a decade younger than most of the German higher commanders—whose average age had remained much higher than in the opposing armies. Nor did he come from the same social level. In this as in other respects he had many similarities to Rommel though he had profited by a more thorough professional grounding. When the big expansion of the army began, with the Hitler régime, Model worked under Brauchitsch in the training department of the War Ministry, and there established close touch with the Nazi leaders. He made a strong impression on Goebbels, who introduced him to Hitler. Later he was put in charge of the inventions department. His technical knowledge was scanty, but he made up for it by imagination and energy, so that, although his enthusiasm was apt to mislead him as to the practicability of various ideas, he did a lot towards developing new forms of equipment.

After being chief of staff of the 4th Corps in the Polish campaign, and then of the 16th Army in the French campaign, he was given command of the 3rd Panzer Division. In the invasion of Russia he distinguished himself by his thrusting power, and led the way in the race to the Dnieper, His extreme energy won quick promotion —first to a panzer corps and then, in the winter, to command of an army, the 9th. He showed much ability here in a defensive rôle under difficult conditions.

In 1943 he was cast for a leading rôle in the summer offensive—as the northern arm of the pincer-stroke against the Kursk salient. Here he lost the best chance by persuading Hitler—contrary to the opinion of Kluge and Manstein—to postpone the stroke so as to accumulate more tanks and strengthen the punch. The delay gave the Russians time to prepare, and Model's eventual attack failed, at heavy cost to break through their well-knit elastic defence. But he did well in checking the dangerous Russian offensive that followed, and in October was promoted to command Army Group "North". In April, 1944, he was transferred to Army Group "South", in place of Manstein, and parried the Russian thrust towards the Carpathian passes. In late June the Russians' summer offensive was launched against Army Group "Centre", which speedily collapsed. Model was sent to take it over. Just as he had checked the Russians along the line of the Vistula, he was despatched to deal with the crisis in the West.

After the failure of the July 20th attempt on Hitler's life, Model had given a lead in reproclaiming his faith in the Führer, and had sent the first telegram of loyalty received from the Eastern front. That assurance reinforced Hitler's confidence in his military gifts. But Model was also one of the few who ventured to disregard Hitler's instructions and act on his own judgment.

In talking to a number of generals who had served under him, I found that all paid tribute to his power of command while emphasizing that he was difficult both as a superior and subordinate. Manteuffel said of him: "Model was a very good tactician, and better in defence than in attack. He had a knack of gauging what troops could do, and what they could not do. His manner was rough, and his methods were not always acceptable in the higher quarters of the German Army, but they were both to Hitler's liking. Model stood up to Hitler in a way that hardly anyone else dared."

In the West it was mainly owing to his efforts and his extraordinary capacity for scraping up reserves, from an almost bare cupboard, that the shattered German forces succeeded in achieving their astonishing rally on the German frontier and frustrating the Allies' expectation of complete victory in the autumn of 1944. He also played the principal executive part in checking the Allies' later offensives and in the Germans' Ardennes counter-offensive of December—although the supreme direction of these final operations in the "Battle for Germany" was in the hands of Rundstedt. For Hitler had called back the "Old Guard" at the moment when Germany seemed about to fall.

"THE OLD GUARD"—RUNDSTEDT

THE wheel had come full circle. In the frantic effort to restore the army's confidence Hitler was driven to put back in the chief military place the man, who, above all others, represented the old Germany and the military tradition—with its devotion to duty, political conservatism, professional exclusiveness, and contempt for amateurs in strategy as represented by Hitler. Moreover Gerd von Rundstedt was a gentleman to the core. His natural dignity and good manners inspired the respect even of those who differed widely from him in views. To such an essential aristocrat the democracy of the Weimar Republic had been unpalatable, but he had found the manners of Nazism far more distasteful.

Now close on his seventieth year, he was almost the same age as Hindenburg had been on attaining supreme command in the previous war. Age and achievement had similarly combined to make him a national idol on something approaching the same scale. But he was a far abler soldier than Hindenburg—abler even than the combination of Hindenburg and Ludendorff—while his achievements were intrinsically finer. That was symbolized in the contrast that his face and figure presented to theirs. As forceful as they had been, in a more refined way, he was lean, ascetic, and thoughtful in appearance—though his thought was confined to his profession. In his devotion to the army, and to Germany, an overriding sense of duty had led him to swallow much that he would have liked to spit out. Here was the root of an inner conflict which revealed itself in the career and in the countenance of this military priest. He despised politics, but they kept on intruding into his seclusion.

By 1932, after successive promotions, he became Chief of the First Army Group Command, covering Berlin. Almost at once he unwittingly acquired a political smell, for it fell to him to carry out the orders of the new Chancellor, Papen, to evict the Social Democratic Ministers of Prussia when they refused to quit office. Then Papen overreached himself and was succeeded as Chancellor by General von Schleicher. But Schleicher could not gain sufficient political support to maintain his position, and thus the way was opened for Hitler to become Chancellor and abolish all parties other than the Nazi. Rundstedt did not like the way things had turned out, and he definitely disliked both the social aims and the manners of the Nazi leaders. But he found satisfaction in the vehement campaign of the Nazis for military expansion, and was even better content when the purge of June 30th, 1934, curbed the power of the storm-troopers. It seemed a healthy sign to his simple soldierly mind that so many military pretenders were wiped off the slate and the professional army freed from the menace of such "brown dirt", as he described them.

He was now able to devote his attention to the development of the Army. In the military sphere he was primarily concerned to revive the power of the infantry, and their confidence in themselves, by modernizing their equipment as well as their training. For while he was receptive to the new ideas of mechanized warfare, and followed with keen interest the British theories and experiments, he was not one of those who fervently embraced them. Rather, he was one of the more progressive leaders of the school that regarded tanks as useful servants, not as the future masters, of the battlefield.

He believed that there was more value in motorization and multiplied fire-power to improve the capacity of the existing arms than in producing completely mechanized forces. Besides his practical steps to overcome the "machine-gun paralysis" that the infantry had suffered in

the last war, he initiated a propaganda campaign to cure
their inferiority complex. But he was too nearly a scientific
soldier to go so far as the British generals who in 1934
contrived that the big exercise of the season should show
that an infantry division could paralyse an armoured
division—and thereby helped to postpone the formation
of Britian's first armoured division for three years more.
Rundstedt favoured the creation of armoured divisions in
the German Army, provided that the proportion was not
unduly high and did not hinder the re-equipment of the
infantry mass. In sum, the extent of his vision and that
of his school accounts for the superiority which the German
Army enjoyed against France in 1940, while the limitations
of their vision explain why it fell short of the technical
superiority that was needed for victory over Russia in 1941.

At the start of 1938 his concentration was disturbed by
another political shock, when Himmler's machinations
provided Hitler with an excuse to turn out Fritsch, the
head of the Army, at the same time as Blomberg, the head
of the whole armed forces, and himself assume the
supreme command. Rundstedt protested to Hitler against
Fritsch's treatment, but, although Fritsch was acquitted
of the moral charge framed against him, such acquittal
did not alter the fact that his post had already been filled.
A few months later Rundstedt endorsed the warning
memorandum drafted by Beck, the Chief of the General
Staff, in an attempt to put a brake on Hitler's war-risking
policy—but that protest merely ended in Beck being driven
to resign office. In the autumn, after the occupation of
the Sudetenland, Rundstedt asked and obtained permission
to retire, on the plea of age.

In August, 1939, he was called back to take command
of an army group on the Polish front. His obedience to
that summons may seem hard to explain, since he had
long insisted that a primary principle of German policy
must be to avoid another war with England. It was a
questionable conception of patriotism which required him

to take a leading part in the kind of war which he had predicted as likely to prove fatal to Germany in the end. To account for it, we need to understand the extremely strait rule of soldierly duty and obedience in which he had been brought up. Beyond that may have been the psychological factor that any ardent soldier finds it hard to resist a professional opportunity.

That opportunity he certainly fulfilled, for it was the army group he commanded which brilliantly carried out the decisive moves in the conquest, first of Poland, and then of France. Yet there were signs that the glory and the pleasure were spoilt for him by an underlying disquietude. In the Russian campaign of 1941 he again proved the outstanding figure, by his direction of the sweeping operations that overturned the Russian armies in the south and gave Germany possession of the mineral and agricultural riches of the Ukraine. But this time even the victories fell short of being a complete success, and in that falling short presaged ultimate disaster. Rundstedt was quick to see confirmation of the apprehensions which had impelled him, beforehand, to offer Hitler unwelcome advice against attacking Russia. When the question of continuing the advance on Moscow was discussed in the autumn, Rundstedt argued in favour not merely of a halt but of a withdrawal to the original starting-line. That advice was still more unwelcome to the Führer. At the same time Rundstedt was growing more and more impatient of "Corporal" Hitler's interference in operational details. Eventually, at the end of November, Rundstedt replied to one of Hitler's orders by telegraphing back that, if the Führer did not trust him to carry out the operation as he judged best, the Führer should find someone else to take command. The offer of resignation was accepted by Hitler with equal alacrity; Rundstedt's doubts and protests had been getting on his nerves, which were already strained by the way that victory was eluding his grasp.

But Rundstedt was not left long on the shelf. Early in 1942 Hitler asked him to take charge in the West, and overcame his hesitation by emphasizing the note of national duty. The entry of the United States into the war created the possibility that American armies might eventually jump off from Britain to invade the Continent, and Rundstedt was very conscious of that risk. He spent the next two years in preparation for the danger he feared, as well as in wrestling with the civil problems arising out of the German occupation of France and the Low Countries. In June, 1944, the danger matured. That part of the story has already been outlined.

Rundstedt was in retirement on the fatal July 20th, so that he had no chance of giving the army a lead against the Nazi régime when the first telegraphic message of the conspirators—saying that Hitler had been killed—reached the higher headquarters in the East and the West. It is thus impossible to say whether he would have acted differently from most of the other high commanders—who, whatever their intentions, became paralysed as soon as second reports indicated that Hitler was still alive. Rundstedt was not associated with the plot, and that is significant.

While many soldiers, knowing his repugnance to Nazism, had been looking to him to give them a lead against Hitler, those who knew him best do not seem to have had any such idea. In the first place, he was regarded as a man so straightforward, so strict in his conception of the soldierly code of honour, as to be unsuitable to participate in a conspiracy which required subtlety. Secondly, because of the symbolical value of his reputation, they wanted to keep it clear of the inevitable taint that any plot carries, even though its object may be good. Beyond that he was more closely watched than others, because of his eminence, by the network of Nazi spies in which all the generals were enveloped.

At the same time a number of the generals had hoped

that Rundstedt would bring about an armistice with the British and Americans, or at least allow them an unopposed entry into Germany, in order to check the Russians. That hope was quenched by his removal early in July, though it revived with his recall in September. In the meantime Kluge had contemplated a similar step on July 20th, but had hesitated to attempt it. The reasons for his hesitation were, first, that it would be a breach of the oath of loyalty to Hitler; second, that the German people had been kept so much in the dark that they would not support such an action; third, that the soldiers on the East front would reproach the West front for betraying them; fourth, the fear of going down to history as a traitor to his country. It was natural that such restraining considerations should have even more influence on a man like Rundstedt when he was summoned back in the September crisis—apart from the practical difficulties of taking such a step when under close surveillance. As a result of that psychological conflict between his judgment and his sense of duty, as well as Hitler's continued interference at every turn, he was virtually in a state of impotence during the autumn months when the Allies imagined him to be conducting the German defence in the West.

His connection with the so-called "Rundstedt offensive" of December in the Ardennes was hardly more than that of a distant and doubting observer. The project was purely Hitler's in respect of aim, timing, and place—though improved by the technical suggestions of Manteuffel, commanding the Fifth Panzer Army. The execution was in the hands of Model and his two principal subordinates, Manteuffel and Sepp Dietrich, commander of the Sixth Panzer Army.

Late in October Hitler sent his plan to Rundstedt. It had the same basic pattern as the 1940 masterpiece. It was designed to profit by the way that the Allies had committed their strength to the push through the Belgian plain towards Aachen and Cologne, and were unlikely to expect a German counter-offensive at this time, particularly in the Ardennes—a psychological calculation that again proved correct. The main effort was to be a double-pronged thrust by the Fifth and Sixth Panzer Armies, with the aim of breaking through the weak American front in the Ardennes, then wheeling north to cross the Meuse and converge on Antwerp. The Sixth Panzer Army was to move on the inner arc of the wheel, past Liège, and the Fifth Panzer on the outer arc, past Namur. The Fifteenth Army was to help the Sixth Panzer Army by a flank thrust north of Liège, while the Seventh Army was to provide flank cover for the Fifth Panzer Army as it wheeled north.

By this scythe-like sweep Hitler hoped to cut off Montgomery's Twenty-first Army Group from its bases and from its American allies, driving it to a Dutch "Dunkirk" even if he could not annihilate it. Britain was now out of reach, but her armies were not—and they were the chosen target of his final fling. But Hitler's executive commanders all regarded the aim as far too ambitious for the resources.

Realizing that a direct protest was hopeless, Rundstedt, Model, and Manteuffel agreed in proposing a more modest alternative plan—to pinch off the American salient east of the Meuse, around Aachen. But Hitler rejected any such limitation of aim, though Manteuffel persuaded him to accept certain changes of timing and method—for Hitler was always more receptive to the arguments of the younger generals than to those of the older generals, and ready to listen to original ideas when he was deaf to counsels of caution. The changes increased the chances of initial surprise, but could not increase the ultimate chances.

The offensive was a gamble—at long odds. All the higher executants realized that Germany was playing her last trump, and that she had not the resources to provide more than a slender chance of success—unless the offensive was accompanied by extraordinary luck or the Allied commanders were extraordinarily inept. That realization was not a good foundation for an offensive. In the event, the stroke threw the Allies off their balance sufficiently to put them in serious difficulties and undue danger. But the German forces were so diminished in strength that they could not afford anything like the normal proportion of checks and slips that occur in the run of any offensive. Manteuffel almost reached the Meuse, but Sepp Dietrich, who had a larger strength and a shorter distance to go, ran into trouble sooner; and when the reserves were switched to back up Manteuffel it was too late for any great results in the face of the Allies' prompt counter-measures. The offensive fell far short of its aims, and when it ended it had fatally impoverished Germany's reserves, leaving her no chance of long-continued defence.

PART II

PRELIMINARIES TO WAR

CHAPTER IX

THE RISE OF HITLER

THE story of Hitler's entry into power has been told from many angles, but not from that of the Reichswehr. Its chiefs have been charged with aiding and abetting his entry, but remarkably little evidence has been produced to support this accusation.

It is obvious that the officers of the Reichswehr were beneficiaries, in their professional prospects, from the expansion of the forces that followed Hitler's advent. Moreover, Blomberg and other generals have admitted that they originally welcomed his régime because it released Germany and the Army from the shackles of the Versailles Treaty. That was a very natural attitude on the part of keen professional soldiers, though one that many of them lived to regret. Others, with more foresight, were apprehensive from the start, for there was good reason to assume that the amateur or "displaced" soldiers who led the S.A. would not be content, once their Party was in power, to see military office remain a privileged preserve of the traditionally conservative Reichswehr.

But evidence that a considerable number of officers were favourably disposed towards Hitler's rise is not equivalent to evidence that they were instrumental in aiding his arrival in power—and still less that the Army in its corporate sense was instrumental. For that would only have been practicable if those who were then in control of the Army were favourably disposed. On this score the cardinal facts seem to point the other way. The political head of the Army at this crucial period was General von Schleicher, who had been made Reichswehr Minister in Papen's Cabinet; under him on that side came Colonel von Bredow, the Chief of the Ministerial Staff (the Ministeramt, which was later developed into the High Command of the Wehrmacht). The military head of the Army was General von Hammerstein (*Chef der Heeresleitung*).

Not long after Hitler came into power, Hammerstein was removed from the command of the Army. Then, in the bloody purge of June 30th, 1934, Schleicher and Bredow were murdered. The steps taken to eliminate these three tends to bear out what other soldiers say—that they had tried to prevent the Nazis' rise to power.

General Röhricht, who was one of Schleicher's assistants at the time, gave me an account of this critical phase, as well as subsequent phases of the conflict between the generals and Hitler. While it runs counter to outside impressions it deserves consideration as the testimony of one of the few surviving witnesses who were on the inside of events during the decisive weeks.

In his preliminary remarks Röhricht sketched the personalities of Schleicher and Hammerstein. This was the description of Schleicher—"He was not so much a soldier as an expert in home politics, though not tied to any party. He was very sympathetic towards, and popular with, the trade unions, while suspected by the Conservatives on account of his tendency to social reforms. He was anything but a 'Junker'. A very skilful and astute political tactician, but without the personality of a statesman that was needed at this period." Speaking of Hammerstein, Röhricht said—"He was gifted and extremely clever, politically level-headed, but a lazy soldier.

He was strongly opposed to National Socialism, and followed Schleicher's political course."

Röhricht's narrative follows:

The Sequence of Events

In their struggle with the National-Socialist Party the Papen-Schleicher Government dissolved the Reichstag and resigned—in October, 1932. The elections, in spite of an obvious loss of votes for the National-Socialists, resulted in a Parliament without any clear basis of confidence and definite majority either for Papen or for the Opposition—which was split into Right and Left. At first the President intended to charge Papen anew with forming the Government. But there was high tension with all circles of revolutionary opposition. During the Berlin transport workers' strike in November, 1932, co-operation between Communists and National-Socialists was apparent. This had to be regarded as a critical symptom.

Based on this alarming situation, a conference and map exercise was held about the 20th November at the Ministeramt of the Reichswehr Ministry, in conjunction with the Ministry of the Interior, in order to examine the question whether the armed forces of the State would be sufficient to break a simultaneous revolutionary assault by the extremists of both the Right and the Left. This situation seemed likely to arise if a new Papen Government relied exclusively on the Conservative Right (Deutsch-Nationale), the Stahlhelm included.

The conclusion reached at this conference was that a general transport workers' strike would paralyse the entire structure and organization of the State and of the armed forces. For the Reichswehr was only motorized to a slight extent, and its emergency-units for technical work (Technische Nothilfe) were not in an efficient state. In Schleicher's opinion we ought to avoid a situation where the troops had to fire on their own countrymen. He did not want to "sit on bayonets".

At this moment, very much against his will, Schleicher was driven to take over the office of Chancellor himself, with the idea that it would be for a limited time. Inasmuch as he was not—like Papen—regarded as a representative of conservative-reactionary circles, but as a neutral soldier, he was accepted as a lesser evil by the Centre Party and the Social-Democrats. The National-Socialists also acquiesced—regarding this stop-gap arrangement as a possible stepping stone to their own coming into power. Thus his appointment at the end of November had a calming effect and provided a breathing space.

Schleicher planned to break the onslaught of the National Socialists by splitting up their faction in the Reichstag. The moment seemed favourable, as the Party was badly disappointed by their electoral setback and worried with financial difficulties. Negotiations started with Strasser and about eighty other M.P.s. The opening of the Reichstag was delayed.

The prospect looked better still when, at the beginning of December, a success was gained in the sphere of foreign affairs—the Disarmament Conference (presumably under the pressure of the stormy domestic development in Germany) conceding to Germany the right of military equality on principle.

But from the start Schleicher met with violent opposition from the Conservatives (Deutsch-Nationale) because his programme contained far-reaching social reforms. Thereupon Schleicher threatened to disclose nepotism in the use of the Eastern Relief funds (Osthilfe). The President—who, on account of his age, was no longer capable of clear judgment—fell under the influence of his contemporary conservative friends, who accused Schleicher of "Bolshevist" tendencies and spread the suspicion that he wanted to pervert the Army for his own political aims. At the same time Papen started an intrigue—negotiating with Hitler—by which he hoped to come back into power with the aid of the National-Socialists, but in the end was cheated himself.

The Hindenburg-Schleicher crisis reacted on Schleicher's attempt to split the National-Socialist Party —by wrecking the discussions, which had opened with good prospects.

Schleicher's situation, therefore, soon appeared hopeless—no support by the President, no prospects of a majority in Parliament. On January 26th or 27th General von Hammerstein, the Chief of the Army Command . . . attempted once more for the last time to change the President's mind, He was sharply rebuffed. Schleicher's resignation on the 29th January was followed by Hitler's appointment as Chancellor on January 30th.

With General von Schleicher the only Chancellor who arose from the Wehrmacht was overthrown. Schleicher was murdered at the first suitable moment (30th June, 1934) by agents of the Nazi Party, together with Colonel von Bredow (apparently overrated as a politician) and Strasser.

By Hitler's appointment the Reichswehr lost their hitherto existing monopoly as the final and decisive instrument of the Government. Their 100,000 men were distributed in small units all over the Reich, whereas the Party dominated the entire apparatus of the State, all the means of transport, public communications and utilities, the opinion of the man in the street, and a large part of the working class. The Army had lost its importance.

In view of these events and facts I venture to suggest that it is historically false to charge the Wehrmacht with having assisted Hitler in his coming into power. The facts point to the contrary.

In this connection I would like to examine the question, whether there was the possibility for the Reichswehr to rise in open rebellion.

The circles around Schleicher and Hammerstein, during the critical days and after the Nazi Party came into power, considered the possibility of a *coup d'état* by the Reichswehr but rejected the idea as hopeless.

These were the reasons. Hitler had been appointed Chancellor by the President as leader of the strongest party according to the constitution—therefore at first in a wholly legal manner. A *coup d'état* by the Reichswehr ordered by Generals von Schleicher and von Hammerstein —who were but little known by the rank and file—would have appeared to be not only against the new Hitler-Papen-Hugenberg Cabinet but also against the greatly respected person of their universally venerated Commander-in-Chief, the President. A political alliance with the Communists was impossible; with the other republican parties it was not prepared. The troops, bound by their oath to Hindenburg, would have declined to follow such an attempt. Besides, the disproportion of power was now still more unfavourable than in November. Finally, the unhappy consequences of a failure could not be overlooked.

THE PERIOD UP TO HINDENBURG'S DEATH
(JANUARY, 1933—AUGUST, 1934)

The Reichswehr stood aside from the political events which changed Germany's features with sweeping revolutionary measures. It was like an island—not commanded by Hitler, but by Hindenburg, who, however, was very old. Hammerstein was replaced by Fritsch on Hindenburg's order.

THE NEW MEN

Von Blomberg was appointed as War Minister ("Reichskriegsminister") in January, 1933. Until then he had been German Representative with the Disarmament Conference at Geneva—and had had no previous relations with Hitler. He was a gifted soldier, a man of the world, widely educated and with many interests, but not a strong character, and was easily influenced.

Von Reichenau was Chief of the Wehrmachtamt, until then the Ministeramt. He was a strong personality and full of initiative, a man of action and instinct rather than of intellect. Ambitious, clever, highly educated, even a poet, he was nevertheless of a sturdy nature and a sportsman. Well acquainted with Hitler for some years, he felt himself bound to the person of Hitler, not to the Party.

Freiherr von Fritsch (Chef der Heeresleitung, later Commander-in-Chief of the Army) was an excellent and distinguished soldier, but his ideas were limited to the military sphere. He was a gentleman from top to toe, and also very religious.

Blomberg and Reichenau had the task of assuring the position due to the Army within the new State—which they had to accept as an established fact—and the task of helping to recover normal public life by eliminating the revolutionary elements of the Party.

The revolutionary S.A., dominating the masses and the Party at that time, was opposed to the Army from the start. The S.A. claimed to form the Army of the new State out of its own ranks. The Army prepared to fight for its position within the new State. Hitler, like every dictator, was forced to rid himself of his S.A. rebels—his Prætorian Guard—who had raised him to power. He sided with the Army and routed the S.A. (Roehm) on 30th June, 1934. without calling in any troops.

The Reichswehr regarded that day as a success—notwithstanding serious excesses (the murder of Schleicher and others). However, it proved a Pyrrhic victory. From that day, with the founding of the Waffen-S.S., dated the rise of an enemy much more dangerous to the Army.

THE PERIOD FROM HINDENBURG'S DEATH TO 1938

Following Hindenburg's death, Hitler declared himself Head of the State—which made him at the same time the titular Supreme Commander-in-Chief of the Wehrmacht.

Re-armament, at first only aiming at equality with Germany's neighbours, began to absorb the entire attention and strength of the troops. Every new stage of re-armament weakened the solid foundations of the hitherto unanimous professional army. The 4,000 professional officers had not only to form the nucleus for the officers of the gradually expanding army, but also for the Luftwaffe. To their numbers were added the newly-reinstated officers, who came from the most varied professions and circles. These—especially the younger ones—brought along their political ideas. The features of the officer-corps were changing, and the Party began to gain ground within the Army. Soon, one could not count any longer on unity of mind.

With the reintroduction of conscription the whole army lost its character as an instrument in domestic struggles. It was further weakened by the formation of the Luftwaffe—which was guided by National-Socialist principles from the outset. For the Luftwaffe, not without purpose, embraced the Flak (A.A.)—a decision which deprived the Army of every means of anti-aircraft defence. The Army's scope of action for domestic struggle grew ever more hopeless.

For all that, the leaders of the Army once more considered the question of a rebellion against Hitler, when, with the fall of Blomberg, there arose a grave conflict over the person of Colonel-General von Fritsch in January and February, 1938. Hitler himself took over direct command of the Wehrmacht in place of Blomberg, and retained Keitel (Reichenau's successor), whose importance never exceeded that of a pliant head-clerk.

The incredible injustice with which the distinguished General von Fritsch was treated, exasperated the generals in positions of high command—no others were ever informed—to great heat.[1] This boiling pot was stirred, already, by a secret group of opposition (Goerdeler, Schacht) which was inclined "to go all out". For decisive action, however, the generals lacked unity in the sense of a solid acting corporation—which had not been attained since the days of Seeckt. They lacked the instrument of power—troops ready to go into action for such a purpose. They lacked political leadership—that was ready for action and ready to take over political power. Rebellion remained untried. On the other hand, Hitler from the outset used his "insertion" within the leaders of the Wehrmacht in order to split up the body of military leaders and to break their back-bone. Each commander was reduced to his own counsel and guidance; it was no longer possible to reckon on uniform and united political action by the Army.

---

[1] Civilian opponents of Hitler, however, complain that the fault of the generals was that they simmered, but never came to the boil.

CHAPTER X

THE RISE OF ARMOUR

WHILE the rise of Hitler changed the map of Europe more quickly than even Napoleon had done—though for a shorter period—it was the rise of armoured forces in the German Army that mainly enabled him to achieve his run of conquests. Without them his dreams would never have turned into realities. More even than the Luftwaffe, and much more than the Quislings, they were his decisive instrument. All his other means of softening opposition would not have sufficed for the quick success he sought without their unique capacity to penetrate and overrun a country. He had had the foresight to back this new development, though he ultimately paid forfeit for not backing it more fully.

The story of the "Panzers" was related in a long account I had in 1945 from General von Thoma who, next to Guderian, was the most famous of the original German tank leaders. (Guderian was a prisoner of the Americans, and I did not get his account until the original edition of this book was published, but such of his evidence as has a bearing on Thoma's account is inserted in brackets.) A tough but likeable type, Thoma was obviously a born enthusiast who lived in a world of tanks, loved fighting for the zest of it but would fight without ill-feeling, respecting any worthy opponent. In the Middle Ages he would have been perfectly happy as a knight-errant, challenging all comers at any cross-road for the honour of crossing spears with them. The advent of the tank in warfare was a godsend to such a man, giving him a chance to re-live the part of the mail-clad knight.

He described the way it was developed in the German

Army after this was released by Hitler from the restrictions of the Versailles Treaty. "It was wonderful to have real tanks for the first time in 1934, after being confined to tactical experiments with dummies for so many years. Until then our only practical experience was in an experimental camp that we had in Russia, by arrangement with the Soviet Government. This was near Kazan, and was particularly for studying technical problems. But in 1934 our first tank battalion was formed, at Ohrdruf, under the name 'Motor-Instruction Commando'. I was in charge of it. It was the grandmother of all the others.

"It was subsequently expanded into a regiment of two battalions, while two more were established at Zossen. They were equipped by degrees, rather slowly, according to the production of the factories—at first with the air-cooled Krupp tank, Pz. I, with only two machine-guns; the next year with the Pz. II, that had a water-cooled Maybach engine and a 20 mm. gun; in 1937–38 came the first Panzer III and Pz. IV, which were both bigger and better. Meantime our organization was growing. In 1935 two tank brigades were formed—one for each of the two armoured divisions that were then created. The German tank officers closely followed the British ideas on armoured warfare, particularly your own; also General Fuller's. They likewise followed with keen interest the pioneer activities of the original British tank brigade." (This was formed in 1931 for experiment, under Colonel (now General) Broad, and given permanent form in 1934 under Brigadier (now General) Hobart.)

I asked him whether the German tank methods had also been influenced by General de Gaulle's well-known book, as has been commonly reported. His answer was: "No, that did not receive much attention then, as we regarded it as rather 'fantastical'. It did not give much tactical guidance, and was rather up in the clouds. Besides, it came much later than the British exposition of the possibilities of tank warfare." (Guderian said:

"Thoma's account was right. I read de Gaulle's book, *Vers l'Armée de Métier*, in 1937, in the German translation. By that time the organization of the German panzer divisions was established and de Gaulle's book did not exercise any influence on the development of the German panzer forces. Nevertheless I read the book with much interest and was curious to see whether the French would accept de Gaulle's ideas. Fortunately they did not.")

Thoma went on to say: "It may surprise you to hear that the development of armoured forces met with much resistance from the higher generals of the German Army, as it did in yours. The older ones were afraid of developing such forces fast—because they themselves did not understand the technique of armoured warfare, and were uncomfortable with such new instruments. At the best they were interested, but dubious and cautious. We could have gone ahead much faster but for their attitude."

Thoma was sent to Spain with a tank battalion in 1936 when the Civil War broke out. "It could be seen that Spain would serve as 'the European Aldershot'. I was in command of all the German ground troops in Spain during the war. Their numbers were greatly exaggerated in newspaper reports—they were never more than 600 at a time." (This excludes air and administrative personnel.) "They were used to train Franco's tank force—and to get battle experience themselves." (A soldier like Thoma could not bear to confine himself to instructional work when there was a chance of fighting, even though the heads of the German Army deprecated such active intervention. General Warlimont, who had been sent in August as military envoy to General Franco, remarked that Thoma was "the soul and substance of all actions of the German ground forces throughout the Civil War".)

Continuing his account, Thoma said: "Our main help to Franco was in machines—aircraft and tanks. At the start he had nothing beyond a few obsolete machines.

The first batch of German tanks arrived in September, followed by a larger batch in October. They were the Pz. I.

"Russian tanks began to arrive on the other side even quicker—at the end of July. They were of a heavier type than ours, which were armed only with machine-guns, and I offered a reward of 500 pesetas for every one that was captured, as I was only too glad to convert them to my own use. The Moors bagged quite a lot. It may interest you to hear that the present Marshal Koniev was my 'opposite number' on the other side.

"By a carefully organized dilution of the German personnel I was soon able to train a large number of Spanish tank-crews. I found the Spanish quick to learn —though also quick to forget. By 1938 I had four tank battalions under my command—each of three companies, with fifteen tanks in a company. Four of the companies were equipped with Russian tanks. I also had thirty anti-tank companies, with six 37 mm. guns apiece.

"General Franco wished to parcel out the tanks among the infantry—in the usual way of generals who belong to the old school. I had to fight this tendency constantly in the endeavour to use the tanks in a concentrated way. The Francoists' successes were largely due to this.

"I came back from Spain in June, 1939, after the end of the war, and wrote out my experiences and the lessons learned. I was then given command of a tank regiment in Austria. I had been offered a tank brigade, but said that I preferred to polish up my knowledge of recent German practice by handling a regiment first, as I had been out of touch so long with what was happening in Germany. General von Brauchitsch agreed. But in August I was given command of the tank brigade in the 2nd Panzer Division, for the Polish campaign.

"That division was in General List's Army on the extreme southern wing, beyond the Carpathians. I was ordered to advance on the Jablunka Pass, but suggested instead that the motorized brigade should be sent there, while I carried out with my tank brigade a flanking move—through thick woods and over the ridge. On descending into the valley I arrived in a village to find the people all going to church. How astonished they were to see my tanks appearing! I had turned the enemy's defences without losing a single tank—after a night approach march of fifty miles.

"After the Polish campaign I was appointed to the General Staff, as Chief of the Mobile Forces. This directorate embraced the tank forces, the motorized forces, the horsed cavalry—of which there was still one division—and the cyclist units. In the Polish campaign we had six armoured divisions and four light divisions. The armoured divisions each had a tank brigade of two regiments with two battalions apiece—the combat strength of a regiment at the beginning was about 125 tanks. After an operation lasting several days, one must, in the light of experience, deduct one quarter from the number of tanks—to allow for those under repair—in reckoning the average combat strength."

As combat strength, Thoma explained, he included only the fighting tanks in the companies (or squadrons). The total number in a regiment, including the light tanks used for reconnaissance, was 160.

"The light divisions were an experiment, and the strength of each of them varied. But the average was two motorized rifle regiments (of three battalions each) and one tank battalion. In addition they had an armoured reconnaissance battalion and a motor-cyclist battalion, as well as an artillery regiment—like the armoured divisions.

"We gave up this experiment after the Polish campaign, and converted them into armoured divisions. For the 1940 offensive in the West we had ten complete armoured divisions. The proportion of medium tanks in a division was increased by that time. Even so, there were too many light tanks."

Thoma then made the surprising revelation that, for

the invasion of France, the Germans had only 2,400 tanks altogether—not 6,000 as French reports at the time stated. He said that he did not count the light reconnaissance tanks, which he called "sardine tins". "The French tanks were better than ours, and more numerous—but they were too slow. It was by speed, in exploiting the surprise, that we beat the French." (Guderian said: "The French tanks were better than ours in armour, guns and number, but inferior in speed, radio-communication and leadership. The concentration of all armoured forces at the decisive spot, the rapid exploitation of success, and the initiative of the officers of all degrees were the main reasons of our victory in 1940." Manteuffel remarked: "In peacetime we all under-estimated the speed of tanks on the battle-field. It is of greater importance than thicker armour.")

Discussing the different types of tank, and their respective qualities, Thoma remarked that if he had to choose between "a thick skin" or "a fast runner" he would always choose the latter. In other words, he preferred speed to heavy armour, having come to the conclusion, from much experience, that speed was a more desirable quality on balance. He went on to say that, in his view, the ideal tank regiment would be made up of two-thirds large tanks, fairly fast, and one-third very fast tanks, lightly armoured.

Talking of the 1940 offensive, Thoma said—"All the tank officers wanted to see Guderian in charge of the panzer army that carried out the thrust through the Ardennes. Kleist had not the same understanding of tanks—he had earlier been one of the chief opponents of them. To put a sceptic, even a converted sceptic, in supreme charge of the armoured forces was typical of the way things were done in the German Army—as in yours. But Guderian was regarded as a difficult sub-ordinate. Hitler had the deciding voice in the issue, and he approved Kleist's appointment. Nevertheless, Guderian was called on to carry out the actual break-through, which he did on the same lines that he had practised in the 1937 Army Manœuvres. After that he continued to lead the drive to the Channel. He concentrated all his thought on exploiting success, and took the attitude 'to hell with what is happening behind'. That thrustfulness was decisive, because it gave the French no time to rally.

"It was commonly said in the German Army that Guderian was always seeing red, and was too inclined to charge like a bull.[1] I don't agree with that opinion. I had personal experience of serving under him on the Smolensk front in 1941, where opposition was very stiff, and I found him a very fine commander under those difficult circumstances."

I asked Thoma what he considered the principal elements in the success of the German armoured forces in achieving such a series of breaks-through as they did in the earlier part of the war. He gave five main reasons:

"1. The concentration of all forces on the point of penetration in co-operation with bombers.

"2. Exploiting the success of this movement on the roads during the *night*—as a result, we often gained success by surprise deep in, and behind, the enemy's front.

"3. Insufficient anti-tank defence on the enemy's part, and our own superiority in the air.

"4. The fact that the armoured division itself carried enough petrol for 150–200 kilometres—supplemented, if necessary, with supply of petrol to the armoured spearheads by air, dropped in containers by parachute.

"5. Carrying rations sufficient for three days in the tanks, for three more days in the regimental supply column, and three more days in the divisional supply column."

Thoma mentioned some of the examples of sustained

[1] I have often noticed that when the senior German generals wanted to convey criticism of some exceptionally vigorous commander who did not conform to their own standards of methodical, and almost chess-like operation, they habitually spoke of him as "a bull". Such a term might be more suitably applied to those who butt at strongly defended positions than to those who loosen opposition by audacity and speed.

speed in long-range drives by the armoured forces. In the Polish campaign, he said, the seven-day march from Upper Silesia to Warsaw averaged about thirty miles a day, fighting included. In the second stage of the French campaign the advance from the Marne to Lyon averaged the same. In the 1941 Russian campaign the advance from Rosslawl to beyond Kiev averaged fifteen miles a day over a period of twenty days, while the thrust from Glukov to Orel covered forty miles a day for three days. The record advance was up to sixty miles in the day. (Guderian gave me the itinerary of his Panzer Group in the invasion of Russia, and this showed an even more rapid rate of advance than the examples which Thoma mentioned. One of Guderian's spearhead divisions penetrated 50 miles on the first day. Minsk, 210 miles from the frontier, was reached on the sixth day—when another 50-mile advance was made.)

Thoma stressed the importance of the commander of an armoured force being well forward—"in the midst of his tanks". He should give "saddle orders", like cavalry leaders of old. "The tactical task for a commander is up in front, and he must be on the spot. He should leave the administrative side to his chief staff officer."

Thoma then talked of the reorganization of the German armoured forces that was carried out before the Russian campaign, and made it clear that he considered it a grave mistake. "The armoured divisions each had one of their two tank regiments taken away from them, in order to form further armoured divisions—making twenty in all. I did not agree with this decision, and protested to Hitler —for he always took a personal interest in technical questions." Thoma argued that the net effect would be disadvantageous on balance, since it meant doubling the number of staffs and auxiliary troops without any effective increase in the armoured punch. "But I could not persuade Hitler—he was obsessed with the advantage of having an increased number of divisions. Numbers always inflamed his imagination. (Guderian remarked: "Thoma is right in his criticism of the reorganization of the German armoured forces before the Russian campaign. Panzer divisions must be strong in tanks. I agree entirely with his views—and with those of General von Manteuffel, who was one of our most active panzer leaders.")

"Hitler had not interfered in the Polish campaign, but the immense public acclaim of 'his' strategy there, and still more after the French campaign, had given him a swelled head. He had a taste for strategy and tactics, but he did not understand the executive details. He often had good ideas, but he was stubborn as a rock—so that he spoilt the fulfilment of his own conceptions.

"Twenty armoured divisions sounded a great increase, but the actual number of tanks was no greater than before. Our combat strength was only 2,434 tanks—not 12,000 as the Russians stated. About two-thirds now were medium tanks, instead of two-thirds being light tanks as in our first campaign."

Discussing the Russian campaign, Thoma said that the German armoured forces developed a new method which they found very successful. "Armoured divisions would break through the Russian front at night, and then go into hiding in woods behind the front. The Russians meantime would close the gap. In the morning the German infantry would launch their attack on this partially cemented sector—which was naturally somewhat disorganized—while the armoured divisions would emerge from the place where they were lying up, and strike the defenders in the rear."

For the 1942 campaign four new armoured divisions were formed—this was achieved partly by breaking up the existing horsed cavalry division, which had not proved effective. Three more infantry divisions were also motorized—in addition to the ten which had been motorized for the 1941 campaign. "But only ten out of the twenty former armoured divisions were brought up to strength again—because, under Hitler's orders, an increase of tank production was neglected in favour of the U-boat programme."

Thoma strongly criticized the failure of the senior generals, and of Hitler, to appreciate the vital importance of the armoured forces, and to develop them in time to the scale that was required, as well as in the form required. "What we had was good enough to beat Poland and France, but not good enough to conquer Russia. The space there was so vast, and the going so difficult. We ought to have had twice as many tanks in our armoured divisions, and their motor-infantry regiments were not mobile enough.

"The original pattern of our armoured division was ideal—with two tank regiments and one motor-infantry regiment. But the latter should be carried in armoured tracked vehicles, even though it entails more petrol. In the earlier part of the Russian campaign it was possible to bring them up in their lorries close to the scene of action before they dismounted. They were often brought up as close as a quarter of a mile from the fighting line. But that ceased to be possible when the Russians had more aircraft. The lorry-columns were too vulnerable, and the infantry had to get out too far back. Only armoured infantry can come into action quickly enough for the needs of a mobile battle.

"Worse still, these clumsy lorries easily became bogged. France had been ideal country for armoured forces, but Russia was the worst—because of its immense tracts of country that were either swamp or sand. In parts the sand was two or three feet deep. When the rain came down the sand turned into swamp."

Thoma added: "Africa was paradise in comparison. Tank troops who had been in Russia found it easy to adapt themselves to the African conditions. It is a mistake to draw lessons from the African campaign and apply them to quite different conditions. For you in future it is only Russia that matters—not the desert any more." It was a characteristic ending.

Thoma emphasized that another great mistake of the Russian campaign was the lack of co-operation between armoured forces and airborne forces. "This forfeited many successes that we might have gained. The cause of it was that the parachute troops formed part of the Luftwaffe, and consequently there were conflicts of opinion in the highest places about their employment. Goering, in particular, was an obstacle. Another handicap was the defectiveness of our self-propelled artillery. This weapon is invaluable. But those we used were only makeshifts, and the chassis was overloaded."

As Thoma was captured at Alamein in the autumn of 1942 he could contribute no evidence based on experience in the last part of the war. But in that period Manteuffel was the outstanding exponent of armoured warfare and his conclusions bore out Thoma's earlier views, on the whole, while supplementing them in certain respects. Manteuffel gave me his views at too great length to set forth here, for non-technical readers, but some of his main points are worth citing—"Tanks *must* be fast. That, I would say, is the most important lesson of the war in regard to tank design. The Panther was on the right lines, as a prototype. We used to call the Tiger a 'furniture van' —though it was a good machine in the initial break-through. Its slowness was a worse handicap in Russia than in France, because the distances were greater."

In comment on the Russian tanks Manteuffel said: "The Stalin tank is the heaviest in the world; it has robust tracks and good armour. A further advantage is its low build—it is 51 cm. lower than our Panzer V, the Panther. As a 'break-through' tank it is undoubtedly good, but too slow."

Manteuffel then spoke of two avoidable handicaps that the German armoured forces had suffered. "Every unit in the division should have its own Mobile Workshop, which should accompany the tactical echelon. Our army made a grave error in thinking that these Mobile Workshops should be kept in the rear. They ought to be well forward, under the command of a tactical leader who is in wireless touch with them. This is essential so that repairs can be done during the night, except in cases of serious damage. Such a system saves many of the accidental casualties that cause wastage. It would have counteracted the pernicious effect that our actual system had in leading the commanders to carry on with a dwindling tank strength because they could not afford to wait for tanks to be repaired. Too often they attempted tasks that were beyond their real strength—because the task was calculated on what a division should be able to achieve on its nominal strength.

"It is essential, too, for an armoured division to have its own air element—a reconnaissance squadron, a tactical bombing squadron, and a liaison squadron of slow-flying aircraft for the use of the commander and staff. The commander of an armoured division should very often direct from the air. In the early part of the Russian campaign, the armoured divisions had their own air contingent. But the High Command took it away from them in November, 1941, in favour of centralized control. That proved a grave mistake. I would also emphasize that the air squadrons should be trained with the divisions in peace time.

"Air transport is also essential—to carry supplies of ammunition, fuel, food and men. For armoured divisions will have to operate at much longer distances in future. They must also be prepared to make advances of 200 kilometres a day. Having read so many of your translated writings in the years before the war, I know what attention you gave to the development of this air side of armoured warfare. This warfare is a different language from infantry warfare—and infantrymen don't understand it. That was one of our great troubles in the war."

Discussing tank design and tactics, Manteuffel spoke

of the value of designing tanks that were low in height, and thus a less visible target. The difficulty was to combine low build with the necessity that the underside of the tank should be sufficiently clear of the ground to avoid becoming "bellied" in crossing obstructions such as bumps in the ground, rocks and tree stumps. "A slight handicap in ground clearance, however, can be overcome by a good eye for ground. That is the most vital quality in handling tanks."

Giving an example, Manteuffel narrated the story of the battle of Targul Frumos, near Jassy in Rumania, early in May, 1944. Here the first Russian drive for the Ploesti oilfields was defeated. The brunt of the attack, by over 500 Russian tanks, fell on the "Gross-Deutschland" Panzer Grenadier Division, which he was then commanding. It comprised some 160 tanks—one unit being equipped with Tiger tanks, two with Panthers, and one with the earlier Mark IVs. "It was here that I first met the Stalin tanks. It was a shock to find that, although my Tigers began to hit them at a range of 3,000 metres, our shells bounced off, and did not penetrate them until we had closed to half that distance. But I was able to counter the Russians' superiority by manœuvre and mobility, in making the best use of ground cover." Even the comparatively small Mark IVs managed to knock out a number of the opposing monsters by getting round behind them and shooting them up from a range of 1,000 metres. Manteuffel said that, when the Russians' attack petered out, about 350 of their tanks had been destroyed and left on the battlefield, while many of those that had got away were damaged. His own definite loss was only ten, though a considerably larger number suffered damage.

Although it was a defensive battle on the German side, its tactics were based on full use of local offensive mobility by the panzer regiment, within the well-chosen defence area held by the two infantry regiments. Manteuffel concluded his account with the emphatic remark: "In a tank battle, if you stand still you are lost." Recalling the memory of that piece of tactics gave him obvious professional satisfaction, and he added: "It would have given you a lot of pleasure to see this fight."

He went on to speak of the importance of the careful selection of tank crews, in order to ensure tactical aptitude and gain the advantage which this offers in modern battle. "With that condition fulfilled, tank design must aim at a careful balance between armour, weapons and speed, taking into account particularly the special risks introduced by air attack, parachutists, and rocket weapons."

Subsequently, Manteuffel gave me his fuller reflections on this subject. "Fire-power, armour protection, speed and cross-country performance are the essentials, and the best type of tank is that which combines these conflicting requirements with most success. In my opinion the German Panzer V, the 'Panther', was the most satisfactory of all, and would have been close to the ideal had it been possible to design with a lower silhouette. A main lesson I learned from all my experience was that much more importance should be placed on the speed of the tank *on the battlefield* than was generally believed before the war, and even during the war . . . It is a matter of life or death for the tank to avoid the deadly effect of enemy fire by being able to move quickly from one fire-position to another. Manoeuvrability develops into a 'weapon' and often ranks equal to fire-power and armour-protection."

It will be noted that Manteuffel's views agreed with Thoma's as to the prime importance of all-round speed across country—what one might call "loco-mobility". The same conclusion was expressed to me by Bayerlein, one of the ablest of the younger panzer generals, who had an exceptionally wide range of experience. He was 1A (operations chief) to Guderian in the invasions of France and Russia, chief of staff to Rommel in the later part of the African campaign, later commanded the picked Panzer Lehr Division in Normandy and the Ardennes counter-offensive, and finally a corps in the Rhineland battles. Bayerlein said: "For future tank design I consider *mobility*, i.e. speed and manœuvrability, the most important factor. Next comes the power of the gun (long range and calibre); and then, armour. 'Greatest mobility' will be decisive in a future war. Movement, action and surprise cannot be too fast."

In another of our talks Manteuffel gave his views on the question of how armies should be organized in the future. "Modern conditions indicate that there should be two classes of army within the Army. The best policy would be to constitute an *élite*. A certain number of divisions should be picked out for this purpose, and they should be given the best possible equipment, ample money for training, and the pick of the personnel. A large country might be able to create an army of up to thirty divisions in this way. Of course, no country could equip an army of millions on this scale. But it is better to have an *élite* army for the main operational purposes than to have a much bigger army that is mediocrely equipped and trained throughout. That *élite* army would have an increased proportion of air support, airborne forces and rocket weapons. The present scale of artillery with armoured forces is a handicap on mobility. It is required by the need for plunging fire, such as only howitzers can provide under existing conditions, but the development of rocket weapons may provide an effective substitute."

Manteuffel went on to say that he agreed with the view I had often expressed in my writings that the basic military problem of the present time was to diminish the proportion of auxiliary troops and vehicles in comparison with the striking arms. "But for such progress to be attained the High Command must learn the new language of mechanized warfare.

"The new model army calls for the design of a new kind of strategy. For these ideas to win acceptance, it is important that all the new type of forces should be under a single chief of adequate status. At the same time in order to foster the *esprit de corps* of the troops composing this *élite* army they should not only have the best of equipment and training facilities but a distinctive uniform—the smartest possible."

After a period of further reflection on his experience in the war, Manteuffel set out his conclusions about the future at greater length and in more detail. The salient points are worth citing.

"The technique of leadership must be of a new conception to that which still prevailed in 1945—to find the means of maintaining strategic mobility in warfare."

"It will be necessary to break completely with old and worn-out practices, as was the case in the German Army with the introduction of strategic tank forces. These produced a new *operational technique*—slowly at first, it is true, but subsequently consolidated: as the successes of 1939–41, and again in 1942 in Africa, clearly proved. In reality, it was a case not only of the introduction of a new arm that utilized motor power for movement and fighting, but of the creation and application of a new operational technique—of which the predominating characteristics were speed in identification, in taking action and in execution, coupled with manœuvrability: resulting in maximum mobility."

"The co-operation of air-landing troops with fast armoured formations will undoubtedly play a very important part in future warfare—because these two arms of the service solve the problems of space and time."

"The artillery of a modern army will be of an entirely different conception to our artillery in 1939–45. Rockets and atomic energy point the way." But Manteuffel also discoursed on possible ways of improving fire control methods to produce greater and more flexible concentration of fire. "With growing power and co-ordination of fire the significance of man to man combat on the ground will sink into oblivion."

"Reconnaissance should nearly always be strong—that is to say, at assault strength—so that on meeting resistance it is capable of attaining its objective by fighting. This principle was not stressed sufficiently in the war . . . Reconnaissance results thus fell short of expectations, with the consequence that the effective employment of the forces frequently suffered."

"Movement and fighting should be carried out more and more during the hours of darkness—above all to diminish the effect of hostile air attack—and this method of combat must be perfected . . . By training and accustoming the troops to this type of warfare, they are the less likely to suffer from its nerve-shaking effect in the event of the enemy practising it on a wide scale—as, for instance, the Russians might."

"I still have very clearly in mind, from my war experience, the importance of the use of artificial fog when going over to the attack. Its importance will be further increased by the two-dimensional conduct of war —from the air and on the ground—and particularly where one's own air force is unable to give effective support at the desired moment and in a limited space. Chemical experts must evolve a low-lying, tenacious smoke that will cover a wide area."

"Tactics has been considered as the art of deploying one's forces on the battlefield at the right time and most favourable spot for the execution of one's plan, thus ensuring the maximum effect from one's weapons. This conception must, in my opinion, now be widened to include petrol in the category of 'combat means' and 'weapon-power' . . . To ensure that ample petrol is available when and where required in battle there must be *tactical control* of its supply."

Dealing with the composition of armies in the future, Manteuffel visualized the continuance of two main types of division: the infantry division, carried in wheeled motor transport, and the armoured division—which he would prefer to call a "mobile division". In discussing the latter type with me when I saw him immediately after the war, his suggested organization (quoted in the original edition of this book) was very similar to that which prevailed in the later stages of the war, though with an increased proportion of half-track transport for the auxiliary elements of the division. But after he had time for more reflection on war experience, he came to the conclusion that a big increase in the scale of tanks was required, while the scale of infantry-men in the division could be reduced if they were given more cross-country mobility by mounting them in full-tracked armoured vehicles. Instead of three tank units, each of 60 tanks, his proposed division would have four tank units each of 100 tanks. Its infantry element would consist of three battalions of armoured infantry, instead of four in half-track vehicles or wheeled trucks. That represents a return to the original proportions of the panzer division, before the war, when tanks were much lighter in weight and armament. "It is a mistaken idea," Manteuffel said, "that the increased effect of more powerful tank guns does not require so heavy a massing of tanks. Moreover, the number of tanks available for action drops alarmingly quickly after a spell of movement and fighting."

He emphasized, like Thoma, the ill-effects of the re-organization before the Russian campaign by which the armoured divisions relinquished half their tanks and were instead given a second infantry regiment. "The armoured division thus lost the impetus and force of penetration of its tank core, whereas everything should have been done to strengthen it. The pace of its attack and much else depended now on the *infantry*, which was—and remains—wrong. In an armoured battle the tanks play the primary rôle, and everything else should take second place. An *armoured* division can only be strengthened by reinforcing the *tank core*." (Guderian, when I got his views later, was also emphatic in his preference for an increased proportion of tanks and likewise specified 400 tanks as the desired scale.)

"It is the massed spearhead of its tanks that lends an armoured division the *impetus* necessary for attack; the infantry's task is to aid the tanks by taking over secondary duties, so as to allow a concentration of as many tanks as possible at the point of main effort. But to employ infantry as a primary support to the armoured divisions conveys a completely wrong picture and means a standstill in their development; it implies that the peak of the armoured force has been reached and passed, which is by no means the case."

As regards the auxiliary elements, Manteuffel said: "The arms accompanying the tank core—Panzer infantry, engineers, artillery—should be made mobile on vehicles that are able to keep up with the pace of the tank on the battlefield. In the war, the Panzer artillery used tank chassis for this purpose; this should be even more feasible in the future, as the artillery will be able to use lighter mountings. Panzer infantry and engineers used the so-called SPW (schutzen-panzer-wagen), a lightly armoured half-track vehicle, with a good cross-country capacity, which proved to have a surprising ability to wade through the deepest mud of the Russian theatre. When panzer divisions were first formed only one infantry battalion and one engineer company could be mounted on half-tracks, but in the course of the war it became possible to increase the scale in some divisions, so that they had one armoured infantry regiment, some units of A.A. artillery and some of field artillery mounted in half-track vehicles—that is, mechanized. In the future, vehicles such as these would suffice for combat echelons of the ordinary infantry. The infantry of armoured divisions, however, need full-tracked vehicles. That requirement applies also to all the other combat elements in the division, while a proportion of the supply vehicles must be of cross-country type. The artillery should be self-propelled, on tank chassis, not tractor-drawn."

PART III

THROUGH GERMAN EYES

CHAPTER XI

HOW HITLER BEAT FRANCE— AND SAVED BRITAIN

THE real story of any great event is apt to be very different to what appears at the time. That is especially the case in war. The fate of millions of people turns on decisions that are taken by one man—who may be influenced by the most curious of motives in reaching a decision that changes the course of history. The way he makes up his mind is known only by a few men behind the scenes, who usually have good reason for keeping it quiet. The truth sometimes leaks out later; sometimes never.

When it emerges it often bears out the saying that "truth is stranger than fiction". A novelist has to appear plausible, and would hesitate to make use of such astounding contradictions as occur in history through some extraordinary accident or twist of psychology.

Nothing could be more extraordinary than the way that the decisive events of 1940 were shaped. France was overcome by an offensive in which few of the higher executants had any faith, and the invasion only succeeded through a belated change of plan on the German side that happened to fit the situation produced by rigidity of plan combined with over-confidence on the French side. Stranger still was the way that the British Army escaped, and Britain herself was preserved from invasion. The truth here runs quite contrary to the popular picture. It would have seemed incredible to the British people at that time, and equally incredible to most of Hitler's ardent followers in Germany. Little indication of it emerged in the revelations at Nuremberg.

The escape of the British Army from France has often been called "the miracle of Dunkirk". For the German armoured forces had reached the Channel coast behind the back of the British Army while this was still deep in the interior of Flanders. Cut off from its own bases, and from the bulk of the French Army, it seemed likely also to be cut off from the sea. Those who got away have often wondered how they managed to do so.

The answer is that Hitler's intervention saved them— when nothing else could have. A sudden order stopped the armoured forces just as they were in sight of Dunkirk, and held them back until the retreating British had reached the port and slipped out of their clutches.

But although the British Army thus escaped from the trap in France, it was in no state to defend England. It had left most of its weapons behind, and the stores at home were almost empty. In the following months Britain's small and scantily-armed forces faced the magnificently-equipped army that had conquered France—with only a strip of water between them. Yet the invasion never came.

At the time we believed that the repulse of the Luftwaffe in the "Battle *over* Britain" had saved her. That is only part of the explanation. The last part of it. The original cause, which goes deeper, is that Hitler did not want to conquer England He took little interest in the invasion preparations, and for weeks did nothing to spur them on; then, after a brief impulse to invade, he veered round again and suspended the preparations. He was preparing, instead, to invade Russia.

Before relating in detail the inner story of these fateful decisions, there is a previous one to reveal. For the real character of earlier events is hardly less amazing than the climax—or anti-climax. While Hitler saved England, France was conquered in spite of his Generals.

When France lay prostrate under the German heel, the men of the victorious Army would have been astonished had they known that their highest military chiefs had not believed such a victory to be possible—and that the victory had been gained by a plan which had been forced on a doubting General Staff as the result of a backstairs approach. Most of them would have been horrified to hear that six months earlier they had nearly been ordered to march on Berlin instead of on Paris. Yet those were the facts hidden behind the triumphant façade.

WHY HITLER DECIDED TO ATTACK

The conquest of the West, although it appeared so irresistible in retrospect, was conceived in an atmosphere of fear and doubt. The preceding period of "the phoney war" was so christened by American commentators in derision of the Allies' inactivity. In that sense it was hardly just, since the Allies lacked the equipment needed to take the offensive—as later events showed. But there *were* "phoney" factors on the German side.

After the conquest of Poland, and the division of the spoils with Russia, Hitler made a bid for peace with the Western Powers—but was rebuffed. Meantime he was growing afraid of what he had started—and of his temporary partner. He expressed the view that a long-drawn-out war of attrition with Britain and France would gradually exhaust Germany's limited resources, and expose her to a fatal attack from behind by Russia. "By no treaty or pact can Russia's lasting neutrality be ensured," he told his generals. His fear urged him to force peace on France by an offensive in the West. He hoped that if the French were defeated, the British would see reason and come to terms. He reckoned that *time* was working against him on every count.

Hitler did not dare to risk playing a waiting game, to see whether the French grew tired of war. He believed that for the moment he had the strength and equipment to beat France. "In certain arms, the decisive arms, Germany to-day possesses clear, indisputable superiority of weapons." Hitler felt that he must strike as soon as possible, before it was too late. His order was: "The attack is to be launched, if conditions are at all possible, this autumn."

Hitler's reckoning, and these instructions were set out in a long memorandum of October 9th, 1939. His analysis of the military factors in the situation was masterly, but it left out of account a vital political factor—the "bull-doggedness" of the British people when aroused.

That may seem strange, since in *Mein Kampf* he had dwelt on the "dogged determination" of the English in war, and warningly spoken of the German tendency to self-deception on this score—"an undervaluation for which we have had to pay a heavy penalty". Did Hitler forget his own earlier warning in the flush of his opening victory? It is more likely that his consciousness of it spurred him on to more desperate measures, once he had taken the fatal step of drawing England into war, even though he still cherished the hope that her people's habit of compromise might eventually prevail over their bull-dog instinct. Moreover it is clear that the language of England's spokesmen made him feel that there was no immediate hope of a compromise even before he attempted his peace bid.

In the last part of September, when Polish resistance was collapsing, Hitler's mind was already turning to the idea of an early offensive in the West. General Warlimont, who was head of the "national defence" section in the O.K.W., told me: "I first heard about this resolution of Hitler's when I was visiting his Headquarters at Zoppot on the Baltic Sea during the last phase of the Polish campaign. Even Keitel, who informed me about this decision, was utterly taken aback—since the German forces were not prepared for such a campaign, either in mind or in fact, and certainly not in planning." The executive heads of the Army were more worried still when, at the end of September, they were informed of Hitler's intention and told to prepare plans. They had been expecting that he would sit tight—leaving time for the Western nations to cool down and count the cost of a prolonged war, or else launch an unpromising attack on the German front that would damp their ardour. Now that the mass of the German forces could be switched back from Poland to the West there was good reason to reckon on being able to repulse any Franco-British offensive.

But Hitler insisted that he could not afford to wait, and that it was necessary to attack in order to protect the industrial districts of the Ruhr and the Rhine, which lay so close to the Belgian frontier. He considered that the Belgians were not really neutral in mind or heart, and pointed to the fact that all their newer fortifications had been built along the German frontier, and none facing France. He cited Intelligence reports of private talks between the French and Belgian Staffs about the possibility of the French and British armies entering Belgium, and emphasized that the strongest part of these armies was concentrated on the Belgian frontier. It was essential, he declared, ·to forestall the danger of them entering Belgium and deploying on the German frontier close to the Ruhr, "thereby bringing the war near to the heart of our armaments industry". (Hitler had some justification for his anxiety, since this was exactly what Gamelin, the French Commander-in-Chief, had proposed on September 1st— as the French documents, and his own memoirs, reveal.)

For these reasons the German offensive would be directed primarily against Belgium, and thence against France—to make its results decisive. Hitler went on to say that he did not expect to attack Holland, but hoped to make a political arrangement with her about the Maastricht strip of territory which intervened between the German and Belgian frontiers. (In the course of October, however, he inclined towards the occupation of Holland, influenced by the requirements of the Air Force.)

SCHISM IN THE COMMAND

Hitler's generals shared his long-term fears, but did not share his short-term confidence. They did not think that the German Army was strong enough to beat France.

On a comparison of numbers their view appeared well justified. For they had no such superiority in total of divisions as was required for success—on any customary basis of calculation. Indeed, they were numerically inferior. The French had mobilized 110 divisions, and might be expected to produce more, from their total of 5,000,000 trained men; of these, 85 divisions (later raised to 101) were concentrated facing Germany. The British had despatched 5 divisions with more to follow (a further 8 arrived during the winter). The Belgians were able to mobilize 23 divisions. On the other hand, the German Army had entered the war with 98 divisions, and only 62 of these were ready for action—the remainder were reserve and Landwehr divisions still incompletely equipped and made up mainly of men over forty who had served in the previous war and required much retraining before they could be effective. Moreover, a considerable number had to be left in the East, to occupy Poland and stand on guard against Russia.

In the light of such a comparison it is not surprising that the senior German generals could see no favourable prospect in an offensive. They did not share Hitler's belief in the power of the new mechanized arms—armoured and air force—to overcome the enemy's superiority in trained manpower. (At the same time, with better reason, they held the view which Beck had so clearly stated in his 1938 memorandum about the danger of bringing on another world war.)

Almost all the generals to whom I talked, including Rundstedt and his chief planner, Blumentritt, frankly admitted that they had never expected such a sweeping success as was achieved. Describing the view that prevailed on the higher levels, Blumentritt remarked: "Hitler alone believed that a decisive victory was possible." But among the younger generals there were two in particular—Manstein and Guderian—who believed that a decisive victory was possible provided that new methods were applied. Through Hitler's backing they were able to prove their point, and thereby changed the course of history.

General Siewert, who had been Brauchitsch's personal assistant from 1939 to 1941, said that no plan for an offensive in the West had even been considered until after the Polish campaign, and gave me an account of Brauchitsch's reaction to Hitler's directive. "Field-Marshal von Brauchitsch was dead against it. All the documents relating to this plan will be available in the archives wherever they are, and they will show that he advised the Führer against invading the West. He went to see the Führer personally, to demonstrate the unwisdom of such an attempt. When he found he could not convince the Führer, he began to think of resigning." I asked on what grounds the objection was made. Siewert replied: "Field-Marshal von Brauchitsch did not think that the German forces were strong enough to conquer France, and argued that if they invaded France they would draw Britain's full weight into the war. The Führer discounted this, but the Field-Marshal warned him: 'We know the British from the last war—and how tough they are.'"

This argument took place on November 5th. It ended in Hitler overriding Brauchitsch's objections and giving the order that the armies were to be ready to attack on November 12th. On the 7th, however, the order was cancelled—when the meteorologists forecast bad weather. The date was put off to the 17th, and then postponed again. Hitler's irritation at the interference of the weather was increased by his awareness that his generals welcomed it. He felt that they were all too ready to grasp at any excuse that would justify their hesitation.

Faced with such doubts on the part of the army chiefs, Hitler summoned a conference in Berlin, on November 23rd, with the aim of implanting his own conviction. I had an account of it from General Röhricht, who was head of the Training Department of the General Staff, and was subsequently responsible for compiling the lessons of the 1940 campaign. Röhricht said: "The Führer spent two hours in a lengthy review of the situation aimed to convince the Army Command that an offensive in the West was a necessity. He answered most sharply the objections which Field-Marshal von Brauchitsch had made beforehand." That evening, after the conference, Hitler repeated his reproaches at a personal meeting with Brauchitsch, who then tendered his resignation. Hitler brushed it aside and told him to obey orders.

Röhricht went on to say that Halder was as dubious as Brauchitsch about taking the offensive. "Both of them argued that the German Army was not strong enough—it was the only line of argument that could have any chance of deterring the Führer. But he insisted that his will must prevail. After this conference many new formations were raised, to increase the Army's strength. This was as far as the Führer would meet the opposing views." (By May, 1940, the total of divisions in the West had been increased to 130. More important, the number of armoured divisions had been raised from six to ten.)

In Hitler's address to the higher commanders he expressed his anxiety about ultimate danger from Russia, and the consequent necessity of being free in the West. But the Allies would not consider his peace offers, and lay behind their fortifications—out of reach, yet able to spring when they chose. How long could Germany endure such a situation? While she had the advantage at the moment, in six months it might no longer be so.

"Time is working for our adversary." There was cause
for anxiety even in the West. "We have an Achilles' Heel
—the Ruhr . . . If Britain and France push through
Belgium and Holland into the Ruhr, we shall be in the
greatest danger. That could lead to a paralysis of German
resistance." The menace must be removed by striking first.

But even Hitler did not display much assurance of
success at this time. He described the offensive as "a
gamble", and a choice "between victory and destruction".
Moreover, he ended his exhortation on the gloomy, and
prophetic note—"I shall stand or fall in this struggle. I
shall never survive the defeat of my people."

A copy of this address was found in the archives of the
Supreme Command after Germany's collapse, and produced at Nuremberg. But there was no mention there of
the opposition that Hitler had met in the discussion, nor of
a sequel that might have cut short his career in the first
autumn of the war.

For the generals were driven by their forebodings to
consider desperate remedies. Röhricht told me: "It was
mooted in O.K.H., by Brauchitsch and Halder that—if
the Führer would not moderate his policy, and insisted on
plans that would involve Germany in an all-out struggle
against Britain and France—they should order the German
Army in the West to turn about, and march on Berlin to
overthrow Hitler and the Nazi régime.

"But the one man who was really vital to the success
of this counter-plan declined to co-operate. This was
General Fromm, the Commander-in-Chief of the Home
Forces, in Germany. He argued that if the troops were
ordered to turn against the régime most of them would
not obey—because they had too much trust in Hitler.
Fromm was only too right on this score. His refusal to co-
operate was not due to any love of Hitler. He disliked the
régime just as much as the others did, and in the end became
one of Hitler's victims—though not until March, 1945."

Röhricht went on to say: "Apart from Fromm's

hesitation, I think that the plan would have failed. The Luftwaffe, which was enthusiastically pro-Nazi, could have broken any revolt which the Army attempted, since it had the *flak* under its control. The original step of making Goering and the Luftwaffe responsible for the anti-aircraft defence of the Army was a very shrewed move in weakening the power of the Army."

Fromm's calculation about the troops' reaction was probably correct. That is admitted by the generals who were upset at the time by his refusal to co-operate, and it tends to be confirmed by our knowledge of how hard it was to loosen the people's faith in Hitler even in the later days of devastation and disaster. But although this 1939 plot might not have succeeded in its immediate object of overthrowing Hitler, the attempt would have been worth while. For at the least it could have so shaken Germany as to nullify Hitler's plans for the conquest of France. In that case all the European peoples would have been spared the misery that befell them as a consequence of that illusory triumph. Even the German people would not have suffered anything like what they did after a long-drawn war, accompanied by ever-multiplying devastation from the air.

Although this plot was still-born, Hitler did not succeed in delivering his offensive in 1939 as he had intended. The weather proved more effective in obstruction than the generals, and an exceptionally cold spell led to a fresh series of postponements during the first half of December. Then Hitler decided to wait until the New Year, and grant Christmas leave. The weather was again bad just after Christmas, but on January 10th Hitler fixed the start of the offensive for the 17th.

A DECISIVE ACCIDENT

On the very day that Hitler took this decision a dramatic "intervention" took place. I relate the story as it was told to me by General Student, the Commander-in-Chief of the German Airborne Forces: "On January 10th a major detailed by me as liaison officer to the 2nd Air Fleet flew from Munster to Bonn to discuss some unimportant details of the plan with the Air Force. He carried with him, however, *the complete operational plan for the attack in the West.* In icy weather and a strong wind he lost his way over the frozen and snow-covered Rhine, and flew into Belgium, where he had to make a forced landing. He was unable to burn completely the vital document. Important parts of it fell into the hands of the Belgians, and consequently the outline of the whole German plan for the Western offensive. The German Air Attaché in the Hague reported that on the same evening the King of the Belgians had a long telephone conversation with the Queen of Holland."

Of course, the Germans did not know at the time exactly what had happened to the papers, but they naturally feared the worst, and had to reckon with it. In that crisis Hitler kept a cool head, in contrast to others. To continue Student's account: "It was interesting to watch the reactions of this incident on Germany's leading men. While Goering was in a rage, Hitler remained quite calm and self-possessed. . . . At first he wanted to strike immediately, but fortunately refrained—and decided to drop the original operational plan entire. This was replaced by the Manstein plan."

That proved very unfortunate for the Allies, even though they were given a further four months grace for preparation—since the German offensive was now put off indefinitely while the plan was being completely recast, and did not come until May 10th. When it was launched, it threw the Allies completely off their balance and led to the speedy collapse of the French armies, while the British barely escaped by sea, from Dunkirk. All these shattering events ensued from that strange accident by which a mere major delivered the original German plan into foreign hands.

It is natural to ask whether it really was an accident. I explored this question after the war in discussion with many of the generals involved. It might be expected that any of them would be only too glad to put themselves in a favourable light with their captors by claiming that they had arranged this warning to the Allies. Yet, in fact, none of them did so—and all seemed convinced that the accident was quite genuine. But we know that Admiral Canaris, the head of the German Secret Service—who was later executed—took a lot of hidden steps to thwart Hitler's aims, and that just prior to the attacks in the spring on Norway, Holland, and Belgium, warnings were conveyed to the threatened countries—though they were not properly heeded. We know, too, that Canaris worked in mysterious ways, and was skilled in covering up his tracks. So the fateful accident of January 10th is bound to remain an open question.

While Hitler benefited so much from the air accident that led him to change the plan, the Allies suffered much from it. One of the strangest features of the whole story is that they did so little to profit by the warning that had fallen into their lap. For the documents which the German staff officer was carrying were not badly burned, and copies of them were promptly passed on by the Belgians to the French and British Governments—revealing clearly the outline of the German plan. But their military advisers, as well as the Belgians, were inclined to regard the documents as having been planted on them as a deception. That view hardly made sense, for it would have been a foolish kind of deception to risk putting the Belgians on their guard and driving them into closer collaboration with the French and British! They might easily have decided to open their frontier and let the Franco-British armies come in, to reinforce their defences, before the blow fell.

Even stranger was the fact that the Allied High Command made no change in its own plans, nor took any precautions to meet the probability that if the captured plan were genuine the German High Command would almost certainly shift the weight of its attack elsewhere.

THE VITAL CHANGE OF PLAN

The original plan, worked out by the General Staff under Halder, was on broadly similar lines to that of 1914, though its aim was less far-reaching. The main weight was to be concentrated on the right wing, for a drive through the plains of Belgium, carried out by Army Group "B" under Bock. Army Group "A" under Rundstedt, in the centre facing the Ardennes, was to play a secondary part. Army Group "C" under Leeb, on the left, facing the frontier of France itself, was simply to threaten and pin down the French armies that were holding the Maginot Line. Bock had the 18th, 6th, and 4th Armies—listing them from right to left; Rundstedt had the 12th and 16th Armies; Leeb had the 1st and 7th Armies. What was more important, the whole of the tank forces was to be concentrated for Bock's blow. None were allotted to Rundstedt, whose task was merely to advance to the Meuse, and there cover Bock's left flank.

In January, Rundstedt's strength was increased by providing him with one panzer corps, and his part in the plan enlarged to some extent—he was to push across the Meuse and establish a wide bridgehead beyond, linking up with Bock's flank and covering it better. But that was only a modification, rather than a radical change. The plan still placed the main weight on the right wing.

It is clear now that if that plan had been carried out it would have failed to be decisive. For the British Army and the best equipped part of the French Army stood in the path. The German attack would have met these forces head on. Even if it had broken their front in Belgium it would merely have pushed them back on their fortified line in Northern France, and closer to their bases of supply.

The inner story of how the plan was changed is an extraordinary one. It was only by degrees that I got on the track of it. From the outset the German generals were very forthcoming in telling me about the military operations—such professional objectivity is a characteristic of theirs. Most of them, I found, were old students of my military writings, so that they were all the more ready to talk and exchange views. They were equally frank in discussing most of the Nazi leaders, whose influence they heartily detested. In regard to Hitler they were more reserved at first. It was obvious that many of them had been so hypnotized by him or so fearful of him that they hesitated to mention his name. As they gradually became convinced that he was dead, this inhibition subsided, and they criticized his actions more freely—Rundstedt was always critical. But they still had a tendency, a very natural one, to cover up cleavages in their own ranks. So it was only after many discussions that I learnt the real truth about the brain-wave that beat France.

The new plan was inspired by General von Manstein, who was Rundstedt's chief of staff at the time. He thought that the existing plan was too obvious, and too much a repetition of the past—so that it was just the kind of move the Allied High Command would anticipate.

If the Allied forces advanced into Belgium, as was expected, there would be a frontal clash. That would not promise decisive results. To quote his own words: "We could perhaps defeat the Allied forces in Belgium. We could conquer the Channel coast. But it was probable that our offensive would be definitely stopped on the Somme. Then there would grow up a situation like 1914, with only the advantage that we would be in possession of the Channel coast. But there would be no chance of reaching a peace."

Another drawback was that the decisive battle would be fought out with the British Army, which, Manstein argued, was likely to be a tougher opponent than the

French. Moreover the German tank forces, on whom the chances of victory depended, would have to make their drive through country which, though flat, was filled with rivers and canals. That was a serious handicap, since the whole issue turned on speed.

So Manstein conceived the bold idea of shifting the main stroke to the Ardennes. He argued that the enemy would never expect a mass of tanks to be used in such difficult country. Yet it should be practicable for the German tank forces, since opposition was likely to be slight during the crucial stage of the advance. Once they had emerged from the Ardennes, and crossed the Meuse, the rolling plains of Northern France would provide ideal country for tank manœuvre and for a rapid sweep to the sea.

In giving me his own account at more length Manstein added: "There was still another part of my plan. I calculated that the French would try to prevent our drive by a counter-offensive with their reserves west of Verdun or between the Meuse and the Oise. Therefore I had proposed that our strong reserves should forestall any such attempt not only by forming a defensive front along the Aisne and the Somme—the solution which was later adopted by Hitler and the O.K.H.—but by overrunning the deployment of every French counter-offensive. I felt that we had to avoid the possibility that the French could build up a new front which might lead to a war of position as in 1914."

After the new plan had evolved in his mind, Manstein took an early opportunity of consulting Guderian about its practicability from a tank point of view. This was in November. Giving me his account, Guderian said: "Manstein asked me if tank movements would be possible through the Ardennes in the direction of Sedan. He explained his plan of breaking through the extension of the Maginot Line near Sedan, in order to avoid the old-fashioned Schlieffen plan, familiar to the enemy and likely to be expected once more. I knew the terrain from World War I, and, after studying the map, confirmed his view.

Manstein then convinced General von Rundstedt and a memorandum was sent to O.K.H. (on December 4th). O.K.H. refused to accept Manstein's idea. But the latter succeeded in bringing his idea to Hitler's knowledge."

The General Staff regarded the Ardennes as unsuitable country for a major offensive, and far too difficult for a tank drive. It was hard to convince them that it was practicable—and they might never have been persuaded about this but for Guderian's authority as a tank expert. The French General Staff held the same view as the German, and clung to it even more stubbornly—with fatal consequences to France. [1]

Warlimont contributed another link in the chain. He told me how Manstein expounded the new project to him when, "about the middle of December 1939, I paid a short visit to Rundstedt's headquarters at Coblenz and was sitting next to Manstein at the dinner-table. . . . After my return to Berlin I mentioned this conversation in my report to Jodl—without his showing any indication of interest in Manstein's idea. Nevertheless I believe it was in this way that Manstein's 'brain-wave' reached the highest headquarters for the first time."

A stronger impetus was produced, a few weeks later, when the airborne staff officer lost his way and carried the existing plan into Belgium. It was only after this "miscarriage", on January 10th, that Manstein's plan really came to the fore. Yet Hitler was still reluctant to make any change that would involve delay in launching the offensive.

---

[1] The same view prevailed in the British General Staff. In several of my books I had strongly disputed that longstanding opinion and argued that "the impassability of the Ardennes has been much exaggerated"—but with little effect. When in November, 1933, I was consulted as to how our fast tank formations—which the War Office was just beginning to form—could best be used in a future war I had suggested that, in the event of a German invasion of France, we should deliver a tank counter-stroke through the Ardennes. I was thereupon told that "the Ardennes were impassable to tanks", to which I replied that, from personal study of the terrain, I regarded such a view as a delusion.

On the 12th, when the weather forecast was again unfavourable, he merely put off "A-day" from the 17th to the 20th. That was the eleventh postponement. But on the 16th another bad weather forecast was reinforced by intelligence reports which seemed to show definitely that his existing plan had fallen into Belgian hands—and he now postponed the offensive indefinitely.

Warlimont says: "It was on this day, January 16th, that the resolution for a thorough change as to date and operations plans for the attack entered Hitler's mind. Even then, this was chiefly due to the air accident and to reports that, on the 15th, complete military preparedness had been ordered in Belgium and in certain parts of the Netherlands."

Another month passed before Hitler swung definitely in favour of Manstein's plan. Jodl's diary shows that on February 13th he submitted to Hitler a memorandum showing how the main concentration of forces could be shifted southward, but his note ends dubiously: "I invite his attention to the fact that the thrust at Sedan is an operational 'secret passage' in which one might be caught by the gods of war."

The final decision was clenched in a curious way. Brauchitsch and Halder had not liked the manner in which Manstein had pressed his "brain-wave" in opposition to their plan. So it was decided to remove him from his post, and send him to command an infantry corps—where he would be out of the main channel and not so well placed to push his ideas. But following this transfer (at the end of January) he was summoned to see Hitler, and thus had an opportunity to explain his idea in full. This interview was arranged on the initiative of General Schmundt, Hitler's chief aide-de-camp, who was a fervent admirer of Manstein and felt he had been badly treated. Manstein's visit was on the 15th, according to his recollection, and produced speedy results.

Warlimont says: "A few days later—when Hitler

pressed more and more for the new idea to be translated into actual planning—Keitel and Jodl had to set about to convince the Commander-in-Chief of the Army and the Chief of the General Staff to follow the new line. This the Army Command did only with the utmost reluctance, yet finally it endorsed the plan and carried it through in one of the finest pieces of general staff work."

Since the Manstein plan had so much of the audacity and originality which always appealed to Hitler it is strange that he was not quicker to embrace it. His impatience to start the attack in the West would seem to be the most likely explanation. But once he had made up his mind to accept the necessity of delay and had adopted the new plan he quickly came to assume, consciously or unconsciously, that he had conceived it. All he gave Manstein was the credit of having agreed with him! For, referring to their discussion, he subsequently remarked: "Among all the generals I talked to about the new plan in the West, Manstein was the only one who understood me."

Hitler was not content with the high credit of having recognized the value of a conception that the General Staff had failed to grasp, and of having pushed the key to victory into their reluctant hands. To share the credit with Manstein might have diminished his own claim to be a supreme strategist; he was the less inclined to do so since he remembered that Manstein had been the right hand of Fritsch and Beck, and regarded him as belonging to the anti-Nazi camp. Significantly, Hitler did not interfere with the action of O.K.H. in moving Manstein out of the main channel.

It is ironical, if only too typical, that the man who produced the battle-winning idea should have been allowed no part in the execution of his own plan. And as Manstein had shown more imagination than any other high member of the General Staff in grasping the potentialities of mobile armoured warfare, it was particularly ironical that he should have been sent to take charge of an infantry corps (which merely played a walking-on part in the initial offensive) just as the new kind of mobility was about to achieve its supreme fulfilment.

It was fortunate for the prospects of the offensive that Guderian was at hand to fulfil the plan, and to give it even more thrust than Manstein could have done. But Guderian might have found the going easier if Manstein had remained at Rundstedt's side.

The further stages in the development of the plan were related to me by Guderian: "On February 7th, a war-game took place at Coblenz under the direction of General Halder, in order to discuss the Manstein plan. My proposal to attack as soon as possible over the Meuse with the panzer corps alone, and without waiting for the infantry, was heavily criticized by Halder. He judged an organized attack over the Meuse impossible before the 9th or 10th day of the campaign.

"A second war-game at General List's headquarters (12th Army) had the same negative results. General List examined the question of stopping the panzers after the arrival on the Meuse and waiting for the infantry to cross the river. General von Wietersheim (XIV Corps) and I protested against this solution. But in the end General von Rundstedt laid down that the panzer divisions should only gain bridge-heads over the Meuse and that no further aims should be aspired to. That was on March 6th. It became clear that General von Rundstedt had no clear conception of the capability of panzer forces. Manstein was needed there!

"On March 15th, General von Rundstedt and his army commanders, with General von Kleist and myself, met Hitler in Berlin. Everyone was to give an account of his task, and the manner of execution he proposed. I was the last to speak. When I had finished Hitler asked me what ought to be done after crossing the Meuse and gaining a bridge-head. I answered that the advance should be continued immediately in the direction of Amiens and

the Channel ports. Hitler nodded, and nobody opposed."
Guderian thus felt that he could go ahead in the way he
proposed when the time came to put the plan into action.
He saw his chance to put into practice the theory of deep
strategic penetration, and was determined to exploit it to
the full. His more orthodox and cautious superiors might
still try to put on the brake, but it would be harder for
them now to halt him.

Throughout these discussions Guderian had insisted, as
an essential condition, that the largest possible armoured
force should be employed in the Ardennes thrust. To use
only a small number of panzer divisions there, as O.K.H.
proposed, might seem less of a hazard, but it would
increase the risk when it came to exploiting the penetra-
tions—and thus be likely to forfeit the chance of any
decisive success. As Guderian remarked to me: "One or
two divisions cannot execute independent operations as
well as a Panzer Army can. The presupposition for independent operations with Panzer armies is sufficient strength
in armour. Therefore in 1940 I asked for all our armoured
forces to execute the raid on the Channel coast—and
succeeded in getting the bulk of them for that purpose."

THE FRENCH PLAN

The shattering effect of the Ardennes stroke owed
much to the design of the French plan—which fitted perfectly, from the Germans' point of view, into their own
remodelled plan. What proved fatal to the French was
not, as is commonly imagined, their defensive attitude or
"Maginot Line complex", but the more offensive side of
their plan. By pushing into Belgium with their left
shoulder forward they played into the hands of their
enemy, and wedged themselves in a trap—just as had
happened with their near-fatal Plan XVII of 1914. It
was the more perilous this time because the opponent
was more mobile, manœuvring at motor-pace instead of

at foot-pace. The penalty, too, was the greater because the left shoulder push—made by the 1st, 7th, and 9th French armies and the British Expeditionary Force—comprised the most modernly equipped and mobile part of the Allied forces, so that once these were deeply committed the French High Command lost most of its manœuvring power.

The supreme advantage of the new German plan was that every step forward that the Allies took made them more susceptible to Rundstedt's flanking drive through the Ardennes. That had been foreseen when the scheme was drafted. Rundstedt himself told me: "We expected that the Allies would try to advance through Belgium and Southern Holland against the Ruhr—and our offensive would thus have the effect of a counter-stroke, with the natural advantages this carries." Such an expectation went beyond the Allies' intentions, but that did not matter. For the opening of the German right wing assault on the frontiers of Belgium and Holland acted like a pistol in starting the Allies' dash forward into those countries, in fulfilment of Plan D—which they had framed in the autumn. Bock's direct thrust drew them out of their defences, and far forward into the open, leaving their flank and rear exposed to Rundstedt's indirect thrust.

THE MATADOR'S CLOAK

Hitler's invasion of the West opened with startling successes on the seaward flank. These focused attention to such an extent as to serve, like a matador's cloak, to distract attention from the thrust that was being delivered through the Ardennes—towards the heart of France.

The capital of Holland and the hub of its communications, at Rotterdam, were attacked in the early hours of May 10th, by airborne forces, simultaneously with the assault on its frontier defences a hundred miles to the east. The confusion and alarm created by this double blow, in

front and rear, were increased by the widespread menace
of the Luftwaffe. Exploiting the disorder, German
armoured forces raced through a gap in the southern
flank and joined up with the airborne forces at Rotterdam
on the third day. They cut through to their objective
under the nose of the 7th French Army which was just
arriving to the aid of the Dutch. On the fifth day the
Dutch capitulated.

The main gateway into Belgium was also forced by a
dramatic opening coup. Airborne troops picked the lock
—by seizing the bridges over the Albert Canal near
Maastricht. By the second day, armoured forces pushed
through into the open, outflanking the fortified bridgehead
of Liége. That evening the Belgian Army was driven to
abandon its fortified frontier line, and fall back westward
as its Allies were rushing up to the line of the Dyle as
planned.

At the same time these direct assaults, on Holland and
Belgium, carried the impression of tremendous strength.
It is remarkable to find how light was the weight put
into these strokes, especially in the case of Holland. The
German 18th Army under General von Küchler, which
dealt with the Dutch, was considerably smaller than the
forces opposing it, and the path of its advance was inter-
sected by a network of canals and rivers that should have
been easy to defend. Its chances turned, primarily, on
the effect of the airborne coup. But this new arm was
astonishingly small.

General Student, its Commander-in-Chief, gave me the
details. "Altogether, we had 4,500 trained parachute
troops in the spring of 1940. To give the offensive against
Holland a fair chance it was necessary to use the bulk of
them there. So we allotted five battalions, some 4,000
men, to that task, supplemented by an air-transported
division, the 22nd, which comprised 12,000 men.

"The limitations of our strength compelled us to concentrate on two objectives—the points which seemed the

most essential to the success of the invasion. The main effort, under my own control, was directed against the bridges at Rotterdam, Dordrecht and Moerdijk by which the main route from the south was carried across the mouths of the Rhine. Our task was to capture the bridges before the Dutch could blow them up, and keep them open until the arrival of our mobile ground forces. My force comprised four parachute battalions and one air-transported regiment (of three battalions). We achieved complete success, at a cost of only 180 casualties. We dared not fail, for if we did the whole invasion would have failed." Student himself was one of the casualties, being wounded in the head by a sniper's bullet, and he was out of action for eight months.

"The secondary attack was made against The Hague. Its aim was to get a hold upon the Dutch capital, and in particular to capture the Government offices and the Service headquarters. The force employed here was commanded by General Graf Sponeck; it consisted of one parachute battalion and two air-transported regiments. This attack did not succeed. Several hundred men were killed and wounded, while as many were taken prisoner."

.   .   .   .   .

In the course of a more detailed account of these operations that Student has given me since his release, he said that he and Sponeck were suddenly called to Berlin on May 2nd, to see Hitler. "We were the first commanders to whom he gave in advance the date intended for the start of the attack in the West—May 6th. Owing to the weather this date was changed to the 10th." Student also mentioned that during this visit Hitler gave them special instructions that they were "to ensure that no harm was done to the Queen of Holland and members of the Royal Household". "In conclusion, Hitler said: 'I will be responsible for everything except that no harm is done to Queen

Wilhelmina, who is so popular with her people and the whole world!' To emphasize the importance of the order it was handed to us in writing."

.   .   .   .   .

The airborne thrusts of the offensive, unlike the armoured thrusts, were directly inspired by Hitler himself —though he found in Student a soldier of imagination to match his own, and a dynamic executant. Student, very honestly, says that Hitler conceived the most striking points of the airborne plan, and also two previous plans which were not carried out. The first had been for the airborne troops to occupy the Belgian "National Redoubt" south-west of Ghent and so cut off the withdrawal of the Belgian forces from their advanced position.

"Hitler personally thought out this plan. It was based on the fact that in 1914 the Belgians escaped under cover of this fortified line and thus extended the Allied front to the coast. Hitler allotted this task to me at the end of October during a lengthy discussion about its execution and chances of success. I then worked out the plan to the smallest details . . . The undertaking was very difficult. But I believed in its success. For the first time in military history a prepared and fortified line far behind the enemy front would be occupied, not by the troops intended to hold it, but by their opponents."

Shortly before Christmas Student received new instructions. He was to work out an alternative plan—for seizing a bridgehead over the Meuse between Namur and Dinant, and opening the way for the advance of Kluge's 4th Army. The choice between the two airborne plans was to be reserved until shortly before the offensive.

Then the whole German plan was changed, following the air accident. While the main armoured thrust was switched southward, the main airborne thrust was switched northward—against "fortress Holland".

.   .   .   .   .

After meeting the paramount needs of the coup in Holland, only 500 airborne troops were left to help the invasion of Belgium, Student told me. They were used to capture the two bridges over the Albert Canal and the Fort of Eben Emael, Belgium's most modern fort, which flanked this waterline-frontier. That tiny detachment, however, made all the difference to the issue. For the approach to the Belgian frontier here lay across the southerly projection of Dutch territory known as the "Maastricht Appendix", and once the German Army crossed the Dutch frontier the Belgian frontier guards on the Albert Canal would have had ample warning to blow the bridges before any invading ground forces could cross that fifteen-mile strip. Airborne troops dropping silently out of the night sky offered a new way, and the only way, of securing the key-bridges intact.

The very limited scale of airborne forces used in Belgium gives a fantastic air to the reports at the time that German parachutists were dropping at scores of places, in numbers that cumulatively ran into thousands. Student provided the explanation. He said that to compensate the scantiness of the actual resources, and create as much confusion as possible, dummy parachutists were scattered widely over the country. This ruse certainly proved most effective, helped by the natural tendency of heated imaginations to multiply all figures.

Student went on to say: "The Albert Canal venture was also Hitler's own idea. It was perhaps the most original idea of this man of many brain-waves. He sent for me and asked my opinion. After a day's consideration I affirmed the possibility of such an enterprise, and was ordered to make the preparations. I used 500 men under Captain Koch. The Commander of the 6th Army, General von Reichenau and his chief of staff General Paulus, both capable generals, regarded the undertaking as an adventure in which they had no faith.

"The surprise attack on Fort Eben Emael was carried

out by a Lilliputian detachment of 78 parachute-engineers commanded by Lieutenant Witzig. Of these, only 6 men were killed. This small detachment made a completely unexpected landing on the roof of the fort, overcame the anti-aircraft personnel there, and blew up the armoured cupolas and casemates of all the guns with a new highly intensive explosive—previously kept secret.

"These 'Hohlladungen' were a surprise-weapon comparable to the 42 cm. howitzers of the First World War which were able to shatter the defence works of Liége and the French fortifications. The surprise attack on Eben Emael was based on the use of this new weapon, which was silently transported to the objective by another new weapon—a freight-carrying glider.

"From the roof of the fort Witzig's detachment kept the garrison of 1,200 men in check until twenty-four hours later, when our ground troops arrived.

"It is worth note that in the Belgian-Dutch area the only bridges that were not blown up by the defenders were those that the parachute troops attacked; all the other bridges were demolished according to plan."

The course of the invasion was described to me by General von Bechtolsheim, the 1A (operations chief) to Reichenau's 6th Army, which carried out this frontal offensive. He was an old acquaintance, having been the German Military Attaché in London before the war.

"The axis of the 6th Army ran through Maastricht to Brussels, its right wing being directed from Roermond past Turnhout to Malines, and its left wing from Aachen past Liége to Namur. Maastricht was the vital point in the first phase—or, to be exact, the two bridges over the Albert Canal west of Maastricht. These were captured, before they could be blown up, by glider-landings on the west bank. Fort Eben Emael was captured in the same way, though not so quickly. The great disappointment of the first day was that the bridges over the Meuse in Maastricht were blown up by the Dutch, thus delaying the advance to support the glider-parties on the Albert Canal.

"However, Hoeppner's 16th Panzer Corps was pushed through as soon as the Meuse had been bridged, although it was strung out in excessive depth, as it had to use a single bridge, and thus had to be passed through a bottle-neck. Once through, it drove towards Nivelles. Progress now became quick.

"Under the original plan there was no intention of attacking Liége. That fortified city was to be by-passed, while screened on the north by our left wing and on the south by the 4th Army's right wing. But our left wing, pushing down towards Liege, succeeded in driving into it from the rear without any serious opposition.

"Our main forces pushed on westward, and made contact with the British Army on the Dyle line. We paused to close up our divisions for the attack, while staging a turning movement from the south, but before it developed the British had fallen back to the Scheldt.

"Throughout our advance to Brussels we were continually expecting an Allied counter-attack from Antwerp against our right flank.

"Meanwhile the 16th Panzer Corps had driven ahead, on our southern flank, and fought battles near Hannut and Gembloux with the French mechanized Cavalry Corps. At first our tanks were outnumbered, but the French tanks fought in a static way that forfeited their advantage, and their lack of enterprise allowed time for the rest of Hoeppner's corps to arrive on the scene. That decided the Gembloux battle in our favour on the 14th. But we were deprived of the chance to exploit our success, for Hoeppner's corps was now taken away to back up the break-through which had been achieved south of the Meuse, in the Ardennes. This decision of the Supreme Command left the 6th Army without any armoured forces."

This order caused much heartburning, and a heated protest from Reichenau. But he was overruled in the

higher interests of the general offensive plan. The 6th
Army had well performed its rôle of attracting the attention
of the French High Command, and distracting their
attention from the greater threat that was developing in
the Ardennes. It had also pinned down the mobile forces
of the Allied left wing during the crucial days. For on the
13th Rundstedt's armoured spearheads crossed the Meuse
around Sedan and burst into the rolling plains of north-
eastern France. When Gamelin, the French Commander-
in-Chief, thought of switching his mechanized cavalry
from the left wing to stem the flood at Sedan he was told
that they were too fully engaged at Gembloux.

Once that object had been fulfilled there was good
reason for reducing Reichenau's punching power, since it
was not desirable to hustle the Allied left wing into too
rapid a retreat before Rundstedt's net had been stretched
across its rear.

Reichenau's air support had been reduced even before
his armour was switched away, Bechtolsheim said. "In
the first phase of the offensive the 6th Army was given very
powerful support by the Luftwaffe, for the crossings of the
Meuse and the Albert Canal near Maastricht, but the
corps of dive-bombers were then concentrated southward
against the crossings of the Meuse near Sedan." I asked
Bechtolsheim whether the freedom from bombing which
the B.E.F. had enjoyed during its advance to the Dyle
was deliberately intended to entice it forward. He replied:
"Not so far as we were concerned at 6th Army H.Q., but
it may have been planned on a higher level."

        .   .   .   .   .

Before passing to the story of Rundstedt's break-through
from the Ardennes to the Channel coast, which trapped the
whole Allied left wing, it is worth giving some of the main
points from Bechtolsheim's account of the 6th Army's later
advance in following up the belated Allied retreat from
the Dyle line.

"The axis of our advance was now directed on Lille, with our right flank moving on Ghent, and our left on Mons and Condé. The first serious contact with the British was on the Scheldt. General von Reichenau wanted to envelop Lille by a turning movement round the north, but O.K.H. ordered the main effort to be made on the other flank—in order to assist General von Kluge's 4th Army (on the right wing of General von Rundstedt's Army Group), which was heavily engaged in the area Roubaix–Cambrai. In this advance our 4th Corps had a tough fight at Tournai, where it did not succeed in penetrating the British defence.

"Better reports then came from the Cambrai area, and General von Reichenau persuaded O.K.H. to approve his plan of swinging round north of Lille towards Ypres. A powerful attack by the 11th Corps broke through the Belgian front here on the Lys near Courtrai. Following this success, we concentrated all possible strength towards Roulers and Ypres. The final overthrow of the Belgian Army was now achieved by the 6th Army.

"On the evening of May 27th word came from the 11th Corps that a Belgian general had arrived at its H.Q. and asked for the conditions of an armistice. This request was referred back to O.K.W., which sent back orders that unconditional surrender must be demanded." This was accepted, and the Belgians laid down their arms early next morning. "I called on King Leopold at Bruges the day after. He did not like the idea of going to the castle of Laeken for internment, and asked if he might go to his country house. I passed on his request, but it was not granted."

I asked Bechtolsheim whether he considered that the Belgian Army could have held out longer. He replied: "I think it could, for its losses were not severe. But when I drove through the lines of Belgian troops most of them seemed to be very relieved that the struggle had ended."

Another question I put was whether he had any news at this time of preparations to evacuate the B.E.F. He said: "We had reports that a large concentration of shipping had been seen at Dunkirk. This led us to suspect that an evacuation was contemplated. Previously, we had expected the British to withdraw southward."

Summing up the brief campaign, he remarked: "The only real difficulty we met was the crossing of rivers and canals, not from opposition. When the 16th Panzer Corps had been taken away, most of our bridging units went with it, and this became a handicap on our subsequent progress."

He also enumerated what he regarded as the four main lessons of the campaign:

"First. The outstanding lesson was the necessity of air-ground liaison in actual battle. This was good in the main efforts, at Maastricht and Sedan, but not in general. At Maastricht the 6th Army had excellent support from and co-operation with Richthofen's Stukas, but these were then subsequently sent to support Kleist's thrust through Sedan. The Air Force should always know when to switch from attacking communications to close co-operation in the battle. There is need for great flexibility.

"Second. Even after the Panzer Group had been taken away, events proved that infantry attack was still possible without tank support—thanks to the way that the infantry had been trained; to well-controlled supporting fire; and to infiltration tactics. Widely dispersed threats create openings for concentrated thrusts.

"Third. When armoured forces are fairly equal, a kind of standing battle develops—where space is lacking for manœuvre.

"Fourth. The need of flexibility in switching forces when they are checked in battle along any particular line of advance."

THE MATADOR'S THRUST

Before dawn of May 10th the greatest concentration of tanks yet seen in war was massed opposite the frontier of Luxembourg. It was poised for a dash through that state and then through Belgian Luxembourg to the French frontier near Sedan, seventy miles distant. Made up of three Panzer corps, these were arrayed in three blocks, or layers, with armoured divisions in the first two, and motorized infantry divisions in the third. The van was led by General Guderian, Germany's chief tank expert, and the whole was commanded by General von Kleist.

"Like a great phalanx, the three blocks stood densely closed up one behind the other"—that was Blumentritt's description. Even so, this armoured array was more than a hundred miles deep from head to tail—which lay nearly fifty miles *east* of the Rhine. A vivid impression of its scale was conveyed in a remark which Kleist made to me: "If this Panzer Group had advanced on a single road its tail would have stretched right back to Koenigsberg in East Prussia, when its head was at Trier."

To the right of Kleist's group lay a separate panzer corps under Hoth, which was to dash through the northern part of the Ardennes, to the Meuse between Givet and Dinant.

These armoured phalanxes, however, formed only a fraction of the armed mass that was drawn up along the German frontier ready to plunge into the Ardennes. According to Blumentritt: "Army Group A had altogether 86 divisions[1] of all kinds closely packed on a narrow but very deep front." He went on: "This advance through the Ardennes was not really an operation, in the tactical sense, but an approach march. In making the plan we had reckoned it unlikely that we should meet any serious resistance before reaching the Meuse. That calculation proved correct. We met no resistance in Luxembourg, and only slight resistance in Belgian Luxembourg— from the *Chasseurs Ardennais* and French cavalry divisions. It was weak opposition, and easily brushed aside.

[1] He was speaking from memory, and would seem to be mistaken in this figure. The documentary records show that at the *start* of the offensive Army Group A comprised 46 divisions, while there were 27 divisions in O.K.H. reserve.

"The main problem was not tactical but administrative —the complicated movement and supply arrangements. It was essential to utilize all roads and tracks that were to any degree practicable. The greatest possible precision was required in plotting the route on the map; in the regulation of traffic; and in the arrangements for protecting the movement against both ground and air interference. The many infantry divisions had to march on field paths and across country, interspersed among the armoured divisions that were using the roads. The most intricate staff work was demanded in laying down start-lines for the successive panzer blocks, while the beginning and end of each division's passage was precisely regulated by the clock. The terrain was difficult—mountainous and wooded —and the roads, though they had a good surface, were often steep and full of bends. The worst problem of all came later, in the passage of these densely-crowded columns of tanks and infantry over the deep-cut valley of the Meuse —a very awkward obstacle."

The chances of success largely depended on the quickness with which Kleist's forces could push through the Ardennes and cross the Meuse near Sedan. Only when they were across that river-barrier would their tanks have room for manœuvre. They must get across before the French realized what was happening, and collected reserves to stop them. But the German air photographs showed what appeared to be a large fortified bridgehead covering the approach to the river at Sedan. Its presence reinforced the doubts of all who questioned the practicability of the Hitler-Manstein plan. They felt that the tanks could not rush such a fortified position, and that the advance would be hung up for days in the effort to capture it.

A few days before the attack was launched, however, an Austrian officer with a flair for interpreting air photographs was given the opportunity to re-examine them. He spotted what no one else had discovered—that the

French fortifications here were not completed, but merely in process of construction. His report was sent off in haste to Kleist. It dispelled the final hesitations. Kleist realized that he could speed up the advance by pushing his armoured and infantry divisions forward simultaneously, without waiting until the latter had cleared the way. The advance to the Meuse became a race rather than a normal military operation.

The race was won, though with little margin. The result might have been different if the defending forces had been capable of profiting from the partial checks caused by demolitions that were carried out according to previous plan. "The destruction of the roads in Belgium did much to delay our march," Guderian said.

But fortune favoured the bold, while heavily penalizing the side that was slow in reaction and old-fashioned in method. Describing the advance of his spearhead corps, Guderian told me: "After penetrating the frontier defences of Belgian Luxembourg—thinly held by the *Chasseurs Ardennais*—we met French cavalry about to instal themselves in a fortified position round Neufchateau. The resisting power of cavalry against panzer divisions proved insufficient! They were dispersed, and retired in the direction of Bouillon on the Semois, pursued by the panzers. They tried to defend the Semois and blew up bridges in the sector of Bouillon. But in the morning of the next day, May 12th, Bouillon was taken by the 1st Panzer Division. The French then made a stand on a fresh line of resistance along their frontier—in prepared positions with barbed wire entanglements and concrete bunkers. This line was immediately broken by our pursuing troops, that same day—and was the last obstacle before the Meuse. It could have been held better if more troops had been available on the French side. The French lacked anti-tank weapons and mines.

"The German advance could have been slowed down by a well-organized defence of the Semois valley or the fortified frontier-line. Further delay could have been caused by a concentrated attack of the Allied bombing forces. But I don't believe that the Allies recognized the German advance to be deadly at that early time."

An armoured counterstroke by the Allies against the flank of the German advance at this stage would probably have paralysed that advance—by its effect on the higher commanders. Even as it was, they were momentarily shaken by the shadow of a stroke from the direction of Montmedy towards Kleist's left flank. Speaking of this, Guderian said: "When, in the course of May 11th, Kleist got the news that French cavalry was advancing from that direction he immediately gave orders that the 10th Panzer Division—my left wing division—was to be stopped and turned against the enemy. This order, if followed, would have made almost impracticable the attack on Sedan and an early break-through. I therefore ordered General Schaal, the commander of the 10th Panzer Division, to continue his march towards Sedan on a line several miles north of his previous route, while asking Kleist to safeguard my left flank by motorized units of Wietersheim's corps and infantry units that were following up my advance."

Rundstedt and Blumentritt were very frank as to their own apprehensions—about such a possible flank counterstroke and other risk. In giving me his account, Blumentritt said: "At the time we feared the Allied air forces. Had you attacked these enormous columns, there would have been terrible confusion. For instance, on the Semois we had a stoppage *without* resistance that lasted twenty-four hours. This could only be discovered and disentangled by an officer in an aeroplane. (The 2nd Panzer Division—Guderian's right wing division—was hung up in consequence, though the 1st had got through.) Our divisions were still new formations and not very practised in march-discipline like our 1914 divisions. But the Franco-British air menace did not have any weight. This was the first miracle!"

Blumentritt also dwelt on the failure of the French to develop their defences, and their folly in not standing on the defence, properly balanced. "The enemy could for months past have been drawn up on the Meuse. He could at the least have prepared field-fortifications on the Meuse as an adequate extension of the Maginot Line. At the same hour that we crossed the German frontier he could have entered such prepared positions and calmly awaited the first arrivals of our troops—on the third or fourth day. Crediting him with such plans, we consequently anticipated on the Meuse the most violent and long-prepared opposition from French forces supported by heavy artillery fire.

"We therefore worked out plans to meet this supposition. According to plan the infantry corps were to attack the Meuse and force a passage for the subsequent crossing of the armoured corps. But this would have occupied nearly a week while the infantry corps were coming up, taking up their positions and making their preparations. Previous to the assault the whole of the artillery would have had to get into position *en masse* and take steps to ensure an ample supply of ammunition.

"Then the second miracle occurred. Receiving word that the panzer divisions were already in position in the large forests on the heights of the Meuse north of Sedan, not only Kleist and I but the Army Group Commander, Rundstedt, drove forward to see them. From there we drove down to the Meuse—where the panzer engineers were already working on a bridge. Here and there a few French machine-guns were firing from small, ludicrous concrete emplacements on the west banks of the Meuse. That was all. We simply could not grasp this miracle—and feared that it was a French ruse. But in fact the dreaded Meuse position was almost non-existent, and only weakly defended. Then the panzer-race across the river began."

There was much justification in the general experience of war for the doubts felt and the caution shown by the German higher command. It is rarely safe to assume that

the opponent is incompetent or paralytic. But in this case
the conjunction of an infantry-time sense on the French
side with a tank-time on the German side, at any rate in
the leadership of the spearhead, produced the most startling
and decisive effects. It is very doubtful, however, whether
they would have arisen except for Guderian's presence
and dynamic influence on the operations throughout.

In giving me his own account of the operation, Kleist
said: "My leading troops, after traversing the Ardennes,
crossed the French frontier on May 12th. General
Schmundt, the Führer's adjutant, came forward to see me
that morning, and asked whether I would prefer to continue the advance at once, and tackle the Meuse, or wait
until the infantry corps came up. I decided to make the
attempt without loss of time. General Schumundt then said
that the Führer would place at my disposal next day, the
13th, the maximum support from the Luftwaffe—including
the whole of Richthofen's air corps, of dive-bombers.
Detailed arrangements were settled at a conference on the
evening of the 12th with General Sperrle, who flew up to see
me for the purpose—my headquarters were then near Bertrix.

"During the day my leading troops had pushed through
the wooded belt north of the Meuse, and reached its
southern edge, overlooking the river. That night the
reserves closed up, ready for an advance in strength. On
the morning of the 13th the infantry regiments of the
armoured divisions pushed down to the river bank. The
Luftwaffe—about a thousand aircraft—appeared on the
scene early in the afternoon. Crossings were achieved near
Sedan, by General Guderian's corps, and near Monthermé,
by General Reinhardt's corps. The one near Monthermé
proved rather harder to exploit, mainly because of the
difficult terrain and steeply winding route of approach.

"The opposition was not serious. That was fortunate,
for my artillery had only fifty rounds per battery—as the
ammunition columns had been delayed by the congestion
on the roads through the Ardennes. By the evening of

the 13th Guderian's corps had established strong bridge-heads over the Meuse. The leading infantry corps only began to arrive on the 14th." (Guderian says it was not before the 15th.)

I asked Kleist about the state of the French defences. He replied: "Along the Meuse there was a moderate amount of fortification, in the way of pillboxes, but these were not properly armed. If the French troops here had been adequately equipped with anti-tank guns we should certainly have noticed it, as the majority of our tanks were of the early Mark I type, and thus very vulnerable! The French divisions in the sector were poorly armed, and of low quality. Their troops, as we repeatedly found, gave up the fight very soon after being subjected to air bombing or gunfire."

On the French side, four 2nd Reserve divisions, of oldish men, were holding a front of over forty miles. Besides being thinly stretched, they were not even provided with the meagre normal scale of anti-tank guns, while lacking anti-aircraft guns. Assailed by swarms of dive-bombers while the Germans were bridging the river and then by masses of tanks, it is not surprising these low-grade French infantry quickly collapsed.

A more specific account of the crossing at Sedan came from Guderian, who also furnished some qualifying comments on Kleist's account. "The detailed arrangements of Generals von Kleist and Sperrle concerning the co-oper-ation between the Luftwaffe and my panzer corps could not be executed, fortunately—for they would have over-thrown the plan settled by General Loerzer and myself. While we had stipulated a continual dive-bombing of the French batteries from the beginning of the attack in the afternoon until nightfall, General von Kleist gave sudden orders for a short bombardment of maximum concentration at 1600 hours. My idea was to keep the French artillerymen down in their dug-outs until dark. If Kleist's orders had been carried out, the effect of the air force would have been limited to twenty minutes in all. The French artillery-men would have been able to recover and go to work during our crossing of the Meuse." Twelve squadrons of dive-bombers were used on this Sedan sector.

Guderian said that he would have preferred to wait until the 14th so as to get all three of his panzer divisions into position—the 2nd was still delayed on the Semois. But Kleist ordered the attack to be launched that afternoon. It was concentrated on a one and a half-mile stretch of the river just west of Sedan—between there and St. Menges—and delivered by the 1st Panzer Division, reinforced by the motorized S.S. Regiment "Gross Deutschland". The 10th Panzer Division had reached the river near Bazeilles, just east of Sedan, and put in an attack there, but Guderian concentrated the fire of his artillery on the sector of the 1st Panzer Division—the preparatory bombardment opening at 2 p.m. When it was found that the opposition was weak he brought the 88 mm. guns of his A.A. regiment down to the river bank to subdue the casemates, or pill-boxes, on the other bank by direct fire at close range—as their concrete had withstood the preliminary bombardment.

The chosen sector provided a perfect setting for forcing a passage. The river bends sharply north towards St. Menges and then south again, forming a pocket-like salient. The surrounding heights on the north bank are wooded, thus providing cover for attack preparations and gun-positions as well as fine artillery observation. From near St. Menges—as I have seen for myself when visiting the scene—there is a wonderful panoramic view over this river-salient, and across to the wooded heights of the Bois de Marfée which form the back-curtain on the far side.

The assault was launched at 4 p.m., led by the panzer infantry in rubber-boats and on rafts. Ferries were soon in operation, bringing light vehicles across. The river-salient was quickly overrun, and the attackers pressed on to capture the Bois de Marfée and the southern heights. By midnight the wedge was driven nearly five miles deep, while a bridge was completed at Glaire (between Sedan and St. Menges) over which the tanks began to pour.

Even so, the German foothold was still precarious on the 14th—with only one division yet across the river, and only one bridge by which reinforcements and supplies could reach it. The bridge was heavily attacked by the Allied air forces, which enjoyed a temporary advantage as the weight of the Luftwaffe had been switched elsewhere. But the A.A. regiment of Guderian's corps kept a thick canopy of fire over the vital bridge, and the air attacks were beaten off with heavy loss. No strong French counter-attack on the ground developed until midday, by which time Guderian's strength had grown and he was better balanced to meet the threat. In the afternoon, when counter-pressure began to subside, Guderian turned sharp right, pushing the 1st and 2nd Panzer Divisions due westward while using the 10th to cover the front facing south—which now became the flank, of his westward thrust. Following this unexpected turn his spearheads secured intact two bridges over the Ardennes canal and by nightfall had extended the bridgehead to a sideways depth of ten miles.

Early on the 15th Guderian resumed his westward thrust. The 1st Panzer Division suffered a check, but then swerved northward in search of a weak spot; converging with the 2nd Panzer Division it broke through at Poix-Terron and then, to widen the gap, swung south on to the backs of the French troops who had checked the advance. With the collapse of this rearward line of defence, the way to the west was open. No further solid resistance was met in the subsequent race to the Channel coast.

Yet that night was a trying one for Guderian—though not owing to the enemy. "An order came from Panzer Group Headquarters to halt the advance and confine the troops to the bridgehead gained. I would not and could not put up with this order, as it meant forfeiting surprise and all our initial success. I therefore telephoned the Chief of Staff of the Panzer Group, Colonel Zeitzler, and getting no satisfaction I then telephoned General von Kleist himself to get the order cancelled. The exchange of views became very lively . . . At last Kleist agreed to permit a continuation of the advance for another twenty-four hours—in order to widen the bridgehead sufficiently to allow the infantry corps to follow us."

The utmost advantage was taken of this cautious permission and full rein was given to the panzer divisions. The westward drive of Guderian's three divisions converged with that of Reinhardt's two divisions from the Monthermé crossing, and also with those of Hoth's two divisions from the crossing near Dinant. It produced a spreading collapse of French resistance, and swept through an empty space. By the night of the 16th the westward drive had gone more than fifty miles farther, towards the Channel, and reached the Oise. Yet once again the brake was applied—not by the enemy, but from above.

A FIRST PAUSE

The higher commanders on the German side were amazed at the ease with which the Meuse had been overcome, and could hardly believe their luck. They were still more surprised that no counter-offensive developed. Rundstedt had feared the delivery of a heavy stroke against his left flank while he was pushing through the Ardennes. "I knew Gamelin before the war, and, trying to read his mind, had anticipated that he would make a flank move from the Verdun direction with his reserves. We estimated that he had thirty to forty divisions which could be used for the purpose. But nothing of the sort developed."

Hitler shared these apprehensions. In consequence he put a curb on the advance—it was the first of two interventions on his part, the second of which had greater consequences. Telling of this first case, from the O.K.H. angle, Siewert said: "The Führer was nervous about the risk that the main French armies might strike westward, and wanted to wait until a large number of infantry divisions

had been brought up to provide flank cover along the
Aisne." Röhricht, then acting as chief liaison officer
between O.K.H. and 12th Army H.Q., was more explicit:
"The 12th Army, which was following Kleist's panzer group,
was ordered to wheel south to the Aisne, when he wheeled
west after crossing the Meuse and headed for the Channel
coast. Weichs's 2nd Army was brought up from the rear to
provide the infantry backing for this seaward drive. In my
opinion this decision was a bad mistake. I reckon it cost us
two days. It would have been better if the 2nd Army had
carried out the wheel south to the Aisne, while the 12th
Army marched straight on to support the armoured forces."

Kleist himself, however, qualified these opinions. "My
forces were actually halted only for one day. The order
came when my leading elements had reached the Oise,
between Guise and La Fère. I was told that it was a direct
order from the Führer. But I don't think it was the
direct consequence of the decision to replace the 12th
Army by the 2nd as our backer-up. It was due to the
Führer's anxiety about the danger of a counter-stroke
against our left flank; he did not care to let us push too
deeply until the situation there was clearer."

Guderian's account shed more light on the pause, from
the front-line point of view, and showed that the hesitation
was not confined to Hitler. "After the wonderful success
on May 16th it did not occur to me that my superiors might
still be thinking on the same lines as before—that of con-
tenting themselves with the bridgehead over the Meuse
and awaiting the arrival of the infantry corps. I wished to
put into operation the idea that I had expounded to
Hitler in March—to exploit the break-through without
halt until the Channel coast was reached. It seemed unimag-
inable that Hitler—who had approved Manstein's daring
plan and raised no objections to my intended deep penetration—might have lost his nerve and stopped the
immediate advance. But here I had made a basic error.
This became clear next morning.

"Early on the 17th I was informed by Panzer Group Headquarters that the advance must be stopped, and that I personally was to await General von Kleist, for an interview on the airfield at 7 a.m. He arrived punctually and began straight away with grave reproaches to the effect that I had disregarded the plans of the High Command." Guderian maintained that he was fulfilling the spirit of the plan and emphasized the danger that a halt would mean losing the initiative, but got no satisfaction. "I asked to be relieved of my post. General von Kleist was slightly taken aback, but then nodded and told me to hand over command to the next senior."

But after reference to Army Group Headquarters, an order came back that Guderian was to stay at his headquarters and await the arrival of General List, the commander of the 12th Army which was coming on behind the panzer group. When List arrived, Guderian reported what had happened. "In the name of General von Rundstedt, he cancelled my removal from command, and explained that the halt order came from the top, so that it had to be enforced. But he recognized my reasons for wishing to continue the advance and gave me permission on behalf of the Army Group to carry on strong reconnaissance."

"Strong reconnaissance" as interpreted by Guderian had an elastic meaning and enabled him to maintain quite a high degree of offensive pressure during the two days' interval before the infantry corps of the 12th Army had begun to form a strong flank shield on the Aisne and he was allowed to race all out for the Channel coast.

So much time had been gained in the preceding stages and so much dislocation had been caused on the opposing side, that the pause on the Oise had no serious effect on the German prospects. Even so, it revealed a significant difference of time-sense on the German side. The gap between the new school and the old school there was greater than that between the Germans and the French.

Gamelin, writing at the end of the war, said of the

Germans' strategic exploitation of the Meuse crossings: "It was a remarkable manœuvre. But had it been entirely foreseen in advance? I do not believe it—any more than that Napoleon had foreseen the manœuvre of Jena, or Moltke that of Sedan (in 1870). It was a perfect utilization of circumstances. It showed troops and a command who knew how to manœuvre, who were organized to operate quickly—as tanks, aircraft and wireless permitted them to do. It is perhaps the first time that a battle has been won, which became decisive, without having had to engage the bulk of the forces."

According to General Georges, who was the executive Commander-in-Chief of the battle-front, it was reckoned that the planned obstruction in Belgian Luxembourg was likely "to retard for at least four days" the Germans' arrival on the Meuse. General Doumenc, the Chief of Staff at G.Q.G. said: "Crediting our enemies with our own procedure, we had imagined that they would not attempt the passage of the Meuse until after they had brought up ample artillery: the five or six days necessary for that would have easily given us time to reinforce our own dispositions."

It is remarkable how closely these French calculations corresponded to those made in the higher quarters on "the other side of the hill". We can see that the French military chiefs had justification—more justification than was apparent immediately after the event—for their basic assumptions about the German offensive. But they had left out of the reckoning an individual factor—Guderian. His adoption of the theory of deep strategic penetration by armoured forces operating independently, his fervent conviction of its practicability, and his consequent impulsion in stretching subordination upset the calculations of the French High Command to an extent that the German High Command would never have done of its own volition. It is clear that Guderian and his tankmen pulled the German Army along after them, and thereby produced the most sweeping victory in modern history.

The issue turned on the time-factor at stage after stage. French counter-movements were repeatedly thrown out of gear because their timing was too slow to catch up with the changing situation, and that was due to the fact that the German van kept on moving faster than the German High Command had contemplated.

THE DRIVE TO THE SEA

The uneasiness in the higher headquarters is understandable, and the more so in proportion to their distance from the front. For the quickness of the French collapse on the Meuse, and the absence of any strong counter-offensive reaction, naturally seemed too good to be true. Events disproved but did not entirely dispel these apprehensions. The shock of the mechanized *blitzkrieg* had paralysed the French Army, which was mentally and materially unfitted to cope with it. In that state of paralysis it was incapable of profiting by the brief relaxation of pressure which Hitler's first intervention provided.

After crossing the Meuse, and turning westward, the German drive met little resistance. The tanks rolled along what was virtually an open corridor, behind the back of the Allied left wing in Belgium. There was no "Battle of the Bulge" such as the official commentators described so graphically at the time. It was a smooth run. The few counter-attacks against its flank were spasmodic and uncoordinated. The first had been at Stonne, just south of Sedan, where the French 3rd Armoured Division caused a momentary jolt before it was itself taken in flank and swept back. The next was near Laon, by the newly-formed 4th Armoured Division, under General de Gaulle. In regard to this Kleist remarked: "It did not put us in any such danger as later accounts have suggested. Guderian dealt with it himself without troubling me, and I only heard of it the day after." Of the two other armoured divisions which the French possessed, the 1st ran out of petrol and was encircled while helpless, while the 2nd was frittered away in packets by the higher command to guard bridges.

The German armoured forces, apart from their brief pause at the Oise, raced westward so fast that their opponents were utterly confused. As an example, Kleist related—"I was half-way to the sea when one of my staff brought me an extract from the French radio which said that the commander of their 6th Army on the Meuse had been sacked, and General Giraud appointed to take charge of the situation. Just as I was reading it, the door opened and a handsome French general was ushered in. He introduced himself with the words, 'I am General Giraud'. He told me how he had set out in an armoured car to look for his Army, and had found himself in the midst of my forces far ahead of where he had expected them to be. My first encounter with the British was when my tanks came upon, and overran, an infantry battalion whose men were equipped with dummy cartridges, for field exercises. This was a sidelight on the apparent unexpectedness of our arrival." The Germans poured like a flood across the back areas of the B.E.F. while the bulk of it was still deep in Belgium.

Kleist continued: "In sum, our advance met no serious opposition after the break-through. Reinhardt's Panzer Corps had some fighting near Le Cateau, but that was the only noteworthy incident. Guderian's Panzer Corps, sweeping farther south, reached Abbeville on the 20th, thus splitting the Allied armies. Wietersheim, with the motorized divisions, was close on its heels, and promptly took over the defence of the sector along the Somme from Peronne to Abbeville, while Guderian turned north next day."[1] He had already cut the B.E.F.'s communications with its bases; he was now aiming to cut it off from retreat to the sea.

[1] Guderian, however, said that the northward advance did not really begin until the 22nd. "For lack of orders there was a halt on the 21st." But he moved his spearheads up to the line of the Authie River, ready to drive north.

As Kleist's panzer group drove into France his flank guards had been relieved in turn by a system of relays—as part of the process of maintaining the momentum of the advance. The infantry corps were backing up his panzer corps, and they came under his orders for a day or two at each stage while they took up defensive positions on the flanks. But, in the later stages, the pace of the panzers became so fast as to leave a dangerous interval behind them. A small British counter-attack force suddenly inserted a wedge into the gap.

Rundstedt told me: "A critical moment in the drive came just as my forces had reached the Channel. It was caused by a British counter-stroke southward from Arras towards Cambrai, on May 21. For a short time it was feared that our armoured divisions would be cut off before the infantry divisions could come up to support them. None of the French counter-attacks carried any serious threat as this one did." (It is remarkable to learn what a jar this gave the Germans and how it nearly upset their drive, for it was delivered by a very small force, part of General Martel's 50th Northumbrian Division with the 4th and 7th Battalions Royal Tank Regiment. It is clear that if there had been two British armoured divisions, instead of battalions, the whole German plan might have been paralysed.)

That proved to be the last effort to cut the net which the Germans had cast across the rear of the Allied armies in Belgium—a net which was soon drawn tighter. The bulk of the French left wing was caught in it, as well as all the Belgians, and the British only escaped through "the miracle of Dunkirk"—an event that seems almost as extraordinary in the light of post-war revelations as it looked at the time of the escape. For it was due to Hitler's intervention.

Up to that point the issue of the invasion had justified Hitler's judgment against that of his chief generals. Yet they were justified in their doubts on any basis of probability. No reasonable estimate of the prospect could have reckoned that the French Commander-in-Chief would have made such an elementary blunder as to leave the hinge of his advance almost uncovered when he rushed the whole of his left wing armies into the central plains of Belgium to meet the threat there. But for that extraordinary oversight, and Guderian's exceptional boldness of thrust, it is almost certain that Hitler's attack would have had only a limited success. If it had penetrated only a short distance over the French frontier, and stuck there, the whole course of the war, and of the world in our time, would have been very different.

Blumentritt said (and others endorsed this): "The fact that Hitler's 'judgment' had been justified in face of his generals intoxicated him, and made it much more difficult for them ever to argue with, or restrain him, again." Thus, in the end, the 13th May proved even more unlucky for them—and for Germany—than it did for France.

The turn of fortune began barely a week later.

HITLER'S "HALT" ORDER

On wheeling north, Guderian's Panzer Corps headed for Calais while Reinhardt's swept west of Arras towards St. Omer and Dunkirk. On the 22nd, Boulogne was isolated by Guderian's advance, and next day Calais. This stride brought him to the Aa at Gravelines, barely ten miles from Dunkirk—the last escape port left to the B.E.F., the bulk of which was still engaged in Belgium. Reinhardt's Corps also arrived on the river and canal-line Aire–St. Omer–Gravelines. At the time there was only one British battalion covering the 20-mile stretch of the Aa between Gravelines and St. Omer, and for a further 60 miles inland the canal line was little better defended. Many of the bridges were not yet blown up, or even prepared for demolition. Thus the German panzer troops had no difficulty in gaining bridgeheads over the canal at a number of places on May 23rd—and it was, as Gort said in his Despatch, "the only anti-tank obstacle on this flank". Having crossed it, there was nothing to hold them up—and stop them establishing themselves astride the B.E.F.'s lines of retreat to Dunkirk.

At that critical moment Kleist received an order that his forces were to halt on the line of the canal. While there are differing accounts of the origin of the order, and the reasons for it, the fact that such a stop was imposed by order is established by ample evidence—from documents as well as witnesses. That order of the enemy high command preserved the British Army when nothing else could have saved it.

Kleist said that when he got the order it seemed to make no sense to him. "I decided to ignore it, and to push on across the Canal. My armoured cars actually entered Hazebrouck, and cut across the British lines of retreat. I heard later that the British Commander-in-Chief, Lord Gort, had been in Hazebrouck at the time. But then came a more emphatic order that I was to withdraw behind the canal. My tanks were kept halted there for three days."

Guderian said: "My repeated protests remained unheard; on the contrary, the cursed order was repeated. Field-Marshal von Brauchitsch, whom I asked after the French campaign why he had agreed to stop the panzer-forces before Dunkirk, told me that it was by order of Hitler—and added that he had hoped somebody would be disobedient." But after what happened when he drove on from the Meuse, even Guderian could hardly venture to court dismissal again by disregarding a definite halt-order.

Thoma, who was chief of the tank side of the General Staff, told me that he was right up forward with Guderian's tanks, near Bergues, where he could look into the town of Dunkirk itself. He sent back wireless messages direct to O.K.H., begging for permission to let the tanks push on. But his appeal had no effect. Referring to Hitler's attitude, he bitingly remarked: "You can never talk to a fool. Hitler spoilt the chance of victory."

Meanwhile the British forces streamed back towards Dunkirk, and cemented a defensive position to cover their re-embarkation. The German tank commanders had to sit and watch the British slipping away under their very noses.

"After three days the ban was lifted," Kleist said, "and the advance was resumed—against stiffening opposition. It had just begun to make headway when it was interrupted by a fresh order from Hitler—that my forces were to be withdrawn, and sent southward for the attack on the line that the remainder of the French Army had improvised along the Somme. It was left to the infantry forces which had come down from Belgium to complete the occupation of Dunkirk—after the British had gone."

A few days later Kleist met Hitler on the airfield at Cambrai, and ventured to remark that a great opportunity had been lost of reaching Dunkirk before the British escaped. Hitler replied: "That may be so. But I did not want to send the tanks into the Flanders marshes—and the British won't come back in this war."

To others Hitler gave a somewhat different excuse—that so many of the tanks had fallen out from mechanical breakdowns that he wanted to build up his strength and reconnoitre the position before pushing on. He also explained that he wanted to be sure of having sufficient tanks in hand for the subsequent offensive against the rest of the French Army.

These explanations did not give much satisfaction to those who had been compelled to stand still and watch victory slipping out of their grasp. The panzer generals with whom I talked said that fresh tanks were arriving daily to replace wastage, and ridiculed the argument about the danger of the panzer force being bogged—they were on the spot at the time, and could judge the conditions better than Hitler. Nevertheless, his explanations seem to have been genuine, so far as they went. Each of the three reasons he gave were in his mind at the time, and weighed on it. But they were not the only factors in his fateful decision.

CHAPTER XII

THE "HALT ORDER" BEFORE DUNKIRK

ONE of the great riddles of the war is the origin of the order by which the German panzer forces were halted outside Dunkirk—the last port of escape left to the British Army.

The first account I had on the subject, just after the war, came from Brauchitsch's adjutant, General Siewert. He was quite definite that the armoured forces were halted on Hitler's personal order; he also related how Brauchitsch and Halder objected to the order and tried to get it cancelled—a statement which is borne out by the documentary records. Then Field-Marshal von Rundstedt and General Blumentritt gave me their respective accounts of how the order had come to Army Group "A"—transmitted over the telephone by Colonel von Greiffenberg at O.K.H., who had conveyed that it was contrary to Halder's view. Blumentritt said that he had himself taken the telephone call.

But Mr. Churchill, in his recent story of the war, says that the halting of the armoured forces "was done on the initiative not of Hitler but of Rundstedt". He bases his conclusion on what the war diary of Rundstedt's Army Group records about the discussion that took place when Hitler visited Rundstedt's headquarters at Charleville on the morning of May 24th.

The weight that Mr. Churchill places on this solitary piece of evidence may seem rather excessive to the critical historian who knows how unit and formation war-diaries are compiled, and has had experience of the way they often err. They are usually kept by junior officers, who have not been present themselves at the crucial discussions, and in periods of great activity and stress both the recording and the checking are apt to be far from adequate. Any such

piece of evidence needs to be treated with care if it stands
alone. Moreover in this case the record itself is by no means
as clear as the conclusion which Mr. Churchill draws from
it. His summary of the record contains these points:

> "At midnight on the 23rd orders came from
> Brauchitsch at O.K.H. . . . for 'the last act' of 'the
> encirclement battle'. Next morning - Hitler visited
> Rundstedt, who represented to him that his armour,
> which had come so far and so fast, was much reduced
> in strength and needed a pause wherein to reorganize
> and regain its balance for the final blow. . . . More-
> over, Rundstedt foresaw the possibility of attacks on
> his widely dispersed forces from north and south. . . .
> Hitler 'agreed entirely' that the attack east of Arras
> should be carried out by infantry and that the mobile
> formations should continue to hold the line Lens-
> Bethune-Aire-St. Omer-Gravelines in order to intercept
> the enemy forces under pressure from Army Group B
> in the north-east. He also dwelt on the paramount
> necessity of conserving the armoured forces for future
> operations."

There is nothing here, however, that shows Rundstedt
taking the initiative in proposing a halt order. The most
that the rather vague diary note shows is that Rundstedt,
in his review of the situation, expressed anxieties that
accorded with Hitler's views. While this is of significance
it is not enough to justify the historian in rejecting the
witness of all the officers concerned that the definite halt
order originated with Hitler himself, and came down from
his headquarters. Moreover, their statements are confirmed
by the more explicit contemporary record in the diary
which Halder kept himself at O.K.H.

Study of this record in conjunction with the other
evidence makes the sequence of events clearer. After the
crossing of the Meuse, Halder's original idea had been

that Rundstedt's Army Group should push *south-west*. Its
axis of advance would run through Compiègne and lead
to the Lower Seine near Rouen (though Halder kept in
mind the possibility, after reaching Compiègne, of wheeling
south-east past Paris). The advance would be in echelon
formation, with the armies on the left "stepped" back,
so that as they advanced they would automatically tend to
protect the neighbour on their right against a blow at his
flank. As the movement progressed, Kluge's army on the
right wing would be transferred to Bock's Army Group,
to help it in completing the round-up of the Allied armies
in Belgium.

But Hitler did not care for the idea of the south-westerly
drive, and had a different conception. He wanted to hold
back the panzer forces until the supporting infantry corps
had established a protective line along the Aisne to cover
the southern flank, and then send the panzer forces in a
north-westerly drive on to the immediate rear of the
Allied armies in Belgium facing Bock. A midday note in
Halder's diary on the 17th—the morning that Guderian
was pulled up—refers to a meeting with Hitler, and says:
"Little mutual understanding. Führer insists main threat
is from south (I see no threat at all)." It then summarizes
the new instructions. A further note later remarks: "Rather
unpleasant day. Führer is terribly nervous. Frightened by
his own success, he is afraid to take any chance and so
would rather pull the reins on us. Puts forward the excuse
that it is all because of his southern flank." (Hitler, however, had a better excuse than Halder recognized—i.e.
Rundstedt's continued expectation that Gamelin would
launch a counter-offensive from the south-east.)

Anxiety over losing time and opportunity pervades
Halder's diary note next morning, the 18th: "Every hour
is precious. Führer H.Q. sees it quite differently. Führer
keeps worrying about south flank. He rages and screams
that we are on the way to ruin the whole campaign. He
won't have any part in continuing the operation in a

westward direction, let alone to the south-west, and still
clings to the plan for a north-westerly drive." After "a
most unpleasant conference", Hitler agreed that the panzer
drive should be westward, though not to it being released.

That evening, however, Halder was able to report to
Hitler that the infantry corps of the 12th Army were
wheeling into line along the Aisne, and he gained
permission to start the panzer drive to the sea.

Halder's next anxiety was whether the Allied armies in
Belgium would be hustled south too fast—"whether Bock
is not already driving the game away, past Kleist. In view
of Bock's ambition to dash out in front such a development
seems fully possible." His worry was needless, for on that
same day, the 20th, Kleist's spearhead under Guderian
reached the mouth of the Somme, severing the enemy's
lines of supply and retreat. Guderian then swung northward. Halder's idea, as a subsequent note indicates, was
that Bock's Army Group should merely pin down the enemy
while Rundstedt's "cuts into his rear and delivers the
decisive blow. . . . I wanted to make AGp A the hammer
and AGp B the anvil".

A complication now developed because the two Army
Groups, instead of advancing parallel, were now converging more and more, while the panzer forces on
Rundstedt's left wing were driving head-on towards Bock's
right wing. To avoid confusion, Brauchitsch wished to
place "the last phase of the encirclement" under Bock's
direction—which entailed changing the boundary line
between the two Army Groups, and transferring Kleist's
panzer forces along with Kluge's army from Rundstedt to
Bock. He gave orders accordingly on the evening of the
23rd.

Halder would have preferred Brauchitsch to co-
ordinate the final phase himself, but could not persuade
him to do so. For once he made a caustic diary comment
on Brauchitsch, saying that it "looks like a device to escape
responsibility. He keeps arguing that he has no choice

but to co-ordinate, either under himself or under Bock—
yet feels unsure about the first alternative, which he should
accept as the logical and manly one. The order goes without my signature, to show my disapproval."

Halder has since explained his reasons more fully to
me: "The means of communication for such a task all
converged at O.K.H. From the psychological standpoint,
too, such a measure would have looked like a lack of
confidence in the able von Rundstedt, though not intended
as such. The highly developed ambition of von Bock
and the not always easy manner of his Chief of Staff,
von Salmuth, made it certain that a serious clash between
the two Army Groups would have resulted from the fulfilment of this order."

It is not difficult to gauge the effect of the order on
Rundstedt, irrespective of personal considerations. He
would naturally become more concerned with the next
stage of the campaign, the advance south, than with the
completion of the encirclement in the north, which was
to be handed over to Bock. That was bound to affect
the trend of his observations on the situation at the conference next morning when Hitler visited his headquarters.
Rundstedt's emphasis on the importance of maintaining
adequate panzer strength for the next stage fitted in with
the current of Hitler's thought. The "hand-over" order
that Brauchitsch issued on the evening of the 23rd forms
a very significant clue to the understanding of the record
of the discussion at Rundstedt's headquarters next morning,
and to the halt-order that Hitler gave in the afternoon.

As early as the 22nd, the day that Guderian's corps
started on its northward drive from the Abbeville area,
Hitler had expressed those doubts at the evening conference with Brauchitsch. He there criticized the basic order
for the encirclement that Halder had just issued, in which
Army Group A was directed to push northwards with the
panzer forces as fast as possible, and to cut the Allied
armies off from the coast. After saying that he considered

it dangerous to use tanks in the low-lying coastal area of Flanders, he had dwelt on the wastage they had already suffered, and gone on to emphasize that he did not want to risk losing more of them, since they would be needed for the second act of the campaign in France.

Hitler's idea was that the panzer forces of Army Group A should be converted from the hammer into the anvil —the back-stop to catch the Allied forces driven southward by Army Group B. Keitel and Jodl shared his doubts and his view. But he did not yet feel able, with merely their support, to overrule Brauchitsch and Halder. Rundstedt represented a much greater weight of strategical authority. The trend of his remarks on the situation and on the need to keep the next act in mind was well appreciated by Hitler, who was skilled in playing off one expert authority against another to gain his own way and justify his decisions. Indeed, it seems likely that Hitler went to see Rundstedt that day in the hope of finding justification for his own doubts and for the change of plan he wanted to impose.

Hitler's first step was to cancel the hand-over order, immediately after the conference with Rundstedt. It was to have come into force that evening, and may have had a preliminary braking effect during the morning, as the commanders who were to be transferred to Bock's control would have a natural tendency to wait for fresh instructions from their new Army Group. (Mr. Churchill himself mentions that "we intercepted a German message sent in clear at 11.42 a.m. on May 24th to the effect that the attack on the line Dunkirk-Hazebrouck-Merville was to be discontinued for the present.")

Brauchitsch was summoned to see Hitler in the afternoon, and Halder accompanied him. Halder's diary records that it was "a very unpleasant interview with Führer", who now gave fresh orders definitely "cancelling yesterday's order. . . . The left wing, consisting of armoured and motorized forces, which has no enemy in front of it, will thus be stopped in its tracks upon direct orders of the Führer. Finishing off the encircled enemy army is to be left to Air Force!"

The halt continued throughout the next day, and then on the 26th Halder's diary has a series of notable entries:

0800 No significant change in situation. Von Bock, suffering losses, is pushing slowly ahead. . . . Our armoured forces have stopped as if paralysed on the high ground between Bethune and St. Omer in compliance with top level orders, and must not attack. In this way, clearing out the pocket may take weeks.

1100 All through the morning ObdH. (Brauchitsch) is very nervy. I can sympathize with him, for these orders from the top make no sense. In one area they call for a head-on attack against a front retiring in orderly fashion, and elsewhere they freeze the troops to the spot where the enemy rear could be cut into at any time. Von Rundstedt, too, cannot stand it, and has gone up forward to Hoth and Kleist to look over the land for the next armoured moves.

1200 A telephone call notifies us that the Führer has authorized the left wing to be moved within artillery range of Dunkirk.

1330 ObdH. summoned to Führer. Returns beaming. At last the Führer has given permission to move on Dunkirk to prevent further evacuations.

But the brake was taken off too late. The Allies had been organizing the defence of a bridgehead round Dunkirk, helped by the precious interval they had been allowed. The morning entry in Halder's diary for the 27th mournfully remarks: "On left wing Kleist seems to encounter stronger resistance than expected. The attack goes slowly." The resistance naturally grew stronger as the main body of the B.E.F. streamed back, bringing reinforcement to the defence of the bridgehead. Between May 26th and the fall of Dunkirk on June 4th 338,000 troops (including 114,000 of the French) were evacuated to England from the beaches and harbour.

If Hitler had felt that Rundstedt had prompted him to halt the armoured forces, he would almost certainly have mentioned it after the British escape among the excuses he gave for his decision, for he was very apt to blame others for any mistakes. Yet in this case there is no trace of him ever having mentioned, in the course of his subsequent explanations, Rundstedt's opinion as a factor. Such negative evidence is as significant as any.

It is also worth taking note of Blumentritt's evidence about the point of Rundstedt's remarks at the conference on the 24th—that in dwelling on the need for a pause to reorganize and regain balance for the final blow Rundstedt was speaking, not of the immediate situation at Dunkirk and the completion of the first phase of the campaign, but of the next phase, the final blow against the rest of the French Army. That seems a very reasonable explanation, and more in accord with the way that Rundstedt talked. Good strategists would never advise delay in completing the last lap of an encirclement, but they would pause to reorganize before launching a fresh offensive. The sooner the battle in the north could be finished the sooner the reorganization for the southward offensive could begin. Halder's diary note on the morning of the 26th indicates Rundstedt's impatience.

Where Rundstedt would seem to have been at fault was in failing to show impatience sooner, or to protest immediately the definite halt order came. Blumentritt says that when he informed Rundstedt and his chief of staff, Sodenstern, of the telephone message "it did not arouse great indignation and excitement with either of them, so far as I remember—whereas vivid and excited enquiries came from the commanders at the front." Blumentritt also told me that throughout the first part of the campaign "Rundstedt was always expecting a great French counter-attack from the South towards Sedan against our extended and thinly-filled flank on the Aisne, since he had a high opinion of the French leadership. During this period he looked much more to the south than to the Channel coast." It is important to realize that Rundstedt's headquarters were still back at Charleville—near Sedan, close behind the Aisne, facing south, and in the centre of the whole German front. That location fostered a tendency to focus on what was in front and give less attention to what was happening on the extreme right flank, where victory seemed to be assured. Dunkirk only came into the corner of his eye.

Kluge and Kleist may also have contributed, more than Rundstedt, to the missed opportunity. Halder's diary contains a significant entry on the afternoon of the 23rd about the report made by the O.K.H. liaison officer with the Panzer Group headquarters: "17.00: von Gyldenfeldt conveys Kleist's anxiety. Kleist does not feel he can carry out his task while the crisis round Arras continues. Panzer losses up to 50 per cent. I point out to him that the crisis will be overcome within 48 hours. I know the measure of the task allotted to him. He must hold out. There is no danger on the Somme." Guderian, too, says: "The advance from Amiens up the Channel coast was conducted very cautiously, by orders of Panzer-Group Kleist. General von Kleist directed the leading divisions from one line to another—for example, from the Authie river to the Canche. He gave orders at what hours the rivers were to be crossed. By this procedure several halts were caused without reason or without being imposed by the enemy. We could certainly have moved faster." General Bayerlein who was 1A of Guderian's corps relates that at the time his chief was "very angry" at these earlier halts as well as at the final one.

Several of the generals also told that 4th Army headquarters were much disturbed by the British tank counter-

stroke at Arras, small though it was, and that Kluge
seriously thought of halting the whole advance. Rundstedt
confirmed this in his account of that crisis.

HITLER'S REASONS

As to Hitler's reasons for giving the halt-order, there is
particular significance in the evidence I had from Warlimont, since he was with O.K.W. After getting word of
the order he asked Jodl for exact information. "Jodl
confirmed that the order had been given, showing himself
rather impatient about my enquiries. He himself took the
same stand as Hitler, emphasizing that the personal
experience that not only Hitler but also Keitel and himself had in Flanders during the First World War proved
beyond any doubt that armour could not operate in the
Flanders marshes, or at any rate not without heavy losses
—and such losses could not be borne in view of the already
reduced strength of the panzer corps and their tasks in
the impending second stage of the offensive in France."
(Warlimont adds that if the initiative for the halt order
had come from Rundstedt, he and the others at O.K.W.
would have heard of it; and that Jodl, who was on the
defensive about the decision, "certainly would not have
failed to point to Field-Marshal von Rundstedt as the
one who had initiated or at least supported that order"—
as that would have silenced criticism, because of Rundstedt's "undisputed authority in operational matters
among all senior general staff officers".)

Warlimont went on to say: "One other reason, however, for the halt order was revealed to me at the time—
that Goering appeared and reassured the Führer that his
air force would accomplish the rest of the encirclement by
closing the sea side of the pocket from the air. He certainly
overrated the effectiveness of his own branch." This
statement of Warlimont's gains significance when related
to the last sentence in Halder's diary note of the 24th,

already quoted. Moreover, Guderian stated that the order came down to him, from Kleist, with the words: "Dunkirk is to be left to the Luftwaffe. If the conquest of Calais should raise difficulties that fortress likewise is to be left to the Luftwaffe." Guderian remarked: "I think that it was the vanity of Goering which caused that fateful decision of Hitler's"— adding: "The 10th Panzer Division, then under my command, took Calais on the 26th May without waiting for the air force—which, by the way, with the bombs available at that time would have had no results against the forts and the citadel of old General Vauban."

THE QUESTION OF CALAIS

Guderian's reference to Calais is also significant in view of the big claims that have been made about the vital effect of its defence on the whole situation. A British infantry brigade and tank battalion was landed there to stiffen the French garrison. Mr. Churchill personally intervened on the 24th to cancel orders for their re-embarkation and insisted that "Calais should be fought to the death and that no evacuation by sea could be allowed to the garrison".

An official account of the defence published in 1941 stated that though the force was annihilated "the fury of its death struggle engaged, during four vital days, the whole strength of at least two Panzer divisions that might otherwise have cut our retreating army's road to the sea. . . . The scythe-like sweep of the German divisions stopped, with a jerk, at Calais. The tip of the scythe had met a stone".

Even in his post-war account Mr. Churchill claims: "Calais was the crux. Many other causes might have prevented the deliverance of Dunkirk, but it is certain that the three days gained by the defence of Calais enabled the Gravelines waterline to be held, and that without this, even in spite of Hitler's vacillations and Rundstedt's orders, all would have been cut off and lost."

While it is natural that Mr. Churchill should wish to justify his personal decision to sacrifice the force landed at Calais, it is hard to understand how he can still make such a claim for the effect of his action. The panzer division which attacked Calais was only one out of the seven in the area. It was employed there because it had nothing else to do during the halt that Hitler had ordered. Otherwise the town could easily have been masked by an even smaller detachment while the bulk of the panzer forces pushed on to Dunkirk. As early as the 23rd they had by-passed Calais and blocked the roads leading out of it.

In commenting on the episode Guderian said: "The British defence of Calais had no effect on the operations against Dunkirk. No delay in the advance arose from the defence of that fortress." But that is apparent without his evidence—from any dispassionate survey of the facts. The gallant stand made by the British troops at Calais cannot obscure the uselessness of the sacrifice they were called on to make.

THE QUESTION OF HITLER'S MOTIVES

The motives behind the Dunkirk halt-order have remained a puzzle to all the generals concerned. The panzer generals are the most puzzled of all, for they saw the ground at the time and could see no justification for halting—as was shown by the way they bombarded higher headquarters with appeals for permission to push on. Nevertheless most of the generals with whom I discussed the question took the view that Hitler's decision was based on military reasons, though they wondered which of the reasons given was uppermost in his mind.

There were some, however, who took a different view, and felt that his decision was inspired or at least influenced by motives of another kind. Halder was one who suspected a political motive—and did so at the time, as his diary shows. In a note written on the morning of May 25th, he emphasizes the reversal of plan caused by Hitler's new order, and remarks that "political command had formed the fixed idea that the battle of decision must not be fought on Flemish soil, but rather in Northern France. To camouflage this political move, the assertion is made that Flanders, criss-crossed by waterways, is unsuited to tank warfare".

Blumentritt, also, was convinced that Hitler's order had an underlying political motive, though a different one. He connected it with the surprising way that Hitler had talked when visiting Rundstedt's headquarters at Charleville.

Hitler was accompanied by only one of his staff, and talked in private to Rundstedt and the two key-men of his staff—Sodenstern and Blumentritt. Here is what the latter told me—"Hitler was in very good humour, he admitted that the course of the campaign had been 'a decided miracle', and gave us his opinion that the war would be finished in six weeks. After that he wished to conclude a reasonable peace with France, and then the way would be free for an agreement with Britain.

"He then astonished us by speaking with admiration of the British Empire, of the necessity for its existence, and of the civilization that Britain had brought into the world. He remarked, with a shrug of the shoulders, that the creation of its Empire had been achieved by means that were often harsh, but 'where there is planing, there are shavings flying'. He compared the British Empire with the Catholic Church—saying they were both essential elements of stability in the world. He said that all he wanted from Britain was that she should acknowledge Germany's position on the Continent. The return of Germany's lost colonies would be desirable but not essential, and he would even offer to support Britain with troops if she should be involved in any difficulties anywhere. He remarked that the colonies were primarily a matter of prestige, since they could not be held in war, and few Germans could settle in the tropics.

"He concluded by saying that his aim was to make peace with Britain on a basis that she would regard as compatible with her honour to accept.

"Field-Marshal von Rundstedt, who was always for agreement with France and Britain, expressed his satisfaction, and later, after Hitler's departure, remarked with a sigh of relief—'Well, if he wants nothing else, then we shall have peace at last.' "

In subsequent reflection on the course of events, Blumentritt's thoughts often reverted to this conversation. He felt that the "halt" had been called for more than military reasons, and that it was part of a political scheme to make peace easier to reach. If the British Army had been captured at Dunkirk, the British people might have felt that their honour had suffered a stain which they must wipe out. By letting it escape Hitler hoped to conciliate them.

This reflection about Hitler's deeper motive was reinforced by his strangely dilatory attitude over the subsequent plans for the invasion of England. "He showed little interest in the plans," Blumentritt said, "and made no effort to speed up the preparations. That was utterly different from his usual behaviour." Before the invasion of Poland, of France, and later of Russia, he repeatedly spurred them on. But on this occasion he sat back.

Since the account of this conversation at Charleville and subsequent holding back comes from a section of the generals who had long distrusted Hitler's policy and became more hostile to him as the war continued, that makes their testimony on this point more notable. They have criticized Hitler on almost every score. It would be natural to expect that, in the post-war circumstances, they would portray him as intent on the capture of the British Army, and themselves as holding back. Their evidence has the opposite effect. They very honestly admit that, as soldiers, they wanted to finish off their victory, and were upset at the way they were checked from doing so. Significantly, their account of Hitler's thoughts about England at the decisive hour before Dunkirk fits in with much that he himself wrote earlier in *Mein Kampf*—and it is remarkable how closely he followed his own bible in other respects.

Was this attitude of his towards England prompted only by the political idea, which he had long entertained, of securing an alliance with her? Or was it inspired by a deeper feeling which reasserted itself at this crucial moment? There were some complex elements in his make-up which suggests that he had a mixed love-hate feeling towards England similar to the Kaiser's.

.   .   .   .   .

There is not sufficient evidence to justify the historian in ascribing Hitler's halt-order to such feelings. But they are worth taking into account, though it is impossible to assess their weight.

Hitler's character was of such complexity that no simple explanation is likely to be true, and no single one adequate. It is far more probable that his decision was woven of several threads. Three are visible—Hitler's desire to conserve tank strength for the next stroke, his long-standing fear of marshy Flanders, the effect on him of Goering's claims for the Air Force. But it is quite likely that some political threads were interwoven with the military ones in the mind of a man who had such a bent for political strategy and so many twists in his thought.

Whatever be the true explanation, we can at least be content with the result. For his hesitations came to Britain's rescue at the most critical moment of her history.

CHAPTER XIII

THE END IN FRANCE AND THE FIRST FRUSTRATION

THE second and final phase of the campaign in France opened on June 5th, when the new German offensive was launched southward over the Somme. That was barely a week after the bulk evacuation of the B.E.F. from Dunkirk had begun, and the day after the last ship had sailed from there.

In their severed left wing the French had lost 30 divisions, nearly a third of their total forces, including the best part of their scanty number of mechanized divisions. They had also lost the help of 12 British divisions, for all that remained in France were two that had not been with the main body of the B.E.F. when the blow fell. Weygand, who had now replaced Gamelin, was left with 66 divisions, mostly depleted or of inferior quality, to hold a stretch that was longer than the original front. The Germans, on the other hand, had now had time to bring up the mass of their marching divisions, which had taken little part in the first offensive.

The most striking feature of the new offensive was in its prelude—the fact that the German armoured divisions, all of which had been engaged in the westward drive to the Channel, could be switched southwards or eastwards in so short a time ready for the next stroke. Such rapidity of reconcentration in a fresh direction was proof that mechanized mobility had transformed strategy.

In the new offensive Rundstedt's Army Group once again played the decisive rôle. It was not definitely cast for that in the plan. While Rundstedt had the larger front and forces, six of the ten German armoured divisions

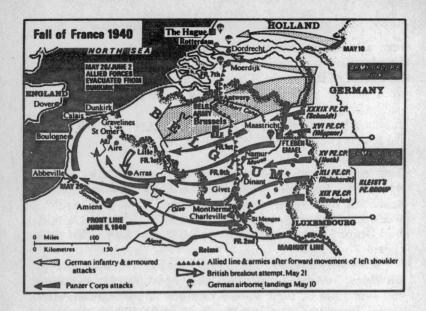

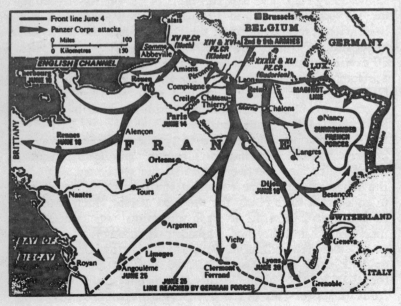

were allotted to Bock's Army Group at the outset. But
the planning was flexible and the pattern developed from
the course of the battle. The change of pattern was another
proof of the power conferred by mechanized mobility.

Nothing could have been more concise than the way
Rundstedt summed up the battle in our first talk—"There
was tough going for a few days but the issue was hardly in
doubt. The offensive was opened by Bock's Army Group,
on the right wing. I waited until his attack had made
headway, across the Somme, before joining in the offensive.
My armies met with strong resistance in crossing the Aisne,
but after that it was easy. The vital thrust was that made
over the Plateau de Langres towards Besançon and the
Swiss frontier, behind the back of the French right wing
in the Maginot Line."

The opening of the offensive, by the German right wing,
had not fulfilled expectations where success was most
desired, though it had surpassed expectations on a secondary
sector where the obstacles had appeared greater.

On the extreme right, between Amiens and the sea, the
attack was delivered by Kluge's 4th Army, as the 18th
Army, originally the right of the line, had been left behind
to clear up the position at Dunkirk. Kluge was given one
panzer corps, and owing to a speedy cut-through by
Rommel's 7th Armoured Division, his advance soon reached
the Seine at and around Rouen. The French troops here
were thrown into confusion and made little attempt to
defend the crossings, so that the Germans got over the
river on the heels of the French.

But it was not here that the decisive stroke had been
contemplated—for no reasonable plan could have reckoned
on such a smooth passage of a broad river-line that was
easy to defend. The main weight of the attack by Bock's
Army Group had been placed with Reichenau's 6th Army,
on the sector east of Amiens, where more decisive results
were anticipated.

What happened here was related by Bechtolsheim,

Reichenau's operations chief. "General von Kleist's Panzer Group was placed under the 6th Army for this attack. Its composition differed from that in the first offensive, for Guderian had been transferred to Army Group "A" in Champagne, and his corps had been replaced by Hoeppner's 16th Panzer Corps. We made a two-pronged thrust. Wietersheim's 14th Panzer Corps attacked from the bridgehead over the Somme that we had gained at Amiens, and Hoeppner's from the bridgehead at Peronne. The idea was that they should converge to join hands on the Oise beyond St. Just-en-Chaussée. After that, the decision was to be taken whether the advance should be pursued east or west of Paris.

"In planning the attack there were some arguments about this method. Personally I should have preferred to concentrate the two panzer corps in a single punch, but in the end General von Reichenau decided in favour of the pincer stroke from the two bridgeheads. The drive might have gone quicker if the weight had been concentrated.

"When the attack was launched it met stiff opposition in the 'Weygand Line' for the first three or four days. As a result, contrary to anticipation, the decisive break-through was not made on our sector, but on the Aisne east of Soissons. Thereupon O.K.H. decided to withdraw General von Kleist's Panzer Group from us, and move it east to exploit this breach. Naturally we were disappointed, for it was a repetition of what had happened to us in Belgium."

Kleist continued the story. "Wietersheim's Corps had actually gained a bridgehead over the Oise at Pont Sainte Maxence, but Hoeppner's advance was delayed by heavy fighting west of Noyon. By this time a break-through had been achieved in Champagne. Although the attack there did not start until the 9th, the passage of the Aisne was quickly forced and Guderian's Panzer Group pushed through the gap made by the 12th Army east of Reims.

The 9th and 2nd Armies had also broken through west of Reims, and I now received orders to pull out of the battle I was fighting, and bring my forces back and round to exploit this opening. We made a long circuit behind the front, north of Compiègne, then crossed the Aisne at Soissons, and next the Marne at Château Thierry, after which we headed for Troyes. By this time the French were collapsing in confusion, so we drove on past Dijon down the Rhône valley to Lyons without check. Another big switch took place before this drive finished, for Wietersheim's Corps was brought back and round for a south-westerly drive to Bordeaux, and then to the Spanish frontier beyond Biarritz."

What had happened in the course of the break-through on the Aisne was told by Blumentritt. "There was only one big strategic decision taken during this offensive. When Guderian's Panzer Group was right through the French front and reached the area between St. Dizier and Chaumont, on the upper Marne, the question arose which of three courses it should take. Should it turn east, over the Plateau de Langres, towards the Swiss frontier, in order to cut off the French armies in Alsace? Should it advance south-east over the plateau to Dijon and Lyon, in order to reach the Mediterranean and to help the Italians over the Alps? Should it turn south-west towards Bordeaux, in order to cut off the French armies retreating from the Paris area to the Loire and beyond? Three short wireless cues were prepared beforehand for this purpose."

In the event, Guderian was directed to follow the first course, while Kleist's Panzer Group, racing up on his right after passing through the gap on the Aisne, carried out both the second and third. For by that time the French armies were breaking up into incoherent fragments, and the Germans could safely take the risk of splitting their own forces.

Guderian was already sweeping across the rear of the Maginot Line when, on June 14th, Leeb's Army Group

"C" joined in the battle by striking at that famous barrier. Significantly, the Germans had not ventured to attack it direct until it was undercut; and even then their efforts were in the nature of probing. The main one was a narrow-fronted assault by Heinrici's 12th Corps (of the 1st Army) near Puttlingen, south of Saarbrücken, while a secondary effort was made a hundred miles to the south, on the 7th Army front, where the Rhine was crossed near Colmar.

Heinrici told me that he broke through the Line in twelve hours. But in further discussion he admitted that this break-through took place only after the defence had been weakened and the French were in process of withdrawing. "On the 14th my troops penetrated at two points, after stiff fighting. I had ordered a continuance of the attack for the 15th when at midnight an intercepted French order was brought to me, showing that the defenders of the Maginot Line had been ordered to withdraw. So our operation next day became a pursuit rather than an assault."

What had been happening meanwhile on the other flank, where the German offensive had started, was described by Bechtolsheim—resuming his account from the point where one of Kleist's panzer corps had gained a bridgehead over the Oise at Pont Sainte Maxence, before being pulled out and switched to the Aisne. "When our infantry relieved the tanks and pushed on beyond the Oise, an awkward problem was presented by the outer line of fortifications covering the approach to Paris that the French had built near Senlis. General von Reichenau was doubtful about the best way of tackling this obstacle, but then decided to turn it by moving round the eastern flank. However, the French retreat saved us trouble. When they abandoned Paris, our right corps was transferred to the 18th Army, which had now arrived from the north, for the move into the capital, while we continued our advance southward. After crossing the Seine at Corbeil and Montereau, we pushed on to the Loire. We found the bridges at Sully and Gien had been blown up, but we captured those at Orleans intact by a *coup de main*. The advance was essentially a pursuit all the way from the Marne to the Cher, where it ended. There was not much fighting."

Summing up the general course of the offensive, Blumentritt said: "Only the crossing of the Aisne, which was strongly defended by the French, involved a serious engagement. Here, the armoured divisions were not launched until the infantry had forced the passage; even so, they had some stiff opposition beyond the river before they broke through. After that, the fighting became less and less strenuous. The armoured divisions pushed on without stopping, or without bothering about their exposed flanks, and flooded the south of France. The German infantry followed them up in forced marches of forty to sixty kilometres a day, liquidating such fractions of the French Army as were still holding out after the tanks had driven on. On many of the main roads our armoured forces advanced without opposition past French columns that were marching back in the same direction.

"During this stage the Luftwaffe worked in close co-operation with the armoured divisions, in a new form of 'street tactics'. When a place was defended, the bombers were called up to attack it, and then the advanced detachment of the division took it; meanwhile the bulk of the division, without leaving the road, usually waited in a long column (nearly a hundred miles in length) until the road ahead was clear. This was possible only because we had air superiority, because the enemy's anti-tank defence was inadequate, and mines were as yet little used.

"In the 1940 campaign the French fought bravely, but they were no longer the French of 1914–18—of Verdun and the Somme. The British fought much more stubbornly, as they did in 1914–18. The Belgians in part fought gallantly; the Dutch, only a few days. *We* had superiority in the air combined with more up-to-date tanks than the French. Above all, the German tank troops were more mobile, quicker and better at in-fighting, and able while in movement to turn wherever required by their leader. This, the French at that time were unable to do. They still thought and fought more in the tradition of the First World War. They were not up to date either in leadership or in wireless control. When they wanted to change direction on the move, they had to halt first, give fresh orders, and only then were they able to start again. Their tank tactics were out of date—but they *were* brave!"

This authoritative German verdict should correct the hasty judgments that the world passed on the defenders of France. While the final collapse was accelerated by a rapidly spreading breakdown of morale, it is clear that the issue of the second offensive was a foregone conclusion. Defeat was inevitable from its outset, though it might have been delayed a little longer.

On an elementary calculation of forces in relation to space—the space that had to be covered between the Somme and the Swiss frontier—Weygand had an insoluble problem to meet. A calculation in terms of quantity multiplied by technical quality only makes the situation look more hopeless. It is more surprising that the British Government, and even part of the French, continued to cherish illusions after Dunkirk, than that soldiers like Weygand and Pétain abandoned hope as soon as the Somme-Aisne line began to crack. But the strangest feature of the whole period is that the German generals should have counted on cutting off the Allied left wing in Belgium, yet not expected a general collapse of French resistance—its almost mathematically calculable consequence. When that collapse came, it was soon clear that they had failed to reckon with such a probability, and were unprepared to follow it up.

RECUMBENT "SEA-LION"

After the collapse of France the German Army relaxed with a happy feeling that the war was over and that the fruits of victory could be enjoyed at leisure. Blumentritt's account of the sequel conveys a vivid impression of the prevailing attitude. "Immediately following the armistice with France, orders came from O.K.H. to form the staff for the victory parade in Paris, and to despatch the troops that were assigned to take part in the parade. We spent a fortnight working on the organization of this parade. Spirits were high, as everyone counted on a general peace. Preparations for demobilization had already begun, and we had received a list of the divisions that were to be sent home for disbanding."

After a few weeks, however, the victory mood began to subside, and a feeling of uneasiness grew in the absence of any sign that Britain was disposed to make peace. Hopeful rumours filled the void. "There was talk of negotiations with Britain being conducted through Sweden; then, through the Duke of Alba." But nothing definite came in the way of confirmation.

On June 29th Halder flew back to Berlin, and visited his dentist. The morrow was his birthday and he spent it at home, but fitted in a visit to Weizsaecker at the Foreign Office. Among the points mentioned in this talk, according to Halder's war diary, was that "Britain probably needs one more demonstration of our military might before she gives in and leaves us a free hand in the East". Next morning, before flying back to France, he saw Admiral Schniewind of the Naval Staff, and had a short talk—"Discussion of basis for warfare against England. Prerequisite is air superiority. (Then perhaps we can dispense with land warfare)". Schniewind then set forth some points about the problem of invasion—weather conditions, routes, and possible assembly of shipping.

Admiral Raeder, the Commander-in-Chief of the Navy, had earlier started to consider the matter, but when he had raised the subject at a conference with Hitler on May 21st and again on June 20th, the Fuehrer had given it scant attention and obviously did not regard invasion as necessary to make Britain accept peace.

After hearing what Schniewind had to say, Halder had a chat with Leeb of the Ordnance Office—"He was told all along that invasion of England was not being considered. I tell him that possibilities have to be examined—for, if political command demands a landing they will want everything done at top speed".

The first indication that Hitler was considering an invasion of England came on July 2nd, when he directed the heads of the three Services to study the problem, and called for intelligence appreciations from them. But he ended by emphasizing that "the plan is in its infancy", and added: "So far it is only a question of preparing for a possible event." Two weeks passed before the next development. Meantime Halder with Greiffenberg and others of his staff at Fontainebleau, was working hard on provisional plans, with August as a broad date-line.

On July 16th, nearly a month after the collapse of France, Hitler issued a directive saying: "Since England, in spite of her militarily hopeless situation, shows no sign of coming to terms, I have decided to prepare a landing operation against England and, if necessary, to carry it out. . . . The preparations for the entire operation must be completed by mid-August." The order, however, sounded very "iffy".

Hitler's disinclination to invade England had been manifest at a conference with the Commander-in-Chief of the Navy, Admiral Raeder, on July 11th. The record of this conference was in the archives captured after the war. Proceedings began with a long discussion, not of the problem of invading England, but of the development of Norway—a matter in which Hitler showed more interest. He expressed his intention of building "a beautiful German city" in the fiord near Trondheim, and ordered plans to be submitted. Later, the question of invading England was discussed. Raeder considered that "an invasion should be used only as a last resort to force Britain to sue for peace". He dwelt on the many difficulties of the venture, and the lengthy transport preparations required, as well as the need for air superiority. When he had finished Hitler expressed his views, which are thus summarized in the record: "The Führer also views invasion as a last resort, and also considers air superiority a prerequisite."

On the 13th Halder flew from Fontainebleau to Berchtesgaden to give a report on the military plans. His diary reads: "*The Fuehrer* is greatly puzzled by Britain's persisting unwillingness to make peace. He sees the answer (as we do) in Britain's hope on Russia, and therefore counts on having to compel her by main force to agree to peace. Actually that is much against his grain. The reason is that a military defeat of Britain will bring about the disintegration of the British Empire. This would not be of any benefit to Germany. German blood would be shed to accomplish something that would benefit only Japan, the United States, and others."

Although the operational directive was issued on the 16th, its tentativeness was emphasized by Hitler's step three days later in making a peace appeal to Britain in his speech to the Reichstag on the victory in France. He struck a remarkably moderate note, deploring the possibility of a war to the bitter end, and dwelling on the sacrifices it would entail for both sides. Even the cynical Italian Foreign Minister, Count Ciano, was impressed and noted in his diary: "I believe that his desire for peace is sincere. In fact, late in the evening, when the first cold British reactions to the speech arrive, a sense of ill-concealed disappointment spreads among the Germans . . . they are hoping and praying that this appeal will not be rejected."

Next morning he called on Hitler, and noted in his diary: "He confirms my impressions of yesterday. He would like an understanding with Great Britain. He knows that war with the British will be hard and bloody, and knows also that people everywhere to-day are averse to bloodshed." On returning to Rome, however, Ciano found that Mussolini was upset by the speech, fearing that the English would respond to Hitler's appeal and consider a negotiated peace. "That would be sad for Mussolini, because now more than ever he wants war."

On the 21st Hitler held a conference of his higher commanders. His opening remarks showed how puzzled he was as to the grounds for Britain's persistence in carrying on the war. He could only imagine that she was hoping that America or Russia would enter the war, but it did not seem likely that either would, though Russia's entry "would be unpleasant for Germany especially on account of the threat from the air". Then he came to the question of invading England, and began by pointing out that it would be "an exceptionally hazardous undertaking, because even if the way is short, this is not just a river crossing, but the crossing of a sea which is dominated by the enemy. Operational surprise cannot be expected; a defensively prepared and utterly determined enemy faces us". He went on to emphasize the difficulties of reinforcement and supply after a landing. He insisted that "complete mastery of the air" was essential before starting, and that as the venture depended on sustained air support, which in turn depended on the weather—which was usually bad during the second half of September—the main operation must be completed by the 15th. The survey ended with the declaration: "If it is not certain that preparations can be completed by the beginning of September, other plans must be considered." The whole address breathed doubt, and the final note implied that his mind was turning elsewhere.

Halder's diary, recording the account he had from Brauchitsch of what Hitler said at this conference, shows Hitler's mingled confidence and perplexity—"Britain's position is hopeless. The war is won by us. A reversal in the prospects of success is impossible." But Hitler went on to emphasize that "invasion is to be undertaken only if no other means is left to come to terms with Britain." After

talking of his "peace feelers", and optimistically dwelling
on signs that British opinion was becoming more peacefully
inclined, Hitler came in conclusion to what he regarded as
the chief hindrance. "Stalin is flirting with Britain to keep
her in the war and tie us down, with a view to gain time
and take what he wants, knowing he could not get it once
peace breaks out." From this came the further conclusion:
"Our attention must be turned to tackling the Russian
problem and prepare planning".

Such plans were initiated immediately. The stated
object was: "To crush the Russian army or slice as much
Russian territory as is necessary to bar enemy air raids on
Berlin and Silesian industries. It is desirable to penetrate
far enough to enable our Air Force to smash Russia's
strategic areas." The idea of an attack on Russia "this
autumn" was mooted, and in that case the "pressure of the
air war on Britain will be relaxed." General Bayerlein told
me that, a few days later, he was sent back to Berlin with the
operational staff of Guderian's panzer group "to prepare
plans for the employment of the panzer forces in a campaign
against Russia," and that the scheme envisaged the use of
four panzer groups for deep thrusts along the same axes
as those that were actually followed a year later.

Hitler changed his mind within a few days about
launching an attack on Russia that autumn—after being
shown what extensive preparations would be needed. He
also yielded to the arguments of the Foreign Office and
O.K.H. for making a further attempt to avert a Russo-
British combination, by offering Russia territorial bribes at
Britain's expense. But the planning for an attack on Russia
continued, and he showed more keenness for it than for the
cross-Channel venture. That bias in his mind was beneficial
to Britain at this crucial time.

It is interesting to look up one's notes of the situation
in England at that time. The Navy's dispositions did not
promise a very prompt intervention in the Channel, for
the British admirals were almost as anxious about the

menace of the German Air Force as the German admirals were about the interference of the British Navy. But on the same day that Hitler's directive was issued, I heard authoritatively that Britain's fighter strength, gravely depleted in covering the evacuation from Dunkirk, had been built up again to its former level—its fifty-seven squadrons now comprised over a thousand machines, with reserves.

During the six weeks since Dunkirk the land forces available to meet an invasion had been so scanty that even a few enemy divisions might have brushed them aside. But although the reorganization and re-equipment of the land forces evacuated from France was still a slow process, one felt that with the restoration of Britain's fighter strength in the air the primary assurance against invasion had been achieved, and that the danger of this succeeding was on the wane. Nevertheless, a glimpse of "the other side of the hill", as an unseen onlooker at Hitler's conferences, would have been still more cheering. So would a glimpse into the reports of the German Intelligence service. For they grossly over-estimated even the strength of Britain's land forces. It is not surprising that Hitler and many of his advisers had growing doubts as they studied the problem.

Goering expressed assurance that the Luftwaffe could fulfil its part—the double rôle of dominating the Royal Air Force and checking the Royal Navy's intervention. That helped to keep the plan alive. But his confidence was by no means common among the leaders of the Luftwaffe—Richthofen, who commanded the dive-bombers, was particularly sceptical.

The German generals and admirals had a common mistrust of Goering's promises, but they did not agree among themselves. A landing force of 40 divisions was originally proposed, but had to be scaled down to 13 divisions because the Naval High Command declared that it was impossible to transport more. The remainder were to be sent over at intervals, in three more waves, if conditions allowed. The panzer menace would not have been

as great as the British expected, for only small elements
were included in the landing force, and the bulk were held
back until a later stage. The Army High Command
insisted that the landings should be made on the widest
possible front—from Ramsgate to Lyme Bay at least—in
order to distract and stretch the British reserves. But the
Naval High Command insisted that they could only protect
a passage and landing on a narrow front, no farther west
than Eastbourne. The argument raged for two or three
weeks. Halder declared that the Navy's proposal spelt
"complete suicide" for the Army—"I might just as well put
the troops that have been landed straight through a mincing
machine." The Naval Chief of Staff retorted that it would
be equally suicidal to cross the Channel on a wider front.

Eventually the controversy ended in a compromise,
ordained by Hitler, that satisfied neither service. By that
time it was the middle of August, and the completion of
the preparations had been deferred until the middle of
September. As Goering had begun his preliminary air
offensive on the 13th, both the generals and the admirals
felt the more inclined to wait and see whether the Luftwaffe
mastered the R.A.F., or whether by failing it conclusively
settled the issue against attempting invasion.

Discussing the invasion plans with Rundstedt, I asked
him about the timing and the reasons for cancelling the
invasion. He replied: "As the first steps to prepare for an
invasion were taken only after the French capitulation, no
definite date could be fixed when the plan was drafted.
It depended on the time required to provide the shipping,
to alter ships so they could carry tanks, and to train the
troops in embarking and disembarking. The invasion was
to be made in August if possible, and September at the
latest. The military reasons for its cancellation were
various. The German Navy would have had to control
the North Sea as well as the Channel, and was not strong
enough to do so. The German Air Force was not sufficient
to protect the sea crossing on its own. While the leading

part of the forces might have landed, there was the danger that they might be cut off from supplies and reinforcements." I asked Rundstedt whether it might not have been possible to keep the invasion forces supplied by air for a time—as was done on a very large scale in Russia during the winter of 1941. He said the system of air supply was not sufficiently developed in 1940 for this possibility to be considered.

Rundstedt then outlined the military side of the plan. "The responsibility of commanding the invasion fell to me, and the task was assigned to my Army Group. The 16th Army under General Busch was on the right, and the 9th Army under General Strauss was on the left. They were to sail from ports stretching from Holland to Le Havre. The 16th Army was to use ports from Antwerp to Boulogne, while the 9th Army was to use the ports between the Somme and the Seine. No landing was to be made north of the Thames." Rundstedt indicated on the map the sector over which the landings were to be made, stretching from Dover to near Portsmouth. "We were then to push forward and establish a much larger bridgehead along an arc south of London. It ran up the south shore of the Thames to the outskirts of London, and then south-westwards to Southampton Water." In answer to a further question, he said the original idea was that part of Reichenau's 6th Army—from Bock's Army Group—was to land on the coast west of the Isle of Wight, on both sides of Weymouth, to cut off the Devon-Cornwall peninsula, and drive north to Bristol. But that was dropped, except as a possible later development.

In further discussion he conveyed that he never had much confidence in the prospects of successful invasion, and that he was often thinking of how Napoleon had been baffled. In that sense the German generals seem to have been hampered by being historically minded—as they were once again in Russia the following autumn.

Brauchitsch seems to have been rather more hopeful than Rundstedt. That is the impression I gathered from General Siewert, who was with him at the time. When I asked him about Brauchitsch's views as to the practicability of the plan, he replied: "If the weather was favourable, and given time to prepare, and considering Britain's great losses at Dunkirk, Field-Marshal von Brauchitsch thought it a possibility." But I gathered that the thought was prompted by the wish, because he could see no other way of gaining peace in face of Mr. Churchill's refusal to consider any proposals for peace. "Our idea was to finish the war as soon as possible, and wé *had* to get across the water to do that." "Then why wasn't it carried out?" I asked. "There were many preparations in progress, but the weather outlook was not good. The attempt was supposed to be carried out in September but Hitler cancelled all the preparations because he thought it impracticable. The Navy's heart was not in it, and it was not strong enough to protect the flanks. Neither was the German Air Force strong enough to stop the British Navy."

What the soldiers told me about the Navy's attitude was amply borne out by the views gathered from a number of admirals, among them Voss, Brinkmann, Breuning, and Engel. One very significant comment seemed to express the common view: "The German Navy was utterly unprepared to hold off the British Navy, even for a short time. Moreover the accumulation of barges brought from the Rhine, the Elbe and the Dutch canals was quite unsuitable." In discussion some said that they did not believe these barges were massed with the idea of using them, and doubted whether an invasion of England was really intended. There was a sense of play-acting—as if most of the higher people concerned were pretending to be more serious about the project than they were. "From what we learnt later about Britain's situation it would seem that the war might have been won in July, 1940, if the German Intelligence service had been better; but most senior naval officers considered it lost on September 3rd, 1939." In other words, from the day Britain entered the war.

General Student gave me details of the part that the airborne forces were to have played in the invasion plan, as well as some more interesting comments on the way he would have wished them to be used. As Student himself was then in hospital, recovering from the head wound he had suffered at Rotterdam, the airborne forces were commanded by General Putzier: "Two divisions[1] were to be employed, as well as 300 gliders—each of these carried a pilot and nine other men, three thousand in all. The intention was to use the airborne force for securing a bridge-head near Folkestone, about twenty miles wide and twelve miles deep. The intended dropping zone was kept closely under air observation. It was seen that obstacles were being quickly prepared—that the suitable landing fields were being filled with upright stakes—and it was assumed that minefields were also being laid there. For these reasons Putzier reported, at the end of August, that an airborne invasion was now out of the question.

"If I had been still on the scene I should have urged the use of the parachute forces against England while your evacuation from Dunkirk was still in progress, to seize the ports where your troops were landing. It was known that most of them had left Dunkirk without any of their heavier weapons.

"Even if this project had been vetoed my plans for the airborne part of the invasion would have been different to what was actually decided. I should have used my force to capture airfields considerably deeper inland than the intended bridge-head. Having captured these, I should have transported infantry divisions over by air, without tanks or heavy artillery—some to turn outwards and attack

[1] The Parachute Division and the 22nd Air-Landing Division, forming the XI Air Corps.

the coast defences from the rear, and some to move on
London. I reckoned that one infantry division could be
brought over by air in a day and a half to two days, and
that this rate of reinforcement could be kept up." It
seemed to me that Student's plan was optimistic, taking
account of the small force that could be carried in this way,
and the time it would take to increase.

"But the best time," Student again emphasized, "was
immediately after Dunkirk—before your defensive measures
were developed. We heard later that the people in Britain
had a parachute psychosis. That amused us, but there
is no doubt it was the best defensive precaution, properly
directed."

The attitude shown in the decision that the airborne
operation should be abandoned was symptomatic.
Although the preparations continued, the nearer they
came to completion the farther the will to invade receded.
The progress of the air offensive was not very encouraging,
and all the doubters in the other services were prompt to
stress that Goering's expectations were not being fulfilled
as quickly as promised. The strain that this "battle over
Britain" was imposing on the defenders was unduly discounted. At the same time the Intelligence reports
emphasized, and exaggerated, the growth of the British
defences on land—there is reason to suspect that this was,
in part, deliberate. Hitler himself tended to emphasize
not only the difficulties, but the ill-effects of failing in an
invasion attempt. The "wait and see" note became louder
as the provisional date approached. Hitler kept on
putting off the crucial decision about fixing a definite
date, and on September 17th decided "to postpone 'Sea-
Lion' indefinitely".

On October 12th he definitely cancelled it, though with
the qualifying remark: "Should the invasion be reconsidered
in the spring or early summer of 1941, orders for a renewal
of operational readiness will be issued later".

Throughout the whole period the minutes of his con-

ferences reek, not only of doubt, but of a deeper disinclination. They tend to bear out the account that Blumentritt
gave me. "Although 'Operation Sea-Lion' was ordered,
and preparations made, the affair was not pushed forward.
Hitler scarcely seemed to bother about it at all—contrary
to his usual way—and the staffs went on with their planning
without any inclination. It was all regarded as a 'war
game'. Field-Marshal von Rundstedt did not take the
affair seriously, and busied himself little with the work.
His Chief of Staff, General von Sodenstern, frequently went
on leave. After about the middle of August no one
believed in its execution any longer, and from mid-
September the means of transport—which were quite
insufficient—were already being silently dispersed. By the
end of September it was quite clear that the plan was not
intended seriously, and it was dropped completely. Among
ourselves we talked of it as bluff, and looked forward to news
that an understanding with Britain had been reached."

Blumentritt's account of the generals' view is called in
question by the evidence of Halder's diary. On August 6th
it contains this significant remark: "We have here the para-
doxical situation where the Navy is full of misgivings, the
Air Force is very reluctant to tackle a mission which at the
outset is exclusively its own, and O.K.W., which for once
has a real combined forces operation to direct, just plays
dead. The only driving force in the situation comes from
us, but alone we would not be able to swing it."

The executive generals, however, seem to have had no
heart in the attempted invasion, and it is clear that the
admirals were even more disinclined to make the venture.
They took the gloomiest view of what the British Navy
could do. When the *Luftwaffe* failed to drive the R.A.F. out
of the sky, all the objections were strengthened. More
significant, however, was Hitler's inward readiness to
accept excuses for a postponement. In this case it was a
permanent postponement. For his mind had an increasingly
eastward slant.

When Hitler, in July, had mooted his project of striking at Russia, it was dubiously regarded by his military chiefs—even though they were at the same time becoming doubtful about the prospect of invading England. Halder's diary records a long discussion he had with Brauchitsch on the 30th. They agreed that "the Navy in all probability will not provide us with the means for a successful invasion of England". But they also agreed in deprecating "a two-front war", if it could be avoided, and in favouring a fresh effort to "keep on friendly terms with Russia". It might be possible to avert the "threatening British-Russian alliance" by facilitating some of Stalin's expansionist aims. "Russia's aspirations to the Straits and in the direction of the Persian Gulf need not bother us. In the Balkans, which falls within our economic sphere of interest, we could keep out of each other's way."

Next day, July 31st, they flew to Berchtesgaden for a conference of the Service chiefs with Hitler. There, Admiral Raeder opened the discussion by dwelling on the difficulties of a sea invasion, said that mid-September was the earliest possible date, and went so far as to propose the spring. Hitler then pointed out further difficulties, but also emphasized that submarine and air warfare might take a year or two to produce a decisive effect. "If invasion does not take place, our action must be directed to eliminate all factors that let England hope for a change in the situation . . . Britain's hope lies in Russia and the United States. If Russia drops out of the picture, America too is lost for Britain, because the elimination of Russia would immensely increase Japan's power in the Far East. Russia is the Far Eastern sword of Britain and the United States, pointed at Japan." Hitler went on to cite intercepted telephone conversation as evidence that the recent recovery in British morale was due to hints of Russia's intervention. "With Russia smashed Britain's last hope would be shattered." Hitler then announced his decision: "Russia's destruction must therefore be made a part of this struggle." But as it was essential to achieve it "with one blow", the invasion of Russia would be deferred until the spring, so as to prepare a stronger blow and ensure a decisive result.

During the weeks that followed, a counter-current was produced by the arguments of the apprehensive chiefs of the fighting and diplomatic Services. The effect is reflected in an entry in Halder's diary for September 30th—"The Fuehrer notified Stalin of the conclusion of the pact with Japan twenty-four hours before it was signed. Now a letter has gone out designed to get him interested in dividing up the estate of defunct Britain; and to induce him to join up with us. If the plan succeeds, it is believed we could go all out against Britain." Thus German policy had for a time a two-way movement. Molotov was invited to Berlin early in November, and official circles clung to the hope that Russia would agree to join the Tripartite Pact. While disappointed at the reservations he made in discussion, they still professed satisfaction with his general attitude. But Hitler found cause only for increased suspicion, and deepened reluctance to change the course on which he himself was now bent.

This turn of his mind and the way it developed were explained by Warlimont, who gave me an account of the period from the O.K.W. angle. Speaking of the plans for the invasion of England, Warlimont confirmed that "Hitler showed unusually little interest in this venture". But he did not share the view of Blumentritt and others that Hitler's invasion measures were a bluff, and felt that the impression was caused by the way that Hitler followed three different courses in rapid succession—first, an intention to avoid any action that would stiffen the British against making peace; second, when he lost hope of this, a resolve to invade England and force peace upon her; third, from doubt of the possibility, a quick turn to take a different route to the same end.

Warlimont's comments are worth quoting at length, and the more so because he was one of the chief protagonists of the invasion plan. "There is no doubt in my mind as to the long-cherished and almost guiding political principle of Hitler's to come to terms with England, on a world-wide and lasting basis. Also I think it true that after the collapse of France he returned to this scheme—but for a short while only, and for the last time. It was during this short period, late in June and early in July, 1940, that he showed himself at first entirely unwilling and later on rather reluctant in taking up the problem of the invasion of England. The only explanation of this unusual attitude came to me at the time from a Foreign Office member of his entourage—he told me about Hitler's intentions of approaching England once more by way of a public peace offer. Hitler's speech, when delivered in the Reichstag on 19th July, seemed to me disappointing. But Hitler in turn may have been still more disappointed that his endeavour met with no response from the British side.

"After this renewed disillusion his further steps were certainly no longer guided by political considerations. On the contrary, it seems to me that subsequent events can be understood only by the underlying idea of how to defeat England in the quickest and most effective way. Hitler pursued this aim in four different ways: the combined air and sea attack against British trade and industry; the air attack as a preparatory step to the invasion of the British Isles; the plan of attacking the British positions in the Mediterranean; and finally the initial preparations for a campaign against Russia, which was deemed 'England's last resort on the Continent'." (It is evident that Hitler's thought ran so closely in Napoleon's groove that he imagined a conspiracy between England and Russia when nothing of that sort existed—and not even a mutually helpful relationship. It is evident, too, that Hitler was resolute only in pursuing the last of the four courses— because his permanent hostility towards Bolshevist Russia was so much stronger than his temporary hostility towards England.)

Warlimont then remarked that the Army High Command, as represented by Brauchitsch and Halder, was at first in favour of a landing in England, provided that the Navy and Air Force fulfilled their part of the requirements. "It was strongly supported by my 'National Defence' directorate (of O.K.W.) whose members, belonging to the three services, did their utmost to bring these to agree on the disputed points, while actual preparations on all sides came close to completion." (On this point Warlimont added: "The shipping needs for an invasion of England had been calculated very carefully, and corresponded to demands. This refers both to quantity and quality as far as transports and cargo-ships of the 7,000 ton class were concerned. The landing craft for the first echelons were, of course, rather improvised devices.")

Warlimont went on to say: "Yet the reluctance of Hitler and his military entourage continued—and that reluctance was due only in part to the unsatisfactory performance of the German Air Force in its efforts to drive the British forces out of the sky. Hitler apparently could not or would not bring himself to believe in the ultimate success of the plan as a whole—at least not in a quick success. And that was what he needed.

"Here, in my opinion, lies the close similarity with the events of the early nineteenth century. Russia had long before begun 'to look over his shoulder', as Stegemann said of Napoleon's case. Had Hitler not reason enough to distrust Russia and the treaty of 1939—and to fear that the Russians were only waiting for the German forces to get again and more deeply engaged in Western Europe? I personally am not of the opinion that a German preventive war against Russia was the only way out of his situation. But I remember Jodl's words when, late in July 1940, he told his staff that fighting against Russia would be unavoidable in the long run, and therefore better disposed of in the course of this war—thus voicing Hitler's estimate of the situation.

"It was Jodl, too, who had a considerable share in killing off the 'sea-lion' when, in the late summer, he summarized his views in a memorandum to Hitler. The plan for an invasion of England, he wrote, would mean from the start a great risk—which had been further increased by the unsatisfactory results of the air offensive, due to the bad weather. If the landing did not succeed, this failure would endanger the whole of the achievements of the war thus far obtained. The invasion should therefore be executed only if there were no other way of forcing England to her knees. Such a way, however, offered itself by attacking and usurping the British positions in the Mediterranean—of which Jodl enumerated Gibraltar, Malta and the Suez Canal. The loss of these positions, he concluded, would bring the war to an end.

"Hitler apparently was only too willing to endorse these considerations against the invasion.[1] From this time on no more serious efforts were made. Early in December the plan was altogether abandoned—the 'sea-lion' was definitely dead."

Its death, however, was followed by its momentary resurrection in a somewhat different form—or, indeed, two different forms in succession. The first began to take shape before "Sea-Lion" was actually buried. It was the project of an occupation of Ireland—as a means to get a

[1] It is clear from the sum of the evidence, however, that Hitler was more inclined to drop the invasion plan than to embrace the alternative plan outlined in this memorandum of Jodl's. While he toyed with the Mediterranean idea in a fitful way, his mind was turning more and more towards a switch against Russia. Raeder and Goering were the chief advocates of the idea of capturing Britain's Mediterranean keys—not least because they were anxious to dissuade Hitler from being involved in Russia. Jodl, though he saw the advantages of such a move, was inclined to share Hitler's fears of an early threat from Russia.

stranglehold of England's seaborne supplies—instead of a direct invasion of England, and may have been generated by Goering.

At a conference on December 3rd Hitler dealt with the subject, and said: "A landing in Ireland can be attempted only if Ireland requests help. For the present our envoy must ascertain whether De Valera desires support . . . Ireland is important to the Commander-in-Chief, Air, as a base for attacks on the north-west ports of Britain . . . The occupation of Ireland might lead to the end of the war. Investigations are to be made." But the Naval Staff made a very damping report on the prospects of any such move, especially if attempted by sea.

That caused Hitler's mind to revert to "Sea-Lion", but with a difference. I had an account of what followed from Student—who, after recovering from the severe wound he had received on the opening day of the invasion of the West, returned to duty at the beginning of January, 1941, and was given command of the new 11th Air Corps composed of airborne troops. Shortly afterwards he received a summons to go along with Goering to see Hitler at Berchtesgaden—it was Student's first visit to that mountain fastness. He was told to come prepared with proposals for how the new corps might be employed in the near future.

"This conference with Hitler and Goering on the Obersalzberg took place in the second half of January, on a day between the 20th and the 25th—I think it was the 25th. At first Hitler developed in detail his *general* views, political and strategical, about how to continue the war against his principal enemy. Herein he also mentioned the issues in the Mediterranean. After that he turned to the question of invading England. Hitler said that during the previous year he could not afford to risk a possible failure; apart from that, he had not wished to provoke the British, as he hoped to arrange peace talks. But as they were unwilling to discuss things, they must face the alternative.

"Then a discussion followed about the use of the 11th Air Corps in an invasion of Great Britain. In this respect I expressed my doubts about using the Corps directly on the South coast, to form a bridgehead for the Army— as the area immediately behind the coast was now covered with obstacles. These doubts were accepted by Hitler. I then proposed that, if it proved absolutely necessary to use the 11th Air Corps on the south coast, then air-fields in the hinterland (25 to 35 miles distant from the coast) should be captured, and infantry divisions landed on them.

"Suddenly Hitler pointed to the waist of the Cornwall–Devon Peninsula, and drew a big circle on his map round Taunton and the Blackdown Hills, saying: 'Your airborne troops could be used here as *flank protection*. This is a strong sector and, besides, this important defile must be opened.' He then pointed to Plymouth and dwelt on the importance of this great harbour for the Germans and for the English. Now I could no longer follow his thought, and I asked at what points on the south coast the landing was to take place. But Hitler kept strictly to his order that operations were to be kept secret, and said: 'I cannot tell you yet'."

Student then put forward the project he himself favoured and had worked out—a surprise descent on Northern Ireland. His idea was that it should be a diversion in aid of, and coincident with, the invasion of southern England. He argued that it would be "not nearly as difficult as if we were to drop on the south coast of England, and would also appeal to the taste of my parachute troops". His aim would be first to secure and then to expand a firm operational base—what he called the "ink on blotting paper" method. Starting from the airfields in Brittany, the drop would be made in a triangular area between Divis Mountain, west of Belfast, and Lough Neagh— capturing the three airfields in that area. A subsidiary drop was to be made at Lisburn, to block that road and rail centre. Large numbers of dummy parachutists were to be dropped in various inaccessible places, such as the Mourne Mountains and Sperrin Mountains, to distract the defending forces. Glider troops could not be used in this operation because of the distance to be covered, but fighter squadrons were to follow in daylight and operate from the captured airfields. In case of failure Student reckoned that his forces would be able to push into Eire, and thus be interned instead of being captured or killed.

Hitler listened attentively to the scheme, but "following his 'wait and see' method, said he must think it over. He then discussed possible operations in the Mediterranean—at Gibralter, Malta, and against the Suez Canal." After that Student withdrew, while Goering continued to confer with Hitler. They travelled back to Berlin the following night, and on parting Goering said: "Don't trouble your-self needlessly about Ulster. The Führer does not wish to invade Britain. From now on Gibraltar will be the main task for you."

Student ended by giving me his personal impressions and reflections on Hitler's attitude to the problem of invasion. "Hitler hesitated to attack—even with the most superior forces—a strong enemy in a prepared position *across the sea.* Such undertakings seemed sinister to him. This was particularly shown in the later cases of Crete and Malta; also in the reverse sense, in the case of "Fortress Europe", which he for a long time considered impregnable. He underestimated the power of the attacker against defended coastlines, and overrated the possibilities of defence behind a water barrier. (Norway was only an "inferior enemy". In that case it was only a question of seizure—which, however, was carried through with great daring.) The problem of *supply and communications* came first with him, and *ruled* all his deliberations. In all airborne and other detached operations his greatest anxiety was that secure land or water communications should be established as quickly as possible. This principle is quite right, but Hitler carried it too far—anyhow in the days of his success.

In those days all undertakings seemed too great a risk to him when it was not possible to lay down exact and absolutely reliable routes of communication. Thus in 1940 he wanted to give up Narvik when the first major crisis occurred.

Student went on to say: "For a possible attack on Great Britain he chose the shortest distances for these reasons. The probability is that he never had a plan for landings beyond the coastal stretch Dover–Land's End. At the conference in January, 1941, I had a definite impression that he was determined to carry out an eventual landing on a *wide front*, not merely on the Dover–Portsmouth sector, and to launch the main attack further west, i.e. Bourne-mouth–Bridport. The 11th Air Corps was to be used accordingly at the narrowest part of the Cornwall–Devon Peninsula for flank protection and forcing access to the Peninsula. But perhaps he wanted to land as far down as Land's End—and the corps was intended for the estab-lishment of communications—or wanted to confine the landing to the Peninsula.

"Moreover it is quite clear to me that, in January 1941, Hitler had not given up the 'Sea-Lion' plan but had only postponed it. Hitler wavered between 'Sea-Lion' —Gibraltar—Russia. Goering wanted 'Sea-Lion' and Gibraltar, but not Russia."

CHAPTER XIV

MISFIRES IN THE MEDITERRANEAN

DISCUSSION with the German generals brought fresh light on many facets of the campaign in North Africa and the war in the Mediterranean as a whole. Here are some of the chief points that came out.

Egypt and the Suez Canal were saved at the time the British forces were weakest, by the Italians' jealousy of the Germans coupled with Hitler's indifference to the opportunity of capturing these keys to the Middle East.

Cyprus was saved by the price the British made the Germans pay for the capture of Crete.

Gibraltar was saved by Franco's reluctance to let the Germans into Spain.

Malta was saved by Hitler's distrust of the Italian Navy.

All that happened during 1941, when Britain's fortunes were at their lowest. In 1942 the tide began to turn, with Russia's sustained resistance to Hitler's invasion, with the entry of America into the war following Japan's assault, and with the growth of Britain's own strength. But there was a long road to travel. It might have been longer but for Hitler's help.

It was Hitler who ensured the British the chance to win such a victory at El Alamein as to decide the war in North Africa. For he forbade his generals to forestall Montgomery's attack by a timely step back that would have preserved them from crushing defeat.

Hitler was drawn, reluctantly, into the Mediterranean. The strongest advocate of that line of operation was Admiral Raeder, who saw very clearly the advantage that might be gained by ousting Britain from her pivotal positions in the

Mediterranean, and the effect it would have on the whole situation. Raeder was supported on this issue by the man whom he most distrusted and despised—Goering. The bitterly opposed heads of the Navy and Air Force were agreed for once, in their common anxiety to divert Hitler from committing Germany to a war with Russia while still engaged with Britain.

Although Hitler was led to embark on a Mediterranean commitment—without foregoing his Russian purpose—his decision was due less to Raeder's arguments than to the pressure of two adverse developments.

The first was Mussolini's sudden invasion of Greece on October 28th—made without warning to his German ally, to snatch some glory for himself. Hitler was furious at the news, since he could see at once that it endangered his own plans. He had wanted to keep Greece neutral, as a safeguard to his flank against British interference in the Balkans and threat to his Rumanian oil supplies. Realizing the hollowness of the Italian show of strength, he now had to face the necessity of taking active measures to ward off British interference on that flank, at the expense of his power of concentration. Mussolini's rash step of independent aggression was most troublesome to Hitler; from it developed his undesired precipitation into a Balkan campaign, and also his subsequent jump on Crete.

The second adverse development was the Italian collapse in North Africa, which started early in December under the impact of the British counterstroke from Egypt.

Thoma gave me an illuminating account of the prelude to Germany's entry into that field. "I was sent to North Africa in October, 1940, to report on the question whether German forces should be sent there, to help the Italians turn the British out of Egypt. After seeing Marshal Graziani, and studying the situation, I made my report. It emphasized that the supply problem was the decisive factor—not only because of the difficulties of the desert, but because of the British Navy's command of the Mediterranean. I said it would not be possible to maintain a large German Army there as well as the Italian Army.

"My conclusion was that, if a force was sent by us, it should be an armoured force. Nothing less than four armoured divisions would suffice to ensure success—and this, I calculated, was also the maximum that could be effectively maintained with supplies in an advance across the desert to the Nile valley. At the same time I said it could only be done by replacing the Italian troops with German. Large numbers could not be supplied, and the vital thing was that every man in the invading force should be of the best possible quality.

"But Badoglio and Graziani opposed the substitution of Germans for Italians. Indeed, at that time they were against having any German troops sent there. They wanted to keep the glory of conquering Egypt for themselves. Mussolini backed their objections. While, unlike them, he wanted some German help, he did not want a predominantly German force."

The importance of this revelation can be better realized if we remember that Thoma's mission to Africa was made two months before O'Connor's brilliant riposte, under Wavell's direction, broke up Graziani's attempted invasion of Egypt. The small and scantily-equipped British forces were capable of smashing the larger but worse equipped Italian Army. But the prospects would have been very dim if a German armoured force had been on the scene.

It is all too likely that a picked force of four armoured divisions, such as Thoma suggested, would have swept into Egypt—any time that winter. For O'Connor's force then consisted of only one armoured and one infantry division, both incompletely equipped .

Now comes another remarkable disclosure. Mussolini got his own way—to defeat—partly because Hitler was not fired by the idea of throwing the British out of Egypt. That was very different to what the British imagined at the time. Yet it may be compared with his equally sur-

THE COAST OF
NORTH AFRICA

MILES

prising attitude to the invasion of England. Thoma was struck by Hitler's indifference, though he was not the sort of man to speculate about the underlying motives.

"When I rendered my report, Hitler said he could not spare more than one armoured division. At that, I told him that it would be better to give up the idea of sending any force at all. My remark made him angry. His idea in offering to send a German force to Africa was political. He feared Mussolini might change sides unless he had a German stiffening. But he wanted to send as small a force as possible." (It is to be noted here that Hitler had already suspended the plans for the invasion of England, and was considering plans for the invasion of Russia.)

Thoma went on to say: "Hitler thought that the Italians were capable of holding their own in Africa, with a little German help. He expected too much of them. I had seen them in Spain, 'fighting' on the same side as we were. Hitler seemed to form his idea of their value from the way their commanders talked when he met them at the dinner-table. When he asked me what I thought of them, I retorted: 'I've seen them on the battlefield, not merely in the Officers' Mess.'" (If Thoma spoke to Hitler like that, it is not surprising that he was out of favour after this talk.) "I told Hitler: 'One British soldier is better than twelve Italians.' I added: 'The Italians are good workers, but they are not fighters. They don't like gun-fire.'"

The German General Staff was also against sending German forces to Africa, either on a big scale or a small scale. According to Thoma, Brauchitsch and Halder did not want to get involved in the Mediterranean at all. "Halder told me that he had tried to impress on Hitler the dangers of extending too far, and had pointedly remarked—'Our danger is that we win all the battles except the last one.'"

But Hitler could not refrain from interfering in the Mediterranean, though he hesitated to go all out there. After Graziani's defeat he sent a picked detachment there, under Rommel, to restore the situation. It was strong enough to frustrate British plans for the conquest of Libya—and to go on frustrating them for more than two years—but not strong enough to be decisive. The battle swayed to and fro, from the spring of 1941 to the autumn of 1942.

Meanwhile Britain's position in the Mediterranean was subject to serious threats elsewhere, though they never matured. That has tended to conceal how deadly they might have been.

The most serious was the projected attack on Gibraltar —which could have barred the Western Mediterranean to Britain. Warlimont told me: "The plan of capturing Gibraltar was dropped when, in mid-December, General Franco informed Admiral Canaris that he no longer agreed to this project, which had been the object of discussions between Franco and Hitler at Hendaye in October, 1940. This sudden refusal came as a surprise to Hitler as, in accordance with the previous understanding, Canaris had been sent to Spain chiefly for fixing the date of the German advance into Spain for early January, 1941." Franco did not definitely refuse, but procrastinated, arguing that it was "impossible for Spain to enter the war on the suggested date"—giving as reasons "the continued menace of the British fleet, incompleteness of Spain's own military preparations, and absolute inadequacy of Spain's provisioning."

In default of permission to pass through Spain, Hitler's mind turned to the possibility of hopping over it. Student told me that in January he was instructed to work out a plan for capturing Gibraltar from the air, by a parachute descent. But after studying the problem he came to the conclusion that it was too big a job to be done by the parachute forces alone. His summing up was, he said: "Gibraltar cannot be taken if the neutrality of Spain is observed by us." His conclusion was accepted, and the project was shelved.

Hitler's attention was henceforth devoted to preparation

for the invasion of Russia and the preliminary step of occupying Greece to keep out the British. Because of fresh developments that step had to be expanded, much to his annoyance, into a bigger move to deal with Yugo-Slavia. Moreover, the Germans' swift success in overrunning both Yugo-Slavia and Greece in April, and evicting the British army which had been landed in Greece, did not solve the problem of safeguarding that flank as effectively as a neutral zone would have done. Still cursing Mussolini's short-sighted initiative, Hitler was led to take further steps to extend the safety curtain and shut out British interference.

From the O.K.W. angle Warlimont said: "When the occupation was completed the "National Defence" directorate had orders from Jodl, emanating from Hitler, to investigate from a strategical point of view whether Crete or Malta should be taken. Our judgment was in favour of Malta. To Hitler, however, Crete seemed much more important—because this island closed the Ægean Sea, and offered a link in a further advance to the Suez area." In comment on the sequel to the capture of Crete, Warlimont added: "Rather soon it became evident that the German Air Force no longer disposed of sufficient strength to avail itself of the advantages offered by the island of Crete as a capital air base in the Eastern Mediterranean. Besides, it turned out to be impossible to supply Rommel's army by way of Crete—because the railway to Athens hardly covered the needs within Greece, and almost no ships were available."

More light on the origins of the project was shed by Student, who made the surprising disclosure that Hitler was not at first keen about the stroke that captured Crete—and gave the British such a shock in the Eastern Mediterranean.

"He wanted to break off the Balkan campaign after reaching the south of Greece. When I heard this, I flew to see Goering and proposed the plan of capturing Crete by airborne forces alone. Goering—who was always easy to enthuse—was quick to see the possibilities of the idea, and sent me on to Hitler. I saw him on April 21st. When I first explained the project Hitler said: 'It sounds all right, but I don't think it's practicable.' But I managed to convince him in the end.

"In the operation we used our one Parachute Division, our one Glider Regiment and the 5th Mountain Division, which had no previous experience of being transported by air. The 22nd Air-landing Division, which had the experience of the Dutch campaign, had been flown to Ploesti in March, to protect the Rumanian oilfields, as the Führer was afraid of sabotage there. He was so concerned with this danger that he refused to release the division for the Crete operation." (Warlimont, however, said: "The true reason was that we did not dispose of any means of transportation in the area to bring the division to Southern Greece in time for the attack.")

The air support was provided by the dive-bombers and fighters of Richthofen's 8th Air Corps, which had played such a vital part in forcing the entry into Belgium and France in turn. Student said: "I asked that this should be placed under my command, as well as the air-borne forces, but my request was refused. Then the higher direction of the whole operation was entrusted to General Lohr, who had been in command of all the air forces taking part in the Balkan campaign. However, I worked out all the plans for the operation—and was allowed a free hand in this respect. The 8th Air Corps was excellent, but its action would have been more effective if it had been placed under my direct control.

"No troops came by sea. Such a reinforcement had been intended originally, but the only sea transport available was a number of Greek caiques. It was then arranged that a convoy of these small vessels was to carry the heavier arms for the expedition—anti-aircraft and anti-tank guns, the artillery and some tanks—together with two battalions of the 5th Mountain Division. Escorted by Italian torpedo-boats, they were to sail to Melos, and wait there until we had discovered the whereabouts of the British fleet. When they reached Melos, they were told that the British fleet was still at Alexandria—whereas it was actually on the way to Crete. The convoy sailed for Crete, ran into the fleet, and was scattered. The Luftwaffe avenged this setback by 'pulling a lot of hair' out of the British Navy's scalp. But our operations on land, in Crete, were much handicapped by the absence of the heavier weapons on which we had reckoned."

Student dwelt on the ill-effects of another mischance, dating back a year earlier. "During the airborne operation against 'Fortress Holland' a German unit carried with it important parts of my operational orders, which were captured by the Dutch on Ypenburg aerodrome near The Hague. From these valuable documents the British quickly ascertained the principles of attack, tactics, and training methods of the new German airborne troops— and used this information in an exemplary manner for their own defence. Unfortunately these facts remained unknown to me until they were discovered from documents captured in Crete. They were one of the most important causes for the heavy German losses in Crete. Had I previously known how much the enemy already knew about us, I would have used different tactics for the attack on the airfields and thus avoided the British defences."

He subsequently added that the main document was a British manual on defence against parachute troops, issued in 1940, which reproduced "important parts of the German operation orders for the airborne attack against 'Fortress Holland', particularly for the capture of airfields by *coup de main*". This manual was found in "one of the caves near Canea (Akortiri Peninsula) where General Freyberg had his headquarters"—but only "after the fighting was over". Until that moment Student was unaware that his operation orders of May, 1940, had fallen into enemy hands, as "the loss had not been reported".

Student may overrate the effect of that accident on the

British anti-paratroop tactics, for there was a good deal of information from other sources and the tactics were based on commonsense principles. But he may be justified in his contention that he would have altered his own tactics if he had known about the lost orders. "Planning the attack, at the beginning of May, I had at first the idea of dropping the paratroops south of Maleme and Heraklion, or the whole mass south and south-west of Maleme only, and making an ordinary ground attack on the airfield—with the help of the air force. There were large plateaux suitable for dropping zones 'outside' the enemy. This method would have been employed by me had I known of the British defence booklet."

Dealing with the actual operation, as carried out, Student said: "At no point on May 20th did we succeed completely in occupying an airfield. The greatest degree of progress was achieved on Maleme airfield, where the valuable Assault Regiment fought against picked New Zealand troops. The night of May 20th–21st was critical for the German Command. I had to make a momentous decision. I decided to use the mass of the parachute-reserves, still at my disposal, for the final capture of Maleme airfield. If the enemy had made an organized counter-attack during this night or the morning of May 21st, he would probably have succeeded in routing the much battered and exhausted remnants of the Assault Regiment —especially as these were badly handicapped by shortage of ammunition.

"But the New Zealanders made only isolated counter-attacks. I heard later that the British Command expected, besides the airborne venture, the arrival of the main German forces by sea on the coast between Maleme and Canea, and consequently maintained their forces in occupation of the coast. At this decisive period the British Command did not take the risk of sending these forces to Maleme. On the 21st the German reserves succeeded in capturing the airfield and village of Maleme. In the evening the 1st Mountain Battalion could be landed, as the first air-transported troops—and so the battle for Crete was won by Germany." (By the 27th the British forces were in full retreat to the south coast, whence the survivors were evacuated to Egypt.)

"Although we succeeded in capturing the island, our casualties were heavy. We lost 4,000 killed and missing, apart from wounded, out of 22,000 men we dropped on the island—14,000 of these were parachute troops and the rest belonged to the Mountain division. Much of the loss was due to bad landings—there were very few suitable spots in Crete, and the prevailing wind blew from the interior towards the sea. For fear of dropping the troops in the sea, the pilots tended to drop them too far inland—some of them actually in the British lines. The weapon-containers often fell wide of the troops, which was another handicap that contributed to our excessive casualties. The few British tanks that were there shook us badly at the start—it was lucky there were not more than two dozen. The infantry, mostly New Zealanders, put up a stiff fight, though taken by surprise.

"The Führer was very upset by the heavy losses suffered by the parachute units, and came to the conclusion that their surprise value had passed. After that he often said to me: 'The day of parachute troops is over.'

"He would not believe reports that the British and Americans were developing airborne forces. The fact that none were used in the St. Nazaire and Dieppe raids confirmed his opinion. He said to me: 'There, you see! They are not raising such forces. I was right.' He only changed his mind after the Allied conquest of Sicily in 1943. Impressed by the way the Allies had used them there, he ordered an expansion of our own airborne forces. But that change of mind came too late—because by then you had command of the air, and airborne troops could not be effectively used in face of a superior air force."

Returning to the events of 1941, Student said: "When I got Hitler to accept the Crete plan, I also proposed that we should follow it up by capturing Cyprus from the air, and then a further jump from Cyprus to capture the Suez Canal. Hitler did not seem averse to the idea, but would not commit himself definitely to the project—his mind was so occupied with the coming invasion of Russia. After the shock of the heavy losses in Crete, he refused to attempt another big airborne effort. I pressed the idea on him repeatedly, but without avail.

"A year later, however, he was persuaded to adopt a plan for capturing Malta. This was in April, 1942. The attack was to be carried out in conjunction with the Italians. My airborne forces, together with the Italian ones, were to be dropped on the island and capture a bridgehead, which would then be reinforced by a large Italian sea-borne force—of six to eight divisions. My force comprised our one existing Parachute division, three additional regiments that had not yet been organized as a division, and an Italian parachute division.

"I hoped to carry out the plan not later than August—it depended on suitable weather—and spent some months in Rome preparing it. In June I was summoned to Hitler's headquarters for the final conference on the operation. Unfortunately, the day before I got there, Hitler had seen General Crüwell, who was just back from North Africa, and had been given a very unfavourable account of the state of the Italian forces and their morale.

"Hitler at once took alarm. He felt that if the British Fleet appeared on the scene, all the Italian ships would bolt for their home ports—and leave the German airborne forces stranded. He decided to abandon the plan of attacking Malta."

That decision was the more significant because Rommel had just won a striking victory over the British in North Africa, turning the Eighth Army out of the Gazala position and capturing Tobruk. Exploiting its confusion Rommel pursued it helter-skelter through the Western Desert. He came within reach of the Nile valley before he was checked on the Alamein line, at the beginning of July.

That was the worst crisis which the British passed through in the Middle East. The situation was made all the more grave by the simultaneous collapse of Russia's southern armies in face of Hitler's new drive to the Caucasus. At Alamein, Rommel was hammering on the front door to the Middle East; in the Caucasus, Kleist was threatening the back door.

Thoma declared, however, that the threat was accidental rather than intended. "The great pincer movement against the Middle East, which your people imagined to be in progress, was never a serious plan. It was vaguely discussed in Hitler's entourage, but our General Staff never agreed with it, nor regarded it as practicable."

Even the threat to Egypt only developed haphazardly —out of the unexpected collapse of the Eighth Army in the Gazala-Tobruk battle. Rommel's forces were nothing like strong enough to attempt the conquest of Egypt. But he could not resist the temptation to push on in the flush of victory. That was his undoing.

I asked Thoma whether it was true that Rommel was so confident of reaching the Suez Canal as appeared in some of the remarks he made to his officers. Thoma replied: "I'm sure he was not! He only expressed such confidence to encourage his troops, especially the Italians. He soon cooled down when he was checked by the British on the Alamein position. He knew that he needed surprise in order to throw the British off their balance, and he didn't see how he could possibly achieve a fresh surprise in face of the Alamein defences. Moreover he knew that British reinforcements were continuously arriving.

"Rommel realized that he had gone too far—with his limited forces and difficult supply line—but his success had caused such a sensation that he could not draw back. Hitler would not let him. The result was that he had to stay there until the British had gathered overwhelming forces to smash him."

Thoma said that he had learnt most of this from Rommel and Rommel's chief subordinates. He himself had only gone to Africa, from Russia, in September. "When I received orders to relieve Rommel, who was sick with jaundice, I telephoned back that I did not want to take the job, saying: 'See what I wrote two years ago.' But back came a message that the Führer insisted on my going, as a personal order, so nothing more could be done. I arrived in Africa about September 20th, and spent a few days discussing the situation with Rommel—who then went for treatment to Wiener Neustadt, near Vienna. A fortnight later General Stumme arrived on the scene, having been appointed to take charge of the African theatre as a whole. This meant that I only had command of our troops at the front, facing the El Alamein position, which limited my capacity to improve the administrative organization. Soon afterwards Stumme had a stroke, and died. All this complicated our measures to meet the British offensive.

"I did what I could to improve our dispositions, under difficult conditions, as any idea of withdrawing before the British offensive opened was vetoed. But we should have had to retreat in spite of Hitler's order but for the fact that we were able to feed our troops with the supplies which we had captured from your stores at Tobruk. They kept us going."

On hearing this, I remarked that it looked as if the loss of Tobruk—disastrous as it seemed at the time—had really helped the British to win the war in North Africa. For if the German forces had retreated from Alamein before Montgomery struck, it was unlikely that they would have been so decisively smashed as they were. This point did not seem to have occurred to Thoma.

Thoma then gave me his impressions of the battle, which opened on October 23, 1942. He said that the

Eighth Army's immense superiority of strength in all the decisive weapons made its victory almost a certainty before the battle opened. "I reckoned that you had 1,200 aircraft available at a time when we were reduced to barely a dozen. Rommel arrived back from Vienna three days after the offensive had begun. It was too late for him to change any of the dispositions. He was in a nervy state, being still ill, and was very apt to change his mind. The British pressure grew heavier, straining us to the limit.

"When it was clear that we could not hope to check the British break-through, we decided to carry out a withdrawal, in two stages, to a line near Daba, 50 miles to the west. That might have saved us. The first stage of the withdrawal was to be made on the night of November 3. It had already begun when a wireless order came from Hitler forbidding any such withdrawal, and insisting that we must hold our old positions at all costs. This meant that our troops had actually to go forward again—to fight a hopeless battle that could only prove fatal."

Thoma then related to me how he himself came to be captured. He had been racing in a tank from one critical point to another during the battle, being hit several times, and in the end was trapped when his tank caught fire and he was pitched out. "I felt it was a fitting finish." He showed me his cap, which had several holes in it—symbols of lucky escapes. With a note of regret he said he had only been able to take part in 24 tank fights during the war—in Poland, France, Russia, and Africa. "I managed to fight in 192 tank actions during the Spanish Civil War."

He was succeeded in command of the Africa Corps by Bayerlein, who managed to extricate what was left of it, evaded the British pursuit, and skilfully conducted the retreat to Tripolitania—under Rommel's general direction.

After being captured Thoma was taken to see Montgomery, and with him discussed the battle over the dinner-table. "Instead of asking me for information, he said he would tell me the state of our forces, their supplies and their dispositions. I was staggered at the exactness of his knowledge, particularly of our deficiencies and shipping losses. He seemed to know as much about our position as I did myself."

Then, speaking of the victor's handling of the battle, he said: "I thought he was very cautious, considering his immensely superior strength, but"—Thoma paused, then added with emphasis—"he is the only Field-Marshal in this war who won all his battles.

"In modern mobile warfare," he concluded, "the tactics are not the main thing. The decisive factor is the organization of one's resources—to maintain the momentum."

CHAPTER XV

HITLER'S INVASION OF RUSSIA

HITLER's gamble in Russia failed because he was not bold enough, and also through conflicting views in the German Command about the direction to be taken. At the critical stage, time was lost that could never be regained. After that he ruined himself, and Germany, because he could not bring himself to cut his losses.

It is the story of Napoleon over again—but with important differences. While Hitler missed the chance of capturing Moscow, he came nearer decisive victory, conquered far more of Russia, and maintained his army there much longer, only to reach an even more catastrophic end.

When launching the invasion in June, 1941, Hitler had counted on destroying the bulk of the Red Army before reaching the Dnieper. When that hope was disappointed—because the Russians proved tougher than expected—he and his generals disagreed on the question of what to do next. Brauchitsch and Halder wanted to continue the advance on Moscow, but Hitler preferred to clear up the situation in the South first, and got his way. After a great victory there, the Kiev encirclement, he let them have their way. The delayed advance on Moscow started with another great victory, but then became bogged in the autumn mud, and finally foundered in the winter snow. It had been launched too late.

But that was not the only cause of failure revealed in what the German generals told me. Sometimes they themselves did not perceive the conclusions, having been too deep "in the trees to see the wood". But they did provide the facts from which conclusions could be drawn.

Here is the most startling of all. What saved Russia

above all was not her modern progress, but her backwardness. If the Soviet régime had given her a road system comparable to that of western countries, she would probably have been overrun in quick time. The German mechanized forces were baulked by the badness of her roads.

But this conclusion has a converse. The Germans lost the chance of victory because they had based their mobility on wheels instead of on tracks. On these mud-roads the wheeled transport was bogged when the tanks could move on.

Panzer forces with *tracked* transport might have overrun Russia's vital centres long before the autumn, despite the bad roads. World War I had shown this need to anyone who used his eyes and his imagination. Britain was the birthplace of the tank, and those of us here who preached the idea of mobile mechanized warfare after 1914–18 had urged that the new model forces should have cross-country vehicles throughout. The Germany Army went further than our own army, or any other, in adopting the idea. But it fell short in the vital respect of developing such cross-country transport. In brief, the German Army was more modern than any other in 1940–41, but missed its goal because it had not yet caught up with ideas that were twenty years old.

The German generals had studied their profession with the greatest thoroughness, devoting themselves from youth on to the mastery of its technique, with little regard to politics and still less to the world outside. Men of that type are apt to be extremely competent, but not imaginative. It was only late in the war that the bolder minds of the tank school of thought were allowed free rein, and then it was too late—fortunately for other countries.

Now for the main points of their evidence on the war in Russia.

THE EFFECT OF THE BALKAN CAMPAIGN

Preliminary to the issues of the Russian campaign itself is the question whether the Greek campaign caused a vital delay in its launching. British Government spokes-men have claimed that the despatch of General Wilson's force to Greece, though it ended in a hurried evacuation, was justified because it produced six weeks' postponement of the invasion of Russia. This claim has been challenged, and the venture condemned as a political gamble, by a number of soldiers who were well acquainted with the Mediterranean situation—notably General de Guingand, later Montgomery's Chief of Staff, who was on the Joint Planning Staff in Cairo.

They argued at the time, and argue still more strongly now, that a golden opportunity of exploiting the defeat of the Italians in Cyrenaica, and capturing Tripoli before German help arrived, was sacrificed in order to switch inadequate forces to Greece that had no real chance of saving her from a German invasion.[1] They emphasize that the Greek leaders were very dubious about accepting the British Government's offer to intervene, and were jockeyed into acceptance by Mr. Eden's persuasiveness, supported by an inflated impression of the extent of help that Britain could provide.

The historian must recognize that this military view was confirmed by events. In three weeks, Greece was overrun and the British thrown out of the Balkans, while the reduced British force in Cyrenaica was also driven out by the German Africa Corps under Rommel, which had been enabled to land at Tripoli. These defeats meant a damaging loss of prestige and prospect for Britain, while bringing misery on the Greek people. Even if the Greek campaign was found to have retarded the invasion of Russia that fact would not justify the British Government's decision, for such an object was not in their minds at the time.

[1] Warlimont remarked: "At O.K.W. we could not understand at the time why the British did not exploit the difficulties of the Italians in Cyrenaica by pushing on to Tripoli. There was nothing to check them.

It is of historical interest, however, to discover whether the campaign actually had such an indirect and unforeseen effect. The most definite piece of evidence in support of this lies in the fact that Hitler had originally ordered preparations for the attack on Russia to be completed by May 15th, whereas at the end of March the tentative date was deferred about a month, and then fixed for June 22nd. Field-Marshal von Rundstedt told me how the preparations of his Army Group had been hampered by the late arrival of the armoured divisions which had been employed in the Balkan campaign, and that this was the key-factor in the delay, in combination with the weather.

Field-Marshal von Kleist, who commanded the armoured forces under Rundstedt, was still more explicit. "It is true," he said, "that the forces employed in the Balkans were not large compared with our total strength, but the proportion of tanks employed there was high. The bulk of the tanks that came under me for the offensive against the Russian front in Southern Poland had taken part in the Balkan offensive, and needed overhaul, while their crews needed a rest. A large number of them had driven as far south as the Peloponnese, and had to be brought back all that way."

The views of Field-Marshals von Rundstedt and von Kleist were naturally conditioned by the extent to which the offensive on their front was dependent on the return of these armoured divisions. I found that other generals attached less importance to the effect of the Balkan campaign. They emphasized that the main rôle in the offensive against Russia was allotted to Field-Marshal von Bock's Central Army Group in Northern Poland, and that the chances of victory principally turned on its progress. A diminution of Rundstedt's forces, for the secondary rôle of his Army Group, might not have affected the decisive issue, as the Russian forces could not be easily switched. It might even have checked Hitler's inclination to switch his effort southward in the second stage of the invasion—an inclination that, as we shall see, had a fatally retarding effect on the prospects of reaching Moscow before the winter. The invasion, at a pinch, could have been launched without awaiting the reinforcement of Rundstedt's Army Group by the arrival of the divisions from the Balkans. But, in the event, that argument for delay was reinforced by doubts whether the ground was dry enough to attempt an earlier start. General Halder said that the weather conditions were not suitable before the time when the invasion was actually launched.

The retrospective views of generals are not, however, a sure guide as to what might have been decided if there had been no Balkan complications. Once the tentative date had been postponed on that account the scales were weighted against any idea of striking before the extra divisions had returned from that quarter.

But it was not the Greek campaign that caused the postponement. Hitler had already reckoned with that commitment when the invasion of Greece was inserted in the 1941 programme, as a preliminary to the invasion of Russia. The decisive factor in the change of timing was the unexpected *coup d' état* in Yugo-Slavia that took place on March 27th, when General Simovich and his confederates overthrew the Government which had just previously committed Yugo-Slavia to a pact with the Axis. Hitler was so incensed by the upsetting news as to decide, that same day, to stage an overwhelming offensive against Yugo-Slavia. The additional forces, land and air, required for such a stroke involved a greater commitment than the Greek campaign alone would have done, and thus impelled Hitler to take his fuller and more fateful decision to put off the intended start of the attack on Russia.

It was the fear, not the fact, of a British landing that had prompted Hitler to move into Greece, and the outcome set his mind at rest. The landing did not even check the existing Government of Yugo-Slavia from making terms with Hitler. On the other hand, it may have encouraged Simovich in making his successful bid to overthrow the government and defy Hitler—less successfully.

Some further information on these preliminary events was provided by Blumentritt after enquiries he made from Halder and Grieffenberg—after being Chief of Operations at O.K.H., Grieffenburg became Chief of Staff to List's 12th Army which conducted the Balkan campaign.

"Remembering the Allied occupation of Salonika, 1915–18, Hitler feared that in 1941 the British would again land in Salonika or on the coast of Southern Thrace. This would place them in the rear of Army Group "South" when it advanced eastward into Southern Russia. Hitler assumed that the British would try to advance into Bulgaria, Rumania, and Yugo-Slavia as before—and recalled how at the end of World War I the Allied Balkan Army had materially contributed to the decision.

"He therefore resolved, as a precautionary measure before beginning operations against Russia, to occupy the coast of Southern Thrace between Salonika and Dedeagach (Alexandropolis). The 12th Army (List) was earmarked for this operation, and included Kleist's Panzer Group. The army assembled in Rumania, crossed the Danube into Bulgaria, and from there was to pierce the Metaxas Line —advancing with its right wing on Salonika and its left wing on Dedeagach. Once the coast was reached, the Bulgarians were to take over the main protection of the coast, where only a few German troops were to remain. The mass of the 12th Army, especially Kleist's Panzer Group, was then to turn about and be sent northwards via Rumania, to go into action on the southern sector of the Eastern Front. The original plan did not envisage the occupation of (the main part of) Greece.

"When this plan was shown to King Boris of Bulgaria, he pointed out that he did not trust Yugo-Slavia. He was afraid that danger might threaten the right flank of the 12th Army from the Yugo-Slav area. German representatives, however, assured King Boris that in view of the 1939 pact between Yugo-Slavia and Germany they anticipated no danger from that quarter. They had the impression that King Boris was not quite convinced.

"In fact, he was proved right. For when the 12th Army was about to begin operations from Bulgaria according to plan, a coup that led to the abdication of the Regent, Prince Paul, was launched in Belgrade quite suddenly and unexpectedly, just before the movement of troops began. It appeared that certain Belgrade circles disagreed with Prince Paul's pro-German policy and wanted to side with the Western powers. Whether the Western powers or the U.S.S.R. backed the coup beforehand, we as soldiers cannot gauge. But at any rate it was not staged by Hitler! On the contrary it came as a very unpleasant surprise, and nearly upset the whole plan of operations of the 12th Army in Bulgaria. For example, Kleist's panzer divisions had to proceed immediately from Bulgaria north-westward against Belgrade. Another improvisation was an operation by the 2nd Army (Weichs), with quickly gathered formations based on Carinthia and Styria, southward into Yugo-Slavia. The flare-up in the Balkans compelled a postponement of the Russian campaign, from May to June. To this extent, therefore, the Belgrade coup materially influenced the start of the attack on Russia.

"But the weather also played an important part in 1941, and that was *accidental*. East of the Bug-San line in Poland, ground operations are very restricted until May, because most roads are muddy and the country generally is a morass. The many unregulated rivers cause widespread flooding. The farther one goes east the more pronounced do these disadvantages become, particularly in the boggy forest regions of the Rokitno (Pripet) and Beresina. Thus even in normal times movement is very restricted before mid-May. But 1941 was an exceptional year. The winter had lasted longer. As late as the beginning of June the Bug in front of our army was over its banks for miles."

Similar conditions prevailed farther north. Manstein, who was then in East Prussia commanding a spearhead panzer corps, told me that heavy rain fell there during late May and early June. It is evident that if the invasion had been launched earlier the prospect would have been poor, and very doubtful whether an earlier date would have been practicable, quite apart from the Balkan hindrance. The weather of 1940 had been all too favourable to the invasion of the West, but the weather of 1941 operated in reverse against the invasion of the East.

THE IMPULSE TO INVADE RUSSIA

As a next stage in my enquiry I sought such light as the generals could shed on the question why Hitler invaded Russia. It was a dim light. Although the project had been incubating in his mind since July, 1940, and had taken definite form before the end of that year, it was remarkable how hazy most of his generals were about the reasons for a step that had decided their fate. Most of them had been apprehensive when they were told of the decision, but they were told very little, and told very late. Hitler was clever in the way he kept his commanders in separate "water-tight compartments"—each was told only what Hitler considered necessary for him to know in carrying out his own localized task. They were almost like prisoners on piecework in a row of cells.

As I heard from all of them that Rundstedt had been the strongest opponent of the invasion—and the first to urge its abandonment—I was anxious to get his views on the question. He told me: "Hitler insisted we must strike before Russia became too strong, and that she was much nearer striking than we imagined. He provided us with information that she was planning to launch an offensive herself that same summer, of 1941. For my part,

I was very doubtful about this—and I found little sign of it when we crossed the frontier. Many of us who had feared such a stroke had been reassured by the way the Russians had remained quiet during our battles in the West, in 1940, when we had our hands full. I felt that our best way of guarding against the danger was simply to strengthen our frontier defence, leaving the Russians to take the offensive if they chose. That would be the best test of their intentions, and less risk than launching into Russia."

I asked him further about the reasons that had led him to discredit Hitler's belief in an imminent Russian offensive. He replied: "In the first place, the Russians appeared to be taken by surprise when we crossed the frontier. On my front we found no signs of offensive preparations in the forward zone, though there were some farther back. They had twenty-five divisions in the Carpathian sector, facing the Hungarian frontier, and I had expected that they would swing round and strike at my right flank as it advanced. Instead, they retreated. I deduced from this that they were not in a state of readiness for offensive operations, and hence that the Russian Command had not been intending to launch an offensive at an early date."

I next questioned General Blumentritt, who at the time was Chief of Staff to Kluge's 4th Army on the main line of attack, and who at the end of the year became Deputy Chief of the General Staff at O.K.H.—where he was in close touch with the records, and the "post-mortems" into the course of the invasion.

Blumentritt told me that the Commander-in-Chief, Brauchitsch, and the Chief of the General Staff, Halder, as well as Rundstedt, were opposed to the attempt to invade Russia. "All three realized the difficulties presented by the nature of the country from their experiences in the 1914–18 war—above all, the difficulties of movement, reinforcement, and supply. Field-Marshal von

Rundstedt asked Hitler bluntly: 'Have you weighed up what you are undertaking in an attack on Russia?' "

Hitler was not moved from his decision. But he was brought to declare that the Russian campaign must be decided west of the Dnieper. He admitted beforehand the difficulties of bringing up, and maintaining, sufficient reinforcements if the advance had to be extended much farther in the face of strong resistance. While the panzer forces on the main line of advance had been told to drive ahead to Smolensk and the Desna, beyond the Dnieper, the idea was that they would create confusion and cut communications while the slow-moving mass of the by-passed Russian armies was rounded up behind them by the German infantry armies. When Hitler found that the Russian armies were not trapped and annihilated west of the Dnieper he was led, like Napoleon, to push on deeper into Russia. That was the most fateful decision of the whole campaign. It was made fatal by Hitler's own indecision as to the best direction to take then.

Further sidelights came in discussion with Field-Marshal von Kleist, who remarked that he was only told of Hitler's intention to invade Russia a short time before the attack was launched. "It was the same with the other high commanders. We were told the Russian armies were about to take the offensive, and it was essential for Germany to remove the menace. It was explained to us that the Führer could not proceed with other plans while this threat loomed close, as too large a part of the German forces would be pinned down in the east keeping guard. It was argued that attack was the only way for us to remove the risks of a Russian attack."

Kleist went on: "We did not underrate the Red Army, as is commonly imagined. The last German military attaché in Moscow, General Köstring—a very able man—had kept us well informed about the state of the Russian Army. But Hitler refused to credit his information.

RUSSIA IN EUROPE

0   100   200   300   400   500 MILES

"Hopes of victory were largely built on the prospect that the invasion would produce a political upheaval in Russia. Most of us generals realized beforehand that if the Russians chose to fall back there was very little chance of achieving a final victory without the help of such an upheaval. Too high hopes were built on the belief that Stalin would be overthrown by his own people if he suffered heavy defeats. The belief was fostered by the Führer's political advisers, and we, as soldiers, didn't know enough about the political side to dispute it.

"There were no preparations for a prolonged struggle. Everything was based on the idea of a decisive result before the autumn." The Germans paid a terrific price for that short view, when winter came.

As regards Hitler's motives for the invasion, a more illuminating view was given me, later, by Warlimont who being at O.K.W., was more closely in touch with the stream of Hitler's thought during the months before it was canalized into a definite decision to direct his forces against Russia.

"The answer to the question why Hitler invaded Russia is, in my opinion, that he found himself in exactly the same situation as Napoleon. Both men looked upon Britain as their strongest and most dangerous adversary. Both could not persuade themselves to attempt the overthrow of England by invading the British Isles. Both believed, however, that Great Britain could be forced to come to terms with the dominating continental power, if the prospect vanished for the British to gain an armoured arm as an ally on the Continent. Both of them suspected Russia of becoming this ally of Britain's. Both recognized this danger to be gradually increasing with the prolongation of the war. Both were convinced that the central European power could not allow the peripheral powers (Britain and Russia) to wait for the most favourable moment in order

to quench the heart of the Continent between them.
Therefore both men, Hitler as well as Napoleon, were of
the opinion that they had to strike in time—being,
consciously or not, in a position of strategical defence.

"These considerations may have been supported, so far
as Hitler was concerned, by a fateful underrating of
Russian military strength and her war potential—prevailing at least in Hitler's entourage. This opinion of
mine is borne out by a statement, probably emanating
from Hitler himself, which was made by Keitel and Jodl in
turn, when they were dealing with the Italians and Finns
prior to the Russian campaign—it read: 'The war has been
won already; it has only to be terminated.'" Warlimont
added that Jodl often made similar remarks in his own circle.

"Intelligence of Russia's military strength always was
extremely poor," Warlimont went on to say, while pointing
out that the estimates discussed in conference, and on
which planning was based, were prepared by the General
Staff—not by Keitel and Jodl. "Only the O.K.H., by its
General Staff work, was able to evaluate the intelligence
reports, and would never have allowed Keitel to promulgate
the results."

It will be observed in Warlimont's account that the
tendency to underrate the Russian strength was not confined to Hitler, nor even to his entourage—contrary to
what Kleist had said (Kleist himself, I found, was always
inclined to rate the Red Army more highly than his
fellows did). The General Staff may not have underrated
the difficulties of a campaign in Russia, but they certainly
under-estimated the number of divisions that the Russians
could bring to meet them. That is clear from documentary
evidence. Very significant is an entry in Halder's diary
after the campaign had been in progress for two months:
"We under-estimated Russia; we reckoned with 200
divisions, but now we have already identified 360."

While the German Intelligence under-estimated Russia's forces, what it did report provided substance for apprehensiveness about the impending danger of a Russian attack. The concentration of divisions in Western Russia (and Russian-occupied Poland) went on rising steadily during the first half of 1941, and by May was double what it had been before the outbreak of war with Poland. The concentration of air force and expansion of airfields was also very marked. All this fomented Hitler's fears. When he talked to his generals and others about the likelihood that the Russians were planning to attack him before the end of the summer, there is little doubt that he was expressing fears that he actually felt, and which a number of his advisers shared. That does not necessarily mean that the fears were correct—Germans have always been apt to overlook the natural reaction that their own measures cause in other people, and this was particularly true of Hitler. On the other hand, it is understandable that with every report of Russia's rising numbers in the frontier zone, Hitler might feel that time was running short.

Even so, it is an astonishing fact that Hitler embarked on the invasion of Russia in face of the knowledge that his forces would be fewer than those opposing him at the outset, and were bound to be increasingly outnumbered if the campaign were prolonged. That alone made the invasion an offensive gamble without precedent in modern history. When Hitler's plan had been unfolded to the generals in February, they had been perturbed by Halder's estimate of the comparative strengths on either side. For, even on his figures, the Red Army had the equivalent of 155 divisions available in Western Russia, whereas the invading forces could muster only 121. (Actually this estimate of the forces immediately available was under the mark.) The assurance that the German forces were "far superior in quality" did not suffice to allay their qualms.

The advantage of the initiative enabled the Germans to

produce a moderate superiority of strength at their chosen centre of gravity—the sector north of the Pripet Marshes where Field-Marshal von Bock's Central Army Group advanced astride the Minsk–Moscow highway. It was given two panzer groups (9 armoured and 7 motorized divisions) to act as spearheads, and 51 divisions in all. But Leeb's Northern Army Group near the Baltic—with one panzer group (3 armoured and 3 motorized divisions) and 30 divisions in all—had bare equality to the opposition. Rundstedt's Southern Army Group was allotted one panzer group (5 armoured and 3 motorized divisions) and 37 divisions in all—and had to play its part with a marked inferiority of strength, especially in armour—the most essential element. Kleist told me that his Panzer Army, which formed Rundstedt's spearhead, comprised only 600 tanks. "That will probably seem incredible to you, but it was all we could assemble after the return of the divisions from Greece. Budenny's Army Group, facing us in the South, had some 2,400 tanks. Apart from surprise, we depended for success simply on the superior training and skill of the troops. These were decisive assets until the Russians gained experience."

In the light of events it becomes clear that Hitler's belief in the power of technical quality to discount superior numbers had more justification than appeared in the final issue of the war. The test of battlefield results for long bore out his assurance of the decisive advantage of quality over quantity. It brought his gamble dangerously near fulfilment. The chances would have been greater if the aim had been more clearly visualized and defined beforehand. Divergence of view on the German side was of great help to Russian resistance in producing a miscarriage of the invasion.

CHAPTER XVI

HOW THE INVASION FELL SHORT OF MOSCOW

"The fog of war" is a phrase that normally signifies the natural unclearness of the situation in war. But in 1941 there was an extra layer of mist that vitally affected the course of events. For in the highest headquarters of the invading army there was an amazing state of haziness about the aims to be pursued. Hitler and the Army Command had different ideas from the start of the planning, and never properly reconciled them.

Hitler wished to secure Leningrad as a primary objective, thus clearing his Baltic flank and linking up with the Finns, and tended to disparage the importance of Moscow. But, with a keen sense of economic factors, he also wanted to secure the agricultural wealth of the Ukraine and the industrial area on the Lower Dnieper. The two objectives were extremely wide apart, and thus entailed entirely separate lines of operation. That was essentially different from the flexibility inherent in operating on a single and central line of operation that threatens alternative objectives.

Brauchitsch and Halder wanted to concentrate on the Moscow line of advance—not for the sake of capturing the capital but because they felt that this line offered the best chance of destroying the mass of Russia's forces which they "expected to find on the way to Moscow". In Hitler's view that course carried the risk of driving the Russians into a general retreat eastward, out of reach. As Brauchitsch and Halder agreed with him about the importance of avoiding this risk, and as he agreed with them about the importance of destroying the enemy's main forces by an early "Kesselschlacht" (battle of encirclement), they shelved a decision on further aims until the first phase of the invasion was completed.

Brauchitsch by his tendency to avoid "meeting trouble half-way" in dealing with Hitler, was apt to run into worse trouble in the end. In this case, by putting off the issue he ran into the trouble midway in the campaign. Moreover, it is evident from the original directive for "Barbarossa" —approved by Hitler and issued on December 18th, 1940— that Hitler's ideas had been clear, while Brauchitsch had bowed to them.

In this directive the aims were thus defined:

"In the zone of operations, divided by the Pripet marshes into a southern and a northern sector, the main effort will be made north of this area. Two army groups will be provided here.

"The more southerly of these two army groups— the Centre one of the front as a whole—will be given the task of annihilating the enemy's forces in White Russia by advancing from the area around and north of Warsaw with specially strong armoured and motorized forces. This will make it possible to switch strong mobile formations northward to co-operate with Army Group North in annihilating the enemy's forces fighting in the Baltic States—Army Group North operating from East Prussia in the general direction of Leningrad. Only after having accomplished this most important task, which must be followed by the occupation of Leningrad and Kronstadt, is there to be a continuation of the offensive operations which aim at the capture of Moscow—as a focal centre of communications and armament industry.

"Only a surprisingly quick collapse of Russian resistance could justify aiming at both objectives simultaneously."

"The Army Group employed south of the Pripet marshes is to make its main effort from the Lublin area in the general direction of Kiev, in order to penetrate quickly deep into the flank and rear of the Russian forces and then to roll them up along the Dnieper River."

Again at the conference of February 3rd, where Halder expounded the O.K.H. plan in detail, Hitler concluded the proceedings by emphasizing: "In carrying it out, it must be remembered that the main aim is to gain possession of the Baltic States and Leningrad."

THE MISCARRIAGE OF THE INVASION

The next question I explored was how the plan went wrong. Kleist's answer was: "The main cause of our failure was that winter came early that year, coupled with the way the Russians repeatedly gave ground rather than let themselves be drawn into a decisive battle such as we were seeking."

Rundstedt agreed that this was "the most decisive" cause. "But long before winter came the chances had been diminished owing to the repeated delays in the advance that were caused by bad roads, and mud. The 'black earth' of the Ukraine could be turned into mud by ten minutes' rain—stopping all movement until it dried. That was a heavy handicap in a race with time. It was increased by the lack of railways in Russia—for bringing up supplies to our advancing troops. Another adverse factor was the way the Russians received continual reinforcements from their back areas, as they fell back. It seemed to us that as soon as one force was wiped out, the path was blocked by the arrival of a fresh force."

Blumentritt endorsed these verdicts except for the point about the Russians yielding ground. On the Moscow route, the principal line of advance, they repeatedly held on long enough to be encircled. But the invaders repeatedly failed to reap the opportunity through becoming immobi-

lized themselves. "The badness of the roads was the worst
handicap, but next to that was the inadequacy of the
railways, even when repaired. Our Intelligence was faulty
on both scores, and had under-estimated their effect.
Moreover the restoration of railway traffic was delayed by
the change of gauge beyond the Russian frontier. The
supply problem in the Russian campaign was a very
serious one, complicated by local conditions." Nevertheless, Blumentritt considered that Moscow could have been
captured if Guderian's unorthodox plan had been adopted,
or if Hitler had not wasted vital time through his own
indecision. Blumentritt's evidence on these issues will be
given later.

Another factor, emphasized by Kleist, was that the
Germans had no such definite advantage in the air as they
had enjoyed in their 1940 invasion of the West. Although
they took such a heavy toll of the Russian Air Force as to
turn the numerical balance in their favour, the diminished
opposition in the air was offset by the stretching of their
own air cover as they pushed deeper. The faster they
advanced on the ground, the longer the stretch became.
Talking of this, Kleist said: "At several stages in the
advance my panzer forces were handicapped through lack
of cover overhead, due to the fighter airfields being too far
back. Moreover, such air superiority as we enjoyed during
the opening months was local rather than general. We owed
it to the superior skill of our airmen, not to a superiority
in numbers." That advantage disappeared as the Russians
gained experience, while being able to renew their strength.

Besides these basic factors there was, in Rundstedt's
opinion, a fault in the original German dispositions that
had a delayed ill-effect on the course of operations subsequent to the initial break-through. Under the plan of the
Supreme Command a wide gap was left between his left
flank and Bock's right flank, opposite the western end
of the Pripet Marshes—the idea being this area could
be safely neglected because of its nature, and the maxi-

mum effort put into the two rapid drives, north and
south of the marsh-belt. Rundstedt doubted the wisdom
of this assumption when the plan was under discussion.
"From my own experience on the Eastern Front in 1914–18
I anticipated that the Russian cavalry would be able to
operate in the Pripet Marches, and thus felt anxious
about the gap in our advancing front, since it left the
Russians free to develop flank threats from that area."

In the first stage of the invasion no such risk
materialized. After Reichenau's 6th Army had forced
the crossings of the Bug, south of the Marshes, Kleist's
armoured forces passed through and swept rapidly forward,
capturing Luck and Rovno. But after crossing the old
Russian frontier, and heading for Kiev, the invaders
were heavily counter-attacked in flank by Russian cavalry
corps that suddenly emerged from the Pripet Marshes.
This produced a dangerous situation, and although the
threat was eventually curbed after tough fighting, it
delayed the advance, and spoilt the chance of an early
arrival on the Dnieper.

While it is not difficult to see how this interruption
weighed on Rundstedt's mind, it is not so clear that the
general prospects of the invasion suffered in consequence.
For no similar interference played any considerable part in
checking Bock's advance north of the Pripet Marches,
where the centre of gravity of the whole offensive lay.

It was here, along the direct route to Moscow, that
the Germans had concentrated their strongest forces, and
had planned to bring off the decisive battle. While the
course of events on that front brought out with even
greater emphasis the difficulties that Rundstedt and Kleist
had encountered on the southern front, it also turned on
more personal factors—of human misjudgment.

A clear picture of the offensive design was given me by
General Heinrici, who traced the moves on the map. He
is a small, precise man with a parsonical manner—he
talks as if he were saying grace. Although he hardly looks

like a soldier, proof of his military ability is provided by the fact that, starting as a corps commander, he finished as Army Group Commander conducting the final battle of the Oder in defence of Berlin. His outline of the pattern of the operation was filled in with fuller details and background disclosures by General Blumentritt, who was Chief of Staff to Kluge's Army throughout the advance from Brest-Litovsk to Moscow. Later, other generals who were on that line of advance supplemented the account, and on some points corrected it.

The plan, in brief, was to trap the bulk of the Russian forces by a vast encircling manœuvre—with the infantry corps moving on an inner circle, and two great panzer groups on an outer circle.

These panzer groups were commanded by Guderian and Hoth respectively. Guderian's comprised three panzer corps, while an infantry corps was placed under him to encircle the frontier fortress of Brest Litovsk, and two further infantry divisions were allotted to his two leading panzer corps for the initial crossing of the Bug. A panzer group was really a panzer army—and was rechristened as such later in the campaign—but initially and intermittently it was placed under the direction of the backing-up infantry army. The ill-defined relationship proved a cause of trouble.

The launching of the invasion took the Russian frontier forces completely by surprise, and the Bug was crossed without difficulty. A number of Guderian's tanks had been water-proofed and adapted for the purpose of driving across the bed of the river under water, "breathing" through a long pipe like the Schnorkel-equipped submarines later in the war. The Russian defence works on the far side were to a large extent unmanned, and very soon the panzer divisions were racing forward through open country. By evening some of the divisions had advanced as much as fifty miles. As they pushed on they met more resistance, though they were often able to by-pass it.

On the 24th the 47th Panzer Corps (Lemelsen) had

some heavy fighting at Slonim with large Russian forces that were trying to break out of the threatened encirclement of the Bialystok area.

The panzer pincers met at Minsk. Hoth's right wing, which started from East Prussia, reached the northern outskirts, on the 26th. Lemelsen's corps, which had farther to go, joined hands with it on the 27th, having covered over two hundred miles in five and a half days. The city fell to the Germans next day. Meanwhile the 24th Panzer Corps (Geyr von Schweppenburg) had been racing on and reached the Beresina that same day, gaining a bridgehead over that historic river. It then drove on to the Dnieper, but found that the Russians had rushed reserves to hold this river line.

Far in the rear, the infantry pincers had closed in at Slonim, but not quite in time to catch the bulk of the Russians in their retreat from the Bialystok pocket. A second attempt, aimed to surround them near Minsk, was more successful, and nearly 300,000 were captured—although large fractions had managed to escape before the encirclement was sealed. The size of the bag gave rise to a wave of optimism, even among the generals who had been apprehensive about Hitler's decision to invade Russia. Halder remarked on July 3rd: "It is probably not an exaggeration when I contend that the campaign against Russia has been won in fourteen days."

These operations, however, had brought out a serious divergence of view about methods among the German commanders. Guderian and Hoth had driven on from Minsk according to their original instructions, leaving minimum detachments to help the backing-up infantry corps in closing the ring. Kluge had wanted to halt the advance until the encirclement battle was completed, and to employ the whole of the panzer forces in that task. But they had already gone ahead, and his unwelcome counter-instructions suffered a convenient miscarriage in transmission. Kluge then appealed to Bock, who acceded to his

desire to pull them back. Brauchitsch would have preferred the panzer groups to continue their thrust, but was
deterred from overruling Bock and Kluge when Hitler
threw his weight on their side. So on July 3rd both panzer
groups were placed under Kluge's direct control. The
surrounded mass of Russians west of Minsk surrendered
on the same day, however, and the panzer groups were
set free again.

Guderian now determined to attempt the crossing of
the Dnieper without further delay, rather than wait a
week or two until the foot-marching mass of the 4th Army
came up—and the Russians, too, had had time to bring
up reinforcements. For the crossing he concentrated his
forces under cover of night, and behind a wide screen, at
three unguarded points. On hearing of his intentions, Kluge
came up to see him and again tried to put on a brake, but
on finding that the stroke was ready for launching he
agreed to the attempt. It proved brilliantly successful, and
after crossing the Dnieper on July 10th Guderian drove on
to Smolensk, undeterred by heavy Russian counter-attacks
from the flanks of the break-through. His left spearhead
reached Smolensk on the 16th, while his centre one
reached the Desna and captured Elnya on the 20th. The
progress of the right spearhead was slowed down by the
counter-attacks of large Russian forces pushing north up
the Dnieper from Gomel.

The invasion had now penetrated over four hundred
miles deep into Russian territory. Moscow lay two hundred
miles farther ahead. For such a deep advance the pace had
been very rapid, though the second stage from Minsk to
Smolensk had taken nearly three weeks compared with
five days on the first stage.

With Hoth's arrival north of Smolensk, a fresh encircling
move was undertaken to cut off the large Russian forces
between the Dnieper and the Desna that had been by-
passed in the panzer drives. The trap was almost closed,
but difficult country and muddy going hampered the

movement, and the Russians succeeded in extricating a large part of their forces. Even so, a total of 180,000 were captured in the Smolensk area.

Blumentritt gave me a vivid description of the conditions under which the advance from Minsk had been carried out, and the way they had become worse beyond the Dnieper and Dvina. "It was appallingly difficult country for tank movement—great virgin forests, widespread swamps, terrible roads, and bridges not strong enough to bear the weight of tanks. The resistance also became stiffer, and the Russians began to cover their front with minefields, It was easier for them to block the way because there were so few roads.

"The great motor highway leading from the frontier to Moscow was unfinished—the one road a Westerner would call a 'road'. We were not prepared for what we found because our maps in no way corresponded to reality. On those maps all supposed main roads were marked in red, and there seemed to be many, but they often proved to be merely sandy tracks. The German intelligence service was fairly accurate about conditions in Russian-occupied Poland, but badly at fault about those beyond the original Russian frontier.

"Such country was bad enough for the tanks, but worse still for the transport accompanying them—carrying their fuel, their supplies, and all the auxiliary troops they needed. Nearly all this transport consisted of wheeled vehicles, which could not move off the roads, nor move on it if the sand turned into mud. An hour or two of rain reduced the panzer forces to stagnation. It was an extraordinary sight, with groups of them strung out over a hundred miles stretch, all stuck—until the sun came out and the ground dried. Hoth, who was advancing from the Orsha-Nevel sector, was delayed by swamps as well as bursts of rain. Guderian made a rapid advance to Smolensk, but then met similar trouble."

Guderian confirmed what Blumentritt had said about

the faultiness of the German maps, and also mentioned the
difficulties caused by swampy areas, but emphasized that
the weather was good during the opening weeks of the
offensive. "What delayed us most during that time was
the hindrance resulting from the doubts of Field-Marshal
von Kluge. He was inclined to stop the advance of the
panzers at every difficulty arising in the rear."

Kluge's particular part in applying the brake was not
brought out by Blumentritt—probably from loyalty to his
former chief. But Blumentritt had been the first to reveal
that, from the start, there was a conflict of ideas about
the method of operation. In giving me an account of it
he said that Hitler and most of the senior generals were
in agreement on planning battles of encirclement—
according to the principles of orthodox strategy. "But
Guderian had a different idea—to drive deep, as fast as
possible, and leave the encircling of the enemy to be
completed by the infantry forces that were following up.
Guderian urged the importance of keeping the Russians on
the run, and allowing them no time to rally. He wanted
to drive straight on to Moscow, and was convinced he could
get there if no time was wasted. Russia's resistance might
be paralysed by that thrust at the centre of Stalin's power.

"Guderian's plan was a very bold one—and meant big
risks in maintaining reinforcements and supplies. But it
might have been the lesser of two risks. By making the
armoured forces turn in each time, and forge a ring round
the enemy forces they had by-passed, a lot of time was lost.

"After we had reached Smolensk there was a stand-still
for several weeks on the Desna. This was due partly to
the need of bringing up supplies and reinforcements, but
even more to a fresh conflict of views within the German
command—about the future course of the campaign.
There were endless arguments."

Bock wanted to push on to Moscow. Endorsing the
views of Guderian and Hoth, he expressed confidence that
another deep penetration by the tank spearheads would

succeed in reaching Moscow. But Hitler considered that the time had come to carry out his original conception of taking Leningrad and the Ukraine as primary objectives. While rating their importance higher than that of Moscow, he was not only thinking of the economic and political effect as most of his critics among the generals tended to assume. He seems to have visualized a Cannae-like operation of super-large dimensions, in which the already created threat to Moscow would draw the Russian reserves to that sector of the front, thus making it easier for the German wings to gain their flank objectives, Leningrad and the Ukraine. And from these flank positions his forces could then converge on Moscow, which might fall like a ripe plum into their hands. It was a subtle as well as a vast conception. In the event it broke down on the time-factor—because Russian resistance proved tougher and the weather worse than had been expected, while Hitler was not prepared to defer its completion until another year. It is evident, too, that the prospects were not improved by the differences of opinion that were prevalent among the generals.

On July 19th Hitler issued a directive for the next stage —to begin as soon as the immediate mopping-up operations between the Dnieper and the Desna had been completed. Part of Bock's mobile forces was to wheel southward to help Rundstedt in destroying the Russian armies facing him, while the other part was to wheel northward to help Leeb's attack on Leningrad by cutting the communications between that city and Moscow. Bock would be left only with foot-marching forces to continue the frontal advance on Moscow as best he could.

Once again Brauchitsch temporized, instead of at once pressing for a different plan. He argued that before any further operations were started, the panzer forces must have a rest to overhaul their machines and get up replacements. Hitler agreed as to the necessity for such a pause. But Russian resistance and counter-attacks delayed the clearance of the area west of the Desna, and it was not until early in August that the panzer forces could be given a rest. At a meeting on the 4th Bock urged the case for an early advance on Moscow, and Guderian said that he would be ready to begin the drive on the 15th. Hitler emphasized, however, that Leningrad was still his primary objective and went on to say that after securing it he would decide between Moscow and the Ukraine—he was inclined to favour the latter as it would open the way for the capture of the Crimea and the air bases there, which he regarded as a potential source of danger to the Rumanian oilfields.

THE SWITCH SOUTH—

FOR THE KIEV "KESSELSCHLACHT"

In the course of the next two weeks the argument was pursued on a higher level. Brauchitsch tried to induce Hitler to sanction the advance on Moscow, but in too mild a manner to make an effective impression. On August 18th the case was more strongly presented in a memorandum that Halder drew up, but on the 21st Hitler turned it down in a fresh directive. This repeated the lines of the one he had issued a month before, except that rather less emphasis was given to Leningrad and more emphasis was placed on an annihilating envelopment of the enemy forces in the Kiev area, on Rundstedt's front. After that Bock might resume the advance on Moscow, while Rundstedt was to push on in the south to cut off the Russians' oil supplies from the Caucasus.

When this directive was received at O.K.H., Halder wanted Brauchitsch to tender their joint resignation. But Brauchitsch said it was useless to do so, as Hitler would merely reject it.

During this prolonged period of discussion, various developments in the situation had tended to confirm Hitler in his decision. Reichenau's 6th Army on Rundstedt's left wing had been blocked in front of Kiev, and the strong

Russian forces that were sheltered behind the eastern end of the Pripet marshes had continued to threaten his left flank, as well as threatening Bock's right flank. On the other hand, Kleist's panzer group had achieved brilliant success in an oblique move. Swerving south-eastward, it drove down the corridor between the Dniester and the Dnieper, on a slant towards the Black Sea and the Dnieper Bend, to cut off the Russian armies that were facing the Rumanians. This combination of events emphasized the possibility, if Kleist turned northward and a strong force from Bock's front was sent southward, of bringing off a double flank stroke that would not only loosen the stubborn resistance of the Russian armies around and above Kiev but also put them in the bag—and thereby eliminate the danger that a drive for Moscow might be upset by a counter-offensive from the south of the Dnieper. The sum of these prospective benefits proved decisive in making Hitler settle on the Kiev operation, as a preliminary to the Moscow advance. Nor was he alone in favouring it.

A significant point about this crucial decision was mentioned by Blumentritt: "Although Field-Marshal von Bock desired to continue the advance on Moscow, von Kluge did not share his view and was strongly in favour of the alternative plan of encircling the Russian forces around Kiev. It was his idea, and desire, that his own 4th Army should swing south to carry out this pincer-movement along with Guderian's panzer forces. When setting forth the arguments for this plan, he said to me, with emphasis: 'It would also mean that *we* should be under Field-Marshal von Rundstedt, instead of Field-Marshal von Bock.' Von Bock was a very difficult man to serve, and von Kluge would have been glad to get out of his sphere. This was an interesting example of the influence of the personal factor in strategy."

It was natural that Rundstedt should welcome a reinforcement from the north to help him in solving the tough problem with which he was faced on his own front, and natural too that he should appreciate the prospect of achieving a great encirclement victory—the soldier's dream. And as Bock's own principal army commander favoured the same course Hitler could feel that he had weighty professional opinion behind him in going contrary to the advice of O.K.H. There was, indeed, much to be said for freeing the southern wing and removing the menace of a counter-stroke from that flank before pressing on to Moscow. Moreover, the relative immobility of the Russian masses increased the advantages of a strategy of switching the concentrated power of the German mobile forces successively from one sector to another, to produce a decisive effect on each in turn. But time for such a procedure was running short, especially as the German army was unprepared for a winter campaign.

It may here be mentioned that Kluge did not attain his desire to get away from Bock. For although he and his staff were withdrawn from the front to prepare the left pincer part of the Kiev operation, their participation in it was cancelled a little later. (Guderian did not mourn the change, even though it diminished the infantry support to his southward drive, for as he remarked to me: "Von Kluge was even more difficult to serve than von Bock.") Kluge was so disgusted that he flew off on leave to visit his family, and occupied himself for several weeks in looking after his estate during the pause in operations on the Moscow front.

While insisting on the Kiev operation, Hitler yielded to the arguments of O.K.H. and Bock on several other issues. Besides leaving the 4th Army with Bock, he abstained from despatching more than one corps from Hoth's panzer group to aid the Leningrad operation. He also agreed that Army Group Centre should prepare to launch a decisive offensive against Moscow, helped by panzer forces from the other army groups, as soon as the Kiev operation was completed. This decision was embodied in a new directive on September 6th. It was hoped that the Moscow advance might begin in mid-September, a logistical calculation that was hardly a logical conclusion from past experience.

The Kiev "Kesselschlacht" itself proved a great success —much the greatest yet attained by the Germans. While Reichenau's and Weichs's armies engaged the Russian armies in front of them, Guderian thrust downward across their rear while Kleist thrust upward from the Dnieper Bend. The two panzer groups met 150 miles east of Kiev, closing the trap behind the backs of the Russians. This time few escaped, and the total bag of prisoners amounted to over 600,000. But it was late in September before the battle ended—poor roads and bad weather had slowed down the pace of the encircling manœuvre, though they failed to prevent its completion.

Autumn had come, bringing its usual impediments to movement. Winter was drawing near, carrying its traditional menace to an invader of Russia.

FORFEIT AT LENINGRAD

Although Hitler's original idea of giving priority to the capture of Leningrad had been contrary to the views of Brauchitsch and Halder, as well as Bock, it had found support among other leading generals. A number of them considered it at the time to be the right course, and still do. Discussing the campaign with me in 1945, Rundstedt said: "The 1941 operations in Russia should, in my opinion, have had their main effort directed, not at first towards Moscow, but towards Leningrad. That would have linked up with the Finns. Then, in the next stage, should have come an attack on Moscow from the north, in co-operation with the advance of Field Marshal von Bock's Army Group from the West."

As the campaign worked out, however, the possibility of pursuing that course suffered not only from opposition but from deflection—towards the Ukraine. Moreover,

Rundstedt himself contributed to the deflection, through his natural concern with the situation facing him on the front of Army Group South. In view of the weight his judgment carried, there might have been a great difference in the general course of events if he had been cast in the first place for the rôle of commander on the northern part of the front.

A concentration of effort southward on the Kiev "Kesselschlacht" was hard to reconcile with a simultaneous push northward against Leningrad. The pressure of O.K.H. and Bock for an early advance on Moscow made it still more difficult—a three-way pull. Thus when Hitler decided to carry out the Kiev manœuvre, it almost inevitably entailed his "primary objective", Leningrad, becoming a secondary one.

But the chance of its early capture disappeared through Hitler's own intervention—according to the accounts I had from several generals. Warlimont said: "Hitler gave another fateful halt-order just when the armoured vanguards of Army Group North had reached the outskirts of the city. Apparently he thereby wanted to avoid the losses of human life and material to be expected from fighting in the streets and squares of this Soviet metropolis against an outraged population, and hoped to gain the same ends by cutting off the city from all lines of supply." Blumentritt's view was that: "Leningrad could have been taken, probably with little difficulty. But after his experience at Warsaw in 1939 Hitler was always nervous about tackling big cities, because of the losses he had suffered there. The tanks had already started on the last lap of the advance when Hitler ordered them to stop—as he had done at Dunkirk in 1940. So no genuine attack on Leningrad was attempted in 1941, contrary to appearances —although all preparations had been completed, including the mounting of long-range artillery that had been brought from France."

The attempt to bring about the fall of the city by

encirclement and blockade did not succeed. Its chances of
succeeding were diminished by the withdrawal of the
mobile forces to take part in the autumn drive for Moscow.
Hoeppner's panzer group, which had been the spearhead
of the advance on the northern front, was sent south to
join Kluge's 4th Army in the centre. Whereas in July
Hitler had opposed the desire of O.K.H. to concentrate
on the capture of Moscow, he now sacrificed his own aims
at Leningrad in order to strengthen the belated effort to
reach Moscow. It would seem that the Germans might
have done better if they had consistently pursued either
the O.K.W. or the O.K.H. aim, whereas their prospects
suffered from the plan being a compromise.

THE AUTUMN PUSH

The disappointing results at Leningrad were obscured
by the triumphant outcome of the Kiev encirclement.
This great success produced such exhilaration as to make
most of the Germans feel that a similar encirclement on
the Desna sector around Vyasma could be achieved, and
would open the way for a rapid drive into Moscow.
Those who had been eager to launch this drive became
even more eager, although it was so late in the season,
while those who had preferred a different course were
now disposed to agree that Moscow was ripe for capture.

Giving me his view after the war, Rundstedt said: "We
ought to have stopped on the Dnieper after taking Kiev.
I argued this strongly, and Field-Marshal von Brauchitsch
agreed with me. But Hitler, elated by the victory at Kiev,
now wanted to push on, and felt sure he could capture
Moscow. Field-Marshal von Bock naturally tended to
concur, for his nose was pointing towards Moscow. So
was General Halder's." From the contemporary records,
however, it does not appear that Brauchitsch really shared
this cautious view when in more eager company. While
the records establish the fact that Rundstedt was the first

to advise a halt, even he does not seem to have emphatically advocated it until early in November.

In the light of the situation then existing, it is easy to understand the prevailing state of confidence and the general pressure for an autumn advance on Moscow. But the two months' grace given to the Russians there had shortened the chances, and they now depended too much on a fair autumn. Contrary to German hopes, it turned out exceptionally wet. As Blumentritt sadly remarked: "We had been halted during August and September—the best two months of the year. That proved fatal."

Hitler's decision to embark on an autumn bid for Moscow was accompanied by another one which involved further complications and a loss of concentration—for he could not resist the temptation to exploit the victory in the South at the same time as he pursued the aim of capturing Moscow.

FRUSTRATION AT THE "GATE TO THE CAUCASUS"

When Hitler made up his mind to push on, he assigned Rundstedt the extremely ambitious fresh task of clearing the Black Sea coast and reaching the Caucasus. The objectives, as Rundstedt traced them for me on the map, were to gain the line of the Don from Voronezh eastward to its mouth near Rostov, and drive far enough beyond it to secure the Maikop oilfields with his right wing and Stalingrad on the Volga with his left wing. When Rundstedt pointed out the difficulties and risks of advancing a further 400 miles beyond the Dnieper, with his left exposed over such a long stretch, Hitler confidently asserted that the Russians were incapable of offering serious opposition and that the frozen roads would enable a quick advance to the objective.

Describing what happened, Rundstedt said: "The plan was handicapped from the start by the diversion of forces to the Moscow front. A number of my mobile divisions were drawn off for a north-easterly advance past Orel towards the southern flank of Moscow. That achieved little, and lost an opportunity. I had wanted von Bock's right wing to turn south-eastward, and strike across the rear of the Russian armies that were opposing me near Kursk, thus cutting them off. It seemed to me a great mistake to swing the offensive centre of gravity north-eastward, as the Russians were much better placed, with the help of the railways radiating from Moscow, to counter a move in that direction." (It will be noticed that Rundstedt's view still differed from that of O.K.H.)

"As it was, my 6th Army on the left wing was blocked beyond Kursk, and fell short of its objective, Voronezh, on the Don. This check reacted on the progress of its neighbour, the 17th Army, and constricted the width of the advance towards the Caucasus. The 17th Army met stiff resistance along the Donetz. It could not push far enough forward to protect the flank of von Kleist's 1st Panzer Army. In consequence, von Kleist's flank was endangered by the strong counter-attacks which the Russians developed in a southerly direction, towards the Black Sea.

"On the other flank, von Manstein's 11th Army pierced the defences of the Perekop Isthmus and broke into the Crimea, quickly overrunning most of that peninsula except for the fortress of Sevastopol and the eastern tip at Kerch. But this divergent move, ordered by Hitler, reduced the strength I had available on the mainland."

The story of what happened to the Caucasus drive is best given in Kleist's own words. "Before we reached the Lower Don it became clear that there was no longer time or opportunity to reach the Caucasus. Although we had trapped most of the enemy forces west of the Dnieper, and thus gained an apparently open path, the Russians were bringing up many fresh divisions by rail and road from the east. Bad weather intervened and our advance was bogged down at a crucial time, while my leading troops ran short of petrol.

"My idea now was merely to enter Rostov and destroy
the Don bridges there, not to hold that advanced line.
I had reconnoitred a good defensive position on the Mius
River, and taken steps to organize it as a winter line. But
Goebbels's propaganda made so much of our arrival at
Rostov—it was hailed as having 'opened the gateway to
the Caucasus'—that we were prevented from carrying out
this plan. My troops were forced to hang on at Rostov
longer than I had intended, and as a result suffered a bad
knock from the Russian counter-offensive that was launched
in the last week of November. However, they succeeded
in checking the Russian pursuit as soon as they had fallen
back to the Mius River line, and although the enemy
pushed on far beyond their inland flank they managed to
maintain their position here, only 50 miles west of Rostov,
throughout the winter. It was the most advanced sector
of the whole German front in the East."

Kleist added: "The German armies were in grave
danger during that first winter. They were virtually frozen
in, and unable to move. That was a great handicap in
meeting and checking the Russian encircling movements."

Rundstedt's account confirmed Kleist's, and also
brought out the story of his own first removal from command. "When I wanted to break off the battle and
withdraw to the Mius River, Field-Marshal von Brauchitsch
agreed, but then an overriding order came from the Führer,
which forbade any such withdrawal. I wired back that it
was nonsense to hold on where we were, and added: 'If you
do not accept my view you must find someone else to
command.' That same night a reply came from the
Führer that my resignation was accepted—I left the
Eastern Front on December 1st, and never returned there.
Almost immediately afterwards the Führer flew down to
that sector; after seeing the situation, he changed his
mind and sanctioned the step-back. Significantly, the
Mius River line was the only sector of the front that was
not shaken during the winter of 1941–42."

From other sources I learnt of two significant supplementary points. When Rundstedt proposed to withdraw to the Mius River, Brauchitsch supported his proposal but then yielded to Hitler's insistence that it should be forbidden—although he did protest at Hitler's promptness to accept Rundstedt's resignation. Reichenau was appointed to succeed Rundstedt, and in conformity to Hitler's desire he at first tried to make a stand on an intermediate position. It was the Russians who, by piercing this line, made Hitler change his mind. Facts were stronger than arguments.

FRUSTRATION AT MOSCOW

The eastward advance on Moscow began on October 2nd, and was carried out by three armies—the 2nd on the right; the 4th in the centre, to which Hoeppner's panzer group was attached; the 9th on the left, with Hoth's panzer group. At the same time Guderian's panzer group, now made an independent panzer army, drove up from the south to strike into the rear of the Russians' line of defence behind the Desna. Its thrust began on September 30th, and was directed north-eastward towards Orel, Tula, and the southern flank of Moscow.

The course of the offensive was vividly described by Blumentritt: "The first phase was the battle of encirclement around Vyasma and Bryansk. This time, the encirclement was perfectly completed, and 600,000 Russians were captured. It was a modern Cannae—on a greater scale. The panzer groups played a big part in this victory. The Russians were caught napping, as they did not expect a big drive for Moscow to be launched at such a late date. But it was too late in the year for us to harvest its fruits"— by a rapid strategic exploitation.

"After the Russian forces had been rounded up, we pushed on towards Moscow. There was little opposition for the moment, but the advance was slow—for the mud was awful, and the troops were tired. Moreover, they met a well-prepared defensive position on the Nara River, where they were held up by the arrival of fresh Russian forces.

"Most of the commanders were now asking: 'When are we going to stop?' They remembered what had happened to Napoleon's army. Many of them began to re-read Caulaincourt's grim account of 1812. That book had a weighty influence at this critical time in 1941. I can still see von Kluge trudging through the mud from his sleeping quarters to his office, and there standing before the map with Caulaincourt's book in his hand. That went on day after day."

This point was of particular interest to me as in August, 1941—when the German tide of invasion seemed to be flowing irresistibly—I had written an article for the October *Strand* on the relation of Napoleon's campaign to Hitler's, basing it on extensive quotations from Caulaincourt, to bring out my implied conclusion. I remarked that we had evidently been thinking on the same lines, though the German generals had begun to remember Caulaincourt a bit late! Blumentritt agreed, with a wry grin.

Resuming his account, he said: "The troops themselves were less depressed than their generals. They could see the flashes of the A.A. guns over Moscow at night, and it fired their imagination—the city seemed so near. They also felt that they would find shelter there from the bitter weather. But the commanders felt that they were not strong enough to push those last forty miles."

On the higher levels, however, a different view prevailed. It is evident from the records that Bock was more insistent than Hitler on pursuing the offensive, arguing that where both sides were so exhausted superior will-power could decide the issue. Brauchitsch and Halder shared Bock's view. Rundstedt and Leeb wished to break off the offensive, but their views had less influence as they were not directly concerned with the Moscow offensive.

Talking to me about the discussions that took place early in November, Blumentritt said: "An important conference was held at Orsha to discuss the future course of operations. All the Chiefs of Staff of army groups and armies were ordered to attend it, to confer with General Halder. It was held in his special train. Field-Marshal von Brauchitsch and the commanders themselves were not present—it was intended to 'feel the pulse' of opinion about the question whether there should be another great offensive along the whole front, or a halt for the winter.

"The Chief of Staff of Army Group South, von Soden-stern, expressed a most emphatic opinion against any further advance. So did the Chief of Staff of Army Group North. The Chief of Staff of Army Group Centre, von Greiffenberg, took a more indefinite line, pointing out the risks but not expressing opposition to an advance. He was in a difficult position. Field-Marshal von Bock was a very capable soldier, but ambitious, and his eyes were focused on Moscow, which seemed so near.

"General Halder then spoke, explaining the Führer's views and his desire to attack again. He said that there was reason to believe that Russian resistance was on the verge of collapse. He went on to tell us that the Führer's plan was to by-pass Moscow and capture the railway junctions beyond it—as O.K.H. had reports that large Russian reserves, amounting in strength to a fresh army, were on their way from Siberia.

"Shortly after this conference we received the fateful order to take Moscow. The plan itself, however, was modified. For Field-Marshal von Kluge had protested that the attempt to penetrate so deep, to reach the railway junctions behind Moscow, was a 'fantasy' at that time of the year. Instead, there was to be a more direct attack, with the aim of occupying Moscow—because of its great importance as a 'symbol' of Russian resistance. The order said that the Kremlin was to be blown up, to signalize the overthrow of Bolshevism.

"While the heads of the army realized the difficulties of attempting the capture of Moscow at this season, none of them expected such a powerful Russian rally as actually developed that winter."

The dispositions were reshuffled before the offensive was launched. On the southern wing it was to be carried out by Kluge's 4th Army, with the 1st Panzer Corps; and on the northern wing by Hoeppner's Panzer Group, with some infantry divisions of the 9th Army. The whole attack was placed under Kluge's direction. This was ironical in view of his disbelief in the possibility of achieving what he must undertake.

Blumentritt continued: "The offensive was opened by Hoeppner's panzer group on the left. Its progress was slow, in face of mud and strong Russian counter-attacks. Our losses were heavy. The weather then turned adverse, with snow falling on the swampy ground. The Russians made repeated counter-attacks from the flank across the frozen Moskwa, and Hoeppner had to divert more and more of his strength to check these thrusts. The 2nd Panzer Division succeeded in penetrating far enough to get a sight of the Kremlin, but that was the nearest it came.

"These unpromising conditions raised the question whether the 4th Army should join in the offensive or not. Night after night Hoeppner came through on the telephone, to urge this course; night after night von Kluge and I sat up late discussing whether it would be wise or not to agree to his insistence. Von Kluge decided that he would gain the opinion of the front-line troops themselves —he was a very energetic and active commander who liked to be up among the fighting troops—so he visited the forward posts, and consulted the junior officers and N.C.O.s. The troop leaders believed they could reach Moscow and were eager to try. So after five or six days of discussion and investigation, von Kluge decided to make a final effort with the 4th Army. The snow was thick on the ground, and the earth was frozen to a depth of several inches. The hardness of the ground was more favourable for artillery movement than if it had been otherwise.

"The attack was launched on December 2nd, but by afternoon reports were coming back that it was held up by strong Russian defences in the forests around Moscow. The Russians were artists in forest fighting, and their defence was helped by the fact that darkness came as early as 3 o'clock in the afternoon.

"A few parties of our troops, from the 258th Infantry Division, actually got into the suburbs of Moscow. But the Russian workers poured out of the factories and fought with their hammers and other tools in defence of their city.

"During the night the Russians strongly counter-attacked the isolated elements that had penetrated their defences. Next day our corps commanders reported that they thought it was no longer possible to break through. Von Kluge and I had a long discussion that evening, and at the end he decided to withdraw these advanced troops. Fortunately the Russians did not discover that they were moving back, so that we succeeded in extricating them and bringing them back to their original position in fairly good order. But there had been very heavy casualties in those two days' fighting.

"The decision was just in time to avert the worst consequences of the general counter-offensive that the Russians now unleashed, and into which Marshal Zhukov threw a hundred divisions. Under their converging pressure our position became daily more dangerous. Hitler was at last brought to realize that we could not check them, and gave reluctant permission for a short withdrawal to a line in rear. We had been badly misled about the quantity of reinforcements that the Russians could produce. They had hidden their resources all too well."

That was the end of Hitler's bid for Moscow—and it proved his last bid on that capital front. Never again would any German soldiers catch sight of the Kremlin, except as prisoners.

CHAPTER XVII

FRUSTRATION IN THE CAUCASUS
AND AT STALINGRAD

WHEN Moscow remained out of reach, and winter set in
at its worst, fear spread among the German troops. With
it grew the danger of a collapse as terrible as befell
Napoleon's *Grande Armée*.

It was Hitler's decision for "no withdrawal" that
averted a panic in that black hour. It appeared a display
of iron nerve—though it may only have been due to sheer
mulish obstinacy. For it was against his generals' advice.

But his success in surviving that crisis was his undoing
in the end. First, it led him to plunge deeper into Russia
the next summer, 1942. He started well but soon went
astray. He missed taking Stalingrad because his eyes were
fixed on the Caucasus, and then forfeited the Caucasus in
belated efforts to capture Stalingrad.

When winter came he was led to gamble again on his
"Moscow" inspiration. This time it produced a disaster
from which he never recovered. Even then, he might
have spun out the war until Russia was exhausted, by
practising elastic defence in the vast buffer-space he had
gained. But he stuck rigidly to his rule of "no withdrawal",
and so hastened Germany's fall.

THE WINTER CRISIS

It is clear from all the generals told me that the German
armies were placed in the gravest danger after being
repulsed before Moscow in December, 1941. The generals
urged Hitler to make a long step back to a secure winter
line. They pointed out that the troops were not equipped

for the rigours of a winter campaign. But Hitler refused to listen. He gave the order: "The Army is not to retire a single step. Every man must fight where he stands."

His decision seemed to invite disaster. Yet the event justified him—once again. The basic reason was brought out by General von Tippelskirch, lean and professorial, a corps and later an army commander there. "Frontal defence was much stronger in this war even than in 1914–18. The Russians always failed to break our front, and although they pushed far round our flanks, they had not yet the skill nor sufficient supplies to drive home their advantage. We concentrated on holding the towns that were rail and road centres, rolling up round them like 'hedgehogs'—that was Hitler's idea—and succeeded in holding them firmly. The situation was saved."

Many of the generals think now that Hitler's decision was the best in the circumstances, though they did not agree with it at the time. "It was his one great achievement," said Tippelskirch. "At that critical moment the troops were remembering what they had heard about Napoleon's retreat from Moscow, and living under the shadow of it. If they had once begun a retreat, it might have turned into a panic flight."

Other generals endorsed this. Rundstedt, however, caustically remarked: "It was Hitler's decision for rigid resistance that caused the danger in the first place. It would not have arisen if he had permitted a timely withdrawal."

Indirect support for that view was provided by the account Blumentritt gave me of what happened on the Moscow front during December. It brought out the needless perils that resulted from Hitler's excessive insistence on rigid defence combined with his unstable way of revoking any concessions he had granted.

"Following the final check before Moscow, General von Kluge advised the Supreme Command that it would be wise to make a general withdrawl to the Ugra, between

J

Kaluga and Vyasma, a line which had already been partially prepared. There was prolonged deliberation at the Führer's Headquarters over this proposal before reluctant permission was granted. Meanwhile the Russian counter-offensive developed in a menacing way, especially on the flanks. The withdrawal was just beginning when a fresh order came from the Führer, saying: 'The 4th Army is not to retire a single step.'

"Our position became all the worse because Guderian's Panzer Group was lying out beyond our right wing, near Tula, and this much-depleted force had to be extricated before the main part of the 4th Army could withdraw. The delay quickly produced a fresh complication, for the Russians attacked Guderian's thin line and rolled it back precipitately over the Oka River. At the same time Hoeppner's Panzer Group on our left was being very hard pressed by the Russians, who threatened to outflank it.

"In consequence the 4th Army became isolated in its forward position, and in imminent danger of encirclement. The rivers were all frozen, so that they provided an inadequate barrier against the Russian thrusts. Soon the danger became acute, for a Russian cavalry corps pressed round our right flank well to the rear of it. This corps was composed of horsed cavalry and sledge-borne infantry, while roping in all the men from the recaptured villages who were capable of carrying a rifle.

"Such was the grim situation of the 4th Army on December 24th—and it had arisen from Hitler's refusal to permit a timely step back. My chief, von Kluge, had gone on the 15th to replace von Bock, who was sick, and I was left in charge of the army. I and my staff spent Christmas Day in a small hut—our headquarters in Malo Yaroslavets —with tommy guns on the table and sounds of shooting all round us. Just as it seemed that nothing could save us from being cut off, we found that the Russians were moving on westward, instead of turning up north astride our rear. They certainly missed their opportunity.

"The situation remained very precarious, for Hitler still delayed a decision, and it was not until January 4th that he at last sanctioned the general withdrawal to the Ugra. I had left just before—to become Deputy Chief of the General Staff—and General Kuebler had arrived to take command. But he soon found that he could not stand the strain and was replaced by General Heinrici, who managed to maintain the new position until spring came, and longer, though it was deeply enveloped on both flanks."

Talking of the conditions under which the forces had to be extricated, Blumentritt said: "The roads were so deep in snow that the horses were up to their bellies. When the divisions withdrew, part of the troops had to shovel a path by day along the route their transport was to move by night. You may understand what their trials were when I mention that the temperature was twenty-eight degrees below freezing, Fahrenheit."

Even though Hitler's decision may have saved a collapse on the Moscow front, a terrible price was paid for it. "Our losses had not been heavy until the final attack for Moscow," Blumentritt told me, "but they became very serious during the winter—both in men and material. Vast numbers perished from the cold." (The records, however, show that the weekly losses were on the average only about half what they had been during the first stage of the campaign—though it is easy to understand how victorious progress made them seem lighter then, whereas the combination of bitter failure with bitter winter made the drain seem more ghastly. The total losses from the start of the invasion up to the end of February were just over a million men. The impression of loss was also increased by the thinning of the ranks, and the delay in filling them up with fresh drafts.)

More specific details came out in discussion with Tippelskirch, who spent the winter as a divisional commander in the Second Corps among the Valdai Hills, between Leningrad and Moscow, and told me that his strength was reduced to one-third of its establishment. "Divisions were down to 5,000 men before the end of the winter, and companies to barely 50 men."

He also threw light on a more far-reaching effect of Hitler's "no withdrawal" policy. "That winter ruined the Luftwaffe—because it had to be used for flying supplies to the garrisons of the 'hedgehogs', the forward positions that were isolated by the Russian flanking advances. The Second Corps required 200 tons of supplies a day, which called for a daily average of 100 transport aircraft. But as bad weather often intervened, the actual number had had to be considerably larger, so as to make full use of an interval of passable weather—on one day as many as 350 aircraft were used to reprovision this single corps. Many aircraft crashed as flying conditions were bad. The overall strain of keeping up supplies by air to all the isolated positions on such a vast front was fatal to the future development of the Luftwaffe."

I questioned the generals about the course and effect of the Russian winter offensive of 1941–42. All testified to the nerve strain caused by the deep flanking threats of the Russian forces, which lapped round their positions and communications, but the general verdict was epitomized in Blumentritt's comment that the direct results were greater than the direct danger. "The principal effect of that winter offensive was in upsetting the German plans for 1942. The weather was a more damaging and dangerous factor than the Russian offensive operations. Besides lowering morale, the weather accounted for the greater part of the German casualties—which were at least as heavy as the Russians' during that winter."

He went on to say that the strain was increased by the way that the German forces were stretched. "The average extent of a divisional frontage was 20 to 25 miles, and even on crucial sectors, such as those near Moscow, they were 10 to 15 miles. That thinness of the front was made more precarious because of the difficulty of bringing up and distributing supplies, which in turn was aggravated by the difficulty of building roads and railways."

I asked him how he accounted for the fact that such thin fronts had, in general, been able to withstand attack, since they were far more widely stretched than what had been regarded in World War I as the limit that a division could hold in defence. He replied: "In that war, the fronts were narrowed by the great depth in which divisions were distributed. New weapons and the improvement of automatic small arms partly accounted for the possibility of holding wider fronts than we could then. The greater mobility of defensive means was the other main reason. If the attackers broke through the front, small detachments of tanks and motorized troops often checked them by mobile counter-moves before they could expand the penetration into a wide breach."

But the way that the disaster was repeatedly averted by this underlying increase of defensive advantage had the ironical effect of encouraging Hitler to gamble more heavily on the offensive. The fact that the crisis was survived exalted Hitler's faith in himself; he felt that his judgment had been justified, against that of his generals. From now on he was less inclined than ever to tolerate their advice.

Brauchitsch's weakness in dealing with Hitler had been increased by his own ill-health, which in turn had been aggravated by the strain of argument with Hitler and the stress of disappointment over the campaign. In November he had suffered a bad heart attack—just when vital decisions were being taken. A few days after the abortive final attack on Moscow, he asked to be relieved of command. A fortnight elapsed before his retirement was announced on December 19th. Meanwhile Hitler had decided to profit by the opening and take over the Supreme Command of the Army (O.K.H.) in addition to his existing position as Supreme Commander of the

Wehrmacht, the forces as a whole (O.K.W.). The announcement that Brauchitsch had been relieved naturally suggested to the German public that he was really being removed for blundering, and that the failure of the campaign was due to the fault of the military chiefs. Hitler had cause to welcome such an interpretation of the reason for Brauchitsch's departure, and it was fostered by his circle. Thus the change in command not only brought him increased power but decreased the resisting power of the generals. An apt comment was provided by Blumentritt: "Only the admirals had a happy time in this war—as Hitler knew nothing about the sea, whereas he felt he knew all about land warfare."

Even the admirals, however, had their troubles. Like Napoleon's admirals, they had to deal with a leader who was too continental-minded to take full account of the obstacles created by British seapower, and its indirect effect on his continental designs. They had not succeeded in making Hitler realize the primary importance of cutting away the bases of that seapower—where these were within reach of landpower—before tackling further objectives.

The generals, on the other hand, were the less able to put a brake on Hitler because their outlook was too exclusively military, besides being continental. That narrowing of vision tended to offset the effect of their greater caution. In this connection, Kleist contributed some significant reflections in the course of one of our talks: "Clausewitz's teachings had fallen into neglect in this generation—even at the time when I was at the War Academy and on the General Staff. His phrases were quoted, but his books were not closely studied. He was regarded as a military philosopher, rather than as a practical teacher. The writings of Schlieffen received much greater attention. They seemed more practical because they were directed to the problem of how an army inferior in strength—which was always Germany's position in relation to the whole—could overcome enemies on both sides who, in combination, were superior in strength. But Clausewitz's reflections were fundamentally sound— especially his dictum that war was a continuation of policy by other means. It implied that the political factors were more important than the military ones. The German mistake was to think that a military success would solve political problems. Indeed, under the Nazis we tended to reverse Clausewitz's dictum, and to regard peace as a continuation of war. Clausewitz, also, was prophetically right about the difficulties of conquering Russia."

PLANS FOR 1942

The question of what should be done in the spring had been debated throughout the winter. The discussion had begun even before the final assault on Moscow. Relating what happened, Blumentritt told me: "A number of the generals declared that a resumption of the offensive in 1942 was impossible, and that it was wiser to make sure of holding what had been gained. Halder was very dubious about the continuance of the offensive. Von Rundstedt was still more emphatic and even urged that the German Army should withdraw to their original front in Poland. Von Leeb agreed with him. While other generals did not go so far as this, most of them were very worried as to where the campaign would lead. With the departure of von Rundstedt as well as von Brauchitsch, the resistance to Hitler's pressure was weakening and that pressure was all for resuming the offensive."

As Blumentritt had become Deputy Chief of the General Staff early in January, under Halder, no one was better placed to know the motives and ideas behind Hitler's decision. He summed them up as follows:

First, Hitler's hope of obtaining in 1942 what he had failed to obtain in 1941. He did not believe that the Russians could increase their strength, and would not listen to evidence on this score. There was a "battle of opinion" between Halder and him. The Intelligence had information that 600 to 700 tanks a month were coming out of the Russian factories, in the Ural Mountains and elsewhere. When Halder told him of this, Hitler slammed the table and said it was impossible. He would not believe what he did not want to believe.

Secondly, he did not know what else to do—as he would not listen to any idea of a withdrawal. He felt that he must do something and that something could only be offensive.

Thirdly, there was much pressure from economic authorities in Germany. They urged that it was essential to continue the advance, telling Hitler that they could not continue the war without oil from the Caucasus and wheat from the Ukraine.

I asked Blumentritt whether the General Staff had examined the grounds for these assertions, and also whether it was true, as reported at the time, that the manganese ore round Nikopol in the Dnieper Bend was vital to the German steel industry. Replying to the latter question first, he said he did not know about this, as he was not acquainted with the economic side of the war. It seemed to me a significant revelation of the way that the German strategists had been divorced from the study of factors that were vital to their planning. He went on to say that it was more difficult to question such assertions by the economic experts as the General Staff was not represented at conferences on these issues—evidence of Hitler's desire to keep them in the dark.

While taking the fateful decision to plunge deeper still into the depths of Russia, Hitler found he no longer had enough strength left for an offensive on the whole front, such as he had carried out the year before. Forced to choose, and hesitating to make another attack towards Moscow, he decided to strike south for the Caucasus oilfields, though it meant extending his flank, like a telescope, past the main body of the Red Army. When his forces reached the Caucasus, they would be exposed to a counterstroke at any point for nearly a thousand miles.

The only other sector on which offensive operations were to be undertaken was on the Baltic flank. The 1942 plan originally included an attempt to take Leningrad in the course of the summer, in order to secure safe communications with Finland and bring relief to her semi-isolated situation. With this exception, the Northern and Central Army Groups were to remain on the defensive, merely improving their positions.

A special Army Group "A" was created for the advance to the Caucasus and placed under Field-Marshal List, while the reduced Army Group South operated on its left flank. Reichenau had replaced Rundstedt in command of the latter, but he died suddenly from a heart attack in January, and Bock was brought back to command it, only to be sacked after the first stage of the 1942 offensive. Kluge remained in command of Army Group Centre, but Küchler had replaced Leeb in command of Army Group North. Warlimont told me: "Field-Marshal von Leeb resigned—after many earlier quarrels—because Hitler insisted upon him maintaining the Demyansk salient, whereas Leeb held the conviction that he could only defend that area by straightening out the line of defence and thus obtaining the reserves that were urgently needed." Blumentritt said that Leeb's general doubts about the Russian campaign made him all the more inclined to give up his command. "His heart was not in it. Apart from regarding it as a hopeless venture on military grounds, he was also opposed to the Nazi régime, and thus glad of a pretext on which he could ask to resign. Resignation would not have been possible without a reason that satisfied Hitler."

In further discussion of the way that the plans for 1942 came to be formulated, Blumentritt made some general observations that are worth inclusion as a sidelight. "My

experience on the higher staffs showed me that the vital
issues of war tended to be decided by political rather than
by strategical factors, and by mental tussles in the rear
rather than by the fighting on the battlefield, Moreover,
those tussles are not reflected in the operation orders.
Documents are no safe guide for history—the men who
sign orders often think quite differently from what they put
on paper. It would be. foolish to take documents that
historians find in the archives as a reliable indication of
what particular officers really thought.

"I began to perceive that truth long ago when I was
working on the history of the 1914–18 war, under General von
Haeften, a very conscientious historian who taught me both
the technique and the difficulties of historical research. But I
came to see it much clearer from my own close observations
of high headquarters in this war—under the Nazi system.

"That system had some strange by-products. While
the German, with his liking for organization and order,
has a tendency to put down in writing more than others
do, still a lot more 'paper' than ever before was produced in
this war. The old army were trained to write brief orders,
that allowed freedom to the executants. In this last war
the practice was changed because mental freedom was
more and more restricted. Every step, and all conceivable
cases, had to be regulated in order to protect ourselves from
penalization. Hence the abundance and length of the
orders—the very contrary to our training. Their often
bombastic language and use of superlatives was against
all the rules of the old style—with its pregnant shortness
and concise phrasing. But our orders now had to be 'stimu-
lating', in the style of propaganda. Many of the orders
of the Führer and O.K.W. were reproduced word for
word in subordinate orders, so as to ensure that, if things
went wrong, the latter could not be charged with having
failed to convey the Führer's intention.

"The conditions of compulsion in Germany under the
Nazi system were almost as bad as in Russia. I often had

evidence of what they were like there. For example, quite early in the campaign, I was present at the interrogation of two high Russian officers who were captured at Smolensk. They made it clear that they were entirely in disagreement with the plans they had executed, but said they had either to carry them out to the letter or lose their heads. It was only in such circumstances that men were able to talk freely—while in the grip of the régime they were forced to echo it and suppress their own thoughts.

"The systems of National Socialism and Bolshevism were similar in many ways. The Führer talking in his own circle one day, when General Halder was present, said how much he envied Stalin, who could deal in a more radical way with the obstinate generals than he could himself. He went on to speak about the pre-war purge of the Red Army Command and how he envied the Bolsheviks who had an army and generals completely impregnated with their own ideology and thus acting unconditionally as one man—whereas the German generals and the General Staff had no similar fanatical beliefs in the National Socialist idea. 'They have scruples, make objections, and are not sufficiently with me.'

"As the war went on Hitler indulged more and more in tirades of this kind. He still needed the class that he personally despised, as he could not carry out his operational functions without them, but he controlled their functions more and more closely. Many of the orders and reports thus bear two faces. Often what was signed did not represent the mind of the man concerned, but he had to sign it unless the too familiar consequences were to follow. Future psychologists, as well as historians, should pay attention to these phenomena."

THE DRIVE FOR THE CAUCASUS

The 1942 offensive had a curious shape, even in its original design. It was to be launched from the backward-slanting line Taganrog–Kursk—the right flank of which,

on the sea of Azov, was already close to the Don at Rostov,
while the left flank at Kursk lay more than 100 miles
behind, to the west. The offensive was to start with a
powerful thrust from this rearward flank. The aims were
mixed, and indefinite. Once again Hitler and the General
Staff had different ideas about the objective, and their
respective ideas were neither clarified nor reconciled
before the offensive was launched. Much trouble arose
from the divergence—as had happened in 1941. This
time the effects were still worse.

When Hitler insisted on resuming the offensive, despite
Halder's doubts, he originally prescribed an advance to
the Volga at Stalingrad. In preparing the operational
plan, Halder treated this as the main objective, and the
advance of the right wing as no more than a secondary
offensive move to provide strong cover for the southern
flank. But in Hitler's mind the purpose of capturing
Stalingrad, apart from its moral value, was to provide
protection on the northern flank so that he could safely
pursue a more far-reaching aim in the south-east—the
capture of the Caucasus.

Kleist, who commanded the armoured drive to the
Caucasus under List's direction, told me how Hitler had
given him personal instructions about his task. As Kleist
understood it: "The capture of Stalingrad was subsidiary
to the main aim. It was only of importance as a convenient
place, in the bottleneck between the Don and the Volga,
where we could block an attack on our flank by Russian
forces coming from the East. At the start Stalingrad was
no more than a name on the map to us." Blumentritt,
however, told me that: "Hitler originally had the idea of
wheeling north from Stalingrad with the aim of getting
astride the rear of the Russian armies at Moscow, but he
was persuaded, after considerable argument, that this was
an impossibly ambitious plan. Some of his entourage
had even been talking about an advance to the Urals,
but that was still more a fantasy."

Even as it was, the plan was a hazardous one, and became more hazardous from the way it worked out in practice.

Kleist said that Hitler sent for him on April 1st—an ominous date. "Hitler said we must capture the oilfields by the autumn because Germany could not continue the war without them. When I pointed out the risks of leaving such a long flank exposed, he said he was going to draw on Rumania, Hungary, and Italy for troops to cover it. I warned him, and so did others, that it was rash to rely on such troops, but he would not listen. He told me that these Allied troops would only be used to hold the flank along the Don from Voronezh to its southerly bend, and beyond Stalingrad to the Caspian, which, he said, were the easiest sectors to hold."

The ultimate course of events bore out such doubts as were felt at the time. Nevertheless, it has to be recognized that this second-year gamble did not fall far short of success. The summer of 1942 saw Russia's tide at its lowest ebb. It was fortunate for her that so much of Germany's initial strength had evaporated. A little greater impetus might have spread the many local collapses into a general collapse.

The summer offensive opened with brilliant success. For the Russians were suffering from their huge losses of men and equipment in 1941, and their newly-raised armies had not yet appeared on the scene. The German left wing made a rapid advance from Kursk to Voronezh. Its progress was helped because the Russian reserves were scanty—they mostly lay farther north in the Moscow sector. Another helpful factor was the Russian offensive towards Kharkov that had been carried out, with great persistence, during the month of May. Referring to this, Blumentritt said: "It used up much of the strength that might otherwise have been available to meet our offensive." He went on: "The 4th Panzer Army was the spearhead of this advance from Kursk to the Don and Voronezh. The

2nd Hungarian Army then took over that sector, while our armoured forces swerved south-eastward along the right bank of the Don."

Remembering the stirring reports at the time about the Russians' stubborn defence at Voronezh and the way it had blocked the German efforts to continue their drive in that sector, I questioned him further on this score. He replied: "There was never any intention of pushing beyond Voronezh and continuing this direct easterly drive. The orders were to halt on the Don near Voronezh and assume the defensive there, as flank cover to the south-eastward advance—which was carried out by the 4th Panzer Army, backed up by the 6th Army under Paulus."

This slanting drive down the corridor between the Don and the Donetz helped in turn to screen, and ease the way for, the thrust of Kleist's 1st Panzer Army, which soon came to assume the principal rôle. Starting near Kharkov, it made a rapid advance past Chertkovo and Millerovo towards Rostov. The 17th Army, south of the Donetz, only joined in the offensive when Kleist approached Rostov. Relating the story of that lightning stroke, Kleist told me that his army crossed the Lower Don above Rostov and then pushed eastward along the valley of the Manych River. The Russians blew up the dam there and the consequent floods threatened to upset the German plans. But his armoured forces succeeded in getting across the river after two days' delay and then swung southward, in three columns. Kleist himself accompanied the right column, which reached Maikop as early as the 9th of August. At the same time his centre and left columns were approaching the foothills of the Caucasus mountains, 150 miles farther to the south-east. This fan-shaped armoured drive was backed up by the 17th Army, which was pushing forward on foot.

Thus in six weeks from the outset the Germans had reached and captured the more westerly oilfields, but they never succeeded in reaching the main sources—which lay beyond the mountains. "The primary cause of our failure," Kleist said, "was shortage of petrol. The bulk of our supplies had to come by rail from the Rostov bottle-neck, as the Black Sea route was considered unsafe. A certain amount of oil was delivered by air, but the total which came through was insufficient to maintain the momentum of the advance, which came to a halt just when our chances looked best.

"But that was not the ultimate cause of the failure. We could still have reached our goal if my forces had not been drawn away bit by bit to help the attack at Stalingrad. Besides part of my motorized troops, I had to give up the whole of my flak corps and all my air force except the reconnaissance squadrons.

"That subtraction contributed to what, in my opinion, was a further cause of the failure. The Russians suddenly concentrated a force of 800 bombers on my front, operating from airfields near Grozny. Although only about a third of these bombers were serviceable, they sufficed to put a brake on my resumed advance, and it was all the more effective because of my lack of fighters and of flak."

Paying tribute to the stubbornness of the Russian defence here, Kleist made an interesting psychological point. "In the earlier stages of my advance I met little organized resistance. As soon as the Russian forces were by-passed, most of the troops seemed more intent to find the way back to their homes than to continue fighting. That was quite different to what had happened in 1941. But when we advanced into the Caucasus, the forces we met there were local troops, who fought more stubbornly because they were fighting to defend their homes. Their obstinate resistance was all the more effective because the country was so difficult for the advance."

Dealing in more detail with the course of operations in the later bound—after the capture of Maikop—he went on to say that the first objective assigned to him was to secure the whole length of the great highway from Rostov across the Caucasus mountains to Tiflis. Baku was to be a second objective. The advance met its first serious check on the Terek. He then tried to cross this river by a manœuvre farther to the east and succeeded. But after this he was held up again in the very difficult country beyond the Terek, which was not only precipitous, but densely wooded. The brake imposed by this frontal resistance was increased by the exposure of his left flank, in the Steppes between Stalingrad and the Caspian.

"The Russians brought reserves round from the southern Caucasus and also from Siberia. These developed a menace to my flank here, which was so widely stretched that the Russian cavalry could always penetrate my outposts whenever they chose. This flank concentration of theirs was helped by the railway that the Russians built across the Steppes, from Astrakhan southward. It was roughly laid, straight over the level plain without any foundation. Efforts to deal with the menace by wrecking the railway proved useless, for as soon as any section of the railway was destroyed a fresh set of rails was quickly laid down, and joined up. My patrols reached the shores of the Caspian, but that advance carried us nowhere, for my forces in this quarter were striking against an intangible foe. As time passed and the Russian strength grew in that area the flanking menace became increasingly serious."

Kleist went on trying to reach his objective until November—by repeated surprise attacks at different points. After failing to get through from Mozdok he made a turning movement from Nalchik on his western flank and succeeded in reaching Ordzhonikidze, in combination with a converging stroke from Prokhladnaya. He traced this multiple manœuvre for me on the map, describing it, with professional satisfaction, as "a very elegant battle". For it, he had at last been given a measure of air support. But then bad weather held him up, and after a short interval the Russians counter-attacked. "In this counter-attack, a Rumanian division, which I reckoned as a good one, suffered a sudden collapse and threw my plan out of joint. After that, a stalemate set in."

The other generals confirmed Kleist's evidence on the causes of the failure, especially the shortage of petrol—the armoured divisions were sometimes at a standstill for weeks on end, waiting for fresh supplies. Owing to this shortage the petrol lorries themselves were immobilized and petrol was brought forward on camels—an ironical revival of the traditional "ship of the desert". Blumentritt furnished a supplementary point in saying that the chance of over-coming the resistance in the mountains was diminished because most of the Germans' expert mountain troops, instead of being used to support Kleist, had been employed to help the 17th Army's advance along the Black Sea coast towards Batum. "That coastal advance was less important than von Kleist's thrust, and it was a mistake to put so much effort into it. When it was checked at Tuapse, and reinforcements were demanded, some of us demurred. The argument went on raging. We used to say, to those who pressed the need of the coastal advance—'Yes, children, but the oil is over there'—pointing to Baku. But the clamour for the reinforcement of the Tuapse operations prevailed, with the consequent splitting of our efforts in the Caucasus, until it was too late."

The divergence of effort that took place in the Caucasus area was repeated, on a greater scale, in the splitting of the forces between the Caucasus and Stalingrad. But on this question, too, Blumentritt differed from the prevailing view. "It was absurd to attempt to capture the Caucasus and Stalingrad simultaneously in face of strong resistance. My own preference, which I expressed at the time, was to concentrate first on taking Stalingrad. I felt that capturing the oil was less important than destroying the Russian forces. Although it was not possible to contradict economic experts who asserted that it was essential to obtain the oil, if we were to continue the war, events disproved their contention. For we managed to carry on the war until 1945 without ever securing the Caucasus oil."

DEFEAT AT STALINGRAD

The supreme irony of the 1942 campaign was that Stalingrad could have been taken quite early if it had been considered of prime importance. Kleist's account revealed this—"The 4th Panzer Army was advancing on that line, on my left. It could have taken Stalingrad without a fight, at the end of July, but was diverted south to help me in crossing the Don. I did not need its aid, and it merely congested the roads I was using. When it turned north again, a fortnight later, the Russians had gathered just sufficient forces at Stalingrad to check it."

Never again did the prospect look so bright for the Germans as in the second half of July. The rapid sweep of the two panzer armies had not only hustled the Russians out of successive positions but created a state of confusion favourable to further exploitation. That accounted for the ease with which the German armoured forces were able to gain crossings over the Lower Don. There was hardly anything to stop them at that moment from driving where they wished—south-eastward to the Caucasus or north-eastward to the Volga. Most of the Russian forces were still to the west of the Lower Don, outstripped in their retreat by the pace of the panzers.

When the 4th Panzer Army missed the chance of taking Stalingrad with a rush, through its temporary diversion south-eastward, the situation began to change. The Russians had time to rally and collect forces for the defence of Stalingrad. The Germans, after their first check, had to wait until the bulk of Paulus's 6th Army had fought its way forward to the Don, mopped up the Russian forces that were cornered in the bend of the river, and were eady to join in a converging attack on Stalingrad. But its arrival on the scene was retarded not only because it was a foot-marching force but because its pushing power dwindled, as division after division was dropped to guard the continually extending flank along the Middle Don.

By the time that the more deliberate bid for Stalingrad began, in the second half of August, the Russians had collected more reserves there. Check followed check. It was easier for the Russians to reinforce Stalingrad than the Caucasus, because it was nearer their main front. Hitler became exasperated at these repeated checks. The name of the place—"the City of Stalin"—was a challenge. He drew off forces from his main line, and everywhere else, in the effort to overcome it—and exhausted his army in the effort.

The three months' struggle became a battle of battering-ram tactics on the Germans' side. The more closely they converged on the city, the narrower became their scope for tactical manœuvre, as a lever in loosening resistance. At the same time, the narrowing of the front made it easier for the defender to switch his local reserves to any threatened point on the defensive arc. The more deeply the Germans penetrated into the densely built-up area of the city, the slower their progress became. In the last stages of the siege the front line was barely half a mile from the west bank of the Volga, but by then the strength of their efforts was fading, as a result of very heavy losses. Each step forward cost more and gained less.

The inherent difficulties of street fighting, in face of stubborn opponents, tended to outweigh the handicaps which the defence suffered in this case. The most serious of these was the fact that reinforcements and supplies had to come across the Volga by ferries and barges, under shell-fire. This limited the scale of the forces that the Russians could use, and maintain, on the west bank for the defence of the city. In consequence the defenders were often hard-pressed. The strain on them was the more severe because the higher command, with cool strategic calculation, reinforced the direct defence as sparingly as

possible—preferring to concentrate most of its gathering
reserves on the flanks, with a view to a counter-offensive.
In the later stages, only on two occasions did it divert to
Stalingrad itself a division from the armies that it was
assembling for the counter-offensive. The margin by
which the gallant defenders of Stalingrad held on was
narrow, but it sufficed.

The story of the prolonged battle for Stalingrad has
been graphically related from the Russian side. On the
German side, detail is lacking because most of the executive
commanders, as well as their troops, fell into the Russians'
hands. So far as it is known, it appears to have been a
rather dull process of battering at blocks of the city, with
diminishing resources. The hopes of the attackers faded
long before the initiative was wrested from them—but they
were forced to continue trying under Hitler's unrelaxing
demands for renewed efforts.

More historical interest lies in the evidence as to the
way that the push for Stalingrad turned into a trap for
the armies engaged. The collapse of the flanks was foreshadowed long before it actually occurred. Emphasizing
this fact Blumentritt said: "The danger to the long stretched
flank of our advance developed gradually, but it became
clear early enough for anyone to perceive it who was not
wilfully blind. During August the Russians by degrees
increased their strength on the other side of the Don, from
Voronezh south-eastward. A number of short and sharp
attacks on their part explored the weaknesses of the German
defence along the Don. These exploratory attacks showed
them that the Second Hungarian Army was holding the
sector south of Voronezh, and the Eighth Italian Army
was holding the sector beyond that. The risk became
worse after September, when the Rumanians took over the
more south-easterly sector as far as the Don bend, west of
Stalingrad. There was only a slight German stiffening in
this long 'Allied' front.

"Halder had sent me on a flying visit to the Italian

sector, as an alarming report had come that the Russians had penetrated it and made a large breach. On investigating it, however, I found the attack had been made by only one Russian battalion, but an entire Italian division had bolted. I took immediate steps to close the gap, filling it with an Alpine division and part of the 6th German division.

"I spent ten days in that sector and after returning made a written report to the effect that it would not be safe to hold such a long defensive flank during the winter. The railheads were as much as 200 kilometres behind the front, and the bare nature of the country meant that there was little timber available for constructing defences. Such German divisions as were available were holding frontages of 50 to 60 kilometres. There were no proper trenches or fixed positions.

"General Halder endorsed this report and urged that our offensive should be halted, in view of the increasing resistance that it was meeting, and the increasing signs of danger to the long-stretched flank. But Hitler would not listen. During September the tension between the Führer and Halder increased, and their arguments became sharper. To see the Führer discussing plans with Halder was an illuminating experience. The Führer used to move his hands in big sweeps over the map—'Push here; push there'. It was all vague and regardless of practical difficulties. There was no doubt he would have liked to remove the whole General Staff, if he could, by a similar sweep. He felt that they were half-hearted about his ideas.

"Finally, General Halder made it clear that he refused to take the responsibility of continuing the advance with winter approaching. He was dismissed, at the end of September, and replaced by General Zeitzler—who was then Chief of Staff to Field-Marshal von Rundstedt in the West. I was sent to the West to take Zeitzler's place.

"Arriving fresh on the scene, and being newly appointed to such a high position, Zeitzler did not at first worry the

Führer by constant objections in the way that General Halder had done. Thus Hitler pursued his aims unchecked, except by the Russians, and our armies were committed more deeply. Before long, Zeitzler became gloomy about the prospect and argued with the Führer that his intention of maintaining our armies forward near Stalingrad throughout the winter was impossible. When the outcome proved the truth of his warnings, the Führer became increasingly hostile to Zeitzler. He did not dismiss him, but he kept him at arm's length."

Summing up the situation Blumentritt said: "There would have been no risk of panic in withdrawing this time, for the German troops were now properly equipped for winter fighting, and had got over the fear of the unknown that had frightened them the year before. But they were not strong enough to hold on where they were, and the Russian strength was growing week by week.

"Hitler, however, would not budge. His 'instinct' had proved right the year before, and he was sure that it would be justified again. So he insisted on 'no withdrawal'. The result was that when the Russians launched their winter counter-offensive his army at Stalingrad was cut off, and forced to surrender. We were already too weakened to bear such a loss. The scales of the war had turned against Germany."

FURTHER REVELATIONS

On the question of the aims in the 1942 offensive, and whether Stalingrad or the Caucasus was the principal objective, General Halder has given me a very significant explanation of that unresolved issue.

"In Hitler's written order to me to prepare an offensive in South Russia in the summer of 1942, the objective given was the River Volga at Stalingrad. The operational order of the O.K.H., therefore, emphasized this objective and held only a protection of the flank south of the River Don to be necessary. This flank protection was to be achieved, firstly, by blocking the eastern part of the Caucasus—which was to be reached by attack; secondly, by holding a strong mobile force at Armavir, and on the high ground eastwards, which was to afford security against possible Russian attack between the High Caucasus and the River Manych. Hitler raised no objections to the executive order of O.K.H. But it seems possible to me that in his over-estimation of his own forces and under-estimation of the enemy forces—so typical of him—he was, early on, inwardly opposed to the limitation in the choice of objectives ordered by the O.K.H. south of the River Don. I remember some critical remarks made just at that time, about the lack of daring and initiative on the part of the General Staff. But Hitler did not connect them with the restriction shown on the subject of objectives south of the River Don. Obviously he was then not yet sure enough of himself to express his objections to the O.K.H. order.

"Later, when the basic operational orders had been issued by the O.K.H. he discussed the subject with those military leaders who were less opposed to his day dreams than the O.K.H. One such man was the very lively von Kleist who—through his Chief of Staff Zeitzler—had in any case a closer contact with Hitler than other Army leaders. In order to find somebody who would agree with his ideas, Hitler seems to have given Kleist another conception of the summer offensive as a whole to the one laid down in the operational order of the O.K.H.

"If the German advance towards Stalingrad was only intended as a protection of the flank of an attack upon the Caucasus—as von Kleist thinks—then von Kleist could rightly expect that the bulk of the forces would be directed towards the Caucasus. Under these circumstances he could agree with Hitler's far-reaching, ambitious plans, and that, obviously, was all that Hitler wanted from his discussions with von Kleist. It is possible, too, that the disastrous influence that Goering and Keitel exerted may have drawn

Hitler's ideas—which were originally directed towards Stalingrad—gradually and imperceptibly in the direction of Baku and Persia.

"I would emphasize again the fact that this attempt at an explanation is only based on knowledge of the persons involved and by no means on documents. I have, however, several times experienced cases in which Hitler succeeded in winning over the consent of leaders of lower rank by clearly misrepresenting those ideas which the O.K.H., as the superior organ, had rejected. I, therefore, think it possible that this was the case here too. It is, anyhow, characteristic of the conditions within the high leadership on the German side that I never came to hear of this discrepancy between the basic operational order of the O.K.H. and the directions given personally to an army commander by Hitler."

Warlimont gave me an illuminating commentary on various aspects of the campaign from the O.K.W. angle—"Hitler's operational plan for 1942 still showed traces of his original idea, namely to push forward on both wings and to keep back the central part of the front. In contrast to the previous year he now shifted the centre of gravity to the southern wing. Plans of advancing on the northern front were shelved until the necessary forces became available.

"The underlying idea was certainly fostered by the prospect of economic gains in the South, especially of wheat, manganese and oil. But to Hitler's mind it was still more important to cut off the Russians from these goods, allegedly indispensable for their continuation in the war, including coal from the Donetz area. Thus he believed he could bring the Russian machine of war to a stand-still. No resistance against Hitler's plans ever came to my ears, though I firmly believe that the general trend of opinion was opposed to resuming the offensive, at least on such a large scale as foreseen by Hitler.

"The course of the summer offensive in 1942 was

influenced by some more instances which may be of interest to you. First, I want to confirm Blumentritt's statement that Hitler did not intend to push beyond Voronezh. I remember that Field-Marshal von Bock was heavily reproached by Hitler because, in his opinion, Bock engaged his forces more than necessary by penetrating too deeply into the town area. (Bock was dismissed and replaced by Field-Marshal von Weichs.) Besides, Hitler had ordered from the start the preparation of a particularly strong reinforcement of anti-tank weapons for the whole defensive wing, from Voronezh to north of Kursk, in anticipation of heavy Russian counter-attacks against this part of the front.

"The ultimate cause of the failure, i.e. the drawing away of forces, had already set in when the first phase of the offensive at Voronezh had been completed. Even before the slanting drive down the corridor between the Don and the Donetz began, an entire panzer corps—the 11th —was assembled in the rear area and put at the disposal of Army Group Centre (von Kluge). The main reason for that was that it seemed impossible to supply the petrol for more than a certain amount of mechanized forces in the southern region. But Hitler once more tried to make amends for this splitting-up of the offensive forces by striving for another goal at the same time; Kluge was ordered to employ the 11th Panzer Corps to straighten out the bulge west of Ssuchinitschi, left over from the winter crisis, while Kluge himself wanted to send the corps farther north in order to check the threatening Russian counter-offensive which had already begun in the Rzhev area.

"The worst mistake of this kind happened in August, 1942—when several armoured divisions south of the Don were at a standstill, waiting for fresh supplies of petrol. Hitler then, on account of the British landing at Dieppe, lost his nerve and gave the order that two of the best divisions, the SS-Leibstandarte and the Gross-Deutschland, were to be transferred to the West. In spite of objections brought forward by Halder as well as by Jodl, Hitler insisted upon his order. Only the Leibstandarte actually reached the Western theatre, while the Gross-Deutschland division on its march to the railheads became entangled in a Russian counter-offensive in the central sector of the front and had to stay there.

"The failure of Field-Marshal List in the Low Caucasus not only led to his dismissal, but to a serious personal crisis in Hitler's headquarters late in September, 1942. Sometime earlier List had received the order to push on over the Low Caucasus towards the Black Sea, using all suitable routes. When he did not succeed in reaching his goal, Hitler once more became utterly impatient and sent Jodl to List's headquarters. On his return Jodl reported to Hitler that List had acted exactly in conformity to Hitler's orders, but that the Russian resistance was equally strong everywhere, supported by a most difficult terrain. Hitler, however, kept on reproaching List with having split up his forces instead of breaking through with concentrated power, while Jodl pointed to the fact that Hitler by his own orders had induced List to advance on a widely stretched front.

"This argument of Jodl's was followed by an unusual outburst of Hitler's. He was so taken aback by the recital of his own previous orders—which he now denied—that Jodl, and Keitel with him, fell in disgrace for a long time to come. Further consequences were that Hitler completely changed his daily customs. From that time on he stayed away from the common meals which he had taken twice a day with his entourage. Henceforth he hardly left his hut in daytime, not even for the daily reports on the military situation, which from now on had to be delivered to him in his own hut in the presence of a narrowly restricted circle. He refused ostentatiously to shake hands with any general of the O.K.W., and gave orders that Jodl was to be replaced by another officer.

"While this was not actually done, the changes in

Hitler's customs were kept up as long as I served with his Headquarters. Jodl, on one of the rare occasions when he talked in confidence to me, was inclined to find an explanation of Hitler's reaction to his report in the psychological field. Jodl had come to the conclusion that a dictator, as a matter of psychological necessity, must never be reminded of his own errors—in order to keep up his self-confidence, the ultimate source of his dictatorial force. My opinion was and is plainer but reaches farther: I am convinced that Hitler, when confronted with the actual situation at the end of the second offensive against Russia, suddenly grasped that he would never reach his goal in the East and that the war would eventually be lost.

"The danger arising for the long-stretched flank west of Stalingrad was evident also to Hitler, particularly because he came to know somehow that it was Stalin himself who had been behind the decisive blow which the Reds administered to the "White Guards" in that region in a rather similar situation of 1919.

"In addition, it became known that the Rumanian divisions, then gradually filling up the defensive front west of Stalingrad, were most inadequately equipped— marching up there from the far-distant railheads, partly without even shoes on their bare feet. Hitler, however, consciously faced the growing danger, trusting that a quick capture of Stalingrad would set free sufficient German forces to relieve the tense situation. But, instead, more and more German troops, finally even single battalions, were drawn away from the defensive wing in order to strengthen the desperate efforts at Stalingrad. At the same time the Russian counter-offensive against Army Group Centre, particularly in the Rzhev area, became a serious threat and caused increasing casualties. It was on this issue that the final clash between Hitler and Halder originated, which led to the latter's dismissal."

CHAPTER XVIII

AFTER STALINGRAD

A QUESTION that I put to many generals was: "Do you think that Germany could have avoided defeat after Stalingrad?" Rundstedt's reply was: "I think so, if the commanders in the field had been allowed a free hand in withdrawing when and where they thought fit, instead of being compelled to hold on too long, as repeatedly happened everywhere." While Rundstedt himself was not on the Eastern front after 1941, his position gave him more detachment of view. Moreover, the fact that he never took an optimistic view throughout, while having unique experience of high command on both fronts, gives a particular value to his opinion on the broad issue. When putting the same question to the generals who stayed in the East, I found them much more definite. All felt that Russia's offensive power could have been worn down by elastic defence—if they had only been allowed to practise it. Some gave striking examples.

Kleist cited his own experience in conducting the retreat from the Caucasus after Paulus's armies had been trapped at Stalingrad. He was promoted to field-marshal for his achievement in conducting that retreat without serious loss, and it would seem to have been better earned than many who have gained their baton for offensive successes, as is the normal rule. For it is difficult to think of any retreat in history that has extricated an army from such a dangerous position under such extraordinary difficulties—with the handicap of distance multiplied by winter, and then again by the pressure of superior forces pressing down on his flank and rear.

Relating the story of that retreat Kleist said: "Although

our offensive in the Caucasus had reached its abortive
end in November, 1942, when stalemate set in, Hitler
insisted on our staying in that exposed forward position,
deep in the mountains. At the beginning of January a
serious danger to my rear flank developed from an attack
which the Russians delivered from Elista westwards past
the southern end of Lake Manych. This was more serious
than the Russian counter-attacks on my forward position,
near Mozdok. But the greatest danger of all came from
the Russian advance from Stalingrad, down the Don
towards Rostov, far in my rear.

"When the Russians were only 70 kilometres from
Rostov, and my armies were 650 kilometres east of Rostov,
Hitler sent me an order that I was not to withdraw under
any circumstances. That looked like a sentence of doom.
On the next day, however, I received a fresh order—to
retreat, and bring away everything with me in the way
of equipment. That would have been difficult enough in
any case, but became much more so in the depths of the
Russian winter.

"The protection of my flank from Elista back to the
Don had originally been entrusted to the Rumanian Army
Group under Marshal Antonescu. Antonescu himself did
not arrive on the scene, thank God! Instead, the sector
was placed under Manstein, whose 'Army Group South'
included part of the Rumanian forces. With Manstein's
help, we succeeded in withdrawing through the Rostov
bottleneck before the Russians could cut us off. Even
so, Manstein was so hard pressed that I had to send some
of my own divisions to help him in holding off the Russians
who were pushing down the Don towards Rostov. The
most dangerous time of the retreat was the last half of
January."

Kleist emphasized how the course of this retreat,
which had appeared hardly possible to achieve, showed
the power of elastic defence. After his forces had got
safely back to the Dnieper, they were able to launch a

counter-offensive that turned the tables on the Russian advance westward from Stalingrad and the Don. This riposte recaptured Kharkov and restored the whole situation on the southern front. A long lull followed, which lasted until after mid-summer 1943.

That breathing space enabled the Germans to consolidate a firm position in the East, and to build up their strength afresh—not to its former level, but sufficient to provide a good prospect of holding the Russians at bay. But Hitler refused to listen to any advice in favour of changing to a defensive strategy. It was he, not the Russians, who took the offensive initiative in the summer. Although his effort was on a more limited scale and frontage than ever, he threw into it all the resources he had—employing seventeen armoured divisions in a converging attack on the Russians' Kursk salient. Talking of this offensive, Kleist said that he had little hope of any good resulting from it, but Kluge and Manstein who were put in charge of the pincers stroke seemed to be quite optimistic beforehand. "If it had been launched six weeks earlier it might have been a great success—though we had no longer the resources to make it decisive. But in the interval the Russians got wind of the preparations. They laid deep minefields across their front, while withdrawing their main forces farther to the rear, so that comparatively few were left in the bag that our high command had hoped to enclose."

MORE EVIDENCE ON THE KURSK OFFENSIVE

Manstein gave me the following explanation of his attitude and also of the delay in launching the offensive: "After the reconquest of Kharkov in March, 1943—the last German victory in the East—I gave Hitler an exposition of the situation to the effect that we could not hope to withstand the Russian attacks purely on the defensive. Our forces were too small to defend the enormous front.

Our only chance would be to utilize our superiority in leadership and the higher fighting value of our troops by a mobile defence.

"There were two possibilities for the conduct of operations in 1943, after the period of mud had passed.

"The first would be to prevent the Russians attacking by a German offensive. In that case our attack should be started at the earliest time possible, before the Russians could make up their losses, especially in tanks. The first step of our offensive should be to cut off the Russian salient at Kursk and destroy their reserves of armoured corps, which would be drawn into the struggle. Then we would have to turn south with all our armoured forces and roll up the Russian front in the South Ukraine. The start of our offensive must be the beginning of May.

"The other way—and the better one—would be to await the Russian offensive, which would certainly be launched against our front in the South Ukraine with the aim of rolling up our front north of the Black Sea. When the Russian offensive started we should give ground, and then —with all our strength—make a counter-attack from the Kiev region against the northern flank of the Russian offensive, with the aim of rolling up their whole front in the south.

"Hitler decided for the first way because he would not abandon the Donetz Basin and because he was not the man to take a big risk in strategy. The offensive against Kursk was to start in the first week of May. But a few days before the time came Hitler decided—under the influence of Model—to wait for more tanks. The offensive was postponed for four weeks in the first place, and then until July 13th, against the judgment of von Kluge and myself.

"It was plain that the offensive would now be very difficult. Nevertheless I had good hope. Indeed, the two armies of my army group that were engaged proved successful. They broke through the Russian front on the south side of Kursk, and had destroyed all the Russian armoured corps that appeared on the battlefield, when Hitler ordered the attack to be broken off. That was a necessity because Model's army (of Kluge's army group) which attacked from the north, had failed to break through, and because the Russians had broken through the front of Kluge's army group. I had to revert to the defensive and hand over several armoured divisions to von Kluge. In consequence my remaining forces did not suffice for the defensive task."

From Warlimont's evidence, however, it appears that the main pressure for the Kursk offensive did not come from Hitler, although he was unwilling to embark on a withdrawal, and that Zeitzler, the new Chief of the General Staff, was the driving force. Warlimont, in giving me his account, said: "Hitler was very reluctant to carry this plan through, though he created it. Zeitzler, in unison with Hitler, held the opinion that the German forces in the East were too weak and the communications too bad to take the risk of leaving it entirely to the Russians to choose when and where they would embark on an offensive of their own. Zeitzler, therefore, exercised much pressure on Hitler in favour of the Kursk attack.

"Jodl, who in the meantime had become Hitler's chief of staff for all the other theatres of war, advised against such a strong commitment in the East—pointing to the need of reinforcements and reserves in Italy and the Balkans, in anticipation of an Allied landing operation in the Mediterranean theatre.

"But Zeitzler was hardly interested in these far-off problems—the fact of being excluded from them, as Chief of Staff of the Army, was a constant source of anger to him. He urged all the more the execution of 'his' offensive, and complained to Hitler of Jodl's intrusion into his sphere of responsibility. Thus it became evident for the first time that the so-called Armed Forces Operations Staff under Jodl had definitely lost its rôle as an over-all advising agency—taking up, instead, the task of a second Army operations branch for all theatres other than the East.

From then on Hitler himself was, in fact, the only man who had a complete insight into the strategical situation.

"In the end, Hitler half-heartedly decided to launch the attack at Kursk—which cost us tremendous casualties. From the start, he did not seem to believe in success. Perhaps his eventual consent to the execution of this attack was mainly due to the fact that, otherwise, he could not have evaded the necessity for a deliberate strategic retreat in the East on a large scale. To consider such a possibility, however, was contrary to his creed—which he then, and later, used to express by the remark: 'The generals want to operate; which, in fact, means to retreat.' For the same reason he repeatedly prohibited any steps to build and fortify rear positions."

SEQUEL TO THE KURSK OFFENSIVE

When this last German offensive had been brought to a halt, the Russians launched theirs—as a counter-offensive. They now had ample resources to maintain the momentum, whereas the Germans in this last gamble had squandered the strength that might still have enabled them to impose a prolonged series of checks, and even produce a stalemate. Almost all the mobile reserves were exhausted. Thus the Russian advance rolled on during the autumn and winter with only short halts—caused more by out-running its own supplies than by the Germans' counter-thrusts. The whole southern front was in a state of flux.

But on the northern front, where the German forces had been allowed to remain on the defensive, the Russian attacks repeatedly broke down in face of the tenacious and well-knit resistance. I had a striking account of this period from Heinrici, who then commanded the 4th Army on the sector from Rogachev to Orsha, astride the great highway from Moscow to Minsk. Mentioning that he had been re-reading what I had written about the trends of modern warfare, he said: "I want to tell you how strongly

I agree, from experience, with your conclusions as to the superiority of defence over attack in the tactical field. The problem turns, as you remark, on the ratio of space to force. I think it may interest you to have some illustrative examples from my experience.

"After the evacuation of Smolensk, the Russians advanced to within twenty kilometres of Orsha, where the troops of the 4th Army were able to check them, after occupying a hastily-prepared position that consisted of only one trench line. That autumn we there had to meet a series of strong Russian offensives, beginning in October and continuing until December. There were five successive offensives. I had ten divisions in my army to hold a sector that was 150 kilometres wide as the crow flies, but actually about 200 kilometres allowing for the irregularity of the front. The 4th Army was without any reserves, and much weakened by the losses it had suffered. But its artillery was intact—that was a vital asset.

"The main objective of the Russians was the great rail centre of Orsha—in order to cut the lateral railway from Leningrad to Kiev. With this aim they concentrated the weight of their assault on a frontage of 20 kilometres astride the main highway. In their first offensive they employed 20–22 divisions; in the second 30 divisions; and in the next three about 36 divisions apiece. Part of them were the original ones, but most of them were fresh.

"To meet this assault I used 3½ divisions to hold the 20 kilometres frontage where the attack came, leaving 6½ to hold the remainder of my very wide front. Every attack was checked. These five successive battles each lasted five or six days, but the crisis usually came about the third or fourth day, after which the attack began to peter out. The Russians did not try any large armoured drive —because no considerable gap was made in the defences. The attacks were supported by up to fifty infantry tanks, but these were always checked.

"The Russians usually made about three tries a day—

the first about 9 a.m., after heavy artillery preparations; the second between 10 and 11; and the third between 2 and 3 in the afternoon. It was almost like clockwork! There was no question of the Russian troops failing to advance, until they were stopped by our fire—for they were driven forward under the compulsion of officers and commissars, marching in rear, and ready to turn their pistols on anyone who shirked. The Russian infantry were badly trained, but they attacked vigorously.

"In my opinion, there were three main factors that contributed to the success of the defence. First, I formed narrow divisional sectors, with a high ratio of force to space, on the actual frontage of the Russian assault. Secondly, I managed to form a very powerful artillery grouping, of 380 guns, to cover the threatened sector. This was controlled by a single commander, at Army Headquarters, and was able to concentrate its fire on any required point of that 20 kilometre frontage. The Russian offensives were supported by up to a thousand guns, but their fire was not so concentrated. Thirdly, the losses of the German divisions engaged—which had to be reckoned as the equivalent of about one battalion per division in each day of battle—were compensated by a system of drawing battalions from the divisions in other parts of the Army front. I always tried to have three fresh battalions —one for each of the divisions holding the battle front— ready behind this before the attack started. The other battalion of the regiment from which it was drawn would follow, together with the regimental staff, and in this way I would get complete fresh regiments incorporated in the front, and then complete fresh divisions. The temporary mixing of divisions was inevitable, and part of the price of the defensive success, but I always tried to restore their integrity as soon as possible."

In May, 1944, Heinrici was given command of the 1st Panzer Army together with the 1st Hungarian Army on the Carpathian front, and with these forces conducted the retreat to Silesia early in 1945 after the German front had collapsed in the north. In March, 1945, he was given command of the Army Group that faced the Russians' final push for Berlin. With this he fought the battle of the Oder and the battle of Berlin.

In this later stage, he said, he had further developed the defensive methods which he had already described. "When the Russians were found to be concentrating for an attack, I withdrew my troops from the first line under cover of night, to the second line—usually about 2 kilometres behind. The result was that the Russian blow hit the air, and its further attack did not have the same impetus. Of course, a necessary condition of success was to discover the actual intended day of the assault, which I sought to do by using patrols to secure prisoners. After the Russian attack had been broken, I continued to hold the second line as my new forward position, while on the sectors that had not been attacked the troops moved forward again to re-occupy the first line. This system worked very well in the battle of the Oder—the only drawback was our scanty strength, after so much had been wasted needlessly by the rigid defence of positions impossible to hold.

"I never suffered defeat during three years of defensive battles when I could base my plan on such methods—and I was proud that I never had to call on the Higher Command to spare me any of its reserves. I found self-propelled guns were of the greatest value in applying these defensive tactics.

"In the light of my experience, I consider that your conclusion that the attacker needs a three to one superiority is under the mark, rather than over it. I would say that, for success, the attacker needs six to one or seven to one against a well-knit defence that has a reasonable frontage to cover. There were times when my troops held their own against odds of 12 to 1 or even 18 to 1.

"The German defeat in the East was, in my opinion, due to one main reason—that our troops were compelled to cover immense spaces without the flexibility, in the command, that would have enabled them to concentrate on holding decisive points. Thus they lost the initiative permanently. I doubt whether we could have worn down the Russians by pure defence, but might well have been able to turn the balance by a more mobile kind of warfare, and by shortening our front so as to release forces that could be used for effective counter-strokes.

"But the army commanders were never consulted about the plan or method of defence. Guderian, when Chief of the General Staff in the last year, had no influence on Hitler. His predecessor, Zeitzler, had only a very slight influence. Earlier still, Halder's advice had been largely disregarded.

"My first experience after taking over command of the 4th Army in 1942, opened my eyes. I withdrew a small detachment from an awkward position it was holding—whereupon I received a warning, conveyed through General von Kluge, then the commander of the Army Group, that if I did anything of the sort again the least that would happen to me would be a court-martial.

"Hitler always tried to make us fight for every yard, threatening to court-martial anyone who didn't. No withdrawal was officially permitted without his approval —even a small-scale withdrawal. This principle was so hammered into the army that it was a common saying that battalion commanders were afraid 'to move a sentry from the window to the door'. These rigid methods cramped us at every turn. Time after time, forces stayed in impossible positions until they were surrounded and captured. But some of us ventured to evade his orders so far as we could."

Such evasion was only possible in a local and limited way. Tippelskirch, who succeeded Heinrici in command of the 4th Army, bore witness to the value of elastic defence, but also to the disastrous consequences of being unable to practise it to an adequate extent. "At Mogilev in March,

1944, I was commanding the 12th Corps—which consisted of three divisions. In the offensive the Russians then launched, they used ten divisions in the assault on the first day, and by the sixth day had used twenty divisions. Yet they only captured the first line, and were brought to a halt before the second. In the lull that followed I prepared a counter-stroke, delivered it by moonlight, and recovered all the ground that had been lost—with comparatively few casualties."

Tippelskirch then went on to relate what happened in the Russians' summer offensive in 1944. He took over command of the 4th Army three weeks before it opened. The army commanders on that front begged for permission to withdraw to the line of the Beresina—a long step back that would have taken the sting out of the Russian blow. But their proposals were rejected. Tippelskirch nevertheless made a short step back on his sector to the line of the Dnieper, and that sufficed to keep his front intact. But the fronts of both the armies on his right and left were ruptured, and a general collapse followed. The retreat did not stop until the Vistula had been reached, near Warsaw.

"It would have been much wiser strategy to withdraw the whole front in time. The Russians always needed a long pause for preparation after any German withdrawal, and they always lost disproportionately when attacking. A series of withdrawals by adequately large steps would have worn down the Russian strength, besides creating opportunities for counter-strokes at a time when the German forces were still strong enough to make them effective.

"Hitler had been justified in his 1941 veto on any withdrawal, but his great mistake was to repeat it in 1942 and later, when conditions were different. For after the first year the German Army was well equipped for winter fighting, and felt quite able to hold its own with the Russians under these conditions. Thus a strategic withdrawal would not have shaken its morale. Our troops were quite capable of carrying out such a manœuvre in winter. Besides economizing their own strength, it would have enabled them to stage a powerful come-back.

"The root cause of Germany's defeat was the way that her forces were wasted in fruitless efforts, and above all in fruitless resistance at the wrong time and place. That was due to Hitler. There was no strategy in our campaign."

Manteuffel said: "There is no doubt that the advance of the Red Armies in the various phases of the war after Stalingrad would have resulted differently if our defence had been more mobile and with a delaying resistance. Time and again this form of fighting has brought me success even against numerical superiority."

General Dittmar contributed some interesting points to the discussion, from his wider and more detached point of view. As a military commentator he was amazingly objective in his broadcast commentaries during the war—more so perhaps than any other military critic anywhere. This was the more notable because he had to expound the situation under restrictions, and dangers, far worse than any Allied commentator had to fear. When I asked him how he was able to speak so candidly on many occasions, he told me that he owed this latitude to Fritsche, the head of radio propaganda, who alone saw his broadcasts before they were delivered. He had the feeling that Fritsche had reached an underlying disillusionment with regard to the Nazi régime, and was glad to give scope to someone who would express what he secretly felt himself. Naturally there were many protests, though Fritsche did his best to shield Dittmar. "I always felt that I was walking a tight-rope with a noose round my neck."

When I asked Dittmar whether he thought that if the Germans had adopted a strategy of elastic defence they could have worn down the Russians, he replied: "I believe we could, and the advantages of elastic defence were clear, but our military chiefs could not apply it properly because

of Hitler's objections. The General Staff were not allowed
to order the construction of lines in rear, or even to discuss
plans in case of being driven back. They were forbidden
to make any preparatory plans for a withdrawal. In
1943, however, they managed to do a little preparatory
work on the quiet, by circulating instructions in discreetly
worded leaflets. These leaflets were distributed among
the various armies, but without any imprint to show that
they emanated from the General Staff."

I asked Dittmar whether any strategic withdrawal was
attempted on the German side, prior to the launching of
the great Russian offensive in July, 1943, or again before
that of January, 1945. He replied: "No. Each was a
case of an absolute break-through, owing to the strategy
that Hitler imposed. Some of the commanders of the
lower formations were shrewd enough to evade his rule
that every place was to be held at all costs, and carried out
short withdrawals on their own, but others clung on in
strict obedience to orders, and as a result their troops were
cut off and captured. The disaster in each case was due
to the fundamental error of a rigidly defensive strategy.
That disaster was all the worse in the case of the Russian
offensive from the Vistula in January, 1945, because the
reserves that had been held ready to meet the threat
were taken away at the critical moment and dispatched
to the relief of Budapest." They comprised three of the
best-equipped armoured divisions available.

"The policy of clinging on at all costs in particular
places repeatedly changed the campaign for the worse.
The attempt to cement one threatened breach in the general
front repeatedly caused fresh breaches. In the end that
proved fatal."

CHAPTER XIX

THE RED ARMY

THE German generals' impressions of the Red Army were interesting, and often illuminating. The best appreciation in a concise form came from Kleist: "The men were first-rate *fighters* from the start, and we owed our success simply to superior training. They became first-rate *soldiers* with experience. They fought most toughly, had amazing endurance, and could carry on without most of the things other armies regarded as necessities. The Staff were quick to learn from their early defeats, and soon became highly efficient."

Some of the other German generals disagreed, and said that the Russian infantry in general remained rather poor, tactically and technically, though the tank forces were formidable. I noted, however, that the more critical opinions came from generals who had been on the northern half of the front—which suggests that the more skilled part of the Red Army operated in the south. On the other hand, the guerrillas seem to have been more active behind the German front in the north, and by 1944 had forced the Germans there to abandon the use of all except a few of the trunk roads as supply routes. Tippelskirch, whose 4th Army was cut off on the northern Dnieper by the Russian summer offensive that year, told me that he extricated it by making a detour southwards towards the Pripet Marches, after the main line of retreat to Minsk had been blocked, moving by way of roads which had long been abandoned because of guerrilla interference. "I found every single bridge on the route had been broken, and had to repair them in the course of my retreat."

Talking of his four years' experience of the Northern front, he remarked: "Our infantry lost their fear of the

Russian infantry in 1941, but they remained fearful of being taken prisoner—and sent to Siberia or worse. This fear helped to stiffen their resistance, but it had an insidious effect as time went on, particularly when they were compelled by Hitler's order to remain in isolated forward positions where they were bound eventually to be cut off."

I asked Rundstedt what he considered were the strong and weak points of the Red Army, as he found it in 1941. His reply was: "The Russian heavy tanks were a surprise in quality and reliability from the outset. But the Russians proved to have less artillery than had been expected, and their air force did not offer serious opposition in that first campaign."

Manteuffel remarked: "In 1941, the Russians found themselves faced with the same problem as we had from 1942 onwards—their infantry, insufficiently equipped with means of anti-tank defence, could not hold on without the help of *mobile* anti-tank defence—i.e. without the support of tanks. As a result armoured combat teams had to be attached to the infantry—which is fatal to the effectiveness of armoured forces, as it entails splitting them up in small packets."

Talking more specifically of the Russian weapons Kleist said: "Their equipment was very good even in 1941, especially the tanks. Their artillery was excellent, and also most of the infantry weapons—their rifles were more modern than ours, and had a more rapid rate of fire. Their T.34 tank was the finest in the world." In several discussions, Manteuffel emphasized the excellent basic qualities of Russian tank design, and particularly the advantage they gained from the fact that "their tracks are strong and broad, enabling the tanks to climb, wade and cross ditches without the tracks coming off". British experts have criticized the Russian tanks for lacking the refinements, and gadgets, desirable in various operational respects. But the German tank experts considered that the British and Americans tended to sacrifice too much in the way of power and performance for these refinements.

As regards the provision of equipment, Kleist said that

the Russians' weakest period had been in 1942. They had not been able to make up their 1941 losses, and throughout the year were very short of artillery in particular. "They had to use mortars, brought up on lorries to compensate their lack of artillery." But from 1943 on their equipment position became better and better. While the inpouring flow of Allied supplies was a big factor, especially in motor transport, the increasing production of the new Russian factories in the East, out of reach, accounted for even more. The tanks employed were almost entirely of their own manufacture.

Guderian said: "The Russians picked up their ideas for the design of their tanks in the U.S.A. The main tank of 1941 was the first Christie Russkij; a development of the U.S.-Christie, and soon after the beginning of the campaign, the well-known T.34, which shows the forms of the Christie. The T.34 tank was first produced in 1941, and first appeared at the front in July, 1941, while the Stalin tank first appeared in 1944.

"I don't think that the Russians are a backward people, since I had the opportunity to see their factory for tractor production at Kharkov, in 1933. In the neighbourhood of this factory for tractor production there was the factory for tank production, and I saw 20 to 25 Christie tanks leave this factory. The Russians told me that this was the case every day—in 1933! The Russians have a special ability to copy foreign models and adapt them to the conditions of their country.

"Thus the T.34 tank was superior to the German tanks in tracks, in motors, in armour and in gun, but inferior in optics and radio—and it had no turret for the tank commander with all-round sight. When—in 1943—the German Panther and Tiger tanks appeared on the battlefields, the superiority passed again to the Germans, but it applied only to the single tank, and not to the quantity. The Russians produced their T.34 tanks without modifications in great series, while Hitler could not be prevented from perpetually changing the types, thus causing repeated reductions of the series.

"Therefore, anxious to learn from history, I give you the warning not to underrate the Russians. They, at least, are able to copy the ideas of others in a very short time."

Some further comments of interest came from Captain von Senger—son of a panzer corps commander—who after commanding a tank unit in Russia, and losing an arm, was adjutant to the Inspector of Panzer Forces in the last part of the war. "The general design of the Russian tanks was good, while simple to the point of crudity. They did not provide comfort for the crews, as the German, British and American tanks did, and the exterior was as rough as the interior—not even painted. But the gun-mounting and other essentials were well-designed. Prior to the summer of 1943 there was wireless only in the tanks of platoon commanders and above, but after that all tanks were fitted with wireless, beginning with the new T.34 which then appeared, the crew being increased from four to five to provide for an operator." (Manteuffel mentioned: "I met, on several occasions, women wireless operators in tanks—they were extremely brave, tough and fanatical.")

Senger emphasized: "The Russians had these principles —to pick up the best type of machine wherever they got it; to have only a very few types; to construct the type as simply as possible; and then to produce these types in large quantities. Our panzer division in 1942 had twelve different types of armoured vehicle and twenty types of other vehicle. The Russian armoured corps then had mostly only one type of tank, the T.34, and one other vehicle, the Ford truck!

"The Russians had only tanks and lorries in their mechanized formations—no cars, motor-cycles or other kinds of vehicle. In the later stages of the war they had a small proportion of jeeps, from American sources, which were used by the battalion commanders, etc. The simplicity of the Russian organization had its drawbacks, but also its advantages, compared with the German—which suffered from having too many types of vehicle, of varying performance and design, thus complicating movement calculations as well as spare part supplies.

"The Russian tank maintenance was also good. The bigger repairs were not carried out as fast as in the German Army, but their normal maintenance service was very efficient, and they had plenty of well-trained mechanics. Indeed, we came increasingly to employ Russian mechanics in our own tank maintenance companies. Before the war it had been a general assumption in Germany, as elsewhere, that the Russians were not mechanically minded or skilled, but this assumption was disproved by experience. They have a natural sense for technical matters, perhaps more so than some Western peoples."

Manteuffel said: "Their salvage and repair services—which in the armoured arm must never be separated from the 'troops'—were very good. They performed extraordinary feats by following the tank troops on foot to tow away and repair the machines. I therefore issued orders that, on principle, tanks were to be set on fire.

"On the other hand, the Russian panzer formations lacked tactical mobility which, coupled with an adequate personnel, is the basis for operative mobility and adaptability. In this respect, by the end of the war they had certainly learnt a great deal but never reached the standard of the German crews and those of the Allies."

More detailed comments on this subject were made by Senger: "Russian tank tactics were of a simple nature, and carried out on a drill pattern that was carefully planned in advance, so as to avoid demanding too much in the way of individual initiative and judgment. For the Russian tank leaders, while efficient within their limits, were not highly intelligent. Before an attack they were given maps on which their routes and objectives were marked by coloured lines—many of these maps were captured, and from them a good idea could be gained of the extent to which tactics were 'planned'.

"Their tactics were, in fact, of an 'infantry support' type, operating in small units. They commonly used a company of tanks—ten machines—to lead and open the way for an infantry company. In attack, they attacked in a long line of tank companies, each closely backed up by infantry. They did not attack in big formations. But after breaking through, the Russian tanks would concentrate and continue the advance in a large formation —until a fresh defensive line was met.

"The Russians had no half-track or full-track armoured vehicles to carry the infantry. They carried a proportion of the supporting infantry on top of the tanks themselves, as long as possible. Apart from these, the Russians depended on motorized infantry divisions, brought up in lorries."

A rather surprising feature of the campaign in the East was that the Russians did not make any effective use of airborne forces, although they had led the world in the development of this new arm—which had played a prominent part in their Army Manœuvres in pre-war years. I discussed this question with Student, who replied: "I often wondered why the Russians never used their parachute troops. The reason, I imagine, may have been that their training was insufficient—due to lack of practice in navigation as well as in dropping. All they did in this way was to drop agents and small parties for sabotage behind our front."

There was one remarkable exception to that rule of abstinence—when the Russians carried out an airborne operation of a highly unconventional kind. As related by Student: "During the Russian winter campaign of 1941–42, several thousand Russians were dropped from the air in the most primitive manner with Russian carelessness behind the German front south-west of Moscow, in support of cavalry forces which had worked their way through. On several clear moonlight nights the Russian transport planes flew over the wide and deep snow-fields. They flew quite slowly a few metres above ground and the Russian soldiers jumped from the aeroplanes without parachutes. It was the simplest form of an airborne operation."

Coming to the question of leadership I asked Rundstedt which were the best of the Russian generals in his experience. He replied: "None were any good in 1941. Of Budenny, who commanded the armies facing me, a captured Russian officer aptly remarked—'He is a man with a very large moustache, but a very small brain.' But in later years there is no doubt of the improvement in their generalship. Zhukov was very good. It is interesting to recall that he first studied strategy in Germany under General von Seeckt—this was about 1921–23."

Dittmar, who in his position as the leading military commentator was best placed to gather the consensus of opinion among the German generals, said that Zhukov was regarded as outstanding. Koniev was good, a clever tactician, but not quite on the same level. "As the war went on, the Russians developed an increasingly high standard of leadership from top to bottom. One of their greatest assets was their officers' readiness to learn, and the way they studied their job." He added that the Russians could afford to make mistakes, because of their immense superiority of strength, in a way that the Germans could not.

This verdict on the Russian generals was questioned by some of their German opponents, especially those who had been on the Northern front. Broadly speaking, the run of opinion seemed to be that the top and bottom of the Russian ladder of command became the strongest sections, while the middle piece was shaky. The top rungs were filled by men who had proved themselves so able that they were allowed to exercise their own judgment, and could safely insist on doing things in their own way. The bottom rungs were filled by junior officers who, within their limited sphere, tended to develop a good tactical sense, because the incompetent soon became casualties in a field that was ruled by the hard realities of the enemy's bullets and shells. But the intermediate commanders, even more than in most armies, were concerned with other factors. Their superiors' orders and judgments were more to be feared than the enemy.

In this connection one of the German army commanders on the northern front made a significant comment: "It was usually safe to encourage the Russians to attack, so long as the defence was elastically designed. The Russians were always very bull-headed in their offensive methods, repeating their attacks again and again. This was due to the way their leaders lived in fear of being considered lacking in determination if they broke off their attack."

As regards the general characteristics of the Russian soldier, Dittmar gave me an illuminating sidelight when I asked him what he considered was the Russians' chief asset. "I would put first, what might be called the soulless indifference of the troops—it was something more than fatalism. They were not quite so insensitive when things went badly for them, but normally it was difficult to make any impression on them in the way that would happen with troops of other nations. During my period of command on the Finnish front there was only one instance where Russian troops actually surrendered to my own. While that extraordinary stolidity made the Russians very difficult to conquer it was also their chief weakness in a military sense—because in the earlier campaigns it often led to them being encircled."

Dittmar added: "On Hitler's specific orders, an attempt was later made in the German Army to inculcate the same mental attitude that prevailed in the Red Army. We tried to copy the Russians in this respect, while the Russians copied us, more successfully, in tactics. The Russians could afford to train their troops in this attitude because losses mattered little to them, and the troops were accustomed to do implicitly what they were told."

That habit of unquestioning obedience was apt to offset the Russians' natural tactical sense, cramping flexibility and making them susceptible to surprise. Tippelskirch, for instance, remarked: "It is not difficult to upset their plans, because they are very rigid. It takes them a lot of time to alter their plans, especially during an action. In my experience I always found that Russian attacks could be stopped and thrown back by resolute counter-strokes, even by far inferior forces—if made immediately—just because they took the Russians by surprise. The Russians are much impressed by unexpectedly strong or energetic resistance, whereas they become more daring if they feel superior. They have a manifest sense for seeking safety when threatened, like wild animals have. It may be the reason why, despite their technical and mechanical sense, their air force was always their weakest side—for an air force is an openly aggressive arm and does not fit their character. But only forces with masterly leadership, first-class training, high morale and excellent nerves can overcome them. Such forces can be inferior in number."

Blumentritt, who was fond of discoursing philosophically and historically on all these subjects, gave me his impressions at greater length, starting with his experience in the First World War.

"In 1914–18, as a lieutenant, I fought for the first two years against the Russians, after a brief contact with the French and Belgians at Namur in August, 1914. In our very first attack on the Russian front, we quickly realized that here we were meeting essentially different soldiers from the French and Belgian—hardly visible, entrenched with consummate skill, and resolute! We suffered considerable losses.

"In those days it was the Russian Imperial Army. Hard, but good-natured on the whole, they had the habit of setting fire on military principle to towns and villages, in East Prussia when they were forced to withdraw, just as they always did thereafter in their own country. When the red glow from the burning villages lit up the horizon at evening, we knew that the Russians were leaving. Curiously, the population did not seem to complain. That was the Russian way, and had been so for centuries.

"When I referred to the bulk of the Russian Army as good-natured, I am speaking of their European troops. The much harder Asiatic troops, the Siberian corps, were cruel in their behaviour. So, also, were the Cossacks. Eastern Germany had plenty to suffer on this score in 1914.

"Even in 1914–18 the greater hardness of war conditions in the East had its effect on our own troops. Men preferred to be sent to the Western rather than the Eastern front. In the West it was a war of material and mass-artillery—Verdun, the Somme, and so on. These factors were paramount, and very gruelling to endure, but at least we were dealing with Western adversaries. In the East there was not so much shell-fire, but the fighting was more dogged, as the human type was much harder. Night fighting, hand-to-hand fighting, fighting in the forests, were particularly fostered by the Russians. In that war there was a saying current among German soldiers: 'In the East the gallant Army is fighting; in the West the Fire Brigade is standing by.'

"It was in this war, however, that we first learnt to realize what 'Russia' really means. The opening battle in June, 1941, revealed to us for the first time the new Soviet Army. Our casualties were up to fifty per cent. The Ogpu and a women's battalion defended the old citadel at Brest–Litovsk for a week, fighting to the last, in spite of bombardment with our heaviest guns and from the air. Our troops soon learnt to know what fighting the Russians meant. The Führer and most of our highest chiefs didn't know. That caused a lot of trouble.

"The Red Army of 1941–45 was far harder than the Tsar's Army, for they were fighting fanatically for an idea. That increased their doggedness, and in turn made our own troops hard, for in the East the maxim held good—'You or I'. Discipline in the Red Army was far more rigorous than in the Tsar's Army. These are examples of the sort of order that we used to intercept—and they were blindly obeyed. 'Why do you fail to attack? I order you for the last time to take Strylenko, otherwise I fear for your health.' 'Why is your regiment not in the initial position for attack? Engage at once unless you want to lose your head.' In such ways we were brought to realize the inexorable character of our opponents. We had no idea in 1941 that within a few years it would be much the same with us.

"Wherever Russians have appeared in the history of war, the fight was hard, ruthless, and involved heavy losses. Where the Russian makes a stand or defends himself, he is hard to defeat, and it costs a lot of bloodshed. As a child of nature he works with the simplest expedients. As all have to obey blindly, and the Slav-Asiatic character only understands the absolute, disobedience is non-existent. The Russians commanders can make incredible demands on their men in every way—and there is no murmuring, no complaint.

"The East and the West are two worlds, and they cannot understand each other. Russia is a dumb question mark on the Sphinx. The Russians can keep their mouths shut, and their minds are closed to us."

Blumentritt's reflections touched on a point that played a part almost as great as morale. For all the generals emphasized that the Russians' greatest asset was the way they could do without normal supplies. Manteuffel, who led many tank raids deep behind their front, gave the most vivid picture—"The advance of a Russian Army is something that Westerners can't imagine. Behind the tank spearheads rolls on a vast horde, largely mounted on horses. The soldier carries a sack on his back, with dry crusts of bread and raw vegetables collected on the march from the fields and villages. The horses eat the straw from the house roofs—they get very little else. The Russians are accustomed to carry on for as long as three weeks in this primitive way, when advancing. You can't stop them, like an ordinary army, by cutting their communications, for you rarely find any supply columns to strike."

CHAPTER XX

THE ALLIED INVASION OF ITALY

WHEN the German-Italian position in Tunisia collapsed in May, 1943, the Allies were presented with a marvellous opportunity. Eight divisions, together with a mass of auxiliary troops, were cut off and taken prisoner in that African "sack". They comprised the bulk of the German troops on the Mediterranean theatre and the best of the Italian divisions. Italy itself now lay open to attack, while stripped of defenders, and Italian morale sank to a new low level. Only a few German troops were immediately available to buttress Italy's defence—two divisions on the mainland, one that was being improvised in Sicily from drafts that had been sent there, and another of the same kind in Sardinia.

Two months passed, however, before the Allies followed up their victory in Tunisia by landing in Sicily, on July 10th. Even then there were only two German divisions on the scene to meet the initial assault of eight Allied divisions. For the Italians mostly collapsed as soon as the Allies had landed. But the Germans, though lacking air support and being reinforced by only two more divisions, succeeded in holding up the more heavily reinforced invading armies. After delaying the Allied conquest of Sicily until the middle of August, they slipped away across the Straits of Messina, under a canopy of *flak*, to the Italian mainland. Field-Marshal Kesselring, the German Commander-in-Chief in Southern Italy, was thankful for the breathing space they had gained for him. But he was also relieved when they got away safely, for he had feared that his opponent would make a further landing on the Calabrian "toe" of Italy and thus block their retreat while they were still engaged in Sicily.

A greater opportunity was missed in the larger field of grand strategy. The Italians' desire for peace had been made manifest by the overthrow of Mussolini on July 25th —as well as by the promptness with which the Italian troops in Sicily had surrendered. But the Allies made little effort to ease the new Government's path to peace, and it was not until September 3rd that the terms of the armistice were settled and signed—behind the Germans' back. It was announced on the 8th, the night before the Allies landed in strength at Salerno, south of Naples. Five days earlier, on the 3rd, the Eighth Army under Montgomery had crossed the Straits of Messina and begun to push slowly up the toe of Italy.

Even then, Kesselring had only seven divisions to guard the whole south and centre of the Italian peninsula, although a further eight German divisions had now arrived in Northern Italy and several more were on the way. The strain on Kesselring's limited strength was increased by the necessity of disarming the Italian forces and keeping guard on them. Fortunately for him the main Allied landing came at a point, Salerno, where he could conveniently concentrate, while the advance up the toe carried no immediate danger to him. He benefited much from the Allied commanders' reluctance to venture outside the limits of air cover—and in his calculations was able to reckon on their consistency in observing such conventional limitations. As a result the Allied landing at Salerno— optimistically styled "Operation Avalanche"—suffered a costly check and courted a disaster, which was only avoided by a narrow margin.

It had seemed to me, beforehand, that the most effective way to take the Germans off their guard, and throw them off their balance, was to make a landing beyond these limits; and I had argued that a landing on the heel of Italy, in the area of Taranto and Brindisi, would be "the line of least expectation" while entailing little risk—and promising the early possession of two fine ports.

Such a landing was added to the plan at the last moment, as a subsidiary move, but the Taranto force consisted only of the British 1st Airborne Division, which was hurriedly collected from rest-camps in Tunisia, and rushed across in such naval vessels as were available at short notice. It met no opposition—but arrived without any tanks, without any artillery except for one howitzer, and with scarcely any motor transport. In sum, it lacked the very things it needed to exploit the opportunity it had gained. After nearly a fortnight had passed, another small force (including an armoured brigade) was landed at Bari, the next port up the east—the Adriatic—coast. It drove north without meeting any serious resistance, and was able to seize the important group of airfields around Foggia—from which the bombing campaign against Germany could be developed from a fresh direction. This indirect advance from the heel of Italy also threatened the rear flank of the German divisions which were facing the Allies near Salerno, and thus helped to loosen their resistance.

On October 1st the Allies entered Naples. In the meantime, however, the Germans had established a firm grip on the rest of Italy, disarmed the Italian forces and nullified the effects of Italy's surrender. They were now able to concentrate on checking the Allies' advance up the peninsula—which was barely a hundred miles wide, while most of that space was filled by the mountain spine and ribs of the Apennines. The Germans had previously hoped for no more than to impose a short delay on the Allies' advance to Rome and gain time to consolidate a defensive front in the north of Italy. But they were encouraged to push reinforcements southwards when they saw that the Allies' progress was slow. It became like the push of a sticky piston-rod in a sticky cylinder against increasingly strong compression.

The advance of General Mark Clark's Anglo-American Fifth Army from Salerno was checked on the line of the Volturno River, twenty miles beyond Naples, and again, more definitely, on the Garigliano in front of Cassino.

Successive attacks in November and December failed to pierce this barrier. Meanwhile, on the eastern side of the Apennines, Montgomery's Eighth Army had advanced from Foggia on October 1st and forced the Biferno River with the help of the leverage exerted by a small landing at Termoli in the enemy's rear. But it was then checked on the line of the Sangro. Montgomery mounted a big attack at the end of November, saying: "The time has now come to drive the Germans north of Rome. . . . The Germans are, in fact, in the very condition in which we want them. We will now hit the Germans a colossal crack." But he was blocked soon after crossing the river, and a deadlock developed—both east and west of the Apennines.

By the end of the year the Allies were only seventy miles beyond Salerno—after four months' pushing. Most of that ground had been gained in September, and since then the rate of progress had been so gradual that the Allied troops had come to describe the method of advance by the term "inching".

At the end of the year Montgomery left the theatre for England, to take charge of the preparations for the landing in Normandy, and several of the most experienced Allied divisions went with him, being replaced by fresh ones. More serious for the prospects of the Italian campaign was the large-scale diversion of landing craft and shipping for the purposes of the Normandy invasion. Sir Oliver Leese succeeded Montgomery in command of the Eighth Army, but Mark Clark remained in command of the Fifth, and Alexander continued to direct the Italian campaign as a whole.

Late in January, 1944, a fresh seaborne manœuvre was tried, with the aim of loosening the enemy's hold on the Garigliano and around Cassino. A strong force was landed near Anzio, twenty-five miles south of Rome. But it was slow to push inland, while the Germans were quick to switch reserves to the threatened spot. Although they failed to drive the Allied force back into the sea, as they had hoped, they bottled it up in a shallow and narrow bridgehead, and at the same time managed to block the renewed assault of the main Allied forces at Cassino.

After four months' pause Alexander mounted a fresh offensive, and for the purpose switched part of the Eighth Army over the Apennines to reinforce the Fifth Army's blow. The ground offensive was preceded by a tremendous air offensive against the enemy's lines of supply. This time the Cassino position was at last forced—with the aid of a flanking thrust over the mountains by General Juin's French Colonial Corps, skilled in mountain warfare. The Allied force at Anzio then chimed in with a stroke from the bridgehead. Under this combination of pressures the Germans were driven to start on a general retreat, and the Allies entered Rome on June 5th—the day before the invasion of Normandy.

Kesselring, however, extricated his forces from their dangerous situation, conducted the retreat with a masterly hand and succeeded in imposing a fresh series of checks on the Allied advance. Once he was established in the mountain-line north of Florence, deadlock set in again. Late in August Alexander switched the weight of the Eighth Army back to the Adriatic coast, and broke through that sector into the valley of the Po, but was brought to a halt by the autumn rains, so that the campaign was prolonged through another winter.

It was only in April, 1945, that the much stretched German front in Italy finally collapsed under the impact of fresh blows—after it had been stripped of reserves and equipment for the sake of bolstering up Hitler's last stand against the double-fronted pressure of the Russian and Anglo-American armies in Germany itself. When the Allies had landed in Italy, after the Italians' surrender, they had not dreamt that it would take them twenty months to clear the Germans out of Italy. Nor had the Germans.

Among the many German generals whom I had an opportunity of questioning in the last half of 1945, few had served on the Italian front and their experience covered only particular sectors and phases of the campaign. For that reason I refrained from dealing with the invasion of Italy in the original edition of this book, as the account would have been fragmentary. Since then, however, I have been able to hear Kesselring's views through the help of his Chief of Staff, General Westphal—as well as gathering the latter's own evidence. Westphal, who was recognized as one of the ablest of all the younger German generals, had been operations chief and Chief of Staff successively to Rommel in North Africa for eighteen months before he became Chief of Staff to Kesselring in the summer of 1943. The following year he succeeded Blumentritt as Chief of Staff to Rundstedt in the West.

Among other valuable fresh sources of information on the Italian campaign was General von Senger, who commanded the German forces in Sicily, then conducted the evacuation of Sardinia and Corsica with marked skill, and from November, 1943, onwards commanded the 14th Panzer Corps on the Italian mainland. He was a Rhodes scholar at Oxford just before World War I, and later became a friend of Kurt Hahn, the progressive German educationalist who created the famous school at Salem, and then a similar school at Gordonstoun in Scotland— after the Nazis came into power. Since the war, Salem is again able to move on free lines, and Senger has taken up a post there.

After this outline, I will now summarize the evidence gathered from "the other side of the hill" about the Italian campaign, expressing it wherever suitable by direct quotation of some of the more significant comments of the generals chiefly concerned—as in the case of the other campaigns.

PRELUDE

The Allied invasion of French North Africa in November, 1942, came as a complete surprise to Hitler, and his military advisers at O.K.W. (Keitel and Jodl both admitted after the war that they had not expected it.) While they had received reports about American plans for a possible landing at Dakar, and also on the islands off the west coast of Africa, they had imagined that the Americans would not go into the Mediterranean itself because of British interests in that quarter! When the vast fleet of transports was reported off the coast of Morocco, they assumed that these were carrying British troops to the Far East. Even when part of the fleet passed through the Straits of Gibraltar, they jumped to the conclusion that it portended an Allied landing in Libya immediately behind the back of Rommel's Army, which had just been driven out of Egypt by Montgomery.

Kesselring took a different view. As Commander-in-Chief of the forces in the central Mediterranean, he was better placed to read the signs, and for a month or two had been acutely apprehensive of an Allied landing in French North Africa. Only three days before it came his warning that it was imminent met continued disbelief in higher quarters, and his urgent appeal for reinforcements was disregarded. No time was lost, however, in reacting to the emergency. German troops were rushed across by air to Tunisia in continuous driblets, and sufficed to check the initial Allied advance from Algiers on Bizerta—though they would hardly have succeeded if the Allied overland advance had not started from a point so far to the west.

As the Allies' strength mounted, the German strength in Tunisia was also progressively increased, and a wide bridgehead built up to cover Bizerta and Tunis. It sufficed to keep the Allies at bay throughout the winter, and to provide shelter in which Rommel's Army, after its long retreat from Alamein, could take refuge. In the end, however, Hitler's forces and his allies paid a heavy price for this belated attempt to save the remnant of Rommel's Army and maintain a foothold in Africa. For when the covering line was pierced early in May, the whole bridge-head collapsed, and all the troops in it were captured—

nearly a quarter of a million men were taken prisoner and of these about two-thirds were German. It was a much bigger bag than the Allies could have hoped to secure if Hitler had been willing to "write off" the remnant of Rommel's Army.

Rommel himself "lived to fight another day". He had fallen sick again just after his Army had reached the frontier of Tunisia, and had been flown home to recuperate —barely a month before the final collapse took place. In September, he was appointed to command the forces in Northern Italy—while Kesselring commanded those in the South. An even more fortunate stroke of "ill" luck came to the rescue of another soldier who was to give the Allies much trouble in the later stages of the war— Hasso von Manteuffel, the panzer army leader who broke through the American front in the Ardennes at the end of 1944. In Tunisia he was commanding an improvised division that held a sector of Bizerta facing the Americans. On the 6th May, the opening day of the final Allied offensive, he was taken ill and evacuated by air to Sicily, along with some of the other sick and wounded. The air transport in which he was flying was attacked three times by Allied aircraft on the way to Trapani, as he told me. When I remarked that he had been lucky to escape, he replied, with a smile: "All the same, I eventually rejoined my comrades at Trent Park, in England, and they had enjoyed a much longer rest!"

The collapse of the bridgehead in Tunisia came as a shock to Hitler and his military advisers. They had reckoned on being able to hold it indefinitely—relying too much on the natural strength of the hill-chain which covered the approaches to Bizerta and Tunis. They took too little account of the wide stretch of the 100-mile perimeter in proportion to the reserves available, or of the shallowness of the bridgehead—which made it highly susceptible to paralysing air attack, while diminishing the chance of a rally once the defensive arc was pierced. The defending army's base was dangerously close to its front; any penetration of the front would soon reach it. When that happened, the loss of the base immediately magnified the German troops' already depressing sensation of fighting with their backs to the sea—a sea dominated by the Allies' sea power and air power. The remote planners at O.K.W. had not given sufficient weight to such moral factors, just as, earlier, they had tended to underrate the difficulty of carrying adequate supplies to any large forces they placed on the far side of the Mediterranean. Kesselring, like Halder and the staff of O.K.H., had been opposed to the North African Campaign and the attempted invasion of Egypt on this very ground. He had argued that it would not be possible to maintain such extended supply lines, and the campaign would thus develop into a "war of supply". This argument of his had brought him in conflict with Rommel. The troubles he had feared became increasingly apparent as the campaign proceeded, and reached a climax by the time the remnants of Rommel's Army were driven back into Tunisia. Even Kesselring himself seems to have erred on the optimistic side when carrying out the original coup in Tunisia and the subsequent large-scale reinforcement of the bridgehead that had there been seized. As he remarked later: "We could not supply our troops, nor could we evacuate them."

THE INVASION OF SICILY

The Allies' conquest of Tunisia cleared the way for their invasion of southern Europe—in a double sense. For the complete round-up of the German-Italian Army in Tunisia left Italy and the Italian islands almost denuded of efficient defending forces. Yet when, in this crisis, Hitler sent a message to Mussolini offering to despatch five fresh and well-equipped divisions to his aid, Mussolini replied that he only wanted three. This reply was sent without consulting Kesselring—who, when he heard of it, regarded it as a political demonstration of Italian desire "to remain masters in their own house". Mussolini's reply also went contrary to the opinion of the head of his own Army, General Roatta, who had urged the necessity of obtaining six panzer divisions, to be distributed in three groups—near Leghorn in the north, Rome in the centre, and Naples in the south. The reduction of the proffered reinforcement was to prove costly to the prospects of resisting invasion.

At the same time the difficulties of the defender's problem were much increased by uncertainty as to where the next attack would come. The Allies had a choice of alternative objectives, and the defender was impaled on the horns of a dilemma—in guessing how and where to distribute his scanty reserves. Hitler's view, influenced by Jodl's opinion, was that the Allies' next step would be to land in Sardinia. The only German force there consisted of the 90th Panzer-Grenadier division, which was in process of formation from drafts that had been assembled there. Reinforcement and supply was difficult because most of the piers in the few harbours had been destroyed by the Allies' air bombing. Hence Hitler decided to move Student's 11th Air Corps, which comprised the two parachute divisions, down to the South of France as a "Führer-reserve", ready to deliver an airborne counter-attack upon Sardinia if the Allies landed there. All the plans for this were made, Student told me.

Kesselring, however, considered it more probable that the next Allied step would be a landing in Sicily. Mussolini and the Italian Command agreed with his view. The only existing German force there was the 15th Panzer-Grenadier division, which had been improvised from drafts, but the "Hermann Goering" panzer division was despatched there. Even with its arrival, there was very small German backing for the ten shaky Italian divisions that were defending the island.

At a conference in Rome on May 13th—the anniversary of the fateful German break-through at Sedan—Kesselring urged that the most hopeful way of relieving the danger to Italy was the indirect way of making a speedy move into Spain. Admiral Doenitz, the new Commander-in-Chief of the German Navy who was present at this conference, agreed with Kesselring. (His predecessor, Admiral Raeder, had repeatedly urged such a move on Hitler after the Allies had landed in French North Africa the previous November.) Doenitz saw Hitler immediately after his return to Germany, and pressed him to adopt this course —as a means of regaining the initiative as well as of threatening the flank of the Anglo-American offensive against Italy. But Hitler felt that the time for such an operation had passed, saying that Franco was much less likely to agree to it than in 1940, and that it could not be attempted without his consent, as the Spanish were tough fighters and could wage a guerilla war against an invader's communications that would make the German position impossible to maintain.

Even so, two months passed before the Allies landed in Sicily, and it is remarkable that so little was done to strengthen the defence of that gateway into Europe. It seems all the more strange because during the month that followed the fall of Tunis, the Allied air forces concentrated on an effort to produce, by sustained air bombardment, the surrender of the fortified island of Pantelleria in the channel between Africa and Sicily. This prolonged "preparation", at immense cost of "ammunition", was mainly effective in dispelling any doubt that Sicily was the Allies' next objective. Yet the enemy High Commands failed to profit by the warning even though they recognized it as such. That failure was largely due to jealousy and mistrust between them. Reviewing events, Kesselring considered that the Allied landings could have been "decisively repulsed" if the two additional German divisions that were hurriedly despatched to Sicily, after the Allies were firmly ashore, had been moved there beforehand—to form, with the two already there, a really powerful and mobile counter-attack force under a single German command. His conclusion seems reasonable.

The chances of a prompt and effective counter to the coming Allied invasion of Sicily were diminished because the Italians rejected their ally's proposal to place the two German divisions in Sicily under a German Corps head-quarters. All they would accept was the appointment of a German liaison officer with General Guzzoni, Commander of the Italian 6th Army in Sicily. Lieut.-General von Senger und Etterlin was selected for this post, being pro-vided with a nucleus operations staff and a signal company so that he might be able in emergency to control the German forces on the spot. As Westphal remarked, this was "a makeshift solution". Only after the Allied landing and the collapse of the Italian 6th Army was a proper German corps staff hastily despatched to Sicily, along with a third German division, the 29th Panzer-Grenadier.

This division was taken from Italy's Adriatic coast, whither it had just previously been sent—to guard the impor-tant Foggia airfields and the "heel" of Italy. Its removal, so soon after arrival, presented the Allies with an opportunity for a stroke at the "heel" of which they were slow to take advantage. In stripping this vital sector Kesselring had reckoned only too well on "the cautious strategy" of the Allies, and their reluctance to venture on any step without ample assurance of air cover.

The course of the invasion of Sicily from the defender's point of view can now be related in the words of General von Senger, who gave me his impression of the salient features. He dwelt particularly on the "armoured" side of the operations, being a general of that arm:

"The Italian-German High Command had, correctly, regarded the south-east corner of the island as the most likely part for landing. It had, however, looked chiefly upon the coastal plains near Gela on the south coast and Catania on the east coast as the most threatened by enemy invasion. These two plains seemed to be the only ones for the employment of armoured formations, as they promised room for deployment from the very moment of the landing, or at least during further advance towards the centre of the island. This view of the details was mistaken. The Allied landing, which took place on the 10th July, extended over the whole of the south-east coast from Syracuse to Licata. It appears that nowhere along this stretch could landings of tank units be seriously checked by the coast defence forces. These forces were second- or third-rate Italian divisions, badly equipped and not backed by any coast batteries fit for this task.

"The Allied High Command refrained from choosing specially tank-suitable stretches of the coast, but rather mixed tank units with all other landing forces along the whole of the landing area. I suppose that it refrained from concentrating tanks on the plains probably for two reasons: the first reason being the predominance of Allied air and sea power, which enabled the Allies to land practically everywhere—thus scattering the defence forces —and to avoid any encounters in the initial stages with enemy tank forces. It is well known that the initial stage of every landing operation is always specially critical. A second reason for the enemy tactics can be seen in the justified view that those plains in the rear of Gela and Catania did not provide ground suitable for rapid tank advances as the large plains in Africa had done.

"Allied tank units accordingly advanced mainly on the roads. They could do so rather rapidly as long as they were backed by their naval artillery and by their air forces. As they were backed by superior air forces also, they made good advances even at later stages where they lacked support by naval artillery and where ground conditions were most unsuitable for mobile tank warfare. Owing to difficult ground conditions, however, they never succeeded in breaking through organized Axis defence lines as had often been the case both in Russia and in Africa, nor did they ever annihilate beaten Axis forces by pursuing them —which they might have done easily on ground more suitable, as in Russia or Africa."

General von Senger then spoke of the action taken by the defending side during the crucial opening phase, and particularly the German tank attack on the American landings near Gela, which cut through to the beaches—the one dangerous counter-stroke that the Allies suffered:

"Defence action was hampered by the fact that Axis forces—as Field-Marshal Montgomery rightly remarks—were scattered. They were scattered because the Axis High Command had to take into account simultaneous landings in the Eastern as well as in the Western part of the island. The main German tank force, a group of Tigers, was concentrated in the East with the "Hermann Goering" division—with the intention of checking (through it, and the tank regiment of the Goering division) any Allied tank advance in either the Gela or the Catania plain. It was launched along with the Goering division to counter-attack from Caltagirone southward. The tanks reached, as witnessed by myself, the dunes south of the Gela-Ragusa road. They checked the Allied advance at this spot, but had rather heavy losses from naval artillery fire. Although they succeeded in forcing the Allied forces to withdraw, and even to re-embark, at this particular spot, their success was of little value strategically as the Allied forces advanced at almost every other sector of the Syracuse-Licata area—all these other routes of advance lying open to them.

"Tiger tanks—the new type with which the German High Command had hoped to re-establish by technical means the lost tank superiority—proved particularly unsuitable for Sicilian ground conditions as, owing to their height and thick armour, they were found particularly clumsy—too large for small roads in the mountainous country, easily spotted by enemy artillery observation planes, vulnerable even to single parachutists landed between the roads and attacking the tanks under cover of the olive-tree-covered country. The ground off the roads was unapproachable by tanks because olive trees in Italy are grown on mountainous slopes with land terraces made of stone walls. Tigers could not turn on the narrow roads. When immovable through even slight damage they could not be hauled except by two other Tigers, the whole forming a wonderfully good target for concentrated artillery fire.

"Tigers and other tanks, however, rendered immeasurable services during the whole of the slow and organized withdrawal across the island—as anti-tank weapons. For this purpose they formed traps, lying camouflaged in ambush alongside those narrow roads to which the attacking tanks of the Allied forces were also tied. The slower the advance became, the more efficient tanks proved as anti-tank weapons. They were not nearly as vulnerable as stationary anti-tank guns, thanks to their armour; they could move from one position to another nearby, thereby avoiding concentrated artillery fire. They always formed a moral backbone for half-demoralized infantry. They facilitated the defence by linking various groups of resistance through their wireless communications. The framework of their companies, even when scattered, often afforded a more reliable picture of the defence positions for higher commanders than the framework of infantry."

The opportunity for that step by step delaying action might not have arisen, however, save for the check that Montgomery's forces suffered in their initial advance up the east coast to Catania—the shortest route to the Straits of Messina. That check was imposed, and could only have been imposed in the circumstances, by the sudden intervention of an airborne reinforcement to the defence of Sicily.

The British forces had established themselves in, and cleared, the south-east corner of the island during the first three days. On the 13th, Montgomery relates: "I decided that we should make a great effort to break through into the Plain of Catania from the Lentini area and ordered a major attack for the night of the 13th July." The key problem was to capture the Primasole bridge over the River Simeto, a few miles south of Catania. A parachute brigade was used for this purpose. Only about half of it was dropped in the right place, but this portion succeeded in securing the bridge intact.

The other half of the story may be told in the account that General Student gave me: "When the Allies landed in Sicily, on July 10th, I at once proposed to make an immediate airborne counter-attack there with both my divisions. But Hitler turned this down—Jodl, in particular, was against it. So the 1st Parachute Division was merely flown (from the South of France) to Italy in the first place—part to Rome and part to Naples—while the 2nd Parachute Division remained at Nimes with me. The 1st Parachute Division, however, was soon sent on to Sicily—for use as ground troops to reinforce the scanty German forces which were there when the Italian troops began to collapse *en masse*. The division was flown by air, in successive lifts, and dropped behind our front in the eastern sector south of Catania. I had wanted them to be dropped behind the Allied front. The first contingent was dropped about 3 kilometres behind our front, and by a strange coincidence it landed almost simultaneously with the British parachute troops who were dropped behind our front to open the bridge across the Simeto river. It overcame these British parachute troops and rescued the bridge from their hands. This was on July 14th."

Although the British, when reinforced, managed to regain the bridge after three days' stiff fighting, their subsequent attempt to push northward was blocked by increasingly stiff resistance, from parachute troops and tanks. This frustrated any hope of a quick drive up the east coast to Messina, sixty miles distant, and Montgomery was forced to shift the weight of the Eighth Army westward for a more circuitous push round the foothills of Mount Etna in combination with the Americans' eastward advance from Palermo. A full month was consumed in this slow push over difficult ground and in face of the delaying tactics that Senger has described. The Germans were able not only to spin out time but to bring away their forces, back to the Italian mainland, "to fight another day".

Greatly to Kesselring's relief, the Allied High Command had not attempted a landing in Calabria, the "toe" of Italy, behind the back of his forces from Sicily—to block their withdrawal 'across the Straits of Messina. He had been anxiously expecting such a stroke throughout the Sicilian campaign, while having no forces available to meet it. In his view, "a secondary attack on Calabria would have enabled the Sicily landing to be developed into an overwhelming Allied victory". Until the close of the Sicilian campaign and the successful escape of the four German divisions engaged there, Kesselring had only two German divisions to cover the whole of Southern Italy.

THE ITALIAN CHANGE OF SIDES—AND THE GERMAN COUNTER-COUP

When Mussolini was deposed on July 25th, Hitler had taken instant alarm—reading this dismissal as a signal that the new Italian Government under Marshal Badoglio, despite its assurances of continued adhesion to the Axis, would be looking for a way out of the war. Hitler's reaction was prompt. On the 27th he ordered the Headquarters of Army Group B under Rommel, which was at that moment taking over command in Greece, to assume responsibility for the defence of Northern Italy—on the pretext of relieving the burden on the Italian forces there, so that they could be used to reinforce the more immediately threatened southern part of their country. Army Group B was to take charge of the area north of the line Elba-Ancona. To fill out the framework, German divisions were scraped from the other fronts and hurriedly railed to Northern Italy.

At the same time, Student and the 2nd Parachute Division were transported by air to Ostia, near Rome. The Italian High Command was given no previous warning of its arrival, but was informed that the division was intended for the reinforcement of Sicily or Calabria. Student, however, was told that "Hitler expected the new Italian Government would capitulate to the Allies". He was instructed to take under his command the 3rd Panzer-Grenadier Division—which had been moved down to Rome from the Orvieto area—and be ready to disarm the Italian forces around Rome, if there was a capitulation.

In contrast to the view of Hitler and O.K.W., Kesselring persisted in the belief that Italy's leaders would remain loyal to their alliance with Germany. He deplored "the extremely chilly attitude of the German Government to the Badoglio Government", fearing that it might drive the latter to break away, and was particularly anxious lest any German move should precipitate such a step. When he received instructions, early in August, that he must be ready to disarm and make prisoner the whole of the Italian forces if the Italian Government capitulated to the Allies, he argued that such a measure was far beyond the capacity of his limited forces. On any calculation of numbers, space, and the risk of Allied intervention, his argument seemed well justified. As he did not succeed in getting the order changed, he decided to confine his action to what appeared practicable.

Westphal says that Kesselring "discarded any idea of taking care of the Italian air formations except those that were in the immediate neighbourhood of German operational stations. He delegated to the German Naval Headquarters in Italy the task of preventing Italian naval units in the Adriatic ports from escaping, as far as this was possible with scanty means—E-boats and U-boats. He instructed 10th Army Headquarters (which was now created to handle the German divisions in Southern Italy) that it should act as the situation required but endeavour to reach an amicable arrangement with the Italian divisions to lay down their arms, bearing in mind their former comradeship. The only definite order he gave in advance was that on no account should the Germans be the first to open hostilities".

Kesselring's problem certainly looked tough beforehand. "In the Rome area there was a strong Italian concentration, of more than five divisions. The German Supreme Command and the Commander-in-Chief tried to induce the Italian Supreme Command to send these divisions to reinforce the Southern front, but all their attempts failed." Badoglio preferred the risk of Allied invasion to that of a German occupation of Rome—the more naturally, since he had already been in touch with the Allies to arrange an armistice and a change of sides. Although Kesselring was unaware of these secret negotiations, he could see that "the strong group of Italian forces near Rome was capable of being a particular danger to the rear communications of the 10th Army".

Eisenhower aptly remarks that: "The Italians wanted frantically to surrender." But the consummation of their desire was unfortunately delayed, partly through defective arrangements and partly through the deterrent effect of the Allies "unconditional surrender" formula. The settlement took longer than was good for the Allies' or the Italians' prospects. The armistice was eventually signed on September 3rd, the day on which Montgomery crossed the Straits of Messina and landed on the toe of Italy. It was to be kept secret until the Allies made a second landing on the shin of Italy—their chosen place being the Gulf of Salerno. They intended at the same time to drop an airborne division near Rome, to help the Italian forces there. But this part of the plan was stillborn. For the Salerno landing started at midnight on September 8th, preceded a few hours by the announcement of Italy's capitulation, whereas the Italian leaders had not been expecting it until several days later. They were caught unready to co-operate, complaining that their preparations were incomplete, and the airborne drop was cancelled. While the Germans were taken even more by surprise, their action at Rome was prompt and decisive, despite the simultaneous emergency at Salerno. As the Italians' deepest wish was to cease fighting, they made their surrender to the Germans in the absence of the Allies!

If the Italians had been as good in action as in acting the outcome might have been different. For in the prologue their performance had gone far to lull the Germans' suspicions and conceal what was impending. There are some piquant features in Westphal's account of those days. "On September 7th the Italian Minister of Marine, Admiral Count de Courten, called on Field-Marshal Kesselring to inform him that the Italian fleet would put out on the 8th or 9th from Spezia to seek battle with the British Mediterranean Fleet. The Italian Fleet would conquer or perish, he said, with tears in his eyes. He then described in detail its intended plan of battle." These solemn assurances made a convincing impression. The next afternoon Westphal drove with General Toussaint to the headquarters of the Italian Army at Monterotondo. "At first we were hindered from proceeding by Italian road blocks north of Rome, but after more than an hour's wait we succeeded in reaching Monterotondo. Our reception by General Roatta was very cordial. He discussed with me in detail the further joint conduct of operations by the Italian 7th and German 10th Armies in Southern Italy. While we were talking a telephone message came through from Colonel von Waldenburg with the news of the broadcast announcement of the Italian capitulation to the Allies . . . General Roatta assured us that it was merely a bad propaganda manœuvre. The joint struggle, he said, would be continued just as had been arranged between us."

Westphal was not altogether convinced by these assurances, and when he got back to his headquarters late in the evening he found that Kesselring had already signalled to all subordinate commands the codeword "Axis"—the pre-arranged signal which meant that Italy had quitted the Axis and that the appropriate action must be taken.

The subordinate commands applied a mixture of persuasion and force according to the situation and their own disposition. In the Rome area, where the potential odds against him were heavy, Student used shock tactics. "I made an attempt to seize the Italian General Headquarters by dropping on it from the air. This was only a partial success. While thirty generals and a hundred and fifty other officers were captured in one part of the headquarters, another part held out. The Chief of the General Staff had got away, following Badoglio and the King, the night before."

Student's forceful reaction to the armistice announcement seems to have given the Italian Command an amazingly exaggerated impression of his strength. Marshal Badoglio tells us that General Roatta told him that he had told General Carboni "to concentrate his forces and to fall back on Tivoli, where the nature of the ground would allow of a much more efficacious defence". Fighting was not much in the minds or in the mood of the Italian forces or their leaders at this time. The retreat not only left the capital in the hands of the Germans but cleared the way for negotiations, where matters could be handled with velvet gloves—even more effectively than with iron fists.

The rest of the story can be related in Westphal's words: "The situation around Rome calmed down completely when the Commander of the Italian forces accepted in its entirety the German capitulation suggestion. This eliminated the danger to the supply of the 10th Army. At the same time the German Command in Italy was freed from the nightmare of having to use weapons against their former allies. The capitulation ensured for the Italian soldiers an immediate return to their homes. This concession had a repercussion because it infringed Hitler's order, according to which all Italian soldiers were to be made prisoners of war. But there can be no doubt that adherence to this order would have held out no inducement to the Italians to accept the German proposals."

"It was a further relief to us that Rome no longer

needed to become a battlefield. In the capitulation agreement, Field-Marshal Kesselring undertook to regard Rome as an open city. He undertook that it should be occupied only by police units, two companies in strength, to guard telephone communications, etc. This undertaking was always observed up to the end of the German occupation. Through the capitulation it was now again possible to resume the wireless signals link with O.K.W. which had been broken off since the 8th. A further consequence of the bloodless elimination of the Italian forces was the possibility of immediately moving reinforcements by road from the Rome area to the 10th Army in the South. . . . Thus the situation around Rome, after so many initial worries, had been resolved in a manner which one could hardly hope to better."

Even O.K.W. does not seem to have had much confidence beforehand that its initial orders could be fulfilled, and the situation restored, if the Allies' landing took place simultaneously with Italy's capitulation to the Allies. According to Westphal, "O.K.W. privately regarded Kesselring's forces as mainly lost. By August this opinion had leaked through to Field-Marshal Kesselring. It was reinforced by the fact that supplies and replacements of personnel, arms, and equipment were almost completely cut off from us from August onward. All demands were at the time brushed aside by O.K.W. with, 'We'll see later on'. This unusually pessimistic attitude probably also played a part in the employment of Army Group B in Upper Italy. It was to take into the Apennine position such parts of our forces as had managed to escape the joint attack of the Allies and the Italians."

"Field-Marshal Kesselring, similarly, took a grave view of the situation. But in his view it was still capable of being mastered in certain circumstances—the farther south that the expected large-scale landing took place, the better the chances would be. But if the enemy landed by sea and air in the general area of Rome, one could hardly bank on

saving the 10th Army from being cut off. The two divisions
we had near Rome were far from sufficient for the double
job of eliminating the strong Italian forces and repelling
the Allied landing—and in addition keeping open the
rear communications of the 10th Army. As early as
September 9th it was becoming unpleasantly apparent
that the Italian forces were blocking the road to Naples,
and thus the supply of the 10th Army. The Army could not
have held out against this for long. And so the Commander-
in-Chief heaved a sigh of relief when no air landings took
place on the airfields round Rome on the 9th and 10th.
On both these days we hourly expected such a landing
to be made, with the co-operation of the Italian forces.
Such an air landing would undoubtedly have given a
great stimulus to the Italian troops and to the civil
population that was unfavourably disposed towards us."

Kesselring's verdict was epitomized in a sentence: "An
air landing on Rome and sea landing nearby, instead of at
Salerno, would have automatically caused us to evacuate
all the southern half of Italy."

THE ALLIED LANDINGS IN ITALY

The days immediately following September 8th were a
period of intense strain for the Germans, and particularly
for Kesselring—whose headquarters were at Frascati, just
south of Rome. Besides the uncertainty whether the
Italians could be quelled and disarmed he had to deal
with a triple invasion—the most immediate threat coming
from the large-scale Allied landing at Salerno.

The opening days were all the more nerve-wracking
through lack of information as to what was happening
there. Never was the "fog of war" so thick—that being
due to the fact that the Germans were fighting in the
country of an ally who had suddenly deserted them. The
effect can best be conveyed by giving Westphal's account—
"The Commander-in-Chief could at first learn very little

about the position at Salerno. Telephone communication broke down—as it was on the Italian postal network. It could not be easily restored, as we had not been allowed to examine Italian telephone technique. Wireless communication could not be arranged at first because the signal personnel of the newly-formed 10th Army headquarters were not familiar with the peculiar atmospheric conditions in the South. Thus the Commander-in-Chief was left, during the first few days, in a state of oppressive uncertainty about the situation at Salerno."

One piece of news that he did get increased his anxiety. For he learned that the arrival on the scene of the divisions that were retreating from Calabria, in front of the British Eighth Army's gradual advance, was being delayed by a shortage of petrol—due partly to an administrative failure.

So he "cast about for other possibilities of feeding reinforcements to the Salerno battle area". Westphal got through on the 9th to Jodl at O.K.W. and asked for the immediate dispatch of two panzer divisions then near Mantua, in Northern Italy. "These requests, as well as a direct request to Army Group B, were refused on the grounds that the troops in question would arrive too late and could not be spared by Army Group B." Kesselring and Westphal felt that neither reason had justification. Although Mantua was 450 miles from Salerno, they reckoned that the two divisions could have reached the battlefield by the 13th, while the issue was still in the balance. "The inferiority of the Luftwaffe and the lack of any means of countering the fire from ships' guns were the prime factors in determining the unfavourable outcome of the Battle of Salerno. But a third reason, following very closely, was the lack of ground forces." In Westphal's view, "these two divisions, despatched in good time, would have turned the Salerno situation in our favour". He says that Jodl subsequently expressed regret that Kesselring's request had not been met.

While Kesselring and Westphal felt that a great

opportunity had been lost of defeating the Allied invasion of Italy at the outset, they also felt that a still greater opportunity had been missed by the Allies. In comment on the campaign, Kesselring remarked: "The Allied plans showed throughout that the Allied High Command's dominating thought was to make sure of success, a thought that led it to use orthodox methods and material. As a result it was almost always possible for me, despite inadequate means of reconnaissance and scanty reports, to foresee the next strategic or tactical move of my opponent —and thus to take the appropriate counter-measures so far as my resources allowed."

The main Allied landing, at Salerno, came exactly where Kesselring had expected it, and where his scanty forces were best placed to meet it. Although these were not sufficient to drive it back into the sea, they were able to check it and ensure that it did not develop into an imminent menace. The Eighth Army's advance up the toe of Italy also ran according to expectation, and presented a still more remote threat. The one serious threat was created by the landing on the heel of Italy, near Taranto, but this was made in such slight strength and with such a lack of mobile transport that the threat was self-stultified.

The view from "the other side of the hill" was given in Westphal's comments to me—"If the forces employed in the landing at Salerno had been used instead at Civitavecchia the results would have been much more decisive. If this latter operation had been carried out, Rome would have fallen into the Allies' hand within a few days at the most. It was well known that there were only two German divisions in Rome and that no others could have been brought up quickly enough to defend it. In conjunction with the five Italian divisions stationed at Rome, a combined sea and air landing would have taken the Italian capital inside seventy-two hours. Quite apart from the political repercussions of such a victory this would have resulted in cutting off at one blow the supplies of the five

German divisions retreating from Calabria, and at the moment reorganizing in the Naples-Salerno sector or on the way there. That would have brought all Italy south of the line Rome-Pescara into Allied hands."

Westphal was equally critical of the way that the Eighth Army pushed up the toe of Italy, through the whole length of Calabria, while the greater opportunity on the exposed heel of Italy and along the Adriatic coast went begging. "The landing of the British Eighth Army should have taken place in full strength in the Taranto sector, where only one parachute division (with only three batteries of divisional artillery!) was stationed. Indeed, it would have been even better to have carried out the landing in the sector Pescara-Ancona, if the lack of harbour facilities could have been offset by maintaining field supplies. No resistance to this landing could have been provided from the Rome sector, owing to our lack of available forces. Likewise no appreciable forces could have been brought down rapidly from the Po plain."

Both Kesselring and Westphal considered that the Allies had paid heavy strategic forfeit for their desire to ensure tactical security against air attack, and that this was an over-insurance in view of the then scanty strength of the German air force in southern Italy. They felt, too, that the Allied High Command's habit of limiting the scope of its strokes to the limits of constant air-cover had been the defenders' salvation, by simplifying the multiple problems of the defence.

Outside Italy itself was the problem of the German detachments that had been sent to Sardinia and Corsica. The Italian surrender had placed them in a very precarious position. Kesselring and Westphal expressed surprise as well as relief at their extrication. "It was completely incomprehensible to us that the withdrawal of the German forces from Sardinia and Corsica could have been carried out with almost no interference by the Allied sea and air striking forces. This enabled over 30,000 soldiers with full equipment to be transferred safely to the mainland." In further comment Westphal said: "It was only too clear to the Commander-in-Chief that a successful execution of the evacuation measures would be very problematical, in face of the enemy's superiority by sea and air. But this counter-action was most surprisingly absent. It only became really threatening when the rear elements of the forces from both islands were assembled in Corsica. The experience gained during the evacuation of Sicily was usefully employed. As already in the case of transportation to Africa, the mass of the personnel was lifted by air. The credit for this completely successful withdrawal operation belongs primarily to the clear, deliberate leadership of General von Senger"— he had been put in charge there at the end of the Sicilian campaign. The 90th Panzer-Grenadier Division reorganized in the Pisa area, and was soon ready for action again. Its return proved of vital importance in the next phase of the campaign on the mainland.

THE BATTLE OF THE SANGRO

Although the Allied Fifth Army was able to establish itself firmly after landing at Salerno, its subsequent push north towards Rome was slow. Kesselring was able to keep it in check at each stage and finally brought it to a halt on the Garigliano, near Cassino. The late autumn assaults on the Cassino position imposed no very dangerous strain on the defence.

But a crisis developed on the Adriatic side of the Apennines, where the Germans were weakest, on the second day of Montgomery's November attack over the Sangro. The attack was launched in the coastal sector with three divisions and an armoured brigade, in the first place. Westphal says: "Only the 65th Infantry Division was available to oppose the attack, its strength being only seven battalions and twelve batteries. Field-Marshal Kesselring and I were with this division the day before the big attack. . . . The division, reformed after Stalingrad and not yet tested in action, was very confident. As yet it did not know the concentrated effect of the enemy's air force and artillery, which hindered every movement on the battlefield and any effective fire on the defender's part. The British technique of attack, battalion after battalion pushed through by joint artillery and air action, was as simple as it was successful. The 65th Division was virtually blown to bits."

The attack had started on the night of November 28th. "By the end of the next day the division was, for all practical purposes, no longer in existence. The way to the north was open, to Ancona at least."

"We rushed the 26th Panzer Division across from the west, and it arrived at the earliest moment it could—but its passage through the mountains could easily have been delayed by well-directed air bombardment. The 90th Panzer-Grenadier Division, which had only just been placed under our command, was brought down from the north but lost time on the way and in coming into action—the divisional commander and leading regimental commander were sacked.

"Until these two divisions arrived the way to the North lay completely open to the British Eighth Army. There was at the moment nothing that could have stopped it. The 90th Panzer-Grenadier Division could not restore the position before it filled the gap in the hitherto continuous front. It could easily have been smashed up and overrun while still on the march. The Eighth Army missed this chance. Thus we were able to avert, quite quickly, the serious crisis on the Adriatic."

A CHANGE OF STRATEGY

The defensive success on the Sangro and at Cassino sealed a decision on strategy to which Hitler had been coming just before these battles opened. He and his military advisers had earlier felt that the only line on which they could hope to halt the Allied advance was the mountain barrier of the Etruscan Apennines north of Florence. As soon as the 10th Army could get back there, it would come under Rommel's Army Group B, and Kesselring's command would cease to exist.

The way in which that plan came to be changed formed an interesting part of the account that Westphal gave me. "When the situation in Southern Italy developed more favourably than O.K.W. had expected, they conceived the wish to set up a front, not initially in the broad Apennine position, but in the narrower stretch south and east of Rome.

"In these calculations, one factor was the desire to keep the Allied air bases farther away from the Reich. Another was that O.K.W. originally hoped that this more southerly front would only require seven infantry divisions, with two mobile divisions in tactical reserves behind each flank. In contrast, the Apennine position would need at least twenty infantry divisions.

"In October Field-Marshal Rommel was asked to state his views on this question. In general he was against the scheme—the main reason being that he could not in the long run guarantee such a risky experiment. The idea now arose of leaving Field-Marshal Kesselring in supreme command after all. Hitler long remained undecided. This was partly because Kesselring had been out of favour since the loss of Tunis. Moreover, as a man with pro-Italian sympathies, he was not felt to be the right man for the post. But now he, too, was listened to. He stated that he was in a position to maintain a defence south of Rome. He had no illusions about the difficulty of carrying out such a task—but, as an air expert, he attached special importance to the need to deny the airfields of Central Italy to the enemy. Apart from this, he took the view that the Apennine position was not tenable with the total forces that were available. . . . Field-Marshal Kesselring believed that with his choice of front he could hold the enemy back from the Apennines for at least another six or nine months of fighting.

"November wore on, and still Hitler could not make up his mind. Then he decided to give Rommel the command in the South, or of the whole. An order to this effect was just being teleprinted when, quite suddenly, Hitler changed his mind again and gave Field-Marshal Kesselring sole military command in Italy. This appointment came into force on November 21st. Army Group B left the Italian theatre, and the troops in northern Italy became the 14th Army, under the Commander-in-Chief South-West (or Army Group C), as Field-Marshal Kesselring's appointment was now renamed." So the Germans were now committed to maintaining a defence as far south as possible for as long as possible—that defence being based on the Bernard Line (which the Allies called the Winter Line) running east and west through Cassino.

Hitler even thought of taking the offensive again in Italy, after the defensive success on the Sangro, with the aim of regaining the Foggia airfields—an idea that was prompted by the Allied air attacks on Southern Germany that were developing from this air base. But when Kesselring reported that for such an offensive he would need a reinforcement of three or four panzer-type divisions and two mountain divisions, Hitler found that he could not provide them, and the plan was put in cold storage.

As it was, the maintenance of an effective defence was handicapped because the German divisions were not only fewer than the Allies', but considerably weaker in manpower and weapon-power. The establishment of the German infantry division had been reduced from 16,000 in 1939 to 12,000 men, while the actual strength was still lower. The Germans were also suffering from a shortage of artillery and tanks, but the worst deficiency of all was in air power. This was made all the worse because the air force in Italy, "Luftflotte 2", had been removed from Kesselring's control at the time of the invasion—"at the instance of Goering, who took the view that he could more effectively direct the operations of Luftflotte 2 from East

Prussia than the Commander-in-Chief—himself an airman
—of the theatre concerned". The Naval forces had at
the same time regained their independence. Although
Kesselring's personal prestige and influence secured a
fair degree of co-operation from other Services, he and his
staff "always envied the clear-cut command system on the
enemy's side—where there was one Commander-in-Chief
for a theatre, and he had everything under command".

THE ALLIED LANDING AT ANZIO

On January 22nd, 1944, the Allies carried out their one
big seaborne outflanking move—by landing an army corps
at Anzio and Nettuno, close to Rome. It started with a big
slice of luck.

How this happened was related by Westphal. "Field-
Marshal Kesselring constantly urged that air interpretations
of the shipping in the port of Naples should be obtained
as frequently as possible, for it was clear that any fresh
enemy landing operation on the West coast of Italy would
have its starting point there." For some months the German
air force seldom got through to Naples, and when it did the
weather conditions or the strong defence prevented it
securing clear air photographs. But at last a successful
photographic reconnaissance of the port was achieved
early in January. "We found in this evidence warning
signs of a probably imminent fresh landing." As a result,
the counter-plans were checked over afresh, and Kesselring
decided to bring the 29th and 90th Panzer-Grenadier
Divisions, from the eastern sector of the 10th Army front,
back into reserve near Rome.

But on January 12th the Allies opened an attack on
the western or Cassino sector, and on the 18th this developed
into a strong offensive across the Garigliano. Fearing that
it would break through into the Liri valley, the Army
Commander asked for the loan of the two reserve divisions,
saying that they would be needed only for a few days.

Kesselring was reluctant to grant his request. But just at this time he received a visit from Admiral Canaris, the head of the German Intelligence Service, and in answer to questions the latter assured him that "there were not the slightest signs of a fresh landing being imminent; shipping in the port of Naples was quite normal". So Kesselring, though still very reluctantly, agreed to release his reserve.

The result was that on landing at Anzio, the Anglo-American force met no resistance, nor found any when they pushed inland and established a covering line for their bridgehead. General Jahn, who arrived on that sector soon afterwards, told me: "At the time of the landing only two German battalions were there. The Allied troops could have reached the Alban Hills with ease." Kesselring's own headquarters lay on the slope of the Alban Hills, close to the road from Anzio to Rome. Westphal said: "The days following the landing were tense for us. Would it be possible to bring up a part of the troops on the way to the scene before the enemy had gained these dominating heights south-east of Rome? This was the decisive question. By any reasonable calculation the answer was really 'No'. On the 22nd, and even on the 23rd, a single unit thrusting forward without delay and attacking boldly—for example, a reinforced reconnaissance regiment—could have penetrated the open city of Rome without any serious hindrance. Even Valmontone could have been taken without trouble on the 22nd—blocking the road and supply line between the Cassino front and Rome. But the enemy, after landing, paused and let time slip away—much to the help of our counter-measures."

These measures were executed with remarkable speed, thanks to previous preparation and emergency organization. Plans had been worked out in advance to counter a landing, in any of five possible areas that had been foreseen, by combing the local reserves from the various sectors of the front and other areas, and switching them to the landing-place. Arrangements were made for sign-posting the march-routes, for emergency refuelling on the way, and for de-icing the passes over the Apennines.

By the evening of the 25th Kesselring and his staff felt that "the acute danger of a break-through to Rome or Valmontone was past". The Allied attack from the bridge-head did not begin until the 30th. It was easily checked, and petered out by February 1st, although the Allied commander now had five strong divisions available. For by this time Kesselring had managed to concentrate a force of almost equal strength, including one division from northern Italy and another from France. General von Mackensen, the Commander of the 14th Army, and his staff were also brought down from the north to direct it.

For Hitler was now pressing for "an early and decisive counter-attack to throw the enemy's landing force into the sea". He even chose and laid down in detail the exact direction and frontage of attack—which was concentrated on a sector only four miles wide. When Mackensen protested that this was too narrow, and was supported by Kesselring, Jodl replied that Hitler "flatly refused to consider any wider extension". Westphal frankly admits that Kesselring and himself were infected by Hitler's confidence, and did not press their objections as they should have done. Even so, the attack on the Allied bridgehead made a momentarily dangerous penetration—though delayed until February 16th by weather and air interference with the build-up of munitions. The Allied air forces played a great part in bringing this attack to a standstill. A further effort was made on the 29th but, as Jahn remarked, "never looked promising". So the Anzio bridgehead remained a thorn in the Germans' side, and from it eventually came a spearthrust in their side. An important indirect effect of the Anzio landing was that it knocked out of Hitler's head a plan, which he had been contemplating, of transferring five of the best mobile divisions from Italy to France in readiness to meet the coming Allied invasion of the West.

Nevertheless, the check to the initial advance of the Allied force from the Anzio bridgehead produced another long delay in the Allied armies' general advance in Italy. A further frontal assault which they made on the Cassino position in February was repulsed with heavy loss. A third offensive was attempted there in March, but again ended in failure, after nine days of battering. After that the Allied High Command paused to build up its resources for another general offensive in May, and meanwhile concentrated on a great air effort to strangle the German armies' supply lines so as to weaken their resistance and retort to the Allies' summer offensive. But the delay in finishing the Italian campaign subtracted very heavily from the total Allied resources, and from the strength they might otherwise have put into their 1944 invasion of the West. It was a much larger subtraction from the total effort than the Germans had incurred by making a stand in Italy.

An historical postscript can now be added to the much-discussed question of the destruction of the historic Bene-dictine Monastery on Monte Cassino as a preliminary step in the Allied offensive there in February. The task was carried out by a large force of American bombers and supporting artillery. According to the announcements of the Allied Command at the time this destruction was ordered because the Monastery, which dominated the approaches to the town, had been "occupied and fortified" by theGermans. These statements were repeated in Field-Marshal Sir H. Maitland Wilson's report published in 1946—which seemed strange in view of earlier testimony from the Vatican and the Abbot himself that the Germans had avoided trespassing on the Monastery, despite the tactical disadvantage which this involved for them. I have had opportunity of discussing the matter with General von Senger, who has since written a detailed account. He was commanding the 14th Panzer Corps on the Cassino sector at the time. "Field-Marshal Kesselring had given express orders that no German soldier should enter the Monastery, so as to avoid giving the Allies any pretext for bombing or shelling it. I cannot testify personally that this decision was communicated to the Allies but I am sure that the Vatican found means to do so, since it was so directly interested in the fate of Monte Cassino. Not only did Field-Marshal Kesselring prohibit German soldiers from entering the Monastery, but he also placed a guard at the entrance gate to ensure that his orders were carried out." Senger's account is borne out by other witnesses whose evidence I have heard independently.

The irony of the bombing was, as both Senger and Vietinghoff remarked, that it turned out entirely to the tactical benefit of the Germans. For after that they felt free to occupy the ruins, and the rubble provided much better defensive cover than the Monastery would have been before its destruction. "As anyone with experience of street-fighting knows, it is only when buildings are demolished that they are converted from mouse-traps into bastions of defence." Batteries posted and concealed in the ruins were able to enfilade and break up the subsequent British attempts to drive through to the town of Cassino. The German generals considered that the only possible way to capture such a position as Cassino was by a wide outflanking movement, and could not understand why the Allies did not do this until the 4th Battle of Cassino.

THE ABANDONMENT OF ROME AND RETREAT TO THE APENNINES

In view of the Allies' superiority of force and the flanking-lever they had now established at Anzio, it would have been wiser on the Germans' part to have fallen back to the main barrier of the Apennines before the Allies were ready to launch their summer offensive. Besides diminishing their own losses and strain they could, by a shrewdly judged step-back when the Allies' armies were obviously inactive, have largely deprived them of the éclat and moral tonic which they gained from the "capture" of Rome. Instead of staying at Cassino and on the Garigliano, it might even have been wiser to make an intermediate withdrawal to an improvised position near Rome. That would have diminished the risks and strain that they suffered by remaining farther south, and might have enabled them to foil the Allies' summer offensive.

Why was no such step taken—either the full step-back or the half step-back? One reason, emphasized at the time, was that the preparation of the Gothic Line in the Apennines north of Florence was still far from complete. But the Line was still incomplete at the time the retreating armies occupied it in the summer, when they were battered and exhausted, yet it sufficed to block the Allies' advance even under those much more adverse conditions. A deeper objection to any timely step-back was not a matter of reason—it sprang from the heart, not the head. Westphal himself, a profound admirer of his chief, put it thus: "Field-Marshal Kesselring was an exceptionally strong-willed personality. Such natures as his, prompted by their own complete and selfless spirit of service, would always like to perform more than is humanly possible with the resources they have. I therefore believe that the desire to hold on to the Rome area, even during this latest battle, had too strong a grip on the Field-Marshal." Westphal's view bore out what I heard from others—Jahn, for instance, declared: "Our High Command had hoped to keep the Allies pinned down indefinitely on the Cassino front."

Such a hope accorded with Hitler's hopes and desires. Indeed, it is likely, in the light of his later objections to any withdrawal, that he would have insisted on the utmost effort to maintain the existing front—and Kesselring was well aware of Hitler's general attitude on the question. But, as it happened, there was no call for such insistence —because of Kesselring's own confidence in the possibility of doing so. That confidence had been fostered by earlier success in defying anticipations. Kesselring's optimism tended to become stronger because of what he regarded as Mackensen's pessimism. Their two temperaments were widely different. Kesselring felt that Mackensen had too little confidence in what could be achieved with the forces available, and "this inevitably caused the Field-Marshal to discount in some degree the anxieties and worries expressed by the 14th Army". Westphal adds that while the 14th Army may have had sufficient strength numerically, for its task of confining the Allied force at Anzio, it consisted mainly of raw infantry divisions whereas the 10th Army was largely made up of seasoned troops.

Even so, the risks on the Anzio sector might never have matured but for the collapse that developed in the south, on the Garigliano. The Germans there were thrown off their balance by the indirect stroke over the mountains, that was delivered by General Juin's French Colonial Corps. Delay in receiving information "on the other side of the hill" accentuated its surprise effect. Kesselring himself said: "Unfortunately, it was only on the third day that I learned of this French attack. The specially organized 'urgent report' system broke down in this instance. On the third day it was no longer possible to put into effect a planned switching of reserves to the mountain positions."

Then, as the Cassino defences were cracking under this outflanking leverage, the Allied force at Anzio started to break out of the bridgehead. Realizing the danger to his supply line, the Commander of the 10th Army, General von Vietinghoff, proposed to make a speedy withdrawal northward to a line about Valmontone, where he could link up with the 14th Army. But, even then, Hitler forbade such a withdrawal. That veto forfeited the Germans' last chance of maintaining a position south of Rome. Instead of a planned withdrawal, there was a spreading breakdown of the Germans' overstretched defence, involving the abandonment of Rome and a far more extensive retreat—to the Gothic Line in the north. The 10th Army managed to extricate itself, by a detour along roads farther inland that the Allies failed to get astride, but the 14th Army was badly cut up. (Some of the German soldiers rather sorely remark that they suffered undue risk, and loss, through Kesselring's insistence on respecting the inviolateness of Rome and preserving the city from damage —combined with the way that the Allies took advantage of the restrictions he had imposed on the German troops. He had given instructions that the bridges over the Tiber were not to be destroyed, on account of their historical value.)

Even so, Kesselring was able to check the Allies' pursuit, and finally brought their advance to a stop on reaching the Gothic Line. There, he succeeded in maintaining his position for nearly another year—until April, 1945— although his forces were increasingly drained of reserves and equipment to fill gaps in the Western and Eastern fronts.

ALLIED STRATEGY— FROM THE GERMAN VIEWPOINT

Giving me his views and Kesselring's on the strategy that the Allies could have followed in Italy with better results, Westphal said: "After the landing at Salerno, the next amphibious operation should not have taken place at Anzio but as far north of Rome as possible—say, at Livorno (Leghorn). There were first-rate landing facilities everywhere in that area. By the end of 1943 the Allied High Command must surely have known how small was the size of the German forces in North Italy, and that the bulk of the forces were tied down on the front south of Rome. Taking account of the situation of the German forces in Italy, and the overall situation of the German forces, it should have been clear that neither from Rome, nor from the north of Italy, nor from anywhere else, could a German counter-stroke in any strength be brought up before the Allies had consolidated such a landing—at Livorno, for instance.

"In the spring of 1944—before the big Allied drive in May—the conditions for such an operation were still more favourable. At that time, apart from two divisions stationed in the Livorno area, the entire available forces were tied down with the 10th and 14th Armies, in the Cassino and Anzio sectors. The Allies' policy on these fronts should have been to keep merely enough forces to contain ours, while employing the bulk for a strategic outflanking manœuvre—and thus to have cut off the mass of the German forces in Italy.

"I can only imagine that operations of this kind, widely separated, were not undertaken on account of the risk of suffering losses from interference by the German Air Force. It must surely have been known, however, that the German Air Force had more or less disappeared from the battle-field—after its severe losses in the African campaign, coupled with the lack of trained flying reinforcements and the inferiority of the German Messerschmidt 109 fighter, as well as the absence of effective bombers.

"Surveying the problem, we came to the conclusion that a large-scale landing in the Livorno-Spezia area could not possibly be prevented—either in the approach or in the disembarkation. Moreover, the enemy would be able, not only to land, but to block the Apennine passes before the German divisions—which mostly had to move on foot—could cover the 200 miles from the front to the scene of the new landing area. Air cover for such a landing could, in our view, be easily provided from aircraft carriers and above all from Corsica—Livorno was only 80 miles from Bastia: less than quarter of an hour's flying distance for a fighter. So can anyone wonder at the responsible commander fearing such a possible landing—which would have crumpled up the whole Central Italian front at a stroke and might very easily have meant a mortal blow to the whole Army Group?

"A landing nearer the front, too, would have unhinged

the 10th and 14th Army sectors, as the total forces were insufficient to repel a frontal attack *and* a landing. One place conceivable for such a landing was south-east of the Anzio bridgehead—with the aim of linking up this bridgehead with the forces attacking the 10th Army and dislodging the right wing of the latter. Another possible place was the Tiber estuary—in 'order to strike the 14th Army in the back. But the worst effects of all would be felt from a landing in the Civitavecchia area, north of Rome. For the weak forces we had there could not hope to hold up the creation of an effective bridgehead until reserves arrived, as the terrain there—as also from Grosseto northward to Livorno—was most suitable for landing operations. Indeed, our only chance of holding up a landing was if it came immediately north and south of the Anzio bridgehead."

THE LAST LONG STAGE

The German commanders heaved a profound sigh of relief when they arrived back in the northern Apennines without being cut off. Their relief was increased when the Allied landing in Southern France took place in August— just after the Allied break-out from the bridgehead in Normandy. For they reckoned, correctly, that no further landing would be attempted behind their backs in Italy. While few of them had any illusions about the outcome of the war, now that the Allied armies had overrun France and reached the Rhine, they felt that they might be able to spin out the time and avoid disaster—in the backwater that Italy had now become.

But their sense of relief evaporated as the inflow of drafts and equipment dwindled while divisions were taken away to bolster up the Rhine and Eastern fronts. The gaps had to be filled with newly raised Italian divisions which Mussolini and Marshal Graziani had formed in the northern part of the country that was still in German occupation. Tippelskirch, who came to Italy to take charge of the 14th Army during the winter, told me that it then consisted of two German and four Italian divisions—a dangerous degree of dilution, even though one of the latter was, he remarked, much better than any of those that had fought with the Italian army in Russia. The 10th Army did not suffer so much from dilution, but was weakened by general shortages—of drafts and equipment.

The course of the last stage may be summarized in the account given me by Jahn, who was then commanding a mixed German-Italian army corps. "We had great difficulty in holding up the Allies' autumn offensive in 1944, and our divisions had heavy casualties. The last few attacks were the most dangerous—but heavy rains, and snow, helped to avert the threatened break-through. Early in 1945, four divisions were taken away and sent to Germany, thus weakening the defensive front. The "Hermann Goering" division, one of the strongest we had, was sent to help in withstanding the Russians.

"While our weakness pointed to the need for a strategic withdrawal to the Alps, O.K.W. was anxious to postpone this as long as possible, because it regarded the retention of northern Italy as vital, both for its armament production and as a source of food supply. But a plan had been made, as far back as October, to withdraw to a new line in the foothills of the Alps in the event of an Allied break-through. When the break-through came, in April, any such withdrawal was made impossible by the shortage of motor transport and petrol, coupled with the speed of the American advance. The American forces, after driving through to Como, turned west and blocked all the passes in the rear of the German forces. We found ourselves cut off from higher headquarters and no orders came through. Hardly any aircraft were left, so that the German forces were rendered blind as well as deaf. The retreating forces wandered 'in the blue' without knowing what had happened or what they were supposed to do—until the order for surrender reached us!"

CHAPTER XXI

PARALYSIS IN NORMANDY

For Britain and the United States the landing in Normandy was the supreme venture. The story of it has been abundantly told from their points of view. It is more illuminating to follow the course of the invasion from "the other side of the hill". During the first month the opposing Commander-in-Chief was Field-Marshal von Rundstedt, who had been in command of the Western theatre since early in 1942. He gave me his account. At the start of the second month Rundstedt was replaced by Field-Marshal von Kluge, who held the post until the collapse came. He is dead—after the collapse he swallowed a dose of poison in despair, and fear of Hitler. But General Blumentritt was Chief of Staff to both throughout this crucial campaign, and I had a very detailed account from him of events during both periods.

Under Rundstedt and Kluge in turn, the battle to check the invasion was conducted by Field-Marshal Rommel commanding Army Group "B", which stretched from Brittany to Holland. Rommel, too, is dead. But I was able to gain light on his part in the Normandy campaign from members of his staff—and get a check on each of the higher commanders' accounts from other generals who were on the scene.

From General Warlimont, now the senior surviving member of O.K.W., I got an insight into the views of Hitler himself and his entourage.

Seeing the battle through the opponent's eyes is the most dramatic way of seeing it. It is different in one important respect from "looking at it through the opposite end of the telescope". For instead of being minimized, the picture is magnified—with startling vividness.

Looking at the invasion problem from the English shore, it appeared tremendously formidable. Looking at it from the French shore, as the enemy saw it, one could better appreciate the very different feelings of those who faced the threat of invasion by Powers which held the command of the sea, and of the air. "I had over 3,000 miles of coastline to cover," Rundstedt told me, "from the Italian frontier in the south to the German frontier in the north, and only 60 divisions with which to defend it. Most of them were low-grade divisions, and some of them were skeletons."

The figure of 60 would not "go" into 3,000 miles on any strategic calculation. It spelt fifty miles per division, even without allowing for the need of reserves behind. That was an impossible proposition. In the 1914–18 war it used to be considered that 3 miles per division was the safety limit against any strong attack. The power of modern defence had increased since then at least double, perhaps treble—even so, the number of divisions available was far too small to cover the whole frontage with any degree of security.

The chances thus depended on guessing correctly where the Allies were likely to make their landing. Unlikely sections of the coastline had to be left almost defenceless in order to have any appreciable cover for the more probable stretches. Even then, these could only be held thinly if reserves were to be kept back for counter-attack at the actual points of landing within the sector—when these were clearly known.

Rundstedt and Blumentritt emphasized to me how much more difficult their problem was made by Hitler's readiness to imagine that the invasion might come anywhere on the circumference of occupied Europe, and his inclination to scout the shipping factors.

PRELUDE

I asked the Field-Marshal whether he had expected an Allied invasion of the West at any time prior to when it actually came. He replied: "I was surprised that you did not attempt an invasion in 1941 while our armies were advancing deep into Russia. But at that time I was myself on the Eastern front, and out of touch with the situation in the West. When I came there, and knew the situation better, I did not expect an early invasion, for I realized that your resources were not sufficient." Rundstedt's reference to his 1941 view would appear to bear out earlier reports that he then got on Hitler's nerves by his warnings about leaving the German rear exposed—a risk which Hitler sought to cover by sending Rundstedt to take charge in the West. Rundstedt's sphere of responsibility stretched from the Dutch-German frontier to the Franco-Italian frontier.

In answer to a further question, the Field-Marshal said he did not imagine that the landing at Dieppe, in August, 1942, portended an actual invasion. He thought it was merely an experimental attack, to test the coastal defences. When I questioned Blumentritt on the same point he gave a somewhat different answer—"I was not in the West at the time, but I heard a lot about the landing after my arrival, at the end of September, to succeed General Zeitzler as Chief of Staff there. The German Command was not sure whether it was merely a raid, or whether it might have been followed up with larger reinforcements if it had been more successful at the outset." It would seem that both Zeitzler and Keitel took a serious view of it. As already mentioned, in Chapter XVII, it led Hitler to order two of his best divisions to be sent to the West just when they might have turned the scales at Stalingrad.

Continuing his account, Rundstedt said: "I expected an invasion in 1943, once we had occupied the whole of

France. For I thought you would take early advantage of this extensive stretching of the German forces in the West."

Blumentritt amplified this point: "After the Allied landings in French North Africa—in November, 1942—the Führer's order for us to advance into the unoccupied part of France was prompted by his conviction that the Allies would go on from Africa to invade southern France. It was reckoned that they would land on the Mediterranean coast, and that the Vichy Government would not oppose them. The occupation took place without any great friction, and the only casualties were caused by partisans—whose activities were already becoming uncomfortable. Field-Marshal von Rundstedt himself went on alone ahead of his troops in order to arrange at Vichy that the occupation should be carried out peacefully, so as to avoid useless losses to both sides. He succeeded in that purpose."

1943—"THE YEAR OF UNCERTAINTY"

"After the fall of Tunis in May," Blumentritt said, "Hitler became increasingly anxious about the possibility of a landing in the south of France. In fact, that year Hitler was constantly on the jump—at one moment he expected an invasion in Norway, at another moment in Holland, then near the Somme, or Normandy and Brittany, in Portugal, in Spain, in the Adriatic. His eyes were hopping all around the map.

"He was particularly concerned about the possibility of a pincer-type invasion, with simultaneous landings in the south of France and the Bay of Biscay. He also feared a stroke to capture the Balearic Islands, followed by a landing at Barcelona and an advance from there northward into France. He was so impressed with the risks of an Allied invasion of Spain that he ordered strong German forces to be sent to the Pyrenees to meet it. At the same time he insisted that the German forces must be careful to observe the strictest neutrality, and avoid any offence to Spain." (Geyr von Schweppenburg, however, told me that in April, 1943—when he was commanding the 86th Army Corps at Dax, near the western end of the Pyrenees—he received instructions to prepare for a dash into Spain. The project was called "Operation Gisela". Five divisions, four of them being mechanized or motorized, were earmarked for what Geyr called "this folly". "One of them was to race for Bilbao and the rest fanwise, the left wing for Central Spain, direction Madrid.")

Continuing his account Blumentritt said: "We soldiers did not share some of Hitler's apprehensions. We thought it was unlikely that the British High Command would attempt a landing in the Bay of Biscay as it was outside the range of air support from England. We also discounted the Spanish possibilities, for several reasons—we doubted whether the Allies would risk incurring Spain's hostility, and in any case it was unfavourable country for large-scale operations, the communications being bad, and the Pyrenees forming a barrier beyond. Moreover we were on friendly terms with the Spanish generals along the Pyrenean frontier, and while they let us know clearly that they would resist any German invasion, they were helpful in providing us with information."

Blumentritt, however, went on to say that while the generals discounted some of the threats that worried Hitler, they thought a landing would come somewhere. "This year showed every sign of being the one for the expected invasion. Rumours grew stronger throughout 1943 that an invasion was coming. They reached us largely from foreign diplomatic sources—from the Rumanian, Hungarian, and Japanese military attachés, as well as from Vichy quarters."

It would seem that rumour was more effective than planned deception in playing on the mind of the enemy command. In one of my talks with Rundstedt I asked him whether he thought that a cross-Channel invasion was coming in September that year—at that time we made an elaborate feint, moving large forces down to the south coast of England, and making an appearance of embarking them. He replied, with a smile: "The movements you made at that time were too obvious—it was evident that they were a bluff."

That too apparent piece of stage-play tended to relieve the anxieties of the German Command, by its indication that the Allies were putting off the attempt. Since autumn gales were about due, it meant that the German garrisons of France might count upon another winter's respite before the storm broke upon them. It was a partial relief after a long period of strained alertness.

"In brief, 1943 might be summed up as 'the year of uncertainty and insecurity'," remarked Blumentritt. "Its difficulties were increased because the Resistance movement in France had by then become very formidable, and was causing us many casualties, as well as serious strain. It had not amounted to much in 1942. It was then divided into three distinct groups—Communists, Gaullists and Giraudists. Fortunately for us, these three groups were mutually antagonistic, and often brought us information about one another's activities. But from 1943 onwards they became united—with Britain directing their operations and supplying them with arms by air."

CHANGING THE GUARD

During 1943 various alterations were made in the defence scheme to meet invasion, under the handicap of limited resources. For France had been used as a convalescent home where divisions exhausted in the Eastern campaign could recuperate and reorganize. Describing the steps, Blumentritt said: "Up to 1943 there had been fifty to sixty divisions in France which were repeatedly being replaced by badly-damaged divisions from the

Russian front. This continual interchange was detrimental to a proper system of defence on the coast. So permanent coast-defence divisions were formed, with a specialized organization adapted to their particular sectors. This system had the advantage of ensuring that they were well acquainted with the sector they had to guard, and it also enabled the most economic use of the limited equipment available in the West. But it had inevitable weaknesses. The officers and men were mostly of the older classes, and their armament was on a lower scale than in the active divisions. It included a large proportion of captured French, Polish, and Yugo-Slav weapons, which fired differing kinds of ammunition—so that supplies were more liable to run out, at awkward moments, than in the case of standard weapons. Most of these divisions had only two infantry regiments, with two field batteries comprising 24 pieces in all, and one medium battery of 12 pieces. As the artillery was horse-drawn it had little mobility.

"Besides these coast-defence divisions there was the coastal artillery. But this, whether naval or military, came under the Naval Command—which was always inclined to disagree with the Army Command."

A fresh complication arose at the end of the year with Rommel's entry on the scene. He had previously been for a short time in command of the German forces that occupied Northern Italy, but in November he was appointed by Hitler to inspect and improve the coast defences from Denmark to the Spanish frontier. After dealing with those in Denmark he moved to France just before Christmas —which brought him into Rundstedt's sphere. He worked under special instructions from Hitler, yet without any clear definition about his relationship to Rundstedt. Controversy naturally developed, and the more inevitably because their ideas differed.

Blumentritt's comment was: "Soon, the armies did not know whether they were under the command of Rundstedt or Rommel, as the latter wanted his ideas on coast defence to be put into practice everywhere. To solve the problem, Rundstedt suggested that Rommel should take over executive charge of the most important sector of the front along the Channel, from the Dutch-German border to the Loire, while the Southern front from the Loire to the Alps would be entrusted to Blaskowitz—both being under Rundstedt as supreme commander. Under Rommel's Army Group "B" would be placed the troops in Holland; the 15th Army, holding from there to the Seine; and the 7th Army, from the Seine to the Loire. Blaskowitz's Army Group "G" comprised the 1st Army, covering the Bay of Biscay and the Pyrenees, and the 19th Army, covering the Mediterranean coast."

According to Rommel's staff, the proposal came from him—"as the only way of putting his ideas into execution quickly". In any case the arrangement was sanctioned, about a month after his arrival. It went some way to ease the situation, although the difference of views about the treatment of the problem was not compatible with a real solution.

Moreover, the new arrangement produced fresh internal complications. All the armoured forces came under Geyr von Schweppenburg, who had recently been made commander of what was called "Panzer Group West". It was natural that he should wish to keep them concentrated. The reorganization not only tended to diminish his authority but produced a clash of convictions, since Rommel favoured a distribution of the panzer divisions that ran contrary to the basic ideas of Geyr, one of the early leaders in that field. Geyr was supported by Guderian, who at this time was Inspector-General of Panzer Forces. Rommel had an equally strong belief in the principle of concentration, but felt that changed circumstances—above all, the Allies' domination of the air—compelled a modification of it in practice.

This conflict of views between experts in armoured

warfare placed Rundstedt in a dilemma. His strategical instinct favoured the principle upheld by Geyr and Guderian, but when it came to deciding on the course to follow he had to recognize that Rommel spoke from experience of fighting the Western powers, with their vastly superior air strength, whereas Geyr and Guderian only had experience of the Eastern front where airpower had played a slighter part. While most accounts of the conflict have portrayed it as an issue between Rundstedt and Rommel, the deeper cleavage on method lay between Rommel and Geyr, supported by Guderian, with Rundstedt as an arbiter—under limitations imposed by Hitler and by circumstances.

Speaking to me of Rommel, Rundstedt said: "He was a brave man, and a very capable commander in small operations, but not really qualified for high command." (That view, although widespread among the senior generals, is strongly controverted, I have found, by most of the commanders who operated under Rommel, and also by the very able General Staff officers who successively served him as Chief of Staff.) Rundstedt had no complaint of Rommel's loyalty: "When I gave an order Rommel obeyed it without making any difficulty."

On the other hand, those who disagreed with the plan adopted complained of Rundstedt's hesitation to overrule Rommel where his own views were basically different, and where Rommel's decisions were bound to have a far-reaching effect on his own measures. Some ascribed the hesitation to Rundstedt being over-scrupulous in refraining from interference in what he regarded as his subordinate's proper sphere of responsibility. Geyr was more blunt: "Von Rundstedt was too weak a personality to enforce his own point of view. In the various conflicts of view he maintained a sort of neutrality. As a result it was quite impossible to get clear-cut decisions on controversial issues. The ship was drifting without a helmsman." In some other comments, Geyr said: "Rundstedt is a gentleman, both wise and clever, but undoubtedly one of the most lazy soldiers I met in higher quarters in my lifetime. And he didn't like my tendency to disturb quiet waters. In 1944 he was an ageing man. Physical ill-health and pyschic resignation certainly had something to do with the state of lethargy of the leading personality."

Geyr's account may underrate the measure in which Rundstedt's mind was changed by Rommel's arguments on practical grounds. General Speidel, Rommel's Chief of Staff, told me that Rundstedt subsequently came to agree with Rommel's ideas, and Geyr admits this, though regarding it merely as evidence of Rundstedt's lack of will "to fight for what he had originally believed in". What is clearer, from all accounts, is that Rundstedt was suffering from fatigue, both of body and spirit, as well as from other troubles. That condition explains much. But the way that such an old and tired man retained the respect of so many who served him, and still made most of them feel that he was irreplaceable, is evidence of an exceptional personality. It shone more strongly again when, with the ending of the war, he had to face as an individual the tribulations of captivity, and he stood up to the test in a most impressive way.

Here I would remark that the more I saw of Rundstedt the better impression he made. That was due to indirect as well as direct evidence. His seniority might have partly explained the high respect, but not the deep affection he inspired among those who shared his captivity. He has a rather orthodox mind, not only in the operational sphere, but it is an able and sensitive mind, backed by a character that makes him outstanding. He is dignified without being arrogant, and essentially aristocratic in outlook—giving that term its best sense. He has an austere appearance that is offset by a pleasant smile and a nice gleam of humour. This frequently comes out. Walking back with him on one occasion to his cramped little room, after passing through the heavily barbed-wire gate into the inner compound, we came to the front door. I motioned him to go in first. He replied to this gesture with a smile: "Oh, no—this is *my* house."

WHERE?

When 1944 came it was clear that the main invasion would be launched from England, because of the scale of the American forces which were being transported there. But it was more difficult to determine where the landings would be made in France. "Very little reliable news came out of England," Blumentritt told me. "All that side of the Intelligence was directed by O.K.W. under Hitler, not by us—and was carried out by a special branch of the S.D. We were dependent on them for our information.

"They gave us reports of where, broadly, the British and American forces respectively were assembled in Southern England—there were a small number of German agents in England, who reported by wireless transmitting sets what they observed. But they found out very little beyond that. We were so weak in the air that reconnaissance over England was very limited. Towards D-day, however, night-flying 'planes reported large movements of transport towards the south-west coast—which they could follow because the vehicles had their headlights on." (Presumably these were American troops, as the western half of Southern England was occupied by them.) "We also intercepted a wireless message from the British Fleet which gave us an indication that something important was about to take place in the Channel.

"Another hint came from the increased activity of the 'Resistance' in France. We captured several hundred wireless transmitters, and were able to discover the bearing of the code phrases used in communicating with England. The messages were veiled, but the broad significance was evident.

"But nothing we learnt gave us a definite clue where the invasion was actually coming. We had to depend on our own judgment in that vital respect."

Blumentritt then told me: "Our Naval Staff always insisted that the Allies would land near a big port. They anticipated an attack on Le Havre—not only because of its value as a port, but because it was the base for our midget submarines. We soldiers did not agree with their view. We doubted whether the Allies would make a direct attack on such a well-fortified place. Moreover, we had information about a big exercise carried out in southern England, where the troops had been disembarked on a flat and open coastline.

"From this we deduced that the Allies would not try to attack a port at the outset. But we had no idea, nor any report, that they were developing artificial harbours— the Mulberries. We thought you were probably intending to lay your ships side by side, to form a bridge over which stores could be unloaded and carried ashore to the beaches."

Rundstedt said frankly: "I thought the invasion would come across the narrower part of the Channel, between Le Havre and Calais—rather than between Caen and Cherbourg. I expected the landing to take place on either side of the estuary of the Somme. I thought the first landing might take place on the west side, between Le Tréport and Le Havre, followed by a further landing between the Somme and Calais."

I asked Rundstedt his reasons for this calculation. He replied: "The Somme–Calais area seemed to us so much better, strategically, from your point of view—because it was so much closer to Germany. It was the quickest route to the Rhine. I reckoned you could get there in four days."

His reasoning suggested that his calculation was governed by a preconceived view, based on the assumption that the Allies would take what was theoretically the best line, regardless of the practical difficulties. I remarked to him that, for the same reasons, it was likely to be the most strongly defended sector—surely a good reason why the Allies were likely to avoid it.

He admitted the point but answered: "The strength o the defences was absurdly overrated. The 'Atlantic Wall' was an illusion, conjured up by propaganda—to deceive the German people as well as the Allies. It used to make me angry to read the stories about its impregnable defences. It was nonsense to describe it as a 'wall'. Hitler himself never came to visit it, and see what it really was. For that matter the only time he came to the Channel coast in the whole war was back in 1940, when he paid a visit on one occasion to Cap Gris Nez." I remarked: "And looked across at the English coast, like Napoleon?" Rundstedt nodded, with an ironical smile.

Rundstedt went on to say that another reason for his anticipation that the invasion would come in the Somme–Calais area was that we should be forced to attack the area where V-weapons were located at the earliest possible moment, in order to save London from destruction. He was told that the effect of these weapons would be much greater than it was in reality. Hitler built excessive hopes on them, and that affected strategic calculations.

It was Hitler, however, who guessed that the Allied landings would come in Normandy. Blumentritt revealed this. "At the end of March O.K.W. issued instructions which showed that Hitler expected an invasion of Normandy. From that time onward we received repeated warnings about it, starting with the words—'The Führer fears . . .' I don't know what led him to that conclusion. But as a result the 91st Air-landing Division with some tank squadrons was moved down there, and posted in reserve behind the Cherbourg Peninsula—near Carentan."

Members of Rommel's staff had told me he likewise anticipated that our landings would take place in Normandy, in contrast to Rundstedt's view. I asked Rundstedt and Blumentritt about this, and they said it was correct.

Rommel came round to that view increasingly in the spring. They did not know how far it was his own judgment, or influenced by Hitler's repeated warnings—"Watch Normandy".

It would seem that Hitler's much derided "intuition" was nearer the mark than the calculations of the ablest professional soldiers. They were unduly influenced by their tendency to go by what was the proper course in orthodox strategic theory—or by a conviction that the Allied planners were sure to do the conventional thing. The value of doing the "unexpected" was overlooked.

In this connection Rundstedt made a significant disclosure in answer to one of my questions. "If the Allies had landed in western France, near the Loire, they could have succeeded very easily—both in establishing a large enough bridgehead, and then driving inland. I could not have moved a single division there to stop them." Blumentritt added: "Such a landing would have met practically no opposition. There were only three divisions covering 300 miles of coast south of the Loire, and two of them were training divisions composed of raw recruits. A company commander on that coast had to cycle all day in covering his company sector. We regarded the Loire area as too far from England for air support, and thus assumed it was unlikely the Allied Command would attempt to land there—knowing how much they were inclined to count on ensuring maximum air cover." (This revelation was of the more interest to me because in January, 1944, I had written a paper suggesting that the Allied landing should be made on the west coast, near the mouth of the Loire, as "the surest way of fulfilling the key principle of 'least expectation', and thereby throwing the enemy off his balance".)

On the same reasoning the German Command, except Rommel, thought that a landing in Normandy was less likely than where the Channel was narrower, and air support easier. Rundstedt said, too: "We thought that any landing in Normandy would be limited to an attempt to capture Cherbourg. The American landing near here was thus less unexpected than the British landing round Caen."

Here we may suitably insert Warlimont's evidence from the O.K.W. angle—"The organization of Intelligence was a source of rivalry and ambitions, and consequently of heavy mistakes on our side. Originally and up to 1944 the 'Office Foreign Affairs and Counter-Intelligence', incorporated in the O.K.W. and conducted by Admiral Canaris, assembled the intelligence and furnished it to the three forces for evaluation. Thus the Armed Forces Operations Staff, in its capacity as the operations branch for the Western theatre, was dependent mainly on the O.K.H. section 'Foreign Armies West', and in addition on the corresponding sections of the Navy and Air Force. Early in 1944 the office of Canaris was dissolved by order of Hitler, chiefly for political reasons, and he himself dismissed. The Intelligence now became a part of the Reichs Security Central Office, headed by the S.D.-Chief, Kaltenbrunner. He, for personal reasons, often deviated from the prescribed official way and sent or delivered important news, or what he deemed such, directly to Hitler or Jodl. In the end, as a natural consequence of such a 'system', there was much trouble and little intelligence. When, finally, on the afternoon of the 5th June, 1944, Kaltenbrunner believed he had sure indications of the impending invasion, and reported them to Jodl, Jodl paid no attention to it—or, at least, informed neither his staff nor Hitler."

"As regards the site of the landing, Hitler was the first who came to the conclusion that Normandy was the most probable spot. On May 2nd he ordered that anti-aircraft and anti-tank weapons were to be reinforced throughout that sector on that calculation. Hitler's view was based on intelligence received as to troop movements in Britain. Two main troop concentrations had been observed there—

one in the south-east, consisting of British troops, and the
other in the south-west consisting of American troops.
The situation of the Americans, in particular, led Hitler
to anticipate an attack launched against the western part
of Normandy. Besides his deductions from troop movements,
Hitler based his conclusions on the consideration that the
Allies, from the outset, would need a big port which had
to be situated in such a way as to be quickly protected
by a rather short front line. These conditions would be
essentially met by the port of Cherbourg and the Cotentin
Peninsula. We were not quite convinced that Hitler was
right, but he kept harping on it, and demanded more
and more reinforcements for the Normandy sector. We
generals figured along the lines of our regular military
education whereas Hitler figured, as he always did, out of
intuition."

This revelation of how Hitler deduced the site of the
Allied landing was also of particular interest to me. For in
the middle of March I had been summoned to the War
Cabinet office, following the proposals I had put forward
for making the landing more unexpected in direction,
and had then, in discussion with General Ismay and
General Jacob, argued that the lay-out of the British and
American forces in the south of England, in relation to the
ports, provided a too obvious indication that our invasion
was planned to come between Cherbourg and the mouth
of the Seine. It is more strange that the German generals
failed to make the right deduction than that Hitler did so.
It was not a matter of intuition in this case, but of
reasonable deduction.

Continuing, Warlimont said: "Hitler became more
and more firm in his conviction, but he believed furthermore, previous to and also for a long time after the
invasion, that a second landing would take place on the
Channel coast. Thus it came about that the small operational reserves which could be spared for the West, and
the invasion, were kept back around Paris. Reinforcements

for the local defence in Normandy were looked for everywhere. But, apart from the so-called 91st Airborne Division,
in fact a newly activated unit, and a certain amount of
anti-aircraft weapons, there were none left to dispose of.
This was the more fateful as Hitler repeatedly reiterated
in my presence: 'If we do not stop the invasion and do not
drive the enemy back into the sea, the war will be lost.'
Hitler himself put all his confidence in the personality of
Rommel, in his Panzer divisions and in the fighting
experience of the German soldier in contrast to that of the
average Allied soldier, forgetting to take the Air Force
into account."

But Hitler showed shrewd judgment when, as Warlimont relates, he declared: "If we succeed in throwing
back the invasion then such an attempt cannot and will not
be repeated within a short time. It will then mean that our
reserves will be set free for use in Italy and the East.
Then we can stabilize the front in the East and perhaps
return to the offensive in that sector. If we don't throw
the invaders back we can't win a static war in the long
run because the material our enemies can bring in will
exceed what we can send to the front. We cannot win a
static war in the West for the additional reason that each
step backward means a broadening of the front lines
across more of France. With no strategic reserves of any
importance, it will be impossible to build-up sufficient
strength along such a line. Therefore the invader must be
thrown back at his first attempt."

THE GERMAN DISPOSITIONS

In June, 1944, there were (to be exact) 59 German
divisions in the West—eight of these being in Holland and
Belgium. More than half the total were coast-defence or
training divisions. Of the 27 field divisions, only 10 were
armoured—three of these were in the south, and one
near Antwerp.

Along the 200 mile stretch of the Normandy coast, west of the Seine, stood six divisions (four of them merely coast-defence). Three of these were in the Cherbourg Peninsula, two held the forty-mile stretch between there and Caen—from the Vire to the Orne—and one was between the Orne and the Seine. Blumentritt commented: "The dispositions would more truly be described as 'coast-protection' rather than as 'defence'! As we did not anticipate that any landing would be made on the west side of the Cherbourg Peninsula, that sector was held very lightly—we even put Russian units there."

There was one armoured division in the forward area, for counter-attack. This was the 21st Panzer Division. "There were prolonged arguments," Blumentritt said, "as to where the 21st Panzer Division should be placed. Field-Marshal von Rundstedt would have preferred it to be south of St. Lo, behind the Cherbourg Peninsula. But Rommel chose to put it nearer the coast and on the other flank, close to Caen. This meant that it was too near the coast to be really available as a reserve for the sector as a whole."

Nevertheless, the presence of that division near Caen proved an important factor. But for it, the British might have captured Caen on the first day of the landing. Rommel begged in vain for a second armoured division to be at hand near the mouth of the Vire—where the Americans landed.

Here we are brought to the great controversy that vitally affected the German plans to meet the invasion. Rundstedt felt that, with forces so limited and a coastline so long, it was not possible to prevent the Allies achieving a landing. He relied, therefore, on a powerful counter-offensive to throw them out—after they had committed themselves, but before they were well established. As already mentioned, Geyr was strongly urging on him that this was the correct strategy with panzer forces.

Rommel, on the other hand, felt that the only chance

lay in defeating the invaders on the coast, before they were properly ashore. "The first twenty-four hours will be decisive," he often said to his Staff. Blumentritt, though of the opposite school, explained Rommel's reasons to me most fairly: "Rommel had found in Africa that the tanks were apt to be too far back for delivering a counter-attack at the critical moment. He also felt that if the panzer reserves were kept far back inland, as the Commander-in-Chief preferred, their move-up would be interrupted by the Allied air force." From Rommel's own Staff I learnt that he was greatly influenced by the memory of the way he had been nailed down for days on end in Africa by an air force that was not nearly so strong as that he now had to face.

Guderian described the development of the controversy as he saw it: "In March, 1944, after a visit to General von Geyr in France, I spoke to Hitler about Rommel's defensive measures and told him that I thought it dangerous to advance the panzer divisions up close to the coast defences, because of their losing their mobility. Hitler was doubtful and ordered me to see Rommel in France and discuss the question with him. This I did in April at Rommel's headquarters at La Roche-Guyon. Rommel explained his views, to me and General Freiherr von Geyr, in a very clear and decided manner." Rommel's argument, as summarized by Guderian, was that the movement of troops would be impracticable by day, and even by night, because of the Allies' air superiority. For this reason Rommel wanted to place all available troops in or immediately behind the front line—the coast. At the time of this discussion, Rommel considered that the most likely scene of the invasion was near the mouth of the Somme, as here the line of communications with England would be short. "I remarked that his reserves would be in the wrong place if his opinion of the presumable landing sector of the Allies should be wrong."

Guderian went on to say: "The visit had no result. I

saw Hitler again in the beginning of May and discussed the question once more, but without result. Hitler refused to oppose the views of the local commander, for he shared Rommel's opinion. Before seeing Hitler, I had co-ordinated my view with that of Field-Marshal von Rundstedt, whom I visited at Paris. It is possible that, towards the end of April, Rommel changed his views and expected an Allied landing towards Normandy, but apparently he did not alter the positions of the panzer divisions at his disposal and therefore failed to have sufficient reserves on the landing front. In practice, movements of panzer divisions have been executed by day and night in spite of the superiority of the Allied air forces. If executed by day, they often suffered heavy losses." (Rommel's staff, however, point out that the range of movement by night was limited, since the nights were short, and that all movements took much longer than had been reckoned—a point which Rundstedt himself emphasizes, as will be seen later.)

As Guderian had failed to convince Hitler, and as Rundstedt was now veering round to Rommel's view, Geyr decided to go up to the Supreme Command himself, and make a personal protest against Rommel's plan. He went to Berchtesgaden for that purpose early in May, and argued that the bulk of the panzer forces should be kept in reserve initially—"under cover from air attack in the forests north-west or south of Paris, from which they could mount their assault when the enemy was deeply committed into the country". Geyr's intervention resulted in a fateful concession. Hitler gave orders that four of the panzer divisions in the West were to be kept in hand as an O.K.W. strategic reserve. That decision had unforeseen effects. It weakened Rommel's capacity to carry out his plan; it left Rundstedt without a reserve under his own control; but it did not lead to the course that Geyr desired. For Rundstedt became convinced of the importance of early counter-attack, before the invaders had established their position, while still maintaining his belief in a concentrated counter-offensive. But he lacked the reserves to carry out both purposes.

As Hitler was unwilling to provide the required reserves at the expense of other theatres, Rundstedt saw that the only way was to create them by a drastic curtailment of his commitments in France. Prompted by Rommel, he therefore put up to Hitler a radical solution for the problem. Telling me about it, Rundstedt said: "Before the Allied invasion I wanted to evacuate the whole of southern France up to the Loire, and bring back the forces there to form a strong mass of manœuvre with which I could strike back at the Allies. This would have provided ten or twelve infantry divisions and three or four armoured divisions to fight a mobile battle. But Hitler would not listen to such an idea—though it was the only way in which I could hope to form a proper reserve. All the newspaper talk about 'Rundstedt's Central Army' was sheer nonsense— that Army did not exist. Worse still, I was not even allowed a free hand with the handful of armoured divisions that were available in France. I could not move one of them without Hitler's permission."

But Rommel was also handicapped in applying his "forward" plan. That was not really due to Rundstedt but to the scanty number of panzer divisions allotted him after the O.K.W. reserve was formed. He had only three for his whole front from the Scheldt to the Loire. It was a very light punch with which to counter a powerful invasion. The handicap proved the greater because Rommel had placed two of his three panzer divisions east of the Seine. Why was it that Rommel did not change that disposition to correspond with his growing conviction that the invasion would come west of the Seine? The reason would seem to be that the two strongest panzer divisions in O.K.W. reserve were placed in the back area of Normandy, and that he counted on early support from them.

So far as Rundstedt was concerned that expectation was justified. For he wished to use them for that purpose—

despite Geyr's objections. But when, in the early hours of
D-day he tried to get them released by O.K.W. he found
difficulty in obtaining permission, and his request was not
granted until the afternoon. (In an effort to make up time
the *élite* Panzer Lehr Division was ordered to move up in
daylight from the Le Mans area, with the result that it
suffered serious damage and more delay. The second day's
march was worse—air attacks were so incessant that the
troops called their route a "bombing race-course".)

Geyr says that he was not informed of this move until
after the "order had been issued", and that he "appealed
to Field Marshal von Rundstedt at least to delay the move
of the second of these divisions (the Panzer Lehr) until
after nightfall", but that "von Rundstedt did not comply
with my request". Bayerlein, who now commanded this
crack division, says that he wanted to wait until dusk, but
that the commander of the 7th Army, Dollmann, insisted
on him moving at 5 p.m.

Whether there would have been any prospects for a
concentrated counter-offensive such as Geyr desired is
doubtful. But it is clear that the far-back position of the
reserves prejudiced the possibility of fulfilling Rommel's
plan of immediate counter-attack. Even apart from the
delay in releasing them, the time required to move them up,
coupled with the scarcity of panzer forces in the forward
area, gravely impaired the chance of repelling the invaders
before they consolidated their position ashore.

The chances were further diminished by earlier neglect
to develop the coast defences. From Rommel's staff I
heard of the feverish efforts he made in the Spring of 1944
to hasten the construction of under-water obstacles, bomb-
proof bunkers, and mine-fields along the Normandy coast
—where, he correctly judged, the invasion would come.
For example, less than two million mines had been laid
along the whole north coast of France in the three years
before he arrived on the scene. In the few months before
D-day the number was trebled—but he was aiming at over

fifty million mines. It was fortunate for the invaders that there was so much more to do than could be achieved in the short time available.

Rundstedt's explanation to me was: "The lack of labour troops and material was the main handicap in developing the defences. Most of the men of the Todt labour force, who had been previously available in France, had been drawn off to Germany to repair air raid damage there. At the same time, the coast defence divisions were too widely extended—often over a forty-mile stretch—to carry out the necessary work themselves. Beyond this, there was not enough material for the job—owing to the constant interference of the Allied Air Forces, which checked both the manufacture and the movement of the necessary material."

But this does not cover the earlier neglect, in 1942 and 1943, of which Rommel complained. In so far as it was not due to lethargy, or to disbelief in the likelihood of an invasion, it may have been due to the fact that Rundstedt and his subordinates, who were exponents of mobile offensive warfare, had little belief in the value of static defences, and so gave too little attention to their construction. That is the view of Rommel's staff, and is in accord with the type of counter-offensive plan originally favoured by Rundstedt, and constantly urged by Geyr.

In sum, the measures to meet the Allied invasion "fell between two stools"—as the result of the conflict of opinion among the military leaders, multiplied by Hitler's tight hand on the reserves. The maladjusted method of defence had more effect in opening the way into France than anything the Allies did to achieve surprise.

THE LANDING

"The coming of the invasion," Blumentritt remarked, "could be recognized by many signs. Increasing disorder in the interior became a serious threat, and caused us considerable loss—through ambushes and raids. There were many derailments of trains that were carrying supplies and reinforcements to the front. Beyond this was the planned destruction by air bombing of the railways in France and Western Germany—especially of the bridges across the Somme, the Seine and the Loire. All these were pointers."

Rundstedt emphasized: "Although we had no definite report of the date of the invasion that did not matter, as we had been expecting it any time from March onward." I asked whether the storm that postponed the launching twenty-four hours, and nearly compelled its cancellation, had not lulled the defenders into a sense of security at the critical moment. Blumentritt replied: "No, it didn't have that effect—because we thougnt the Allies were sure to have the kind of vessels that would not be affected by heavy seas. So we were always on tenter-hooks, and just as ready at one time as another."

Rundstedt went on: "The one real surprise was the time of day at which the landing was made—because our Naval Staff had told us that the Allied forces would only land at high water. A further effect of your choice of low tide, for the landing, was that the leading troops were protected from fire to a considerable extent by the rocks.

"The scale of the invading forces was not a surprise—in fact we had imagined that they would be larger, because we had received exaggerated reports of the number of American divisions present in England. But that over-estimate had an indirect effect of important consequence, by making us the more inclined to expect a second landing, in the Somme–Calais area."

Blumentritt related to me the story of D-day, from the point of view of the German Headquarters in the West—which was located at St. Germain, just west of Paris. (Rommel's Headquarters, at La Roche-Guyon, was midway between Rouen and Paris.)

"Soon after 9 p.m. on June 5th we intercepted messages

from England to the French Resistance Movement from
which it was deduced that the invaders were coming.
Our 15th Army east of the Seine at once issued the 'Alarm',
though for some reason the 7th Army in Normandy
delayed doing so until 4 a.m.[1] That was unfortunate.
Soon after midnight news came that Allied parachute
troops had begun dropping.

"Time was vital. The nearest available part of the
general reserve was the 1st S.S. Panzer Corps, which lay
north-west of Paris. But we could not move it without permission from Hitler's headquarters. As early as 4 a.m.
I telephoned them on behalf of Field-Marshal von Rundstedt and asked for the release of this Corps—to strengthen
Rommel's punch. But Jodl, speaking for Hitler, refused to
do so. He doubted whether the landings in Normandy were
more than a feint, and was sure that another landing was
coming east of the Seine. The 'battle' of argument went
on all day until 4 p.m., when this Corps was at last released
for our use.

"Then further difficulties interfered with its move. The
Corps artillery had been kept on the east bank of the Seine
—and the Allied Air Forces had destroyed the bridges.
The Field-Marshal and I had seen some of them being
smashed. The artillery thus had to make a long circuit
southward by way of Paris before they could get across the
Seine, and was repeatedly bombed on the march, which
caused more delays. As a result two days passed before
this reserve was on the scene, ready to strike."

By that time the Allied forces were well established
ashore, and the chances of an early counter-stroke had
faded. The armoured divisions became absorbed in the
fight piecemeal, in the effort to check the invaders from
spreading farther inland, instead of being used to drive
them back into the sea.

Two startling revelations about the opening day are

[1] According to 7th Army records, however, the alarm there was
issued at 1.30 a.m.

that Hitler himself did not hear of the landing until very
late in the morning, and that Rommel was off the scene,
as at Alamein. But for these factors, action might have
been more prompt and more forceful.

Hitler, like Churchill, had a habit of staying up until
long after midnight—a habit very exhausting to his staff,
who could not sleep late but were often in a sleepy state
when they dealt with affairs in the morning. It appears
that on D-day Jodl, reluctant to disturb Hitler's late
morning sleep, took it upon himself to resist Rundstedt's
appeal for the release of the O.K.W. reserves. Warlimont
told me how Jodl spoke to him after Blumentritt had been
on the telephone from France, and said that he (Jodl)
"did not yet feel sure that the real landing operation had
begun". The daily conference on the situation took place
about noon—at Klessheim castle near Salzburg. Warlimont
recalled that Hitler, on entering the room, said "in an
unusually strong Austrian dialect, laughing oddly: 'So,
anganga ist's' ('So, at last it's begun')".

It was after this conference that Hitler sanctioned the
release of the divisions from O.K.W. reserve, for which
Rundstedt had begged. It is possible that they would have
been released earlier if Rommel had not been absent from
Normandy. For, as Blumentritt said: "Rommel always
had very close direct connection with O.K.W. and often
spoke to Hitler himself on the telephone, which Rundstedt
never did; and Rommel, having been in the Führer's
Headquarters at the start of the war, knew everybody
there very well."

But Rommel had left his headquarters on the morning
of June 5th on a trip to Germany. Blumentritt said:
"Rommel was 'quietly' given leave by O.K.W. to attend
his wife's birthday celebrations. His home was near Ulm
on the Danube, whither he travelled by car. The Commander-in-Chief, West, *knew* this." Speidel, however, says
that Rommel intended to go on to see Hitler at Berchtesgaden next day. "The journey was made by car as the

high military leaders were forbidden to travel by plane on account of the enemy's superiority in the air." Soon after 6 a.m. on the 6th, Speidel telephoned him at Herrlingen to say that the invasion had begun. Rommel at once set off back to Normandy and arrived at his headquarters by tea-time. It is not easy to determine how serious was the effect of his absence during the first twelve hours of the invasion. While the initial counter-measures had long been arranged, and were duly put into effect, it is possible that he might have accelerated them by personal influence, or taken other measures.

There were certainly some bad hitches in the chain of command that day. The 21st Panzer Division, the only one near the scene, lay between Caen and Falaise. Its commander, Feuchtinger, had news soon after midnight of the airborne landing on the seaward side of Caen. But no orders came at all until 7 a.m., and then he was merely notified that he was placed under command of the 7th Army. (Geyr says that from 2.15 a.m. onwards the Chief of Staff of the 7th Army had "made repeated requests that the panzer division be permitted to go into action".)

Half an hour earlier Feuchtinger had decided on his own initiative to move forward up the east bank of the Orne and attack the airborne invaders. Just before 10 a.m. he was told that he had been placed under command of the 84th Corps, holding the coastal sector, and received his first operational order—to strike at the British forces which had landed from the sea on the west side of the Orne. (Geyr says that the change of direction was ordered by the 84th Corps contrary to the intentions of the 7th Army). This meant that he had to break off his attack on the airborne force (the British 6th Airborne Division) and switch the van of his division across the river. Its intervention checked the invader's advance on Caen (by the 3rd British and 3rd Canadian Divisions), but at the forfeit of the chance of wiping out the bridgehead east of the Orne.

Moreover, although the panzer thrust actually reached

the coast at some points, in the afternoon, the invaders
were well enough established ashore to frustrate the
German aim of driving them back into the sea. The thrust,
besides being late, was on too small a scale for the purpose. The leading element of the 12th S.S. Panzer Division
did not begin to arrive until late that night and an attack
it made next day was hampered by lack of petrol, while
the Panzer Lehr Division did not begin to arrive until
late on June 8th. Three vital days had been lost. After
that the three panzer divisions, and those that followed,
were frittered away in efforts to fill gaping holes—as the
infantry divisions that held the coast had been shattered.

If the three panzer divisions had been close enough at
hand to come into action on the first day, the invaders'
airborne bridgehead east of the Orne and both the sea-
bridgeheads west of the Orne might have been broken up
before they were consolidated. It was the one real chance
that the Germans had of repelling the invasion. In retrospect
it becomes as clear as anything can be that Rommel's plan,
applied in full, offered the only hopeful prospect.

I asked Rundstedt whether he had hopes of defeating
the invasion at any stage after the landing. He replied:
"Not after the first few days. The Allied Air Forces
paralysed all movement by day, and made it very difficult
even at night. They had smashed the bridges over the
Loire as well as over the Seine, shutting off the whole
area. These factors greatly delayed the concentration of
reserves there—they took three or four times longer to
reach the front than we had reckoned."

Rundstedt added: "Besides the interference of the Air
Forces, the fire of your battleships was a main factor in
hampering our counter-stroke. This was a big surprise,
both in its range and effect." Blumentritt remarked that
army officers who interrogated him after the war did not
seem to have realized what a serious effect this naval
bombardment had.

But there was still another cause of delay. Rundstedt

and Blumentritt said that by the second week they came to the conclusion that the expected second landing east of the Seine was not coming, but Hitler's headquarters were still convinced it was, and were reluctant to let them move forces westward to Normandy from the Calais area. Nor were they allowed to reshuffle their forces in Normandy as they wished. "In desperation, Field-Marshal von Rundstedt begged Hitler to come to France for a talk. He and Rommel together went to meet Hitler at Soissons on June 17th, and tried to make him understand the situation. Although Caen and St. Lo, the two pivots of the Normandy position, were still in our hands, it was obvious they could not be held much longer. The two Field-Marshals were now in full agreement as to the only step that might save the situation short of a big retreat—which they knew Hitler would not permit. They wanted to withdraw from Caen, leave the infantry to hold the line of the Orne, and pull out the armoured divisions to refit and reorganize. Their plan was to use the latter for a powerful counter-stroke against the Americans' flank in the Cherbourg Peninsula.

"But Hitler insisted that there must be no withdrawal—'You must stay where you are.' He would not even agree to allow us any more freedom than before in moving the forces as we thought best.

"The Field-Marshal and I had come to realize more and more clearly, since the second week, that we could not drive the invading forces back into the sea. But Hitler still believed it was possible! As he would not modify his orders, the troops had to continue clinging on to their cracking line. There was no plan any longer. We were merely trying, without hope, to comply with Hitler's order that the line Caen–Avranches must be held at all costs."

While referring sympathetically to the sufferings of the troops, Blumentritt remarked: "They did not stand artillery fire as well as our troops had done in the last war. The German infantry of this war were not as good as in 1914–18. The rank and file had too many ideas of their own—they were not so disciplined and obedient. The quality of the army had suffered from its too rapid expansion, which did not allow time for a thorough disciplinary training."

At the conference on the 17th Hitler swept aside the field-marshals' warnings about the critical situation at the front by assuring them that the new V weapon, the flying bomb, would soon have a decisive effect on the war. The bombardment of London had begun in the first hours of the previous day. The field-marshals then urged that, if this weapon was so effective, it should be turned against the invasion beaches—or, if that was technically difficult, against the invasion ports in southern England. Hitler insisted that the bombardment must be concentrated on London "so as to convert the English to peace". But when Rommel finished his survey of the situation by urging that the war should be brought to an end, Hitler cut him short with the retort: "Don't occupy yourself with that issue— look after your invasion front".

All that Rundstedt and Rommel obtained from this interview was an assurance that Hitler would come forward to some point near the front to meet a number of the fighting commanders, and hear their views for himself. But next day a telephone message came that Hitler had returned to Berchtesgaden during the night. This hasty departure, Speidel told me, followed the explosion of a flying bomb just outside Hitler's command-post at Soissons. It was presumably one of the many that lost direction— but the direction it took excited alarm and suspicion.

In the last week of June Rundstedt and Rommel went to Berchtesgaden to see Hitler, but their hope of making him face the realities of the situation was again disappointed. He kept them waiting for several hours and then behaved as if the purpose of the meeting was merely to give them an injection of optimism, accompanied by an admonition to "hold out in all circumstances".

This second meeting with Hitler, on the 29th, was

followed by Rundstedt's removal from command—for the time being. "Field-Marshal von Rundstedt had flatly said that he could not carry on unless he had a free hand. In view of this, and of the pessimistic tone of his reports on the situation, Hitler decided to find a new commander. He wrote the Field-Marshal a letter, which was quite pleasantly worded, saying that he had come to the conclusion that, in the circumstances, it was best to make a change."

That decision of Hitler's was influenced by another piece of plain speaking on Rundstedt's part, according to Blumentritt. Keitel had rung him up to ask about the situation, and after hearing Rundstedt's gloomy report, had plaintively asked: "What shall we do?" Rundstedt pungently replied: "End the war! What else can you do?"

Geyr was also sacked. He had written a report, which Rundstedt approved and forwarded, urging the abandonment of Caen and the need to practise "elastic defence", while stating that the panzer divisions were "melting away" as a result of the policy insisted upon by O.K.W. Hitler was furious over their frank criticism and warning —and gave orders that Geyr was to be replaced forthwith.

COLLAPSE UNDER BACK-AND-FRONT STRAIN

Field-Marshal von Kluge happened to be visiting Hitler's headquarters at that moment. He had been on the sick list for nine months recovering from the injuries sustained in a bad air crash in Russia, but Hitler had sent for him at the beginning of July in view of the precarious situation on the Eastern front. Hitler's idea was to send him back there to replace Busch, as commander of the Central Army Group, which was cracking under the strain of the Russian summer offensive that had just opened. According to Blumentritt, Kluge was actually with Hitler, when Keitel came in and told Hitler what Rundstedt had said on the telephone. Thereupon Hitler at once decided that Kluge must go to take charge in

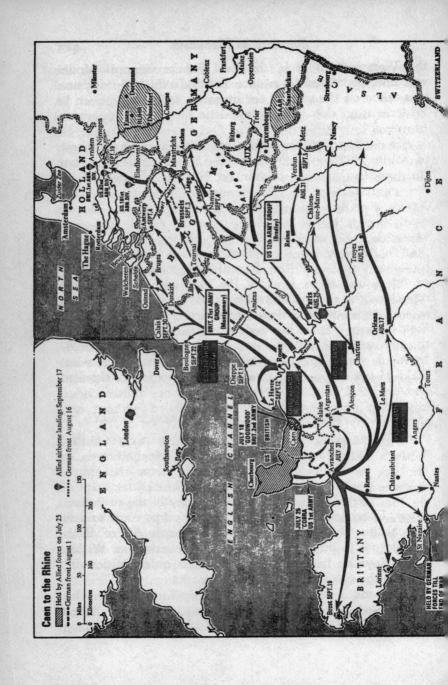

Caen to the Rhine

▨ Held by Allied forces on July 25   ● Allied airborne landings September 17
⎯⎯ German front August 1   ······ German front August 16

Miles 0 50 100 200
Kilometres 0 100 200 300

N O R T H   S E A

E N G L A N D

London

Southampton

Dover

E N G L I S H   C H A N N E L

Cherbourg

US

JULY 25 'COBRA' US 1st ARMY

JULY 18 'GOODWOOD' BRIT. 2nd ARMY

BRITISH

Caen

Avranches

Falaise

Argentan

Alençon

Le Mans

BRITTANY

Rennes

St Nazaire

Nantes

Brest SEPT.19

Lorient

HELD BY GERMAN FORCES TILL END OF WAR

Châteaubriant

Angers

Tours

L O I R E

Orléans AUG.17

Chartres

Dreux

US 3rd ARMY (Patton)

US 1st ARMY (Hodges)

Le Havre SEPT.12

Dieppe SEPT.1

Rouen

CAN. 1st ARMY (Crerar)

Boulogne SEPT.22

Calais SEPT.30

Dunkirk

Ostend

Bruges

BRIT. 2nd ARMY

Amiens

Somme

Oise

Seine

Seine

Paris AUG.25

Troyes AUG.25

Dijon

F R A N C E

BRIT. 21st ARMY GROUP (Montgomery)

Lille

Tournai

Brussels SEPT.3

Antwerp SEPT.4

Beveland

Walcheren

Schelde

Rotterdam

The Hague

Amsterdam

Zuider Zee

H O L L A N D

Arnhem SEPT.19

Nijmegen

RUHR

Dortmund

Münster

Düsseldorf

Cologne

Rhine

US 82nd ABN. DIV.
US 101st ABN. DIV.
BRIT. 1st ABN. DIV.

Eindhoven

Maas

Albert Canal

Meuse

Liège

Namur SEPT.4

Maastricht

Aachen

B E L G I U M

Sambre

Meuse

Ardennes

LUX.
Luxembourg

Bitburg

Trier

Verdun

Metz SEPT.5

Nancy

Mosel

Moselle

Châlons-sur-Marne

Reims

Meuse

AUG.31

US 12th ARMY GROUP (Bradley)

G E R M A N Y

Coblenz

Mainz

Frankfurt

Oppenheim

Saarbrücken

SAAR

Strasbourg

A L S A C E

Rhine

S W I T Z E R L A N D

the West instead of in the East (where General Model was now promoted to replace Busch). While the decision was taken on the spur of the moment, it had long been in Hitler's mind that Kluge should be Rundstedt's deputy if the need arose.

"Field-Marshal von Kluge was a robust, aggressive type of soldier," Blumentritt remarked. "He arrived at our headquarters at St. Germain on July 6th to take up his new appointment as Commander-in-Chief in the West. At the start he was very cheerful and confident—like all newly-appointed commanders. Indeed, he was almost gay about the prospects.

"In our first talk he reproached me because we had forwarded, and endorsed, Rommel's report on the gravity of the situation in France. He said such a pessimistic report ought not to have been sent to the Führer but should have been modified by us before it was forwarded. Field-Marshal von Rundstedt was still at St. Germain at the moment—he stayed there for three days after Field-Marshal von Kluge arrived. When I told him what Field-Marshal von Kluge had said, he was rather shocked and declared emphatically: 'It was proper that such an important document should be forwarded without any alteration by a superior headquarters.'

"While Field-Marshal von Kluge clearly thought at first that the dangers of the situation had been exaggerated, his view soon changed. For he was quick to visit the front, as was his habit. While there he saw the Commander of the 7th Army, Hausser, the Commander of the 5th Panzer Army, Eberbach, and then the various corps commanders —including the 1st and 2nd S.S. Corps. All of them pointed out to him the seriousness of the situation. Within a few days he became very sober and quiet. Hitler did not like the changing tone of his reports.

"On the 17th Rommel was badly injured when his car crashed, after being attacked on the road by Allied 'planes. Hitler then instructed Field-Marshal von Kluge to take charge of Army Group 'B' for the moment, as well as being Commander-in-Chief."

Then, three days later, on July 20th, came the attempt to kill Hitler at his headquarters in East Prussia. The conspirators' bomb missed its chief target, but it had terrific repercussions on the battle in the West at the critical moment.

"Field-Marshal von Kluge was at the front that day and I was not able to get into touch with him until the evening. By that time he had already had the messages about the attempt—first that it had succeeded, and then that Hitler was still alive. The Field-Marshal told me that, more than a year before, some of the leading officers who were in the plot had approached him, and that he had received them twice, but at the second meeting he had told them that he did not want to be mixed up with the plot. He knew, however, that it was continuing. The Field-Marshal had not said anything to me about it before, and I had not been aware of the plot.

"When the Gestapo investigated the conspiracy, in the days that followed, they found documents in which Field-Marshal von Kluge's name was mentioned, so he came under grave suspicion. Then another incident made things look worse. Shortly after General Patton's break-out from Normandy, while the decisive battle at Avranches was in progress, Field-Marshal von Kluge was out of touch with his headquarters for more than twelve hours. The reason was that he had gone up to the front, and there been trapped in a heavy artillery bombardment. At the same time his wireless tender was destroyed by bombing, so that he could not communicate. He himself had to stay under cover for several hours before he could get out and start on the long drive back to his headquarters. Meantime, we had been suffering 'bombardment' from the rear. For the Field-Marshal's prolonged 'absence' excited Hitler's suspicion immediately, in view of the documents that had been found. A telegram came from

Hitler peremptorily stating 'Field-Marshal von Kluge is at once to extricate himself from the battle area around Avranches and conduct the battle of Normandy from the tactical headquarters of the 5th Panzer Army'.[1]

"The reason for this order, as I heard subsequently, was that Hitler suspected that the Field-Marshal's purpose in going right up to the front was to get in touch with the Allies and negotiate a surrender. The Field-Marshal's eventual return did not calm Hitler. From this date onward the orders which Hitler sent him were worded in a brusque and even insulting language. The Field-Marshal became very worried. He feared that he would be arrested at any moment—and at the same time realized more and more that he could not prove his loyalty by any battlefield success.

"All this had a very bad effect on any chance that remained of preventing the Allies from breaking out. In the days of crisis Field-Marshal von Kluge gave only part of his attention to what was happening at the front. He was looking back over his shoulder anxiously—towards Hitler's headquarters.

"He was not the only general who was in that state of worry for conspiracy in the plot against Hitler. Fear permeated and paralysed the higher commands in the weeks and months that followed. The influence on the generals of July 20th is a subject that would form a book in itself."

After General Patton's break-out from Normandy, and the collapse of the front in the West, Field-Marshal Model suddenly arrived on August 17th as the new Commander-in-Chief. "His arrival was the first news of the change that Field-Marshal von Kluge received—this sudden arrival of a successor had become the customary manner of dismissal at this time and had already happened in the case of the commanders of the 19th and 15th Armies. At that moment Field-Marshal von Kluge was at Laroche-Guyon, the head-

---

[1] General Speidel confirmed this account, but said that the order told Kluge to leave "the Falaise pocket", and that the date of the incident was August 12th.

quarters of Army Group 'B'. He stayed on there for twenty-four hours putting Field-Marshal Model in the picture.

"I went over there from St. Germain to say good-bye to him, and saw him alone. As I went in he was sitting at his table with a map in front of him. He kept tapping it at the point marked 'Avranches'—where Patton had broken through—and said to me: 'That is where I lose my reputation as a soldier.' I tried to console him, but with little effect. He walked up and down the room ruminating gloomily. He showed me the letter from the Führer, that Field-Marshal Model had brought him. It was written in quite polite terms—the Führer saying that he felt the strain of the battle was too much for the Field-Marshal and that a change was desirable. But the last sentence of the letter had an ominous note—'Field-Marshal von Kluge is to state to which part of Germany he is going.' The Field-Marshal said to me: 'I have written a letter to the Führer in which I have explained to him clearly the military position, and also other matters'—but he did not show me this letter."[1]

[1] The letter was found by the Allies in the captured German Archives. After acknowledging the order for his replacement, and remarking that the obvious reason for it was the failure to close the gap at Avranches, it went on to say—"When you receive these lines . . . I shall be no more. I cannot bear the reproach that I have sealed the fate of the West through faulty measures, and I have no means of defending myself. I draw a conclusion from that and am dispatching myself where already thousands of my comrades are. I have never feared death. Life has no more meaning for me, and I also figure on the list of war criminals who are to be delivered up." The letter then went on to a long and detailed exposition of the practical impossibility of averting the collapse at Avranches, and a mild rebuke to Hitler for not attending to the warnings he had been given both by Rommel and Kluge himself as to the critical position.

"Our appreciations were *not* dictated by pessimism but by sober knowledge of the facts. I do not know if Field-Marshal Model, who has been proved in every sphere, will still master the situation. From my heart I hope so. Should it not be so, however, and your cherished new weapons not succeed, then, my Fuhrer, make up your mind to end the war. The German people have borne such untold suffering that it is time to put an end to this frightfulness. There must be ways to attain this end, and above all to prevent the Reich from falling under the Bolshevist heel." The letter ended with a final tribute to Hitler's greatness and affirmation of Kluge's loyalty even in death.

"Field-Marshal von Kluge left for home next day. On the evening of the day after his departure I had a telephone call from Metz to say that he had had a heart attack, and had died. Two days later came a medical report stating that his death was due to a cerebral hæmorrhage. Then came word that he was to have a State Funeral, and that Field-Marshal von Rundstedt had been instructed by the Führer to represent him in laying a wreath and delivering the Funeral Oration. Then came a sudden order that there was to be no State Funeral. I then heard that Field-Marshal von Kluge had taken poison, and that this had been confirmed by a post-mortem. Like other generals who had been on the Eastern front, he had carried poison capsules in case of being captured by the Russians—though many did not take them even when they were captured. He had swallowed one of these capsules in the car and was dead before he arrived in Metz. My opinion is that he committed suicide, not because of his dismissal, but because he believed he would be arrested by the Gestapo as soon as he arrived home."

While Kluge committed suicide of his own accord, Rommel was compelled to swallow a similar dose, just over a month later, while he was still convalescing from his accident. Two fellow-generals visited him, under orders from Hitler, and took him out for a drive and there confronted him with Hitler's decision that he must commit suicide or be brought to trial—with the certainty of a degrading execution. He had been more definitely implicated in the plot. A realization of the hopelessness of the situation in the West had brought him into revolt at an earlier stage. I was told by his staff that he had little confidence in the prospect even before the Allies landed and thereafter became increasingly critical of Hitler's lack of a sense of reality.

After the Allies had succeeded in establishing their bridgehead in Normandy he said to one of his staff: "All is over. It would be much better for us to end the war now, and live as a British dominion, than to be ruined by continuing such a hopeless struggle." Realizing that Hitler was the main obstacle to peace Rommel openly said that the only thing was to do away with him and then approach the Allies. That was a remarkable change of attitude in Hitler's favourite general. It cost Rommel his life, but it was too late to save Germany.

Talking of the general breakdown which followed Patton's break-out from the Normandy bridgehead, Blumentritt made another significant revelation. "Hitler and his staff at O.K.W. had been deluded, in postponing a withdrawal so long, by their belief that our forces would have time to get back and occupy new lines in rear, if the need arose. They counted on the British advance being deliberate, and on the Americans being clumsy. But Pétain, who was an old acquaintance of Field-Marshal Rundstedt's, had several times warned him not to under-rate the speed with which the Americans could move, once they had gained experience. The event proved it. The lines in rear which O.K.W. had reckoned on holding were successively outflanked by Patton's dash before they were even occupied."

Warlimont gave me a long account of this last crucial phase from the O.K.W. angle, throwing light on the reactions in Hitler's Headquarters. "In July a tremendous pressure on Hitler and all concerned arose from the simultaneous Russian offensive and the subsequent break-down of Army Group Centre on that front. In this way, for the first time, a strategic co-operation of the Allies on both the main fronts developed, while the plot of July 20th increased the general perturbation.

"During these days late in July, Field-Marshal von Kluge almost every morning round 10 o'clock called me on the telephone and gave me a vivid personal picture of the ever more threatening situation in Normandy. Why he made these reports to me and not to Hitler himself or to Jodl in person, I can only guess. (Jodl used to work until late in the night, having adapted himself to Hitler's customs.) I put down the telephone messages of Kluge's in writing as carefully as possible and sent them over to Jodl for the noon situation report to Hitler. Prior to this time no decisions were made.

"All my efforts to fly to France, to gain a personal impression of the situation in Normandy, had been banned so far by Jodl. Under the impression of Kluge's telephone messages I repeated my endeavours and finally got permission to leave for France on August 1st, after the Allied break-through at Avranches.

"Before I left, I asked Jodl for instructions as to the general operational course which Field-Marshal von Kluge was to follow, if he did not succeed in closing the gap at Avranches. This question, of course, had come up at O.K.W. over and over again—in contrast to the opinion expressed by Blumentritt. But up to this moment it had not been possible for me, as the Assistant Chief of Operations at O.K.W. and as a participant of the daily situation reports to Hitler, to gather even a general outline of further intentions and much less to obtain a directive thereon. Jodl, according to his customary attitude, remained rather taciturn about my question, but arranged for a special meeting with Hitler late in the night. Hitler's directives to me were very short and simple: 'You may tell Field-Marshal von Kluge that he has to keep his eye on his front line only. It is not his business to bother with anything in the rear. That will be taken care of by O.K.W.'

"When I stopped on the night of August 1st at an airfield near Munich, Jodl called me on the telephone and asked me to pay special attention to the attitude of the higher officers in the West about the plot against Hitler of July 20th. I did not know then what Jodl told me only after the war, that Hitler had summoned him to his hut shortly after I had left, and had told him to call me back at once—because Hitler suspected that I was going to see Kluge only in order to arrange a new plot against him. Jodl at that time had succeeded in calming Hitler's suspicions and had contented himself with giving me the warning on the telephone. However, during the eight days of my absence, I had constantly to report my whereabouts to Jodl and was finally ordered by him to return at once.

"I came to Kluge's Headquarters at La Roche-Guyon late in the afternoon of August 2nd after a short stay with Blumentritt at St. Germain. The tense situation of the front in Normandy had become still worse. Single German infantry battalions, mostly taken from the coast defence in Brittany, were holding a thin line in the extreme south-west corner of Normandy, but they were much too weak to resist the impending break-out from the peninsula. On other parts of the front, particularly around Caen, the German troops continued clinging on to their cracking line with their last effort. The sky was entirely dominated by the invaders.

"Early on August 3rd, before I left for a visit to the 7th Army, Kluge showed me a teletype order from O.K.W. directing him to close up the gap at Avranches by a counter-stroke, which was to be conducted from east to west. The idea, so obviously desirable, had already been considered by Kluge himself, but he had abandoned this plan for lack of means. Now he was ordered to execute this counter-stroke, but without being given any additional troops or even supplies. Hitler in this case proved once more that he took no pains to comply with the fundamental rules of conducting operations, i.e. not only to give a directive or an order, but also the indispensable means for carrying it out.

"Kluge now at once, in the early morning hours, set about to have these means assembled from other sectors of the front in Normandy, after the responsibility of running this risk had been taken from him by Hitler's order. In the course of this and the following days I had the professional pleasure of observing how the commanders concerned—Kluge, Hausser, Eberbach, Funck, whom I saw in turn—prepared the counter-stroke in spite of the tremendous difficulties. They all felt that the outcome would decide the fate of the army in Normandy, and in all probability much more, and they acted accordingly. All their efforts, however, could not make amends for the much too low figures of tanks and artillery, and, above all, for the almost complete lack of air force.

"Before the offensive started, early on August 7th, I had to leave for East Prussia. Its failure was already known at Headquarters when I returned there on August 8th about noon. In addition Hitler, the same morning, had sent another general of the O.K.W. to Kluge, carrying the order with him that after the failure of the first counter-stroke a second one had to be delivered, but again without assigning any additional means to the already defeated army.

"The new plan was based on the assumption that the break-out from Normandy could no longer be prevented, and that Patton's army would turn in the general direction of Paris. The idea now was to strike against the flank and the rear of the east-bound American drive, with one panzer group advancing from east of Avranches and with another one from Falaise in the general direction of Mayenne. This idea had no relation to realities and I do not believe that Kluge took it seriously. Besides, he was advised by this order to *wait* for weather conditions that would prevent the enemy from using their domination of the sky!

"When, on the afternoon of August 8th, I had to report to Hitler on my observations in Normandy I laid special emphasis on the way that Kluge had done everything in his power to carry the counter-stroke at Avranches to a final success. Hitler listened nervously, but without interrupting or asking any question. After I had finished, he only said in an ice-cold manner: 'Success only failed to come because Kluge did not want to be successful.'

This drastic remark of Hitler's shed a tragic light on the relationship between the German Commander-in-Chief and his generals."

.   .   .   .   .

After following the course of the decisive break-through as the German High Command saw it, it is worth while to supplement it by a short account of how it appeared, and felt, to the fighting commanders on the spot.

A graphic impression of the American break-through at Avranches as it looked from the German side was given me by General Elfeldt who commanded the 84th Corps, holding that sector, at the foot of the Cherbourg Peninsula. He was only sent there to take over charge just as the decisive offensive was opening. Until then he had been commanding the 47th Division, which held the Calais-Boulogne sector. "It was on the 28th July, so far as I remember, that orders came for me to go at once to Field-Marshal von Kluge's headquarters. On arrival he told me that I was to take over command of the 84th Corps from General von Choltitz. He said he did not agree with the defence policy of the latter, but did not say in what respect. The Corps, he told me, comprised the remnants of seven divisions. He also said that the 116th Panzer Division was to counter-attack westward to relieve the pressure, and would be under my command. After spending the night with the Field-Marshal I drove in the morning to Le Mans and on to the tactical headquarters of the 7th Army, which was then 10 to 15 kilometres east of Avranches. From there I was directed to my own corps headquarters. I do not remember exactly where it was, as it was hidden in the trees, away from any village. Everything was confused, and the Allied air force dominated the area. On the following day I went round my troops. They were very weak and there was no continuous front. Some of the divisions had only about three hundred infantry left, and the artillery was much depleted.

"The first order I gave was that all the troops south of the River La See, near Avranches, were to defend the south bank, while the troops from the east were to hang on where they were until the 116th Panzer Division arrived that night; they were then to join in its counter-attack. But the 116th did not arrive, as it was diverted to another danger point while on the way. On the morning of the 31st American tanks drove towards Brescy, on the River See, 15 kilometres east of Avranches. At that moment my headquarters was north of Brescy, and was nearly cut off by this flank thrust. My headquarters personnel were in the fighting line all day. Luckily the Americans were not very vigorous in their thrust here.

"In the next two days I was reinforced by two new divisions which were nearly up to strength, as well as by the 116th Panzer Division. I formed the remnants of the other seven divisions into a single one. My orders were to stop a further break-through between Brescy and Vire, and to delay the expected American thrust south-east-wards from Avranches, as a powerful counter-thrust was to be made by a panzer corps, under General von Funk. This was subsequently reinforced, to provide a counter-stroke of bigger scale, by all the tanks that could be made available from Eberbach's 5th Panzer Army."

Elfeldt went on to describe at length the even more precarious situation that developed, after the armoured stroke had failed to reach Avranches, and his left flank was increasingly outflanked. He wheeled back gradually to the eastward, and the difficulties of the withdrawal were the greater because the armoured forces retired through his front, creating confusion. Fortunately the American pressure on his front and immediate flanks was not too dangerous—Patton's 3rd Army was moving on a wider circuit. "The American troops, of the 1st Army, on my front were not at all clever tactically. They failed to seize opportunities—in particular they missed several chances of cutting off the whole of my corps. The Allied air force was the most serious danger.

"By the time we had got back to the Orne the whole front had become much narrower than before, so my corps headquarters had become superfluous and was temporarily withdrawn from the line. But the following morning the Canadians broke through southwards to Falaise and I was at once ordered to form a front to check them. The available troops were very scanty and we had no communications. The Canadian artillery fired all day into my headquarters, but fortunately did no damage at all although they fired about a thousand shells. These fell all round the small house in which I was, but no one was hurt. During the day I was able to re-form a continuous line, but beyond my right flank I could see the British tanks driving down the other side of the River Dives towards Trun. Thus our line of retreat was blocked.

"The next day I was ordered to break out *north*-eastward, behind the backs of these armoured forces. It was soon clear that this was not possible, as the British were now there in strength. So I proposed to the army commander, General Hausser, that my troops should be placed at the disposal of General Meindl, who was commanding the parachute forces, to help the latter to break out near St. Lambert, *south*-eastward. It seemed to me that one strong thrust might have a better chance than a number of small ones. Meindl succeeded in breaking out, but when I reached St. Lambert myself next morning the gap was again closed. I tried an attack with all I had left —a couple of tanks and two hundred men. It started well but then ran into part of the 1st Polish Armoured Division. After a two-hour fight our ammunition began to run out. Then the troops which were following behind me surrendered, thus leaving me with a handful of men at the cut-off tip of the wedge. So we had to surrender in turn. The Commander of this Polish division was a fine-looking man and a gentleman. He gave me his last cigarette.

His division itself was in an awkward situation and had run out of water—the forces of the two sides were extraordinarily intermingled."

. . . . .

I took the opportunity of asking Elfeldt what he thought about the German soldier in this war compared with the previous war. His views differed in some respects from those of Blumentritt (*see page* 409). "The infantry were quite as good as in 1914–18, and the artillery much better. Weapons had improved, and so had tactics. But there were other factors. In the last two years of the first war, the morale of the troops became affected by the spread of Socialistic ideas that were pacifist in trend. In this war, National Socialism had the opposite effect—it fortified their morale."

"How did discipline compare in the two wars?" "That is more difficult to answer. National Socialism made the troops more fanatical—which was both good and bad for discipline. But relations between officers and men were better than in 1914–18, and that helped discipline. The improved relationship was due partly to the new conception of discipline that was inculcated in the Reichswehr, based on the experience of 1914–18, and partly to the subsequent influence of National Socialism in diminishing the gulf between officers and men. The ordinary soldiers showed more initiative, and used their heads better in this war than they did in the last—especially when fighting on their own or in small parties." On this score Elfeldt's opinion corresponded with the judgment of British commanders, who often remarked how the German soldiers excelled their opponents when operating alone or in pairs—a verdict that was in surprising contrast to the experience of 1914–18, as well as to the continuing popular view that the Germans were no good as individualists. Since National Socialism made so strong an

appeal to the herd instinct, the natural assumption was
that the generation which grew up under it would show
less, not more, individual intiative on the battlefield than
their fathers. I asked Elfeldt if he could suggest an explanation. He said that he himself was puzzled, but added,
"I think it may have been due to the kind of scout training
these young solders had received in the 'Hitler Youth'
organization."

The question how the German soldier of the two wars
compared came up again, a few days later, in a discussion
with Heinrici, Röhricht, and Bechtolsheim. Heinrici's
view was that the German Army was better trained in
the first war, but he did not consider that the discipline
had been better. Röhricht and Bechtolsheim agreed, and
Röhricht added: "The Army needed a long interval
between the Polish and the Western campaigns to develop
its training—especially the training of the non-commis-
sioned officers. As head of the Training Department of the
General Staff, I was in close touch with this question. But
morale, and discipline, were better in the later part of this
war than in the later part of the first war. Between 1916
and 1918 the soldiers' morale was gradually undermined
by the infiltration of Socialistic ideas, and the suggestion
that they were fighting the Emperor's war, whereas this
time they had and kept such extraordinary confidence in
Hitler that they remained confident of victory in face of
all the facts."

Heinrici and Bechtolsheim endorsed this statement of
Röhricht's, who went on to say: "Nevertheless the morale
of the Army was gradually weakened by the effects of
overstrain, and by the tendency of the S.S. to grab the
best men. On the Eastern Front the divisions never got
a rest, and that became a debilitating factor."

In reply to a further question about the effect of
National Socialism on the Army, Röhricht said: "It had a
mixed effect. It created difficulties for us, and weakened
our control, but it fostered an ardent patriotic spirit in

the soldiers, which went deeper than the spirit of 1914—for this time there was no enthusiasm for war such as there had been then. That spirit had greater endurance under reverses." Heinrici agreed with Röhricht, while emphasizing that faith in a personality counted for more than the system. "The troops' tremendous confidence in Hitler was the dominant factor, whether one liked it or not."

. . . . .

What did the German generals think of their Western opponents? They were diffident in expressing an opinion on this matter, but I gathered a few impressions in the course of our talks. In a reference to the Allied commanders, Rundstedt said: "Montgomery and Patton were the two best that I met. Field-Marshal Montgomery was very systematic." He added: "That is all right if you have sufficient forces, and sufficient time." Blumentritt made a similar comment. After paying tribute to the speed of Patton's drive, he added: "Field-Marshal Montgomery was the one general who never suffered a reverse. He moved like this"—Blumentritt took a series of very deliberate and short steps, putting his foot down heavily each time.

Giving his impression of the different qualities of the British and American troops, Blumentritt said: "The Americans attacked with zest, and had a keen sense of mobile action, but when they came under heavy artillery fire they usually fell back—even after they had made a successful penetration. By contrast, once the British had got their teeth in, and had been in a position for twenty-four hours, it proved almost impossible to shift them. To counter-attack the British always cost us very heavy losses. I had many opportunities to observe this interesting difference in the autumn of 1944, when the right half of my corps faced the British, and the left half the American."

In subsequent comment on the broad strategic situation after the collapse of the front in France, Blumentritt said: "The best course of the Allies would have been to concentrate a really strong striking force with which to break through past Aachen to the Ruhr area. Strategically and politically, Berlin was the target. Germany's strength is in the north. South Germany was a side issue. He who holds northern Germany holds Germany. Such a break-through, coupled with air domination, would have torn in pieces the weak German front and ended the war. Berlin and Prague would have been occupied ahead of the Russians. There were no German forces behind the Rhine, and at the end of August our front was wide open.

"There was an operational break-through in the Aachen area, in September. This facilitated a rapid conquest of the Ruhr and a quicker advance on Berlin. By turning the forces from the Aachen area sharply northward, the German 15th and 1st Parachute Armies could have been pinned against the estuaries of the Maas and the Rhine. They could not have escaped eastwards into Germany."

Blumentritt considered that the Allied offensive had been too widely and evenly spread. He was particularly critical of the attack towards Metz, pointing out that the forces available to defend this sector along the Moselle were better relatively than elsewhere. "A direct attack on Metz was unnecessary. The Metz fortress area could have been masked. In contrast, a swerve northward in the direction of Luxembourg and Bitburg would have met with great success and caused the collapse of the right flank of our 1st Army followed by the collapse of our 7th Army. By such a flank move to the north the entire 7th Army could have been cut off before it could retreat behind the Rhine. Thus the bulk of the defeated German armies would have been wiped out west of the Rhine. Then the Allies' main attack could have continued towards Magdeburg and Berlin, while the side-attack converged in the same direction past Frankfurt-on-Main and Erfurt.''

All the German generals to whom I talked were of the opinion that the Allied Supreme Command had missed a great opportunity of ending the war in the autumn of 1944. They agreed with Montgomery's view that this could best have been achieved by concentrating all possible resources on a thrust in the north, towards Berlin.

Student, who was placed in charge of that flank with the so-called "1st Parachute Army", emphasized this point. "The sudden penetration of the British tank forces into Antwerp took the Führer's Headquarters utterly by surprise. At that moment we had no disposable reserves worth mentioning either on the western front or within our own country. I took over the command of the right wing of the western front on the Albert Canal on September 4th. At that moment I had only recruit and convalescent units and one coast-defence division from Holland. They were reinforced by a panzer detachment—of merely twenty-five tanks and self-propelled guns!" His front stretched a hundred miles.

CHAPTER XXII

THE ANTI-HITLER PLOT—
AS SEEN FROM H.Q. IN THE WEST

THE story of the 20th July Plot has been told from many
angles, but not from that which has the closest bearing
on the military issue. A fairly clear picture has emerged
about what happened after the bomb exploded at Hitler's
headquarters in East Prussia, and failed to kill him; also
about the course of events in Berlin, and how the conspirators there failed to seize their momentary opportunity.
To complete the picture it is important to trace what
happened on that fateful day at German Headquarters
in the West. I had a long account of this, and the subsequent reactions, from General Blumentritt which is worth
giving in full—not only for its direct evidence, but for
the atmosphere it conveys.

BLUMENTRITT'S ACCOUNT

During the early months of 1944 there were many
visitors to Supreme Headquarters, Western Front, at
St. Germain, and long discussions of the war-situation.
A matter that was often mooted was whether the field-
marshals should jointly approach Hitler and urge him to
make peace.

One day, about the end of March, Field-Marshal
Rommel came to St. Germain accompanied by his Chief
of Staff, General Speidel. Just before they left, Speidel
said he wanted to have a word with me in private. When
we had withdrawn, Speidel told me that he was speaking
on Rommel's behalf and then said: "The time has come
when we must tell the Führer that we cannot continue

430

the war." It was agreed that we should broach the matter
to Field-Marshal Rundstedt, and this was done. We
found that he was of the same opinion. A telegram was
then sent to O.K.W., asking the Führer to come to St.
Germain "in view of the serious situation in France".
But no reply was received.

General Speidel came to see me again about the matter,
and in the course of our conversations told me that there
were a number of people in Germany who were intending
to tackle Hitler. He mentioned the names of Field-Marshal
von Witzleben, General Beck, General Hoeppner, and
Dr. Goerdeler. He also said that Field-Marshal Rommel
had given him a few days leave to go to Stuttgart to
discuss the matter with others there—both Speidel and
Rommel came from the State of Württemberg, and had
long known Goerdeler. But in these conversations Speidel
never indicated that the assassination of Hitler was
contemplated.

Nothing further developed before Field-Marshal von
Kluge arrived to replace Field-Marshal von Rundstedt
as Commander-in-Chief in the West—following the latter's
heated telephone talk with Field-Marshal Keitel, in which
he had insisted that the war ought to be brought to an
end. I would add a little more about this change. Hitler
knew that Field-Marshal von Rundstedt was much
respected by the Army, and by the enemy. Allied propaganda broadcasts often suggested that the views of the
Field-Marshal and his staff differed from those of Hitler.
It was notable, too, our headquarters was never subjected
to air attack. Nor was the Field-Marshal ever threatened
by the French Resistance Movement—presumably, because
it was known that he had always been in favour of good
treatment for the French. All these things were brought
to Hitler's notice, of course, in reports from his own
agents. While he treated the Field-Marshal with respect
—more respect than he showed other soldiers—he kept
him under careful watch. Then, the Field-Marshal's

emphatic advice about seeking peace provided Hitler with a suitable ground for replacing him.

Field-Marshal von Kluge arrived at St. Germain, to take over, on July 6th. On the 17th Field-Marshal Rommel was knocked out. Thereupon von Kluge moved to Rommel's headquarters at La Roche-Guyon, to conduct the battle from there, leaving me in charge at St. Germain.

JULY 20TH

The first news of the attempt on Hitler's life reached me about 3 p.m.—from Colonel Finck, the Deputy Chief of Staff, who had been transferred from the Eastern front about six weeks earlier. Colonel Finck came into my room and said: "General, the Führer is dead. A Gestapo mutiny has taken place in Berlin." I was very surprised, and asked how he had heard. Finck replied that it had come from General von Stülpnagel, the Military Governor of Paris, on the telephone.

I tried to get hold of Field-Marshal von Kluge on the telephone, at La Roche-Guyon, but was told that he was visiting the front. I then told Speidel in very guarded terms—as we were talking over the telephone—that there were serious developments, and that I would drive over myself to tell him what had happened. I left St. Germain about 4 p.m. and arrived at La Roche-Guyon about 5.30 p.m.

Field-Marshal von Kluge had just returned there. When I went into his room I saw that he had in front of him an extract from the German Radio to the effect that an attempt had been made on the life of the Führer, but that it had failed. Von Kluge told me that he had previously had two telephone messages from Germany, but without any indication of the sender's identity, which said: "The Führer is dead and you must make a decision." Von Kluge went on to say that, about a year before, Witzleben, Beck and others had come to his home to sound him about an approach to the Führer and how it should be conducted. He also said that he had made notes of these discussions.

While we were talking a telephone message from St. Germain was brought in. It said that an anonymous telegram had arrived there stating that Hitler was dead. Kluge was puzzled as to which of the statements were true, and wondered whether the Radio was merely putting out a false report. After some further discussion I put a telephone call in to General Warlimont, Jodl's deputy, at O.K.W. It was a long time before the call came through. Then the reply was merely that Warlimont was not available, as he was engaged with Keitel.

So von Kluge and I put our heads together, and discussed whom we could try next. We telephoned the Chief of the S.S. in Paris. He replied that he did not know anything beyond the radio announcement. We then telephoned General Stieff—the Chief of the Organization Department—at O.K.H. I knew Stieff well, but had no idea that he was in the inner circle of the conspiracy, as later emerged. Stieff at once asked: "Where did you get the news that the Führer was dead?" He added: "The Führer is quite well, and in good spirits"—and then rang off. We felt very uneasy about this telephone call afterwards, realizing how suspicious it must have appeared in the circumstances.

Stieff's answer and manner were so curious as to suggest a likely explanation, and I remarked to von Kluge: "This is an attempt that failed." Von Kluge then said to me that, if it had succeeded, his first step would have been to order the discharge of the V 1's against England to be stopped, and that his second step would have been to get in touch with the Allied Commanders.

Von Kluge then instructed me to telephone General von Stülpnagel, and tell him to come to La Roche-Guyon. I was also to summon Field-Marshal Sperrle, commanding the Luftwaffe in the West.

General von Stülpnagel arrived first, about 7.30 p.m., accompanied by Lieut.-Colonel Hoffacker. They sat round a table with the Field-Marshal, Speidel and I—all the circle are dead now, except Speidel and me. Von Stülpnagel began by saying: "May Lieut.-Colonel Hoffacker explain matters." It soon became clear that Hoffacker knew all about the attempt, and was the link between von Stülpnagel and von Witzleben. He traced how the plot had developed from an intended petition into a *putsch*—as it was realized that Hitler would not listen to argument, and that the Allies would not listen to any peace offer from Hitler. He told how von Stauffenberg had organized the actual attempt, and gave us the details.

When he had finished, von Kluge, with obvious disappointment, remarked: "Well, gentlemen, the attempt has failed. Everything is over." Von Stülpnagel then exclaimed: "Field-Marshal, I thought you were acquainted with the plans. Something must be *done*." Von Kluge replied: "Nothing more can be done. The Führer is still alive." I noticed that von Stülpnagel had begun to look very uncomfortable. He got up and walked out on the verandah. When he returned, he said very little.

Then Field-Marshal Sperrle arrived—and only stayed a few minutes. He refused von Kluge's invitation to remain for dinner. I felt that Sperrle did not want to get drawn into the discussion, or be a witness of anything that transpired.

The rest of us now went in to dinner. Von Kluge seemed very vivacious and unworried in manner, whereas von Stülpnagel was taciturn. After a while he turned to von Kluge and said: "May I speak to you privately again." Von Kluge agreed—and said to me, "You come too." We went into a small room. Here von Stülpnagel told me that he had taken "the first precautions" before leaving Paris. Von Kluge exclaimed: "Heavens! What have you been doing?" "I gave orders for all the S.S. in

Paris to be arrested"—by this he meant not the Waffen S.S., but the S.D., or Security Service.

Von Kluge exclaimed: "But you can't do that without my orders." Von Stülpnagel replied: "I tried to telephone you this afternoon but you were away from your H.Q., so I had to act on my own." Von Kluge remarked: "Well, that's your responsibility." After that, they didn't go back to finish their dinner.

Von Kluge then told me to telephone to von Stülpnagel's Chief of Staff in Paris and ask whether steps had actually been taken to arrest the S.S. This was Colonel von Linstow—who is also dead.[1] He told me that steps had been taken, adding, "And nothing can stop them." Von Kluge then said to von Stülpnagel: "Look here, the best thing you can do is to change into civilian clothes and go into hiding." He told von Stülpnagel to release all the arrested S.S. at once.

After von Stülpnagel had gone, I said to von Kluge: "We ought to do something to help him." Von Kluge pondered my suggestion and then told me to drive after von Stülpnagel, and advise him to disappear somewhere in Paris for a few days. Strictly, of course, von Kluge should have placed him under arrest.

I drove to St. Germain first. On arrival there my staff brought me fresh telegrams which had come while I had been away. One was from Field-Marshal Keitel; it said that all reports of the Führer's death were false; and all orders sent on that assumption were to be ignored. Another was from General Fromm, saying that Himmler had just taken over command of the home forces from him— Hitler no longer trusted any of the generals in Germany. A third was from Himmler—simply saying that he had taken over command of the home forces. While I was reading the telegrams a telephone call came from Admiral Krancke, the Naval C-in-C in the West—the Field-Marshal

[1] Blumentritt's narrative was punctuated with repetitions of "tot" (dead).

had not thought of calling him to the conference—to ask if I would drive into Paris to see him.

About an hour after midnight I set off for Paris, where I found all the Naval H.Q. staff assembled. Admiral Krancke showed me a long telegram he had received from Field-Marshal von Witzleben, saying that the Führer was dead, and that a new government was being formed, under himself for the time being. Thereupon Krancke had telephoned O.K.W. and by chance had been put through to Admiral Doenitz, who said that it was untrue.

I then went on to the H.Q. of the Security Police. They were just coming back from prison. The first officers I saw wanted to know what had happened and why they had been arrested without any reason. Their attitude was very decent, and they showed a willingness to help in hushing things up. I asked where Obergruppenführer Oberg, the Chief of the Security Police, was at the moment. I was told that he was at an hotel, along with von Stülpnagel.

I went on there, about 2 a.m., and found what was almost like a party in progress—including Abetz, the Ambassador in Paris. Oberg took me aside into another room, and told me that he had no idea what was behind the situation, but that we must agree as to what ought to be done next. I must say that, throughout, Oberg behaved very decently, and tried to smooth things over for the sake of the Army. He suggested that the regiment that had carried out the arrests should be confined to barracks, and that the men should be told that it had been merely an exercise. But von Stülpnagel considered that it was impossible to prevent a leakage. I then conveyed von Kluge's advice to von Stülpnagel—that he should disappear. But when I got back to St. Germain I found that a message had already come from O.K.W. saying that he was to proceed to Berlin at once, to render a report.

Later in the day von Stülpnagel set off for Berlin by car, by way of Verdun and Metz. He was accompanied

by one man besides the driver, as an escort in case they
met French partisans. Just before Verdun was reached,
he ordered the car to stop, and said that as they were just
coming to the partisan area it would be a good thing
for them to get out and fire their pistols at a tree, to make
sure they were in working order. After that they drove
on, but he stopped the car again when they came to the
old Verdun battlefields—where he had fought in the
previous war—and said that he would like to show them
round. After going a short way he said to them: "You
stop here, I'm going on alone to look at a point I know."
They suggested they ought to accompany him in case of
meeting partisans, but he said it was not necessary. Shortly
afterwards they heard a shot. They ran forward and
found him floating in a canal. He had shot himself after
getting into the water—so that he would drown if the
first shot did not succeed. But his attempt at suicide
had not succeeded. The two men fished him out and
took him to hospital. He had shot one eye out, and the
other eye was so badly damaged that it had to be removed.

I heard these details subsequently from Oberg, who,
feeling that von Stülpnagel was probably mixed up in the
attempt on Hitler, had driven to Verdun to see von
Stülpnagel in hospital, still in the hope that he might be
able to keep things quiet. Von Stülpnagel, however, had
refused to say anything, Oberg told me. After about a
fortnight in hospital, von Stülpnagel was removed to
Berlin on orders from there. He was brought to trial,
condemned and hanged.

Meanwhile there was something like a panic in Paris
among the Staff—as to who were suspect. Oberg received
a string of telegrams to arrest various people—first,
Hoffacker, then Finck; and in all about thirty or forty
people, both soldiers and civilians. A few days later
Oberg telephoned me to come and see him, and told
me that Hoffacker had mentioned von Kluge's name in

his preliminary interrogation. Oberg said that he could not believe that von Kluge was implicated.

I accompanied Oberg when he went to see von Kluge and make a report. Von Kluge told Oberg: "Carry out these interrogations as your sense of duty tells you." Oberg remarked to me that he did not like the task, but as it could not be avoided he wanted to conduct the interrogations in a gentlemanly way. So it was arranged that, as an assurance, one of the officers of my staff should be present during them. Here it is worth mentioning that neither Speidel nor I had breathed a word to anyone about the conference on the evening of July 20th.

Soon after this, von Kluge visited Rommel in hospital in Paris. On his return he told me that Rommel had expressed surprise that there had been an attempt to kill Hitler, as distinct from putting pressure on him to sue for peace.

In the days that followed I noticed that von Kluge began to look more and more worried. He often talked about himself and his own affairs. On one occasion he remarked, sombrely: "Events will take their course." Then Field-Marshal Model suddenly arrived to replace him. On his way home, as I have already related, von Kluge was found dead in the car, having swallowed a poison capsule.

Apart from the conversation we had on the evening of July 20th, von Kluge never said anything to me about a plot to tackle or overthrow Hitler. I had left von Kluge's staff in January, 1942, and had no close relations with him again until July, 1944. General von Tresckow was IA to von Kluge, and may have been taken more into his confidence—but he is dead.[1]

I was in Schleswig with General Dempsey after the capitulation in May, 1945, and saw very clearly that even

[1] Tresckow was a determined opponent of Hitler, from religious conviction, but had been left in the East when his chief was transferred to the West. Thus his influence was missing at the crucial moment.

then the civil population was divided in their view of Hitler. One half was shocked that the German generals had taken part in the attempt to overthrow Hitler, and felt bitterly towards them in consequence—the same feeling was manifested in the Army itself. The other half complained that the generals had not turned out Hitler before.

THE AFTERMATH

After taking over command in the West, Field-Marshal Model stayed at the H.Q. of Army Group "B". Telephoning me from there a day or two later, he said that he had just received a disconcerting message from the Führer's H.Q. "All *they* can talk about and think about is the 20th July, and now they want to take Speidel away, as a suspect." He had emphatically told Keitel that he could not spare the Chief of Staff at Army Group H.Q. when the situation was so critical. As a result, Speidel was left there until the first week of September. He was then relieved, and came to see me, telling me that he had been ordered to return home. On arrival there he was arrested by the Gestapo.

After General Speidel had gone, a telegram came which said that I was to be relieved by General Westphal, and was to report to the Führer's H.Q. on the 13th September. I felt somewhat depressed! On setting off, I went first to see Field-Marshal von Rundstedt at Coblenz, where he had just established his H.Q. on being recalled to take supreme command in the West. Field-Marshal von Rundstedt was very annoyed to hear that I was being taken away from my post just as he had returned to command. He at once protested to O.K.W. and asked that he might retain me as his Chief of Staff. But the answer came back that the request could not be granted. The reason given was that I had repeatedly expressed a desire for a fighting command. This did not sound very convincing in the circumstances.

I left Coblenz on the 9th September, and took the opportunity to visit my family—at Marburg—in case of what might happen. I spent Sunday, the 10th, at home. I felt a quiver every time the telephone rang or the sound of a car was heard approaching the house—and went to the window to look out.

On the 11th I took the train for Berlin. The train was held up by an air raid at Kassel, so I telephoned from there to say that I was delayed, and would thus miss the special courier train that ran nightly from Berlin to East Prussia. Continuing in the train to Berlin I had to get out at Potsdam, because of bomb damage on the line. Just as I got out of the train I suddenly heard a voice in the dark saying: "Where is General Blumentritt?" I felt another quiver. After I had answered, an officer came up to me, accompanied by a soldier who was carrying a tommy gun. The officer addressed me politely, and said he had orders to escort me to a hotel in Berlin—the Adlon. On arrival there, the hall porter told me there was a sealed envelope awaiting me. I opened it—all that it contained was my ticket to Angerburg in East Prussia. That was rather an anti-climax. But it brought only a temporary sense of relief. I still had to wait and wonder what was in store for me at the Führer's H.Q.

The following night I caught the special train thence, arriving at Angerburg on the morning of the 13th. I was met by Field-Marshal Keitel's adjutant, who took me to Keitel's special train; here I had breakfast and left my baggage. I was told that the Führer was too tired to receive me, but that I could attend the daily conference at midday if I liked. I decided to do so.

In front of the house where the conference was held I found a group of generals. I went up to them and reported to General Guderian, who had become Chief of the General Staff. I noticed that he did not attempt to shake hands, while Keitel and others stood aloof. Guderian said to me, in a loud voice: "I wonder you dare to come

here after what has happened in the West."[1] I showed
him the telegram ordering me to report. Then an S.S.
officer arrived and said that, after all, the Führer had
decided to attend the daily conference. A few minutes later
we saw Hitler walking through the forest, with tired and
slow steps, accompanied by an escort of five or six men.

Guderian turned to me and said, grimly: "Now you
can report yourself to the Führer." But to my surprise
Hitler greeted me in a pleasant manner, saying: "You've
been having a very hard time in the West. I know the
Allied air forces are on top and what it means. I'd like
to have a talk with you after the conference."

When the conference ended Guderian said to me:
"Come and have a talk with me about the Eastern front."
I replied: "It doesn't interest me in the least at the
moment." I then had ten minutes' talk with Hitler,
alone, and he was again very nice.

When I came out, the other generals were all waiting,
and at once asked me: "What did the Führer say to
you?" I replied: "He was very pleasant." Thereupon
they all became very pleasant, and Keitel invited me to
have tea with him. I replied that I should like to get
away that evening and go home, adding: "It's two years
since I spent a leave with my wife and children." At
that, Keitel said: "I don't think it is possible." I said:
"But the Führer told me I could go on leave, and was then
to report to Field-Marshal von Rundstedt, who would
give me command of an army corps in the West." Keitel
told me to wait half an hour. After seeing the Führer,
he came back and told me I could go.

During our conversation, this time, Keitel spoke of
von Kluge, and remarked that they had documentary

[1] Guderian told me: "I don't remember the scene related by
Blumentritt. I never was prejudiced against him". He felt that
Blumentritt, being in a state of acute anxiety, had misunderstood
his manner or a bantering remark he may have made. (I have
noticed myself that Guderian, who has a keen sense of humour,
often indulges in banter.)

evidence about his treasonable activities. Keitel said that they had intercepted a wireless message from some Allied H.Q., which asked to be put in touch with von Kluge. Keitel added: "And that's why he was missing so long that day near Avranches." Protesting that this suspicion was unjust, I related how von Kluge had been forced to take cover, and how he had been unable to get in touch with his own H.Q. for hours, because his wireless tender had been knocked out. But it was obvious that Keitel did not believe this explanation.

I also paid a call on Jodl before leaving. Jodl said to me, without shaking hands: "That seems to be a bad show of yours in the West." I retorted: "It might be well for you to come yourself and have a look at the situation." Jodl was surprised to hear that I was going on leave that evening.

After that I went back to Keitel's train to pick up my baggage. An orderly there gave me a bottle of claret to take away, remarking at the same time: "Where you had breakfast this morning you were sitting in the same seat where Colonel Steiff last sat." I felt that I had had a lucky escape. Even after I reached my home at Marburg I still jumped when the telephone rang. I did not begin to feel at ease until I got back to the front, and took over command of my new corps. An underlying anxiety continued.[1]

[1] From other sources I have since heard that Blumentritt's personal anxiety was needless. "His replacement only took place because the O.K.W. considered that a firmer control in the West was needed, and that Westphal was more suited on the ground of his three years fighting experience in Africa and Italy. Blumentritt was summoned to East Prussia only because Hitler wanted to confer the Knight's Cross of the Iron Cross upon him in person. Blumentritt was one of the very few of whom Hitler remained fond, without Blumentritt himself doing anything towards that end. His South German descent may have played a decisive part in that respect."

This correction of Blumentritt's apprehensions does not diminish its significance. That a man whom the dictator wished to honour should have been reduced by the summons to such palpitating nervousness is striking evidence of the prevailing condition.

From then on to the end of the war many of us felt that we were under a cloud of suspicion. In March, 1945, when I was commanding the army in Holland, I received a telegram from O.K.W. telling me to report at once the whereabouts of my family. That sounded ominous—as if they might be taken as hostages. I looked at the map and saw that the American forces were approaching Marburg—being already less than sixty miles away. So I didn't send an answer to this telegram! I felt that my family would be safer with the Americans.

*   *   *   *   *

From the night of July 20th onwards the German generals often used to discuss among themselves whether they should get in touch with the Allies—as von Kluge had thought of doing that evening, when he thought Hitler was dead. The reasons that checked them from doing so were:

(1) Their oath of loyalty to the Führer. (They now argue: "We gave our oath of loyalty to the Führer. If he is dead that is cancelled." So most of them want to believe that he is dead.)

(2) The people in Germany had not realized the truth of the situation, and would not understand any action the generals took towards making peace.

(3) The troops on the East front would reproach the West front for letting them down.

(4) The fear of going down to history as traitors to their country.

CHAPTER XXIII

HITLER'S LAST GAMBLE—
THE SECOND ARDENNES STROKE

IN the dark, foggy morning of December 16, 1944, the German Army struck in the Ardennes. The blow came as a shock to the Allies, for some of their highest commanders had been confidently saying that the Germans would never be capable of another offensive. It soon became a greater shock, for the blow burst through the American front in the Ardennes and threatened to sever the Allied armies. Alarm spread behind the front, and was worse still in the Allied capitals. It was like a nightmare. Fears were voiced that the Germans might reach the Channel coast, and produce a second Dunkirk.

It was Hitler's last big gamble—and the rashest of all.

Everything looked very different from the German end of the telescope. The offensive was not only a long-odds chance, but an incredible muddle. The Allies spoke of it as the "Rundstedt offensive". That title acts on Rundstedt like the proverbial red rag, for his feelings about the plan were, and remain, very bitter. In reality he had nothing to do with it except in the most nominal way. Having failed to dissuade Hitler from attempting it, and feeling that it was a hopeless venture, he stood back throughout and left Field-Marshal Model to run it.

The decision was entirely Hitler's own, and so was the strategic plan. It would have been a brilliant brain-wave *if* he had still possessed the forces and resources to give it a fair chance of success in the end. That it gained a startling initial success was largely due to tactics suggested by the young General von Manteuffel—an army commander at forty-seven—who persuaded Hitler to adopt them. Hitler would never listen to the arguments of the older generals, whom he distrusted, but he had a very different attitude towards newer men and ideas. He regarded Manteuffel as one of his discoveries. He loved revolutionary ideas.

The surprise achieved at the start also owed much to the extreme secrecy in which the design had been hidden. But this was carried so far that it became more hindrance than help. It caused many of the muddles which forfeited such chance as the attack gained. But long after the plan had miscarried, Hitler insisted on pursuing the attack. He forbade any timely withdrawal. If the Allies had moved quicker, his armies might have been trapped. Even as it was they were badly hammered. The losses they suffered were fatal to the prospects of the continued defence of Germany.

It is instructive to follow the course of events through the eyes of some of the chief German commanders concerned. At the top came Rundstedt, who had been restored to his old place as Commander-in-Chief in the West early in September—when the Allies were approaching the Rhine, and Hitler needed a symbol that would rally the confidence of his shattered armies. Under Rundstedt came Model, who was not a great strategist, but who had a ruthless energy in scraping up reserves from a bare cupboard, and was one of the few generals who dared to argue with Hitler. Model committed suicide at the end of the war. Under Model came the two Panzer Army commanders, Sepp Dietrich and Manteuffel. Sepp Dietrich was an S.S. leader, formerly a rolling stone in various business jobs, who had caught Hitler's fancy by his aggressive spirit. Rundstedt regarded him as responsible for fumbling the crucial part of the offensive. Manteuffel was a professional soldier of the younger school, and an aristocrat. A man of quiet dignity, similar to Rundstedt's, he was also a dynamic exponent of new methods. Within a year he had risen from command of a panzer division to command of an Army. Besides being the designer of the tactics of the Ardennes offensive, it was his thrust that proved by far the most threatening feature. For these reason I give the story largely in his words, checked and supplemented by evidence gathered from other sources.

Manteuffel is keenly professional enough to enjoy "fighting his battles over again" in discussion, while philosophical enough not to dwell disproportionately on how things went wrong. He has a pleasant vein of humour, too. It survived the hard conditions of the camp where the generals were then confined, as well as the strain of anxiety which all of them felt about the fate of their families, and whether they would ever see them again. That cheerless camp deep in a remote mountain valley was depressing enough, even without the barbed wire, to induce claustrophobia. Visiting it on one of the dreariest of mid-winter days, I remarked to Manteuffel that Grizedale was not a pleasing place at such a time of the year, but that it would be better in summer. He replied, with a smile: "Oh, it might be worse. I expect we shall be spending next winter on a barren island, or else in a ship anchored in mid-Atlantic."

THE PLAN

"The plan for the Ardennes offensive," Manteuffel told me, "was drawn up completely by O.K.W. and sent to us as a cut and dried 'Führer order'. The object defined was to achieve a decisive victory in the West by throwing in two panzer armies—the 6th under Dietrich, and the 5th under me. The 6th was to strike north-east, cross the Meuse between Liége and Huy, and drive for Antwerp. It had the main rôle, and main strength. My army was to advance along a more curving line, cross the Meuse between Namur and Dinant, and push towards Brussels— to cover the flank. On the third or fourth day the 15th Army, using the specially reinforced 12th S.S. Corps under

General Blumentritt, was to make a converging thrust from the north-east towards the Meuse at Maastricht—to assist the 6th Panzer Army's drive on Antwerp. The Führer's idea was that the Ardennes offensive would by then have drawn off a large part of the reserves to the help of the Americans, so that this secondary stroke, although lighter, should have a chance of success.

"The aim of the whole offensive was, by cutting off the British Army from its bases of supply, to force it to evacuate the Continent."

Hitler imagined that if he produced this second Dunkirk, Britain would virtually drop out of the war, and he would have breathing space to hold up the Russians and produce a stalemate in the East.

The plan was unfolded on October 24th. Describing his reactions, Rundstedt told me: "I was staggered. Hitler had not consulted me about its possibilities. It was obvious to me that the available forces were far too small for such an extremely ambitious plan. Model took the same view of it as I did. In fact, no soldier believed that the aim of reaching Antwerp was really practicable. But I knew by now it was useless to protest to Hitler about the *possibility* of anything. After consultation with Model and Manteuffel I felt that the only hope was to wean Hitler from this fantastic aim by putting forward an alternative proposal that might appeal to him, and would be more practicable. This was for a limited offensive with the aim of pinching off the Allies' salient around Aachen."

Manteuffel gave me a fuller account of their discussion and conclusions. "We were agreed in our objections to the plan. In the first place the strategic dispositions were faulty, and there would be grave risk to the flanks unless these were buttressed. Beyond that, the ammunition supplies were not sufficient for such extensive aims. Beyond that again, the Allies' air superiority would be too great a handicap in attempting such aims. Moreover, we knew that strong Allied reinforcements were available back in

France, and also in England. I myself stressed the point that we must expect intervention from the airborne divisions that were ready in England. I also emphasized how the good network of roads beyond the Meuse would facilitate the Allies' counter-moves.

"We drafted a report to O.K.W. emphasizing that the forces were not adequate to deliver an offensive on the lines laid down. At the same time we suggested a modified plan. In this, the 15th Army, with a strong right flank, would deliver an attack north of Aachen, towards Maastricht. The 6th Panzer Army would attack south of Aachen, and cut in behind that place with the eventual objective of establishing a bridgehead over the Meuse in the Liége area. The main aim here was to fix the Allies' attention. The 5th Panzer Army would strike from the Eifel through the Ardennes towards Namur, with the aim of gaining a bridgehead there. The armies would then turn north and roll up the Allied position along the Meuse. If opposition seemed to be collapsing, they could exploit their success by an advance towards Antwerp, but otherwise they could limit their risks."

The most that they really hoped, Manteuffel said, was to pinch out the American forces that had pushed beyond Aachen as far as the River Roer. But he would have preferred to wait until the Allies started a fresh offensive, and keep all the German armoured forces in hand for the delivery of a concentrated counter-stroke. Rundstedt was of the same opinion, as Blumentritt independently confirmed—"The Field-Marshal was really against any further offensive on our part. His idea was to defend the Roer and hold all the armoured divisions in readiness behind that line, as a powerful reserve for counter-attack against a break-through. He wanted to pursue a defensive strategy."

Since Hitler rejected such an idea, the only hope seemed to lie in subtly inducing him to modify his offensive design to a form that would offer a chance of moderate success without involving too heavy risks.

Manteuffel explained that the scope and direction of the thrusts suggested was close enough to Hitler's design as to appear not so very different. In putting forward the alternative plan, they tried to increase its appeal by suggesting that, if opposition seemed to be collapsing, they could then exploit the success towards Antwerp. "On November 4, so far as I remember, this alternative plan was sent to O.K.W. for submission to Hitler. It was emphasized that we could not be ready to launch the attack before December 10—Hitler had originally fixed the date as December 1."

Manteuffel went on: "Hitler rejected this more moderate plan, and insisted on the original pattern. Meanwhile, knowing that he usually kept us waiting for an answer we had begun our own planning—but only on the narrower basis of our own proposals. All the divisions of my own 5th Panzer Army were assembled, but kept widely spaced, between Trier and Krefeld—so that spies and the civil population should have no inkling of what was intended. The troops were told that they were being got ready to meet the coming Allied attack on Cologne. Only a very limited number of staff officers were informed of the actual plan."

The 6th Panzer Army was assembled still farther back, in the area between Hanover and the Weser. Its divisions had been drawn out of the line to recuperate and be re-equipped. Curiously, Sepp Dietrich was not informed of the task that was intended for him nor consulted about the plan he would have to carry out, until much closer to the event. Most of the divisional commanders had only a few days' notice. In the case of Manteuffel's Army, the move down to the starting line was made in three nights.

THE FLAWS

This strategic camouflage helped surprise, but a heavy price was paid for the extreme internal secrecy—particularly in the case of the 6th Panzer Army. Commanders who were informed so late had too little time to study their problem, reconnoitre the ground, and make their preparations. As a result many things were overlooked, and numerous hitches occurred when the attack began. Hitler had worked out the plan at his headquarters in detail, with Jodl, and seemed to think that this would suffice for its fulfilment. He paid no attention to local conditions or to the individual problems of his executants. He was equally optimistic about the needs of the forces engaged.

Rundstedt remarked: "There were no adequate reinforcements, no supplies of ammunition, and although the number of armoured divisions was high, their strength in tanks was low—it was largely paper strength." (Manteuffel said that the actual number of tanks in the two panzer armies was about 800—which puts a different complexion on the Allied statement, based on the number of divisions, that this was the most powerful concentration of tanks ever seen in the war.)

The worst deficiency of all was in petrol. Manteuffel said: "Jodl had assured us there would be sufficient petrol to develop our full strength and carry our drive through. This assurance proved completely mistaken. Part of the trouble was that O.K.W. worked on a mathematical and stereotyped calculation of the amount of petrol required to move a division for a hundred kilometres. My experience in Russia had taught me that double this scale was really needed under battlefield conditions. Jodl didn't understand this.

"Taking account of the extra difficulties likely to be met in a winter battle in such difficult country as the Ardennes, I told Hitler personally that five times the standard scale of petrol supply ought to be provided. Actually, when the offensive was launched, only one and a half times the standard scale had been provided. Worse still, much of it was kept too far back, in large lorry columns on the east bank of the Rhine. Once the foggy weather cleared, and the Allied air forces came into action, its forwarding was badly interrupted."

The troops, ignorant of all these underlying weaknesses, kept a remarkable trust in Hitler and his assurances of victory. Rundstedt said: "The morale of the troops taking part was astonishingly high at the start of the offensive. They really believed victory was possible—unlike the higher commanders, who knew the facts."

NEW TACTICS

At the start, the chances were improved by two factors. The first was the thinness of the American defences in the Ardennes sector. The Germans had good information about this, and knew that only four divisions covered the 75-mile stretch of front. It was Hitler's keen sense of the value of the unexpected which led him to exploit this weakness, and its indication that the Allied High Command was unprepared—despite the lesson of 1940—for a large-scale German offensive in such difficult country.

The second favourable factor lay in the tactics that were adopted. These were not part of the original plan. Manteuffel told me: "When I saw Hitler's orders for the offensive I was astonished to find that these even laid down the method and timing of the attack. The artillery was to open fire at 7.30 a.m., and the infantry assault was to be launched at 11 a.m. Between these hours the Luftwaffe was to bomb headquarters and communications. The armoured divisions were not to strike until the break-through had been achieved by the infantry mass. The artillery was spread over the whole front of attack.

"This seemed to me foolish in several respects, so I immediately worked out a different method, and explained it to Model. Model agreed with it, but remarked sarcastically: 'You'd better argue it out with the Führer.' I replied: 'All right, I'll do that if you'll come with me.'

So on December 2, the two of us went to see Hitler in Berlin.

"I began by saying: 'None of us knows what the weather will be on the day of the attack—are you sure the Luftwaffe can fulfil its part in face of the Allied air superiority?' I reminded Hitler of two occasions in the Vosges earlier where it had proved quite impossible for the armoured divisions to move in daylight. Then I went on: 'All our artillery will do at 7.30 is to wake the Americans—and they will then have three and a half hours to organize their counter-measures before our assault comes.' I pointed out also, that the mass of the German infantry was not so good as it had been, and was hardly capable of making such a deep penetration as was required, especially in such difficult country. For the American defences consisted of a chain of forward defence posts, with their main line of resistance well behind—and that would be harder to pierce.

"I proposed to Hitler a number of changes. The first was that the assault should be made at 5.30 a.m., under cover of darkness. Of course this would limit the targets for the artillery, but would enable it to concentrate on a number of key targets—such as batteries, ammunition dumps, and headquarters—that had been definitely located.

"Secondly, I proposed to form one 'storm battalion' from each infantry division, composed of the most expert officers and men. (I picked the officers myself.) These 'storm battalions' were to advance in the dark at 5.30, without any covering artillery fire, and penetrate between the Americans' forward defence posts. They would avoid fighting if possible until they had penetrated deep.

"Searchlights, provided by the flak units, were to light the way for the storm troops' advance by projecting their beams on the clouds, to reflect downwards. I had been much impressed by a demonstration of this kind which I had seen shortly beforehand, and felt that it would be the key to a quick penetration before daylight." (Curiously, Manteuffel did not seem aware that the British had already developed such "artificial moonlight". And although he spoke to me of the impression made on him by a little book of mine, *The Future of Infantry*, which appeared in 1932, he had forgotten that this new development was one of the principal suggestions in that book.)

Resuming his account, Manteuffel said: "After setting forth my alternative proposals to Hitler, I argued that it was not possible to carry out the offensive in any other way if we were to have a reasonable chance of success. I emphasized: 'At 4 p.m. it will be dark. So you will only have five hours, after the assault at 11 a.m., in which to achieve the break-through. It is very doubtful if you can do it in the time. If you adopt my idea, you will gain a further five and a half hours for the purpose. Then when darkness comes I can launch the tanks. They will advance during the night, pass through our infantry, and by dawn the next day they will be able to launch their own attack on the main position, along a cleared approach."

According to Manteuffel, Hitler accepted these suggestions without a murmur. That was significant. It would seem that he was willing to listen to suggestions that were made to him by a few generals in whom he had faith—Model was another—but he had an instinctive distrust of most of the senior generals, while his reliance on his own immediate staff was mingled with a realization that they lacked experience of battle conditions.

"Keitel, Jodl, and Warlimont had never been in the war. At the same time their lack of fighting experience tended to make them underrate practical difficulties, and encourage Hitler to believe that things could be done that were quite impossible. Hitler would listen to soldiers who had fighting experience and practical ideas."

What these tactical changes did to improve the prospects of the offensive was offset, however, by a reduction of the strength that was to be put into it. For the executive

commanders soon had damping news that part of the forces
promised them would not be available—owing to the
menacing pressure of the Russian attacks in the East.
The result was that Blumentritt's converging attack on
Maastricht had to be abandoned, so leaving the Allies
free to bring down reserves from the north. Moreover,
the 7th Army, which was to advance as flank cover to the
other wing of the offensive, was left with only a few divisions
—and without any tanks. Manteuffel was the more
dismayed to hear this, because he had told Hitler, on the
2nd, that in his view the Americans would launch their
main counter-stroke from the Sedan area towards Bastogne.
"I pointed out the way that so many of the roads converged
on Bastogne."

Yet the ambitious aims of the offensive were not
modified. Curiously, too, Hitler and Jodl did not seem
to realize the effect on the momentum of the advance.
"The time of reaching the Meuse was not discussed in any
detail," Manteuffel told me. "I imagined that Hitler must
realize that a rapid advance would not be possible under
winter conditions, and these limitations, but from what I
have heard since it is clear that Hitler thought the advance
could go much quicker than it did. The Meuse could not
possibly have been reached on the second or third day—as
Jodl expected. He and Keitel tended to encourage Hitler's
optimistic illusions."

Rundstedt receded into the background after Hitler's
rejection of the "smaller" plan, leaving Model and Manteuffel, who had more chance of influencing Hitler, to
fight for the technical changes in the plan that were all
Hitler would consider. Blumentritt bitterly remarked:
"The Commander-in-Chief in the West was not, in fact,
consulted any more. He was expected to carry out the
offensive in a mechanical way in accordance with the
Führer's operation orders—which regulated the smallest
details—without being able to interfere in any way himself." Rundstedt took only a nominal part in the final

conference, held on December 12th in his headquarters at Ziegenberg, near Bad Nauheim. Hitler was present, and controlled the proceedings.

THE MISSING CARD

As the start of one of my talks with Manteuffel I raised a question about the use of the airborne forces. I said that in travelling over a large part of the Ardennes before the war I had been struck by the fact that its possibilities for tank movement were greater than was generally supposed, especially by the conventionally-minded French high command. At the same time there was an obvious difficulty in the way that the roads descended into steep valleys at the river crossings, and these might form tough obstacles if stoutly defended. It had seemed to me that the offensive answer to this defensive problem was to drop airborne forces on these strategic defiles, and seize them ahead of the tank advance. That was why in my commentary when the Ardennes offensive opened I had assumed that the Germans were using their airborne troops in this way. But it now appeared that they did not do so. Could he, Manteuffel, tell me something about this.

Manteuffel's reply was: "I entirely agree with your definition of the nature and problem of the Ardennes, and I think it would have been an excellent idea to use parachute forces in the way you suggest. It might have unlocked the door. But I don't remember it being mooted when the plan was being discussed, and in any case the available parachute forces were very scanty. Our parachute forces were hampered by a shortage of transport aircraft, above all, but also by a lack of men at the time when this offensive was launched. The dangerous situation on the Eastern front had led Hitler to use them as ordinary infantry, to cement breaches. Other divisions had been drawn away to Italy and absorbed in the battle there.

The result of all these factors was that only about nine hundred parachutists were available for the Ardennes offensive, and they were used on the front of the 6th Panzer Army."

Manteuffel went on to talk of the neglect to make any effective use of Germany's parachute forces after the capture of Crete in 1941—how they had been earmarked for a stroke against Malta or Gibraltar which never came off; how Student had wanted to use them in Russia, and had been thwarted by Hitler's preference for keeping them in reserve for some special coup; and how, in the end, they had been frittered away in the rôle of ordinary ground troops instead of being employed in their own proper rôle. He concluded by saying: "In my view, there could be nothing better than a combination of panzer and parachute troops."

On this subject Thoma told me, earlier: "Guderian always worked well with Student, who trained the parachute forces, but Goering blocked proposals for combined action with the panzer forces. He always wanted to keep up the strength of the Luftwaffe, and was therefore niggardly with such air transport as he had to provide for the parachute forces."

From General Student I got details of how the parachute troops were employed in the Ardennes offensive. When the German front in France collapsed and the Allies dashed forward into Belgium, at the beginning of September, he was sent to form a fresh front in southern Holland. For this purpose he was given command of a scratch force that was imposingly named the 1st Parachute Army. It consisted of a number of depleted infantry divisions supplemented by a sprinkling of parachute units that were then in course of training under him. After the new front had been established, and the Allied advance checked, the German forces in Holland were constituted as Army Group 'H', comprising the 1st Parachute Army and the still more newly created 25th Army. Student was given command of this army group in addition to his other function of Commander-in-Chief of the Parachute Forces.

On December 8th he was told of the intended offensive in the Ardennes and instructed to collect what he could in the way of trained parachutists in order to furnish one strong battalion. That was barely a week before the offensive was launched. The battalion comprised about 1,000 men under Colonel von der Heydte, and it was sent to the sector of Sepp Dietrich's 6th Panzer Army. On getting in touch with the Luftwaffe command, von der Heydte found that more than half the crews of the aircraft allotted had no experience of parachute operations, and that necessary equipment was lacking. It was not until the 13th that he managed to see Sepp Dietrich, who said that he did not want to use parachute troops for fear that they might give the enemy a warning, but that Hitler had insisted.

The task eventually assigned to the parachute troops was, not to seize one of the awkward defiles ahead of the panzer advance, but to land on Mont Rigi near the Malmedy-Eupen-Verviers cross-roads, and create a flank block to delay Allied reinforcements from the north. Von der Heydte was ordered, despite his protests, to make the drop at night instead of at dawn, to avoid putting the enemy on the alert. But on the evening before the attack the promised transport did not arrive to take the companies to the airfields, and the drop was postponed until the next night—when the ground attack had already started. Then, only a third of the aircraft managed to reach the correct dropping zone, and the strong wind dragged the parachutes so that many of the troops were killed or injured in landing on the wooded and snow-covered heights. By this time the roads were filled with American columns streaming south, and as von der Heydte had only been able to collect a couple of hundred men he could not gain the cross-roads and establish a blocking position. For several days he harassed the roads with small raiding parties, and then, as there was no sign of Sepp Dietrich's forces arriving to relieve him, he tried to push eastward to meet them, but was captured on the way.

"This was our last parachute operation," said Student. "On D-day we had had 150,000 parachute troops, and six organized divisions. Of the total 50,000 were trained, and the rest under training. We were not able to complete their training as they were constantly committed to ground fighting, and by the time they were needed for the Ardennes offensive, five months later, only a handful were available —because they had been used up as infantry instead of being kept for their proper rôle."

THE BLOW

The blow that gave the Allies their biggest shock since 1942 had no such weight behind it as they pictured at the time. That is now clear from the German order of battle, though Manteuffel did not emphasize it—he gave his account with marked restraint, and is the type of man who dislikes to offer excuses, however justifiable.

The offensive was launched on December 16th along a seventy-mile stretch between Monschau (south of Aachen) and Echternach (just north-west of Trier). But the 7th Army's attack on the southern sector did not really count, as it could only employ four infantry divisions. The intended main punch was delivered on a narrow front, of barely fifteen miles, by Sepp Dietrich's 6th Panzer Army, which was composed of the 1st and 2nd S.S. Panzer Corps, supplemented by the 67th Corps (of infantry). Although it had more armoured divisions than the 5th Panzer Army it was a light-weight for its purpose.

Sepp Dietrich's right-hand punch was blocked early by the Americans' tough defence of Monschau. His left-hand punch burst through and, by-passing Malmedy, gained a crossing over the Ambleve beyond Stavelot on the 18th—after a thirty-mile advance from the starting line. But it was checked in this narrow defile, and then cornered by an American counter-move. Fresh efforts failed, in face of the Americans' rising strength as reserves were hurried to the scene, and the 6th Panzer Army's attack fizzled out.

Manteuffel's 5th Panzer Army attacked on a broader front, of some thirty miles. He sketched out for me its dispositions and course. The 66th Corps (of infantry) was on his right wing, facing the direction of St. Vith. "It was purposely put there because the obstacles were greater, and the chances of rapid progress less, than farther south." The 58th Panzer Corps was in the centre, between Prüm and Waxweiler. The 47th Panzer Corps was on the left, between Waxweiler and Bitburg, facing the direction of Bastogne. At the start these two corps included only three armoured divisions, and despite recent reinforcement the latter only had a strength of between sixty to a hundred tanks each—one-third to a half of their normal establishment. Sepp Dietrich's armoured divisions were not much stronger in tanks.

On Manteuffel's front the offensive had a good start. "My storm battalions infiltrated rapidly into the American front—like rain-drops. At 4 o'clock in the afternoon the tanks advanced, and pressed forward in the dark with the help of 'artificial moonlight'. By that time bridges had been built over the Our river. Crossing these about midnight, the armoured divisions reached the American main position, at 8 a.m., then called for artillery support, and quickly broke through.

"But Bastogne then proved a very awkward obstacle. Part of the trouble was due to the way that the 7th Army had been reduced in strength, for its task was to block the roads running up from the south to Bastogne." After crossing the Our at Dasburg, the 47th Panzer Corps had to get through another awkward defile at Clervaux on the Woltz. These obstacles, combined with winter conditions, caused delay. "Resistance tended to melt whenever the tanks arrived in force, but the difficulties of movement offset the slightness of the resistance in this early stage. When they approached Bastogne resistance increased."

On the 18th, the Germans came close to Bastogne—after an advance of nearly thirty miles from their starting line. But during the night before, General Eisenhower had placed the 82nd and 101st Airborne divisions, then near Rheims, at General Bradley's disposal. The 82nd was sent to stiffen the northern sector, while the 101st was rushed up by road to Bastogne. Meanwhile part of the 10th U.S. Armoured Division had arrived at Bastogne just in time to help a battered regiment of the 28th Division in checking the Germans' initial threat. When the 101st Airborne Division arrived on the night of the 18th, the defence of this vital road-centre was cemented. During the next two days thrusts were made against it, from front and flanks, but all were foiled.

On the 20th Manteuffel decided that no more time must be lost in trying to clear away this obstacle. "I went forward myself with the Panzer Lehr Division, led it round Bastogne, and pushed on to St. Hubert on the 21st. The 2nd Panzer Division pushed round the north side of Bastogne. To cover these by-passing advances I masked Bastogne, using the 26th Volksgrenadier Division to surround the town, with the help of a panzer grenadier regiment from the Panzer Lehr Division. The 58th Panzer Corps meanwhile pressed on through Houffalize and Laroche, after momentarily swinging north to threaten the flank of the resistance that was holding up the 66th Corps near St. Vith, and help it forward.

"Even so, the masking of Bastogne entailed a weakening of my strength for the forward drive, and thus diminished the chances of this reaching the Meuse at Dinant. Moreover, the 7th Army was still back on the Wiltz, which it had not been able to cross. The 5th Parachute Division, on its right, came through my sector and pushed forward close to one of the roads running south from Bastogne, but was not across it."

The situation was now less favourable, and potentially more dangerous than Manteuffel realized. For Allied reserves were gathering on all sides in a strength much exceeding that which the Germans had put into the offensive. Field-Marshal Montgomery had taken over temporary charge of all the forces on the north flank of the breach, and the 30th British Corps had been brought down to the Meuse, as a support to the 1st American Army. On the south flank of the breach two corps of General Patton's 3rd American Army had swung northward, and on the 22nd one of them launched a strong attack up the road from Arlon to Bastogne. Although its advance was slow, its menacing pressure caused an increasing subtraction from the forces that Manteuffel could spare for his own advance.

The days of opportunity had passed. Manteuffel's swerving thrust towards the Meuse caused alarm at Allied Headquarters, but it was too late to be really serious. According to plan, Bastogne was to have been gained on the second day, whereas it was not reached until the third, and not by-passed until the sixth day. A "small finger" of the 2nd Panzer Division came within a few miles of Dinant on the 24th, but that was the utmost limit of progress, and the finger was soon cut off.

Mud and fuel shortage had been important brakes on the advance—owing to lack of petrol only half the artillery could be brought into action. That deficiency was not compensated by air support. While the foggy weather of the opening days had favoured the German infiltration by keeping the Allied air forces on the ground, this cloak of obscurity disappeared on the 23rd, and the scanty resources of the Luftwaffe proved incapable of shielding the ground forces from a terrible pummelling. That multiplied the toll for time lost. But Hitler was also paying forfeit for the decision that had led him to place his main strength on the northern wing, with the 6th Panzer Army, where room for manœuvre was much more cramped.

In the first week, the offensive had fallen far short of what was hoped, and the quickened progress at the start of the second week was illusory—for it only amounted to a deeper intrusion between the main road-centres, which the Americans were now more firmly holding. On Christmas Eve, Manteuffel got through on the telephone direct to Hitler's headquarters, to represent the realities of the situation and to make a proposal. Speaking to Jodl, he emphasized that time was running short, that Bastogne was causing a lot of trouble, that the 7th Army was not far enough forward to cover his flank, and that he expected a massive Allied counter-stroke very soon, driving up the roads from the south. "Let me know this evening what the Führer wants. The question is whether I shall use all my strength to overcome Bastogne, or continue masking it with small forces and throw my weight towards the Meuse.

"I then pointed out that the most we could hope to do was to reach the Meuse—and gave my reasons. First, because of the delay at Bastogne. Second, because the 7th Army was too weak to bar all roads from the south. Third, because after eight days of battle the Allies were sure to be on the Meuse in strength, and it would not be possible to force a crossing in face of strong opposition. Fourth, because the 6th Panzer Army had not penetrated far, and was already held up on the line Monschau-Stavelot. Fifth, it was clear that we should have to fight a battle this side of the Meuse. For I had picked up wireless messages from the Allied Traffic Control at Huy, which was sending regular reports of the passage of reinforcements across the bridge there—we were able to decipher the code."

After that, Manteuffel made his own proposals—for a circular stroke northward on the near side of the Meuse, to trap the Allied forces that were east of the river, and sweep the bend clear. This would establish the German forces in a stronger position, which they might hope to hold. "With this aim, I urged that the whole of my army, reinforced by the O.K.W. reserves and by the 6th Panzer Army's reserves, should be concentrated south of the Ourthe, around Laroche, and then wheel round in a circuit past Marche towards Liége. I said: 'Give me these reserves, and I will take Bastogne, reach the Meuse, and swing north, so helping the 6th Panzer Army to advance.' I finished by emphasizing these points—I must have a reply that night; the O.K.W. reserves must have sufficient petrol; I would need air support. Up till then I had only seen the enemy's aircraft!

"During the night Major Johannmeier, the Führer's adjutant, visited me and after discussion telephoned Jodl. At the end I came to the telephone myself, but Jodl said that the Führer had not yet made a decision. All he could do for the moment was to place at my disposal one additional armoured division.

"It was not until the 26th that the rest of the reserves were given to me—and then they could not be moved. They were at a standstill for lack of petrol—stranded over a stretch of a hundred miles—just when they were needed." (The irony of this situation was that on the 19th the Germans had come within about a quarter of a mile of a huge petrol dump at Andrimont, near Stavelot, containing 2,500,000 gallons. It was a hundred times larger than the largest of the dumps they actually captured.)

I asked Manteuffel whether he felt that real success would have been possible as late as December 24th—even if he had been given the reserves immediately, and they had been provided with petrol. He replied: "I think a limited success would still have been possible—up to the Meuse, and perhaps the capture of bridgeheads beyond it." In further discussion, however, he admitted that such a belated attainment of the Meuse would have brought more disadvantage than advantage in the long run.

"We had hardly begun this new push before the Allied counter-offensive developed. I telephoned Jodl and asked him to tell the Führer that I was going to withdraw my advanced forces out of the nose of the salient we had made —to the line Laroche–Bastogne. But Hitler forbade this step back. So instead of withdrawing in time, we were driven back bit by bit under pressure of the Allied attacks, suffering needlessly heavy losses. On January 5th the situation was so serious that I feared Montgomery would cut off both our Armies. Although we managed to avoid this danger, a large part of them were sacrificed. Our losses were much heavier in this later stage than they had been earlier, owing to Hitler's policy of 'no withdrawal'. It spelt bankruptcy, because we could not afford such losses."

AFTERMATH

Manteuffel summed up the last stage of the war in two sentences: "After the Ardennes failure, Hitler started a 'corporal's war'. There were no big plans—only a multitude of piecemeal fights."

He went on: "When I saw the Ardennes offensive was blocked I wanted to carry out a general withdrawal—first to our starting line, and then to the Rhine, but Hitler would not hear of it. He chose to sacrifice the bulk of his main forces in a hopeless struggle on the West bank of the Rhine."

Rundstedt endorsed this verdict. But he also made it clear that, although the German Army's leading exponent of offensive warfare, he had never seen any point in this offensive. "Each step forward in the Ardennes offensive prolonged our flanks more dangerously deep, making them more susceptible to Allied counter-strokes." Rundstedt traced the effect, on the map, as he talked. "I wanted to stop the offensive at an early stage, when it was plain that it could not attain its aim, but Hitler furiously insisted that it must go on. It was Stalingrad No. 2."

The Ardennes offensive carried to the extreme of absurdity the military belief that "attack is the best defence". It proved the "worst defence"—wrecking Germany's chances of any further serious resistance. From that time on, the main concern of most of the German commanders seems to have been, not whether they could stop the Allies' advance, but why the Allies did not advance faster and finish the war quicker.

They were tied to their posts by Hitler's policy, and Himmler's police, but they were praying for release. Throughout the last nine months of the war they spent much of their time discussing ways and means of getting in touch with the Allies to arrange a surrender.

All to whom I talked dwelt on the effect of the Allies' "unconditional surrender" policy in prolonging the war. They told me that but for this they and their troops—the factor that was more important—would have been ready to surrender sooner, separately or collectively. "Black-listening" to the Allies' radio service was widespread. But the Allied propaganda never said anything positive about the peace conditions in the way of encouraging them to give up the struggle. Its silence on the subject was so marked that it tended to confirm what Nazi propaganda told them as to the dire fate in store for them if they surrendered. So it greatly helped the Nazis to keep the German troops and people to continue fighting—long after they were ready to give up.

CHAPTER XXIV

HITLER—
AS A YOUNG GENERAL SAW HIM

In the course of one of my talks with Manteuffel about the Ardennes offensive he gave me a military character-sketch of Hitler that differed markedly from the impression of him that the older generals conveyed. It is worth reproducing because it goes further to explain the sources of both his power and his failure.

The way in which Manteuffel attracted Hitler's notice is also illuminating. In August, 1943, he had been given command of the 7th Armoured Division—which Rommel had led in 1940. It was in Manstein's Army Group. That autumn the Russians surged over the Dnieper and captured Kiev, then rolled on rapidly west towards the Polish frontier. Manstein had no formed reserve left to meet this fresh crisis, but charged Manteuffel with the task of collecting such odd units as he could find for an improvised counter-stroke. Manteuffel broke in behind the rear of the advancing Russians, ejected them from Zhitomir junction by a night attack, and drove on north to recapture Korosten. By dividing his meagre forces into a number of small mobile groups Manteuffel created an impression out of proportion to his strength, and the sudden riposte brought the Russian advance to a halt.

After that, Manteuffel further developed this method of penetrating raids that cut in between the Russian columns and struck at them from the rear. "It was handicapped by the Russians' lack of dependence on a normal system of supply —I never met any supply columns on these 'interior' raids— but I caught staff and signal centres besides striking bodies of troops in the back. These penetrating raids proved very effective in spreading confusion. Of course, for operations of this kind an armoured division must be self-contained for supplies, carrying with it what it needs, so as to be free from dependence on communications during the whole course of the operation." (It is evident that Manteuffel practised what General (then Brigadier) Hobart demonstrated with the 1st Tank Brigade in the Salisbury Plain area in 1934–35—though without convincing the British General Staff that such a form of strategy was practicable.)

Hitler was delighted with the new method, and eager to hear more about it. So he sent an invitation for Manteuffel and the commander of his tank regiment, Colonel Schultz, to spend Christmas at his headquarters near Angerburg, in East Prussia. After congratulating Manteuffel, Hitler said: "As a Christmas present, I'll give you fifty tanks."

Early in 1944 Manteuffel was given command of a specially reinforced division, the "Gross-Deutschland", and with this he was sent to different sectors to check a breakthrough or to release forces that had been trapped by the Russian tide of advance. In September, after he had cut a way through to the German forces that were hemmed in on the Baltic coast round Riga, he was given a big jump in promotion—to command the 5th Panzer Army, in the West.

Throughout 1944, Manteuffel saw more of Hitler than did almost any other commander, as Hitler frequently summoned him to his headquarters to discuss these emergency missions and to consult him on armoured warfare problems. This close contact enabled Manteuffel to get under the surface that terrified or mesmerized other generals.

"Hitler had a magnetic, and indeed hypnotic personality. This had a very marked effect on people who went to see him with the intention of putting forward their views on any matter. They would begin to argue their point, but would gradually find themselves succumbing to his personality, and in the end would often agree to the opposite of what they intended. For my part, having come to know Hitler well in the last stages of the war, I had learnt how to keep him to the point, and maintain my own argument. I did not

feel afraid of Hitler, as so many did. He often called me
to his headquarters for consultation, after that Christmastide
I had spent at his headquarters by invitation, following the
successful stroke at Zhitomir that had attracted his attention.

"Hitler had read a lot of military literature, and was also
fond of listening to military lectures. In this way, coupled
with his personal experience of the last war as an ordinary
soldier, he had gained a very good knowledge of the lower
level of warfare—the properties of the different weapons; the
effect of ground and weather; the mentality and morale of
troops. He was particularly good in gauging how the troops
felt. I found that I was hardly ever in disagreement with his
view when discussing such matters. On the other hand he had
no idea of the higher strategical and tactical combinations.
He had a good grasp of how a single division moved and
fought, but he did not understand how armies operated."

Manteuffel then went on to talk of how the "hedgehog"
system of defence had developed, and how Hitler was led
to carry it too far. "When our troops were being forced
back by the Russian attacks, they were attracted, as by
magnets, towards the defended localities that had been
prepared in rear. Falling back on these, they found it
natural to rally there, and put up a stubborn resistance.
Hitler was quick to see the value of such localities, and the
importance of maintaining them. But he overlooked the
need of giving the sector commanders reasonable latitude
to modify their dispositions, and to withdraw if necessary.
He insisted on having the question submitted to him in
every case. Too often, before he had made up his mind,
the Russians had broken through the over-strained defence.

"He had a real flair for strategy and tactics, especially
for surprise moves, but he lacked a sufficient foundation
of technical knowledge to apply it properly. Moreover,
he had a tendency to intoxicate himself with figures and
quantities. When one was discussing a problem with him,
he would repeatedly pick up the telephone, ask to be put
through to some departmental chief, and enquire—'How

many so and so have we got?' Then he would turn to the man who was arguing with him, quote the number, and say: 'There you are'—as if that settled the problem. He was too ready to accept paper figures, without asking if the numbers stated were available in reality. It was always the same, whatever the subject might be—tanks, aircraft, rifles, shovels.

"Generally, he would ring up Speer or Buhle—who was in charge of factories. Buhle always kept a little note-book beside him, with all the figures ready for which Hitler was likely to ask, and would answer pat. But even if the numbers had actually been produced, a large part of them were still in the factories, and not with the troops. In much the same way, Goering said he would provide ten divisions of ground troops from the Luftwaffe at short notice, for the Russian front—forgetting that the officers had been trained only for air operations, and would need a lengthy fresh training before they would be fit for land operations."

I remarked to Manteuffel that the more I heard about the German side of the war the more the impression had grown that, on the one hand, Hitler had a natural flair for strategy and tactics of an original kind, while the German General Staff, on the other hand, were very competent but without much originality. I felt that, from the way many of the generals had talked, Hitler's misunderstanding of technical factors so jarred on them that they tended to discount the possible value of his ideas, while he was angered by their orthodoxy and lack of receptivity. In this way, it seemed to me, that a tug-of-war had developed, instead of a good working combination. Manteuffel said that he agreed completely with that definition of the situation. It summed up the trouble on the military side. "I said much the same thing to Hitler myself when I spent Christmas with him in 1943, when discussing the difference of outlook between the tank leaders and those who had grown up with the older arms. The more senior generals could not get into the mind of the fighting troops under the new conditions of warfare.'

CONCLUSION

SURVEYING the record of German leadership in the war, and the course of operations, what are the conclusions that emerge? An utter failure on the plane of war policy, or grand strategy, is seen to be accompanied by a remarkable, though uneven, run of performance in strategy and tactics. The explanation is also of a dual nature. The older professional leaders trained under the General Staff system tended to prove highly efficient, but lacking in genius—save in the sense of "an infinite capacity for taking pains". Their immense ability carried its own limitation. They tended to conduct war more in the manner of chess than as an art, unlike the old masters of war. They were inclined to frown on fellow-professionals who had novel ideas, and were more contemptuous when such ideas came from amateurs. Most of them, also, were limited in understanding of any factors outside the military field.

Hitler was quicker to spot the value of new ideas, new weapons, and new talent. He recognized the potentialities of mobile armoured forces sooner than the General Staff, and the way he backed Guderian, Germany's leading exponent of this new instrument, proved the most decisive factor in the opening victories. Hitler had the flair that is characteristic of genius, though accompanied by liability to make elementary mistakes, both in calculation and action. The younger soldiers he picked out and pushed on were often akin to him in these respects—especially Rommel, the most favoured military "upstart". Such men had an instinct for the unexpected and a greater sense of its incalculable value in paralysing opponents. They brought back into warfare, in a new guise, the classical ruses and stratagems which the established military teachers of the last half-century had declared out of date and impossible to apply in modern operations. By Hitler's success in demonstrating the fallacy of orthodoxy he gained an advantage over the military hierarchy which he was quicker to exploit than to consolidate.

Sometimes the intuitive amateurs were justified by events; sometimes the mathematically calculating professionals—the latter more, naturally, in the long run. But the jealousy between them, and the way it aggravated inevitable clashes of opinion, proved more fatal to Germany than the actual errors of either side. For that, the primary responsibility lay with the established hierarchy, as it always does. The result may have been inevitable, for war is not an activity that teaches wisdom to its priests or the quality of reconciling contrary views. In view of Hitler's policy and his temperament, he would have been very difficult to restrain in any circumstances; but the attitude of the professions and the frequency with which his insight proved more correct than theirs made him uncontrollable. But neither side was conscious of its own limitations.

The German generals of this war were the best-finished product of their profession—anywhere. They could have been better if their outlook had been wider and their understanding deeper. But if they had become philosophers they would have ceased to be soldiers.

TABLE OF THE GERMAN HIGH COMMAND

C-in-C of the Combined Forces (Wehrmacht)	1933–38, Blomberg	1938–45, Hitler {Keitel	
C-in-C of the Army	1933–38, Fritsch	1938–41, Brauchitsch	1941–45, Hitler
Chief of the General Staff	1933–38, Beck	1938–42, Halder	1942–44, Zeitzler	1944–45, Guderian

POSTS HELD IN THE WAR BY SOME OF THE OTHER GENERALS MENTIONED

Rundstedt	Army Group South in Poland, 1939	Army Group A in West, 1939–40	Army Group South in Russia, 1941		C-in-C West 1942 to 2.7.44 and 4.9.44 to 18.3.45
Bock	Army Group North in Poland, 1939	Army Group B in West, 1939–40	Army Group Centre in Russia, 1941		Shelved early in 1942
Leeb		Army Group C in West, 1939–40	Army Group North in Russia, 1941		Resigned early in 1942
Reichenau	10th Army in Poland, 1939	6th Army in West, 1940, and in Russia, 1941	Army Group South in Russia, Dec.		Died. Jan. 1942
Kluge	4th Army in Poland, 1939	4th Army in West, 1939–40	4th Army in Russia, 1941	Army Group Centre in Russia 1942–43 (Injured in air crash)	C-in-C West July–Aug. 1944 Removed and committed suicide
Kleist	Pz. Corps in Poland, 1939	Pz. Group in West, 1940	Pz. Group in Russia, 1941	1st Pz. Army in Russia, 1943	Army Group A in Russia, Oct.

(name cut off)	Staff in Poland and West, 1939–Jan. 1940	West, 1940; 56th Pz. Corps in Russia, 1941	…sia, Sept. 1941– Nov. 1942	…Army Group… in Russia, 1943	…eved in March, 1944
Rommel	7th Panzer Div. in West, 1940	Africa Corps and then Pz. Army Africa, 1941–4.43	Army Group in N. Italy, 1943	Army Group B in West, 1944	Injured in July and compulsory suicide in Oct.
Thoma	German troops in Spain, 1936–39	Pz. Bde. in Poland, 1939	Director, Mobile Forces, General Staff, 1940	Pz. Div. & Corps in Russia, 1941–42	Africa Corps Sept.–Nov. 1942. Captured at Alamein
Model	Chief of Staff, 16th Army (Busch) in West, 1940	3rd Pz. Div. and Pz. Corps in Russia, 1941	9th Army in Russia, 1942–43	Army Gps. North, South, Centre in turn, Russia, Oct. 1943–Aug. 1944	Army Group B in West, 1944–45 (temp. C-in-C West late Aug. 1944)
Heinrici	12th Corps in West, 1940	43rd Corps in Russia, 1941	4th Army in Russia, 1942–May, 1944	1st Pz. Army, 1944–45	Army Group W, covering Berlin, March 1945
Tippels-kirch	30th Inf. Div. in Russia, 1941–42	12th Corps in Russia, 1943–44	4th Army in Russia, May–July 1944 (injured in air crash)	14th Army in Italy, early 1945	4th Army in E. Germany, April 1945
Manteuffel	Motor Inf. Regt. in 7th Pz. Div. (Rommel) in West, 1940, and Russia, 1941	Motor Inf. Bde. in 7th Pz. Div. in Russia, 1942	Mixed Div. in Tunisia early 1943	7th & G.D. Pz. Divs. in Russia, 1943–44	5th Pz. Army in West, Sept. 1944–45
Blumentritt	Chief of Staff, 4th Army (Kluge) in Russia, 1941	Rundstedt's 1A (Ops. Chief) in Poland, 1939; and in West, 1940	D.C.G.S. (Ob.Q.I.) 1942	Chief of Staff, West, Sept. 1942 –Sept. 1944	Corps & Army in West, Oct. 1944– May 1945

INDEX